Understanding Social Policy

Eighth Edition

Michael Hill and Zoë Irving

WILEY-BLACKWELL

A John Wiley & Sons, Ltd., Publication

Understanding Social Policy

Contents

List of Tables

Preface to the Eighth Edition

This book is an introduction to the study of social policy. It reflects a concern that the study of social policy needs to be approached with confidence – no one is untouched by social policy, it matters to everyone and most people know more about it than they think. Knowledge however, is advanced by *understanding* and thus the book is also based on the view that those who study this subject need to consider the way in which policy is made and implemented, as well as to learn about the main policies and their limitations and to locate what is learned in a social context. It has been written for people who have had no previous training in the social sciences, with the needs of social workers, nurses, health visitors and other social policy 'practitioners' very much in mind, as well as those of undergraduates.

The first edition of this book was published just after the election of a new Conservative government led by Margaret Thatcher in 1980. The fact that it has now been seen as necessary to produce an eighth edition is testimony to the hyper-active policy change that has characterized government, both Conservative and Labour since that time. But over a period of nearly 30 years it is not only policy that has changed, but also the teaching of social policy. When the publishers suggested that Michael Hill should produce a further revision of the book, he expressed concern that, while continuing to monitor developments in policy and undertaking a variety of teaching on social policy around the world, he had for some time ceased to be engaged in introductory teaching of the subject. It was agreed therefore that he should seek a co-author with that more direct involvement. Messages to friends produced a variety of suggestions and it was through the good offices of Alan Walker that he was introduced to Zoë Irving, who, having used the previous editions of *Understanding Social Policy* as both a student and a teacher was very pleased to be involved in the preparation of an eighth edition.

This revised version of *Understanding Social Policy*, whilst taking largely the same shape as its predecessors, therefore benefits from the perspectives of two people rather than one, and parts of it – particularly at the beginning and the end – have been reshaped to relate it better to contemporary teaching needs. The historical chapter, which had grown rather incrementally as the year history 'stopped' moved forward, has been rewritten to give a broad overview, with rather less detail than in the past. A chapter that put the UK policy into comparative perspective – an innovation in the seventh edition – has now become a chapter which puts it into *global* perspective. The pattern of chapters on substantive issues remains much the same, except that a formal institutional change – the break up of social services into adult and children's services with the latter linked to education – has been followed by a similar reshaping. With these changes it is hoped that an appropriate balance between depth and breadth has been achieved.

At this stage in the history of a textbook, Michael Hill finds it impossible to acknowledge satisfactorily all the people who have helped to shape the previous editions. He wishes to continue the book's dedication to his wife Betty who, when she was a health visitor student, first helped him to identify the gap in the market. Nowadays her practical understanding of the social policy system comes rather more from the consumer end. He is proud of his family of 'practitioners' still upholding the public service tradition, who keep him in touch with the real world of social policy. He has benefited from his daughter Julia Regan's involvement in local authority scrutiny work and is grateful to her husband Shaun for putting him right on some aspects of housing policy while David and Teresa Lavelle-Hill regularly update him on what is going on in the new Education and Children's departments.

Zoë Irving would like to thank colleagues Bob Deacon and Susie Molyneux Hodgson for helpful comments on two of the chapters and Kevin Farnsworth for collegiality. In respect of Zoë's contribution to the book thanks are owed to all her teachers at the University of Edinburgh (1988–1992) for assisting her own understanding of Social Policy and especially Adrian Sinfield whose enthusiasm for the subject at a 'fresher's fair' was what convinced her she needed to change her original degree course before she'd actually started it. Zoë would also like to acknowledge David Keighley whose approach to making social policy 'real' for students attending open days is apparent in Chapter 1, Pat Young whose insight into learning and teaching has, she hopes, helped to improve her own practice, and also the students to whom she has taught introductory Social Policy over the last 15 years. Zoë's personal thanks go to her family: Mark for making sure she's always reminded of what goes on in the 'real world', Ellice for caring about whether she'd had a nice day writing her story, Louis for constantly testing her powers of explanation, Robyn for always having a smile and to Pam Irving for support despite difficult times. Zoë would like to dedicate her writing here to Stan Irving (1934–1997), a welfarist through and through.

Both authors would like to extend special thanks to Justin Vaughan and Ben Thatcher at Blackwell/Wiley Publishers, as they have played a particularly helpful role in the planning of this edition, consulting the market extensively. We are also grateful to Sarah Dancy for her work in steering this text through the production process.

M.H. and Z.I.

Chapter 1
Studying Social Policy

- Introduction
- The Individual and Society
- Rights and Obligations
- Social Policy: Magpie, Jelly-baby or Side-salad?
- The Content of this Book
- Suggestions for Further Reading

Introduction

Many students come to social policy with a rather sketchy idea of what it entails. Some may have covered particular aspects of welfare such as 'education' or 'the family' as part of previous sociological studies, while others may have engaged with some of the more applied areas within a health and social care framework. Others still, with no previous experience of the subject may embark on courses either because social policy study is a requirement of their particular course of study (for example on a health studies degree) or because it sounded like an interesting option. The range of directions from which students arrive at the study of social policy is illustrative of the beauty of the subject. You can be sure that even if the term 'social policy' has never previously crossed your academic radar, that you have been exposed to it throughout your entire life. From Child Benefit to GCSEs, GP services to the care of elderly relatives, social policy impacts on our security, development and happiness. However, social policy also touches our lives in more unexpected ways such that areas as diverse as food consumption, discipline within families and global economic competitiveness are all matters of social policy. This chapter will examine further some of the issues, concerns and topics with which a student of social policy can expect to become acquainted in the course of her or his studies. Rather than beginning with an excursion into the 'meaning' or 'definition' of social policy, which tends to construct artificial and restrictive subject boundaries, the aim of this chapter is to demonstrate the depth and breadth of enquiry, what is possible rather than what the limitations or boundaries are.

The Individual and Society

> ### Box 1.1   Daniel: What is to be done?
>
> Daniel has been described in his local paper as a 'one boy crime wave'. At the age of 15 his offences already include truancy, vandalism, criminal damage, assault, assaulting a police officer and affray. It is reported that he has made the lives of members of the community in which he lives a misery. In addition to the offences with which he has been charged, he is reported as being abusive to his neighbours, intimidating local residents as part of a local gang and being involved in bullying at school where his level of educational achievement is well below his peers.
>
>   Daniel's father, who works away a lot of the time, believes that his behaviour is just teenage high spirits, while his mother who has a serious heart condition and spends much of her time travelling to and from hospital admits that Daniel seems to dislike authority but is at a loss as to how to change his behaviour. Daniel himself can't see that he has any problems except boredom and the unwelcome attention of the adults around him.

What should be done with or about a boy like Daniel? At a personal level it might be hard to find the desire to do anything *for* him since his behaviour might suggest that he is not a particularly sympathetic character. However, his actions clearly have an impact on the lives and well-being of those with whom he comes into contact as well as affecting his own future. Popular and ideological responses to a 'problem' like Daniel can be found in the pages of newspapers and in the speeches of politicians. There are regular calls for the reintroduction of national service in the tabloid press for example, while the present Labour government has embarked on a project of 'responsibilization' though various educational, family and criminal justice policy measures. In a rather unlikely contrast, David Cameron, as Leader of the Conservative Party, once advocated a more understanding and caring approach towards young people, which was captured in the sound bite 'hug a hoody'. In considering Daniel and the challenges he represents for social policy, it is helpful to separate considerations into different levels of analysis which in some ways correspond to a timeframe – what should be done in the short, medium and long term, but also illustrate the depth and breadth of the issues that arise in relation to a single individual's place in society. In this way it is possible to examine the relationship between 'subjects' of social policy (as both individuals and members of social groups), the institutions and policy measures set up to respond to them and also how these fit into a wider picture of human development.

   At the meta or macro level, the framework for a societal response to any particular problem, and in fact the ways in which issues come to be seen as problems in the first place, depends very much on underlying visions of the 'good society', the kind of social world we aim to shape. These visions also reflect our beliefs in relation to human nature, whether we view humans as essentially good, or altruistic, but corrupted by circumstance, or whether we are essentially bad or self-interested and restrain our unpleasant tendencies due to the existence of social sanctions. This of course also requires consideration of the relationship between structure and agency in human action. Debate around the relative importance of environment and our 'place' in the social structure (our class, gender or ethnic group for example) and our capacity to determine our own progress (our individual agency) within the social world, is not necessarily polarized into an argument that we are *either* passive victims of circumstance *or* free agents. Even Marx, concerned to stress the impact of social structure, recognized that as individuals we 'act', but not, he suggested, in circumstances of our own choosing. At the individual or micro level, it is impossible to measure accurately the extent to which level of income or education, or standard of housing or health influence what a person chooses to do with her or his life, but there is plenty of evidence to show that these factors do influence the scope of choices to be made – people's life chances. Poor health measured as lower life expectancy for example, is more likely to be found amongst people with low incomes. At one level, lower life expectancy amongst one social group as compared to another is itself an effect of structural conditions (social stratification in this case). However, once analysis shifts to the specific causes of poor health and early death (environmental factors, diet, smoking and so on) the debate between those who emphasize 'structure' in the form of unequal access to the labour market, health services and education for example, compared to those who prefer more individualized explanations around health behaviour, becomes much more complex and heated. Headlines such as 'Obese told: "it's up to you"' (*Observer* 18.01.04) reflect the increasing dominance of individualized explanations of social problems and their influence on government responses. At the same time however, the tacit recognition that humans (especially children) are not necessarily free agents is also clear in more recent moves to ban the television advertising of junk food during the hours when children could be watching. Thus in this example where social class differences in obesity can be demonstrated, there is a clear case for examining the relevance of food consumption under advanced capitalism (at the macro level) rather than simply opting to shift the blame for ill-health onto sufferers themselves (focusing on the micro level).

A second point to make in relation to the significance of macro and micro level questions around structure and agency relates to one of the core considerations in the study of social policy which is the distribution of resources or 'who gets what'. David Donnison, an important contributor to social policy, has suggested that this distributional concern, with resources, opportunities and life chances, is, in fact, what makes a policy 'social'. At the macro level again, analysis concerns the principles which underpin the patterns and processes of distribution and of course, questions of 'fairness' are at the centre of debate. Views on the fairness of inequalities depend very much on the extent to which these inequalities are considered to be the products of individual choices or to result from forces beyond individual control. For example, a person may have sufficient command over resources to participate in the property market but rather than buying a house may choose to rent a caravan because she or he prefers a more transient lifestyle. Most people would find this kind of housing inequality perfectly acceptable. If the caravan dweller was restricted to this form of housing because she or he did not earn enough to participate in the property market this would begin to raise questions around individual choice and the reasons why it might not be enjoyed in the same way by all individuals. However, if the caravan dweller's situation was replicated in a number of other cases then the fairness of the general distribution of housing and employment would clearly be more questionable still. A more detailed discussion of the significance of 'personal troubles' compared to 'public issues' can be found in Robert Page's chapter in May et al. (2001), but what should be clear is that in attempting to seek out policy solutions to social issues, an exclusive focus on the individual can never provide a sufficient basis for action. To return to Daniel, our views on his actions and how society should respond to them also depend on the extent to which he is considered to be a product of his environment (has he been damaged in some way through his early life experience?) or an essentially bad person (and can we say this for definite given that he is still legally a child?). In fact, in the area of crime and criminal justice policy, there is a much greater focus on individual agency and, while an individual's particular emotional circumstances are sometimes considered in mitigation for crimes committed, public issues such as unemployment are not. Subjective, micro-level considerations are also made in relation to the treatment of individuals such as Daniel. The societal response to his behaviour depends on an assessment of his needs (for anger management or literacy classes for example) balanced against the needs of society (the need for others to feel secure and protected). These needs can be conflicting and are not necessarily recognized by those who are viewed as possessing them. Daniel may not accept that he needs to control his aggressive behaviour for example. Consideration of the societal response to social problems and the individuals and groups at whom they are targeted requires us to focus our analysis on the 'meso' level.

At the 'meso' level we find the central aspects of Social Policy study, the institutions and structures which mediate the more abstract social, political or ideological values, and translate these into action in the form of policies intended to shape individual lives to achieve some kind of collective aim. Although the main policy areas covered in this book are those associated with state welfare provision, policy, and especially social policy, is not restricted to the activities of the state. Social policy also concerns action undertaken by our families, friends and community, collectively, sometimes called the 'informal' sector, as well as voluntary or 'not for profit' organizations, and, increasingly, the private sector through for example the perks of employment (from occupational pensions to gym membership) as well as newer forms of commercial involvement in the provision of services. Thus there are a number of different social policy actors or agencies of welfare, each having contrasting values and aims in terms of their role in provision, depending on the historical circumstances of their involvement and their relationship to the people to whom the provision of welfare is directed. The relationship between a mother and her child for example is clearly different to the relationship between an employer and employee, or a volunteer support worker and her or his client, or a school teacher and pupil. For most people, the largest share of individual welfare provision is undertaken in the home within households and families and includes basic need fulfilment such as the provision of food but also aspects of health, education, personal care and emotional well-being. We don't, for example, present ourselves at our local accident and emergency department every time we catch a cold. However, there are many ways in which informal welfare provision is insufficient to meet needs since it relies on the existence of both material and non-material resources that are not universally available or adequate. It is for this reason that historically, individuals have sought and continue to seek collective solutions to the meeting of social needs through both voluntary and political action. Those, on the other hand who regard informal provision as insufficient but who do have access to material resources, have sought individual solutions in the market for private provision.

Consideration of Daniel in the context of meso-level analysis would lead us to explore both the range of institutions which might be called upon to intervene in his life, and also the nature of that intervention. A response to Daniel's behaviour could involve both formal state agencies in the areas of education, social work and criminal justice such as his school and his area Youth Offending Team, but at the same time his family and local community might also be called upon if, for example, his parents or guardians were required to attend parenting classes or if he were served with an Anti-Social Behaviour Order (ASBO) which local residents were encouraged to monitor. From these responses to the 'problem' of Daniel we can see that a mixture of rights and obligations is operating in the form of societal expectations regarding the roles and behaviour of Daniel, his family and his local community and the expectations of each of these groups and individuals regarding support that can or should be provided by the state. Our responsibilities towards each other and the treatment we can expect, whether as close family members, acquaintances or as strangers we have never met, are also part of the essence of social policy.

Rights and Obligations

The case of Sarah outlined in Box 1.2 raise some central issues in social policy debate around questions of rights and responsibilities. In the post-war context, lone parents became a (some would argue 'soft') target for criticism during the late 1980s when the Conservative government, influenced specifically by Charles Murray (1990) and other US commentators, took a condemnatory stance towards unmarried mothers in particular. The argument ran that young women were deliberately choosing to raise children without their fathers because generous social security and housing provision encouraged them to do so. These mothers and their children were blamed for many social ills from youth crime to poor educational attainment to the general breakdown of the moral fabric of society. What the government of the time lacked in evidence and policy ideas it made up for in harsh words and the demonization of what is a very diverse and fluid social category. We will return to the substance of family change in Chapter 12 but it is useful here to highlight the key features of this

Box 1.2   Sarah: What is to be done?

Sarah is a 36 year old divorced lone parent with a son aged 11 and a daughter aged 13. The family live in a privately rented house, the costs of which are met in full via Housing and Council Tax Benefit. The children's father lives close by but pays no maintenance because he suffers from mental health problems, is unable to work and receives Incapacity Benefit. Sarah has a new long-term partner but they live separately because she thinks this is better for the children. Sarah's weekly income therefore consists of the means-tested social assistance benefit Income Support (IS) and the universal but categorical Child Benefit. She is also entitled to some NHS related 'passport' benefits (such as free prescriptions) and free school meals and bus passes for the children.

Sarah left school at 16 with one O level and does not drive, but has since completed a mature access course at her local college which qualifies her for entry to University. For the last 8 years Sarah has worked for 2 hours per week running a local youth club where she earns £20 per week. This money is declared and is allowed under the 'earnings disregard' attached to IS. She is also very active in the local community, working voluntarily for the residents' association and other local groups. Sarah is not ambitious or materialistic and is happy with the roles she plays in relation to her family and community.

debate because it symbolizes significant contests around the understanding of concepts such as 'dependency' and 'participation'. This is particularly important because although the moral critique of lone parents has waned, their economic position is of continued political interest. This interest has finally found substance in the most recent policy changes regarding the employment status of lone parents where Labour, following the release of their 2007 White Paper, *Ready for Work: Full Employment in Our Generation*, are planning to restrict by the child's age, the point at which full-time (lone) parenthood is legitimate insofar as honouring social security claims is concerned. By the end of 2010, lone parents will be expected to become jobseekers when their youngest child reaches the age of 7 years.

One of the fundamental issues at stake here, the obligation to undertake paid work, is bound up with broader question of what 'citizenship' means in twenty-first century UK society. In his influential essay on 'Citizenship and Social Class' written in the immediate post-war context, T. H. Marshall (1963) argued that in addition to the civil and political rights gained in earlier centuries, the twentieth century witnessed the establishment of a set of social rights to health, education and other social services and a 'modicum' of economic welfare, which enabled both social participation and the expression of equality in status of each individual. While Marshall did not explicitly set out a set of obligations concomitant to the rights he identified, it is 'the duties we owe' that have come to overshadow social policy under Labour, and the duty to be employed is arguably the most significant of these. There are two other issues that arise in examining this question, and Sarah's case captures both of these.

Firstly, there is clearly a gender dimension in the obligation to take paid work, particularly in the case of lone parents, who are predominantly women (male-headed lone parent families have only made up between 1–3 per cent of all families since the early 1990s). If Sarah is expected to take employment then who is to provide the care and support required by her children while she is at work? If she is only expected to work part-time then will the UK's tax credit system guarantee her an acceptable reward for her work? Given that she has limitations on the employment she could seek (she would be unable to access the graduate employment market, she can't drive and she has childcare commitments) what kind of economic independence could she secure? Ultimately, is it fair that because Sarah is living alone with her children that she is denied the choice to be a full-time parent when this choice may be available to women in two-parent households? At the macro level these questions relate to the way that production (economic activity) is valued above social reproduction (raising children and maintaining households over time). Sarah may well be doing an important job in raising her children but in the UK the state is less and less inclined to support this role as a 'status'. While T. H. Marshall's account of citizenship did not recognize the ways in which the role of carer filters access to social rights (see Ruth Lister's (2003) *Citizenship: Feminist Perspectives* for further discussion of this topic), the 'new' Labour version represents an approach to 'adults' that assumes an equality of gender relations which doesn't exist.

Secondly, there is a question related to the valuing of paid and unpaid work in the context of voluntary activity. Sarah's participation in supporting the well-being of her local community through her voluntary and youth work is both an important source of welfare and an expression of the civic virtue often seen as part of the obligations of citizenship. Labour have been very keen to encourage this form of activity and a role for voluntarism was built into the UK welfare state from its inception. Voluntary and charitable activities do, of course, save the government money which would otherwise have to be allocated to the provision of often very specialized welfare services, and so it is debatable whether Sarah's shift from a voluntary worker claiming social security benefits to a part-time employee claiming tax credits would actually serve any economic purpose at all. Certainly a shift such as this would not assist in improving social welfare generally since Sarah's voluntary and youth work may well contribute to the achievement of 'neighbourhood renewal' (which is a government aim) as well as perhaps the prevention of teenagers following Daniel's path. Thus we can see from Sarah's case that our rights and obligations towards the state and collectivities closer to home are both complicated and conflicting. The presence of children in Sarah's case, and her status as a benefit claimant might make a difference to the kinds of rights and obligations which are publicly and politically acceptable, but in Edith's case (see Box 1.3) the responsibilities of individuals and the state have a very different basis.

The UK is considered to be an 'ageing society' in that the proportion of the population that is beyond retirement age is increasing and will continue to do so.

Box 1.3   Edith: What is to be done?

Edith is 84 and lives alone in a ground floor local authority flat, which she shared with her husband until he died several years ago. Edith has had both hips replaced and the local authority has made some adaptations to her flat in order to facilitate her mobility. A local authority funded carer also visits in the morning and evening to assist Edith with housework and bathing. Edith has three children, a daughter and two sons and several grown-up grandchildren with children of their own but none of this immediate family lives close by. Despite it being a two hour round trip, her daughter, who is retired, visits two or three times a week to do Edith's shopping, to help with other day to day activities and to provide some company, and her sons visit from time to time. Other than this Edith's only visitors are her carer and a niece who lives a short walk away.

Recently Edith has begun to forget things and feels depressed, and she has not been eating properly although she is able to cook for herself. She has been prescribed some anti-depressants by her GP who has also suggested that it might be time to think about an alternative living arrangement.

The official UK statistical service (the Office for National Statistics) reports that while the proportion of people aged 65 and over in 2006 was 16 per cent, by 2031 this will rise to 22 per cent. Thus there will be more and more people in situations similar to that of Edith, for whom decisions about care arrangements and living accommodation will at some point become pressing. Edith's case raises another set of issues relating to our expectations of state assistance and involvement in our lives and thus questions about our rights to care and support particularly in later life, but equally at any time that we require support to enable us to maintain our independence. However, Edith's case also illustrates the ways in which social policy is entwined with provision for emotional, intellectual and very personal needs for both day to day physical activities and the more general need for human dignity and the support of our interpersonal lives. It is relatively simple to meet physical needs through the fitting of handrails and walk-in baths for example, but provision to meet our needs for autonomy, self-worth and the respect of others is not so easy to specify.

Had Edith been a homeowner, perhaps in receipt of a private occupational income or with other sources of income, then the state's obligations to support her care and accommodation needs would be minimal. As a local authority tenant with a funded carer, Edith is much more likely to qualify for state funded care and accommodation in a range of residential settings depending on her needs and their availability in her area. The range of options open reflects the fact that in the UK, as in other developed welfare states, a 'mixed economy' of care exists which means that needs are met via a selection of care providers, both voluntary or charitable and private or commercial organizations, as well as through directly provided state services. In fact, the latter are becoming less and less important as changes in the nature of state intervention brought about in attempt to reduce costs, mean it has become more of a funder than a provider. However, most decisions on questions of care and accommodation are based on considerations beyond the cost, and bring into play our intimate relationships with family and significant others.

The obligations of kinship are a central part of social anthropological study and in relation to social policy tell us much about the kinds of welfare arrangements we might expect to find in any society. In a post-industrial, increasingly atomized society such as the UK where labour mobility has been encouraged to support economic growth, we find that 'families' are much more geographically dispersed. It is thus not unusual to find that, as with Edith's family, the children of those over retirement age do not live in close proximity to their parents or even their own children. The reasons for this and the more general implications are discussed in more detail in Chapter 12, but here the point is that for Edith (and other people in her situation), there is no guarantee that the obligations of kinship exist, or that even if they do, that a theoretical guarantee can result in practical care and support. Comparative research indicates that the UK is well below the southern European countries in terms of social visiting (an unpublished study at the time of writing, on which one of the authors worked, of the social networks of people over 50 shows that 67 per cent in Britain but 89 per cent in Spain see a close relative (other than spouse) once a week or more) and there are regular reports in the British media of mostly older people dying alone without anyone to notice their passing. While these cases are extreme, they are symptomatic of the challenges and failures faced by society at the macro level in terms of how we construct our social relationships, but also of social policy at the meso level in terms of how our obligations towards each other as humans can be mediated via the collective provision of public services.

In Edith's case, it is the intervention of her GP, a 'gatekeeper' insofar as access to other health and social care services is concerned, that acts as a catalyst to changes in her daily life. The fact that her daughter has taken a caring role may mean that familial obligation falls upon her in relation to the more intensive care that Edith will require from now on. This might reflect what Land and Rose (1985) termed 'compulsory altruism' in respect of the gendered nature of caring within families and women's lack of choice in taking on the caring role. However, bound up with its gendered characteristics, caring is an expression of emotional ties and so a process of moral rationality (Duncan and Edwards, 1997) operates in parallel to the economic rationality that may inform the decisions about Edith's care. The financial costs will not necessarily be foremost in the considerations of Edith's care where her family are concerned even though this may be the most important element of discussion of her case by her local authority representatives. The involvement of a number of different people, representing different agendas and with different perspectives on Edith's welfare again highlights the contested arena within which social policy is practised.

As someone who is already in receipt of public assistance, a 'case conference' to discuss Edith's future arrangements might involve both family and local authority representatives such as social workers and housing officers in combination with input from her GP. If Edith were a homeowner with no previous involvement with public services, then decisions regarding her welfare may well be taken by herself and her family alone. Thus we can see that our position in terms of social class and as a welfare service user has implications for the normative definition of our needs and consequently the experience of 'independence' and 'autonomy'. This is not suggesting that families are likely to be any less paternalistic than state agencies but that in the current situation where health and social care services operate within a market, those with greater financial independence will be able to exercise greater power in decisions regarding their care.

The three case studies we have introduced provide food for thought in relation to many of the fundamental concepts, themes and questions which arise in the study and practice of social policy. The next section considers some of the ways in which social policy fits into wider study in the social sciences.

Social Policy: Magpie, Jelly-baby or Side-salad?

In research undertaken amongst academics teaching social policy, the subject was variously referred to in the terms above (Irving and Young, 2004) and it should be clear from the preceding discussion that the theoretical and material concerns of social policy range widely in scope and draw on knowledge and understanding developed across the social sciences from moral philosophy to micro-economics. In this way, social policy, as an academic endeavour, is said to be a magpie, a social science pickpocket taking concepts, methods and theories wherever it sees fit and using them to whatever purpose it sees fit. Some regard this as a disadvantage, with no emblematic key thinkers in the same way that Marx, Weber or Durkheim are for sociology, and allegedly no core area of enquiry which it can call its own. It is not the place here to elaborate on what makes a discipline. Sociology could also be subject to a similar critique regarding its disciplinary provenance. For students, it is less important whether social policy has disciplinary status than whether the right questions are being addressed. In fact, there are many important theorists who have contributed to the study of social policy, too many to list here (many will be found in the references in later chapters), but suffice it to say that what is significant about theorizing in social policy is that it is never concerned with abstraction alone. Social policy is normative, that is, it is concerned with changing the world rather than simply describing it. It is particularly difficult to study social policy from a position of political ambivalence or disinterest and even the pseudo-neutrality implied by the recent governmental reliance on what is termed 'evidence-based policy' is exposed in the thinking around the macro-level questions referred to earlier – the answers to which inform the policy that the 'evidence-base' is established to support. This is not to say that social policy analysis and research is partisan and thus spurious; the academic study of social policy entails working from a constructively critical stance and seeking to both improve understanding and initiate change and influence the direction of that change. As Paul Spicker has aptly noted: 'There would be something distasteful about rummaging through the chronicles of human misery without trying to produce any positive effect' (Spicker, 1995, p. 7).

For students of social policy, part of its appeal is that it is an academic jelly-baby that can be moulded to fit the disciplinary goals of historians, geographers, economists and so on. At the same time the subject maintains its own empirical concerns and as noted in the previous section, social policy is applied. In view of this it can also be regarded as a side-salad in the sense that along with the aspects of 'deep-theory' found in sociology, the social theory of political science and the modelling of economics, it acts as the real life accompaniment, the set of specific social issues and problems to which more abstract concepts, principles and theories can be applied. Methodologically, social policy study is equally at home in the statistical pictures created through large survey techniques as it is in qualitative and ethnographic research stories, and this has been the case throughout the subject's century-long history. Many social policy researchers contribute to the annual statistical analyses produced by the Office for National Statistics, such as *Social Trends*, while at the other end of the spectrum, journalists produce work which is grounded in the academic study of social policy but which reports the human condition in ways which are popularly identifiable. An example of this would be Polly Toynbee's book *Hard Work* (2003) which provides excellent social policy insight in a narrative form. This kind of reporting actually has a long, and sometimes controversial history: some arguing that Henry Mayhew's work on the London poor for example, pandered to the prurient tendencies of the Victorian middle class, while others believe Mayhew's work, and the popular reporting of other social commentators, were influential in the germination of welfare policies. The academic study of social policy has evolved from its early twentieth century roots in the study of 'social administration' at the Department of Social Science at the London School of Economics. Consequently it is linked very directly to the practice of social work but its purpose was as much to train social researchers in an attempt to inform the work of social welfare professionals as it was to teach frontline professionals themselves. Thus social policy (and administration) has an 'empiricist tradition' concerned with the establishment of social 'facts' which in the early years directed the forms of methodological enquiry towards social surveys and the approach to analysis towards a search for immediate and small-scale 'solutions' rather than calls for social transformation.

No wonder then that the question 'What is social policy?' continues to be the subject of perennial disagreement, and that its status as a discipline or field of study comes under regular scrutiny by those involved in its analysis. What we can be sure of is that we are engaged in the study of human welfare, that we need to know what has been done to improve welfare, who has influenced the directions and forms of development, whose interests policies serve, what the impact of policy has been and how policy changes shape in the light of social, political and economic change. Three decades ago, Mishra defined social policy as 'those social arrangements, patterns and mechanisms that are typically concerned with the distribution of resources in accordance with some criterion of need' (Mishra, 1977, p. xi). This statement neatly captures the scope of study, but within this distributional arena, debate and conflict is found in the construction of needs (cf. Edith's case in Box 1.3), whether they are expressed or imposed and the kinds of responses proposed to meet them: should they be interventionist or 'light-touch', should there be more regulation of behaviour or less, should there be greater investment (and higher taxation to pay for it) or more efficient use of existing funds?

The answers to these kinds of questions are now much more theoretically informed since the arrival of 'critical' social policy in the late 1970s and 1980s. Although the early Fabian influence was based in social criticism, the development of analyses of welfare states and state welfare from Marxist, feminist and anti-racist (Gough, 1979; Pascall, 1986; Williams, 1989) perspectives and more recently from constructivist perspectives which emphasize diversity, identity and culture (see for example chapters in Lewis et al.'s *Rethinking Social Policy*, 2000) have contributed much to the broadening of social policy horizons. Fiona Williams (1989) for example, demonstrated that although historically the aims and outcomes of policy have been linked to economic structures, or the needs of capitalist production (for an educated, healthy workforce and enough social security to prevent social unrest), that social divisions of gender and 'race' and ethnicity, are also built in to the architecture of the welfare state. Examples of social policy research in the 1980s into areas such as the impact of residency rules on social security entitlements, differences in social housing allocations between different ethnic groups, issues of differential educational achievement and differences of treatment within health services all pointed to the operation of racially discriminatory practices and the existence of institutional racism long before the Macpherson Report into the racist murder of Stephen Lawrence (Macpherson, 1999) established this term in mainstream policy discourse. A final point to consider then before moving on to outline the more specific contents of this book, is that social policy is not always a benign force and that social progress is not always its goal or outcome. Social policy has always been somewhat of a double-edged sword, a 'handmaiden of industry' and social control on the one side, and a product of the struggles for social amelioration on the other.

The Content of this Book

In this book, analyses are mainly focused on the meso level, and also on the key areas of state welfare provision: social security, health, social care, education, and housing. The decision to concentrate on these more traditional areas of social policy is to some extent arbitrary, but at the same time reflects the view that these areas can be subject to a critical and theoretically informed examination which recognizes that social policy is much more than state social policy, and that 'social' policy is much more than that directly concerned with the provision of welfare services. The final chapter will return to some discussion of the nature of social policy in the modern world and thus the scope and concerns of study will re-emerge. In the meantime, we can give some indication of what can be found in this book and what will have to be found elsewhere. Given that we have begun with an example which highlights the problem of crime and what is now termed anti-social behaviour, it might considered odd that there is no chapter on criminal justice in the book. The omission is deliberate for two main reasons. Firstly, that the field of criminology has expanded rapidly over the last decade and this expansion has necessarily given rise to the publication of a wealth of introductory literature addressing both sociological enquiry into crime and the analysis of crime policy. Secondly, and related to this sudden interest in crime and its perpetrators, under the Labour governments from 1997, the boundary between social and crime policy has become extremely fuzzy to the extent that crime policy often takes primacy in the design of policies which are only indirectly concerned with the prevention and treatment of crime. This is particularly the case in relation to housing, regeneration and social exclusion policies, but can also be identified in policies from asylum to maternity services. It is important that the study of social policy continues to question such trends rather than reinforcing state directed shifts in the politics of welfare. Therefore, while we recognize that all criminal justice policy has social significance, we are interested in it here only as it intersects with other areas of welfare provision such as housing and social work services.

The policy areas covered in this book do, ostensibly, fit the traditional and sometimes criticized 'classic welfare state' model of social policy, but in attempting to build understanding of a subject it is important to focus on depth rather than breadth, to develop a sense of principles and themes across a limited range of topics, rather than gather a vast range of knowledge. Given that beyond the traditional areas covered here, social policy analysis can arguably be undertaken in relation to any action that has an impact on quality of life and the distribution of welfare, it would be impossible and unwise to attempt to address every aspect in a single text. For a student new to the subject, it would also be overwhelming to find that the field of study appeared to cover 'everything' and so we begin with tradition and hope that having got to grips with the basics, that students can then use their understanding to take social policy study in the direction of their choice.

The policy areas explored in this book are those developed in the aftermath of the Second World War in response to the existence of 'five giants' identified by the main architect of the British welfare state, William Beveridge, as the great social evils which had to be eliminated for successful post-war reconstruction: want, ignorance, idleness, disease and squalor. The 1942 Beveridge Report is regarded as having provided the blueprint for British welfare arrangements although his plans were never brought to full fruition, and were subject to many amendments, omissions and oversights between the publication of the report, the enactment of legislation such as the 1944 Education Act, and the actual implementation of policy. In addition to the areas of social security, education and children's policy, employment, health and housing, this book also contains a chapter on social care of adults. These kinds of localized caring services, emerging from family and community support systems, have formed the basis of social intervention throughout the period of industrialization and thus are at the heart of social policy study.

It would be impossible to come to a reasonable understanding of current and recent policy without some exploration of the both the historical and political context in which it has evolved. So much of what we experience of twenty-first century social policy is steeped in the welfare struggles of the past, and despite over a century of political change and concomitant welfare reform, many of the principles which underpin welfare arrangements in the UK, are those established in England's pre-modern existence. However, although a historical perspective assists in explaining the shape of the present (the subject of the next chapter), history does not determine current or future developments. The role of politics in explaining the means by which policy is made and the ways in which it is interpreted and delivered is essential (see Chapters 3 and 4). Through engagement with these two approaches to analysis we can uncover the power relationships between interested actors, the structures and institutions via which power is exercised and the difference between what is intended through policy and what is actually achieved. It is important to note here that because of political change, and the historical relationships of the four constituent countries of the UK, the terminology used in the rest of the book will vary depending on topic and context and thus readers will find references to the UK and (where services diverge across the countries) concentration on much the largest of the countries (England) but references to special features of the others.

This book also contains a chapter dealing with the comparative dimension of social policy study. Although the preceding chapters are focused on social policy in the UK, it is clear that national welfare concerns are subject to increasing levels of external influence. This is not to say that learning from abroad is new or that nation states are politically immobilized. Economically advanced countries have always looked to one another for social policy ideas; the pension system introduced in early twentieth-century Britain had been informed by the late nineteenth-century systems of social provision introduced in Bismarck's Germany for example, and it is important that the political effects of the current phase of global economic development are not overstated. What is significant for social policy is the greater intensity of cross-national exchange and the establishment of new forms of international and trans-national relationships which give rise to new forms of inequality and new ways to respond to them. In the light of these changes, it is imperative that students of social policy are aware of the comparative context from the outset, and that UK based students can place the content of their own country's welfare arrangements in the context of the wider world. Despite the similarity of social problems across national borders (poverty, powerlessness, ill-health and so on) the social policy response is neither uniform nor universal.

The final chapter considers some of the themes which are apparent throughout the discussions of policy context and policy areas, and links these to the topic of social change, which also represents a significant element of any understanding of social policy. Many social policies are implemented in order to bring about social change, as discussed in relation to rights and responsibilities above. But policy operates within frameworks of power relations both passively, reflecting patterns of domination and subordination and also actively in reinforcing unequal relationships and sometimes establishing new forms of inequality, for example between people who are eligible for support and those in similar situations who are not. Thus social change is not always equivalent to social progress. The aspects of change explored in the concluding chapter are directly linked to much longer established analyses of social division. Inequality, despite its contested nature, is a fundamental concern of social policy and the transformation of families, work and the age and ethnic composition of populations has fundamental implications for the nature and form of inequalities. For social policy there is a double challenge, firstly to understand the nature of change, its good and bad points, and secondly to actively respond to it using measures which are designed to be either supportive or to arrest what are regarded as negative developments.

Suggestions for Further Reading

A good introduction to the key issues in social policy is to investigate the various ideological perspectives on its role in society. George and Wilding's *Welfare and Ideology* (1994) offers an excellent overview of this subject. Fiona Williams's *Social Policy* (1989) also offers an introduction to the ideological debate but with an emphasis on the need to take account of gender, class and race in both historical and contemporary social policy analysis. Issues about the relationship between social problems and social policy are explored in May, Page and Brunsdon (eds.) *Understanding Social Problems* (2001). An overview of the whole field of social policy is offered in an edited volume by Alcock, Erskine and May (eds.) (2008). Alcock, Erskine and May have also produced a valuable reference book *The Blackwell Dictionary of Social Policy* (2002). Hartley Dean's (2006) *Social Policy*, is published as part of a series of short introductions, and provides an account of social policy which is both educative and entertaining.

The Social Policy Association has a good web site with many links to other useful sites at www.socialpolicy.net. There is also a government website that provides a gateway to sites for individual departments, agencies, local authorities and some international organizations at www.direct.gov.uk.

Chapter 2

The Shaping of Contemporary Social Policy

- Introduction
- Poverty and the State before the Welfare State
- The Emergence of a 'Welfare State' in the Early Twentieth Century
- Beveridge's 'Five Giants'
- The Welfare State after Beveridge
- Suggestions for Further Reading

Introduction

The shaping of UK social policy and social provision over the last five hundred years is not well depicted by the term 'development' since this tends to imply a well-planned journey with various pre-determined stopping points and a safe arrival at the intended destination. This uncomplicated and comfortable picture couldn't be further from the truth. The kinds of social policies that affect everyday life today exist because of, and in some cases in spite of, the outcomes of social and political progress and decline, people's struggle and sacrifice, altruism and self-regard. This chapter provides an entry point into the colourful and fascinating history of the evolution of social policy: the provision of welfare prior to and during the period of industrialization, the establishment of the British 'welfare state' in the mid twentieth century and the events since that time which have altered the direction of policy and impacted on social welfare in Britain. As we have seen in Chapter 1, social policy is concerned with far more than poverty alleviation, but the main focus of this chapter is the state's response to the problem of poverty. The reason for this is that the existence of poverty, questions around what to do about it and the solutions adopted by those with political power have been fundamental to the evolution of welfare provision in all advanced economies. An examination of the state's relationship with the poorest members of its population gives insight into significant aspects of social policy study and allows us to consider some enduring themes. These themes include questions of:

- Morality and social justice – the separation between the 'deserving' and 'undeserving' or the extent to which those in political power distinguish between types of poverty. Those deemed to be 'the deserving poor' being seen to have come to be in need due to circumstances beyond their individual control (through ill-health or disability for example) and the undeserving through individual failing (idleness or fecklessness for example).
- Family obligation – the extent to which kin obligations are codified into policy, the breadth of kin relationships to which obligations apply (parents, children, grandparents and beyond for example) and the relationship between obligation to support and legal marriage (in respect of children born outside marriage for example).
- Settlement – the extent to which social responsibility is dictated by geographical location and links established to location through birth, marriage or other family connections.
- Stigma and social control – the extent to which policy is used as a negative force to prevent or repress social disharmony or to reinforce individualistic and residualist ideology which represents reliance on public support as shameful.
- The relationship between work and welfare – the fundamental economic and ideological questions around the necessity to maintain work 'incentives', societal contribution and low wages.
- Administrative architecture and bureaucratic procedure – the strengths and weaknesses of centralization versus local administration, rules and discretion in the provision of public support and the politics of implementation.

Attention to these themes enables us to take the 'long view' in the exploration of welfare state development, and to understand the influences which have shaped social policy, as well as showing how the policies enacted in Britain today, such as changes to child maintenance and support systems, disability benefits and public health for example, have their roots in national culture and political and economic relationships which stretch far back into history.

Poverty and the State before the Welfare State

The tale of state involvement in social policy usually begins in the sixteenth century when legislation began to be enacted, designed to deal with the 'problem' of poor people through registration of paupers, the raising of local taxes and the criminalization of begging for example. Around this time a number of factors led to a serious shortage of employment and a consequent change, both qualitative and quantitative, in the characteristics of poor people. Previously poverty and the related condition of homelessness (or 'vagrancy' as it was then known) had been much more dependent on not being able-bodied and thus being unable to take on paid work, usually agricultural work, though either ill-health or disability or old age. In the latter years of the 1500s, although Elizabeth's rule saw England become a relatively strong economy within Europe, harvests were poor, and the economy had moved away from the feudal system where, despite the acute social division, aristocratic landowners had duties to protect their workers (vassals, peasants and serfs), towards an economy based much more on the production of goods such as textiles, which created significant regional inequalities as some English counties were better able to enter these markets than others, and also a shift away from agriculture towards wool production which had an impact on both the amount of work and the amount of food available to the rural population. So although this change led to the development of an expanding middle class of merchants, it also led to increasing numbers of able-bodied people, especially men, who, unable to secure their livelihoods in their local villages, began to travel the country in search of work. In a similar way to the unease with which groups of men in public places are regarded today (think of football supporters or 'gangs' of young people congregating on street corners), the observation of groups of vagrants roaming the countryside, hungry and with nothing to lose began to worry the political establishment. Whereas the giving of alms to the poor and the collective local support of those unable to support themselves had been undertaken as a religious duty in medieval times, by the end of the 1500s, attitudes to the suddenly apparent able-bodied pauper were not so charitable. This group were much more problematic in the eyes of the state since they were a source of potential unrest and therefore a threat to the newly established social order that the monarchy, which had greatly increased powers in the Tudor period, had a particular interest in maintaining. The level of taxation was as much an issue in the sixteenth century as it is now, and England's economic strength was regarded by many economists of the time to be partly a result of the low levels of taxation. Thus in addition to the perceived problem of social control was the threat of rapidly expanding *numbers* of poor people – the losers in the economic shift away from agricultural production – who were likely to place increasing pressure upon local tax payers, representing a different source of political disorder.

This combination of social and political instabilities culminated in the 1601 Act for the Relief of the Poor (otherwise known as the 43rd of Elizabeth), which had been preceded in Scotland by the 1574 Scottish Poor Law Act. Historians tend to suggest that the provisions enacted in this Elizabethan response to poverty were in fact more paternalistic and less harsh than had been the case in the reigns of her predecessors where vagrancy had been punished with time in the village stocks, public beatings and even time in slavery, but nevertheless these provisions laid the way for an approach to poverty that continues to permeate policies concerning 'workfare', homelessness, lone parents and low wages in the twenty-first century. What is important in looking at the contribution of the 1601 Act to the foundations of British social policy are:

• The setting up of a national administrative structure (for England and Wales) which relied on local administration of the Act's provisions at Parish level. The nature of this system had consequences for both tax obligations as local rates were levied on householders according to the value of the property in which they resided, and issues of 'settlement', i.e. the determination of a person's origins and residence and thus responsibility for her or his welfare.

- The statement of family obligation or in the language of today the 'liability of dependents' insofar as individuals' welfare was reliant upon their parents and grandparents or children and grandchildren.
- The distinction between classes of poor people which while recognizing that poor people required collective support, differentiated between people who were incapacitated through old age, illness or disability and those regarded as 'able-bodied'. This latter group were regarded with suspicion and shame, ensuring that self-support was always preferable to public relief (both materially and psychologically).
- The introduction of 'workfare' or, as it was then called, 'setting the poor on work' and the responsibilities of parishes to provide the means for the destitute to work and apprenticeships for children (see Box 2.1)

In addition to its administrative and social influences, the 1601 Act also attempted to set a trend towards institutional support, called 'indoor relief' rather than the existing and numerically expanding forms of 'outdoor relief' or direct payments made to poor people within local parishes. Indoor relief was expected to take place in existing and especially constructed houses of correction and poorhouses. Interestingly, in the contemporary context of a mixed economy of welfare where private and voluntary providers are subcontracted by local authorities to undertake social care and health services (see Chapters 7 and 8), in the 1600s, 'farming the poor' took place where subcontractors would feed and house poor people and charge local parishes for these services. Jeremy Bentham (1748–1832), the renowned philosopher and social commentator would later further develop this idea in his pauper management plan for a national chain of private workhouses each holding 2,000 inmates. Fortunately, this plan was never taken on board by government, but clearly the role of the private sector in welfare provision is nothing new.

Box 2.1   The 43rd of Elizabeth

'Overseers of the poor . . . shall take order from time to time, by and with the consent of two or more Justices of Peace . . . for setting to work of the children whose parents shall not by the said churchwardens and overseers or the greater part of them be thought able to keep and maintain their children. And also for setting to work all such persons married or unmarried having no means to maintain them or no ordinary and daily trade of life to get their living by, and also to raise weekly or otherwise (by taxation of every inhabitant . . .) a convenient stock of Flax, Hemp, Wool, Thread, iron and other necessary ware and stuff to set the poor on work and also competent sums of money for and towards the necessary relief of the lame, impotent, old, blind and such other among them being poor, and not able to work and also for putting out of such children to be apprentices'

Excerpt from what is believed to be the text of the original Reginae Elizabethae Anno 43, the 1601 Act for the Relief of the Poor with modernized spelling. www.sochealth.co.uk/history/poorlaw.htm

The local implementation of the 1601 Act never matched its centralizing aims (see Chapter 4 for some discussion of these issues), the system of poor relief remained uneven and fragmented and the nature and generosity of provision depended entirely on the overseers and Justices within each parish who were responsible for its administration, and, given the regional economic disparities in the seventeenth and eighteenth centuries, the location of the parish. As mentioned previously, popular views towards alms-giving had begun to change and resistance to taxation was as present in Elizabethan times as it is in the 2000s. As a result many disputes occurred around the question of the parish 'ownership' of paupers and the spatial dimensions of social obligation were set out in the Acts of Settlement from 1662 onwards. Settlement depended on either paternal birthplace or place of employment for 365 days or, for women, their husband's birthplace. The 1662 Act allowed the removal of people to their place of settlement if local parish Justices suspected they were likely to become paupers. The parish support of destitute children who had been born outside marriage and thus whose fathers could not necessarily be traced was also often a source of hot dispute as parishes, relying on patrilineal assessment of residence, attempted to avoid the cost of poor relief. Parishes were keen to obtain the removal of unmarried pregnant women before their babies were born (and became the responsibility of the parish), and these women were also excluded from later protections afforded to mobile labour. In 1743, the 'illegitimate' child's settlement became that of her or his mother rather than place of birth, and so began a long history of the public humiliation of unmarried mothers based upon questions of economic support. From 1732 pauper women were legally required to name the father of a child born outside marriage so that he could be forced to reimburse the parish for the cost of the child's relief. This issue has remained a feature of social assistance, subject to controversial efforts to modernize it in recent times (see Chapter 5, pp. 114–16).

The linking of shame, a significant social tool, with collective support was not restricted to lone mothers however, and in 1697 it became law that paupers should wear a badge with the letter 'P' printed on it and the initial of their parish to avoid any confusion around responsibilities for support. This marking of paupers served not only as an administrative convenience but also as a way to reinforce the stigma associated with being poor. The stigmatization of poverty and the labelling of those who are poor as 'workshy', 'feckless' and generally inadequate has travelled down through the years and continues to be reflected in British social security and employment policy (the New Deal, the detection of benefit fraud, changes to incapacity benefits for example) which assumes that given the choice people will choose the 'dole' rather than work. This approach to the treatment of poverty in society is associated with the liberal welfare regimes found in most of the Anglophone world (see Chapter 11 for further discussion). It draws from an individualist ideology informed by Protestantism and contrasts with arrangements for public support which have developed in continental European, Nordic or East Asian countries which are infused with different forms of collectivism and influenced by other aspects of religion and political patterns.

The eighteenth century was a time of great hardship and hunger for the English labouring population who endured the consequences of the loss of common land through enclosure and instability in the price of wheat, the staple of their diets. Through to the nineteenth century, unemployment also began to rise, particularly in the South as agricultural labour was squeezed out of the national economy and industry moved North, leaving behind the unskilled agricultural labourers whose labour mobility was restricted through the Acts of Settlement. In the late 1600s around half the total population of England were either labourers or paupers (around 2,575,000 people) and in fact many historians have argued that the inmates of poor-houses would in all likelihood have been better fed than the majority of the labouring population who struggled to maintain the self-sufficiency which had characterized life in an agrarian economy (Cole and Postgate, 1971). It is perhaps for this reason that the use of stigma and harsh treatment were used so widely as a deterrent for claiming public relief as parishes saw the numbers of paupers rise dramatically. In an effort to address the consequences of social change and relieve starvation, in the 1790s the parish of Speenhamland in Berkshire introduced a system of relief which other parishes also copied. Put simply, this system provided a wage subsidy based upon family size and the price of bread and provides an illustrative example of several themes which endure in social policy across the world. Firstly, the notion of publicly financed wage subsidies for the low paid which has made a significant comeback in the form of tax credits in the UK and other industrially advanced countries. Secondly, the notion that family size has an impact on households' command over resources which was a finding of the groundbreaking poverty studies at the turn of the twentieth century, and became a principle underpinning the welfare legislation enacted following the Second World War. Thirdly, in a similar vein, the linking of general welfare to food and its security, which has also formed an important part of both poverty studies over the last century, and the design of the levels of benefit paid today.

The 1601 Act lasted through two centuries but by the 1820s it was clear that it was ill-equipped to respond to the changes in work and life brought about by urbanization and industrialization. Poor people were beginning to become politically organized and to combat this the state had begun to use increasingly repressive measures to control the population, which were unsustainable in the long term. There was also change amongst those with political power however, as capitalist economic development continued and the new economic liberalism gained political strength. The cost of poor relief had reached around 20 per cent of national expenditure by 1832 and influenced by the economists and popular authors of the time (Ricardo, Malthus and Samuel Smiles for example) came a more punitive and less tolerant approach to the existence of pauperism. As Michael Rose (1972, p. 10) observes 'poverty had been regarded by many writers as a necessary element in society, since only by feeling its pinch could the labouring poor be inspired to work. Thus it was not poverty but pauperism or destitution which was regarded as a social problem.' The latter was viewed as an individual failing – 'indolence, improvidence or vice' – rather than a result of circumstance, and the solutions were based upon punishment, deterrence and the inculcation of the work ethic, preferably involving hard work. These views, involving a moral separation of the 'dangerous classes' from the 'respectable poor', were publicized and taken on board by both politicians and the burgeoning middle class, despite the fact that most labouring men were working around 12 hours a day with women and children still only just beginning to feel the effects of the factory acts reducing their working hours. We can also detect echoes of these debates in Conservative government concern in the 1980s with the rise of a 'dependency culture' resulting from the supposed cushion provided by the modern welfare state and Labour's more recent wish to remove the 'perverse incentive to act morally' from the current benefit system.

It is unsurprising then that the most significant piece of social policy legislation since the 1601 Act, the Poor Law Amendment Act of 1834 or the 'New Poor Law', represented an attempt to translate these views into policy. As an 'Act for the amendment and better administration of the laws relating to the poor' (to give it its proper title) it is clear that the *administration* of poor relief was seen to be part of the problem and restructuring part of the solution, a theme taken up in Chapters 5 and 6. In an effort to achieve both centralization and uniformity of provision, the act set up a national Poor Law Commission to superintend the system, and formed the parishes into groups known as Poor Law Unions. This important step towards the development of a national system provoked local opposition and was only a limited success. However, the Act's main contributions to the development of policy were the 'workhouse test' and the doctrine of 'less eligibility'. The aims of these were to curb indiscriminate 'outdoor' relief and thus reduce costs through the restriction of relief to that provided 'indoor' in the workhouse. Thus the 'workhouse test' stipulated that people declaring themselves destitute had to be sufficiently desperate to enter the workhouse otherwise they could not be really in need. The system was intended to ensure that those who received public support were worse off ('less eligible') than the poorest people in work and this principle continues to underpin the payment of unemployment benefits today. In the period following the Act the statistics gathered did seem to suggest that the costs of poor relief had fallen, however social historians now argue that in reality, the poor simply turned to any other means of survival rather than enter the workhouse. Henry Mayhew, who published a journalistic account of 'London Labour and the London Poor' in 1851, describes in detail a huge range of marginal economic activities undertaken by the poor from street sellers selling flowers and sheep's trotters to those called 'toshers' – the sewer hunters who searched for metal objects and rope and 'pure' finders who collected dog excrement from the streets and sold it to the tanners yards. Clearly the fact that people would rather do these kinds of jobs suggested a fear of something worse in the workhouse and the workhouse test became a point of strong resistance around which working class movements organized and protested, sometimes violently, before and after the passing of the Act.

Resistance to the Poor Law reforms came in the wake of a much more sinister piece of legislation which in many ways was more symbolic of the deep class divisions and the lack of humanity afforded to the poor during the nineteenth century. The development of medical science in the 1800s, and particularly the Schools of Anatomy which provided the training for physicians and surgeons, created a need for bodies on which students could practise dissection and examine the human anatomy. However, due to the desire of most people for a Christian burial intact, there were few cadavers available apart from those of hanged murderers who forwent their posthumous rights. This led to a booming market for 'resurrectionists' (bodys-natchers), who disinterred and stole corpses, and for the even more unsavoury activity of 'burking' which described murder with the intention of selling the victim's body and was so-called after the infamous Burke and Hare who murdered at least 16 people in Edinburgh and sold their bodies to the anatomy school operated by Dr John Knox. In the 1830s 'Burkophobia' had taken hold, particularly amongst the poor and itinerant since they were the most likely victims of 'Burkers' and whose bodies, as Ruth Richardson comments, were worth more dead than alive. A 'scare' in Shadwell workhouse where an inmate alleged that the cook had made 'nattomy soup' for the inmates (broth which as well as meat, contained human remains), demonstrates that despite the unlikelihood of truth, amongst the inmates, 'the suspicion itself is testimony to the poor's understanding that they were regarded as bestial by their social superiors' (Richardson, 2001 p. 222). The 1832 Anatomy Act confirmed that the poor were indeed considered less human as it allowed the work-house overseers to sell the bodies of paupers for dissection (adding further to the popular fear of a 'pauper funeral'). This state sanctioned threat to bodily integrity (even be it after death) and its restriction to one class of people (those reliant on public support) created a huge swell of disquiet amongst working-class people, particularly in the North, who, given the economic vicissitudes of the time, were all potential inmates of the workhouse. By the time that the reforms to the Poor Law emerged this disquiet was easily transformed into serious unrest and uprising, culminating in the creation of the Chartist movement for democratic reform in favour of social equality, and in many areas the implementation of the reforms was prevented for several years.

It is easy to understand why resistance to the reforms was so strong: combined with the symbolism of the workhouse, the actual conditions within were indeed something to be feared. Entering the workhouse was the ultimate degradation, often physical, but inmates were also denied privacy, dignity and family life as families were separated and men and women inhabited separate wards. Able-bodied inmates were required to work, undertaking tasks such as rock breaking or picking oakum and given the poor sanitation and spread of disease encouraged by institutional living, in all likelihood those who entered the workhouse had a good chance of dying there. The workhouses were supposed to provide minimum adequate sanitation, food, shelter and medicines to sustain their inmates but the number of scandals reported in the press during the latter half of the nineteenth century suggest otherwise (see Box 2.2).

In practice, many Poor Law Unions failed to implement the 'workhouse test' as strictly as had been intended and outdoor relief continued to be paid. Some Unions were unwilling to invest in the building of new workhouses while in others, the parish guardians (the new overseers) were either opposed or too frightened of local unrest to impose the Act's provisions. By the end of the nineteenth century more working class and female guardians had been appointed to the Poor Law boards and

Box 2.2   The scandal at Huddersfield workhouse

The following is an extract from the overseers' report which was requested by Huddersfield Township in response to allegations of ill-treatment of inmates in Huddersfield Workhouse:

> ... that patients have been allowed to remain *for nine weeks together* without change of linen or of bed clothing: that beds in which patients suffering in typhus have died, one after another, have been again and again and repeatedly used for fresh patients, without any change or attempt at purification; that the said beds were only bags of straw and shavings, for the most part laid on the floor, and that the whole swarmed with lice ... and that it is a fact that a living patient has occupied the same bed with a corpse for a considerable period after death; that the patients have been for months together without properly appointed nurses to attend to them ... they have been suffered to remain in the most befouled state possible, besmeared in their own excrement, for days together and not even washed.

The following is an extract from a supplement to the Leeds Mercury in 1848 giving details of the official investigation:

> ... the house is, and has been for a considerable period, crowded out with inmates; that there are forty children occupying one room eight yards by five; that these children sleep four, five, six, seven, and even ten, in one bed; that thirty females live in another room of similar size; and that fifty adult males have to cram into a room seven and a half yards long by six yards wide; that the diet of the establishment has been and still is, insufficient; that four shillings worth of shin of beef, or leg offal, with forty-two pounds of potatoes, have been made to serve for 'soup' for 150 inmates ... that the clothing of the establishment is miserably deficient; that there is no clothing in stock; that a great proportion of the inmates are obliged to wear their own clothes; that others have little better than rags to cover them; that instances have been known where the nakedness of even females has not been covered ... and that there are throughout the entire establishment the most unmistakable signs of bad arrangement, shortsightedness, real extravagance, waste of the rate-payers' money, and want of comfort, cleanliness, health, and satisfaction amongst the poor.

A web of English History www.historyhome.co.uk/peel/poorlaw/huddscand.htm

this alongside public outcry at the horrific workhouse conditions still being reported, served to create a groundswell of support for change in the treatment of and attitudes towards poverty in British society, and it is to the convergence of factors which assisted this development that we now turn (see Box 2.3).

Box 2.3   From succour of last resort to first port of call: How a building can change

The more wealthy Poor Law Unions such as Sheffield had purpose-built workhouses such as 'Fir Vale', opened in 1881, housing over 1,500 inmates in a range of wards designed for different groups ('casuals', children, women and so on) and providing a hospital, school and chapel. This building still stands today as the Northern General Hospital. In less than a century the building was transformed from a prison for poor people to a fundamental element of a comprehensive health service free at the point of access. Workhouses in most towns and cities have found renewed life within the more positive provisions of the modern welfare state while some have merely provided some civic revenue through their sale. To identify and examine the fate of workhouses all over the UK visit Peter Higginbotham's site: www.workhouses.org.uk

The Emergence of a 'Welfare State' in the Early Twentieth Century

It is convenient, for the presentation of historical accounts, when a specific date can be identified as a watershed. It further adds neatness when that date is the beginning of a century. While there is always an arbitrary aspect to the choice of such dates, particularly in social history, the dividing point between the nineteenth and twentieth centuries seems a particularly significant one. At this time, political change and challenges to the strength of Britain as an economy and imperial power combined with the development of a social conscience to create the conditions under which the collectivization of social provision began to occur. The large male working-class element added to the electorate in 1885 was just beginning to influence political thinking. The Labour Representation Committee (LRC) was set up in 1899 to try to elect more working men to Parliament and was successful in that over 50 MPs returned to parliament after the 1905 election were Labour or 'Lib/Lab'. The LRC became the Labour Party in 1906. The major political parties, the Conservatives and the Liberals, were increasingly aware of both the need to compete for working-class support and also the fear of the rise of Socialism in Europe felt by the British establishment. For the Conservatives, the formula was an interesting blend of imperialism and social reform (Semmel, 1961). The Liberals had a radical wing, temporarily disadvantaged by a conflict over home rule for Ireland and the jingoism of the Boer War, but ready to push the party towards acceptance of a package of new social measures.

Late in the nineteenth century, the UK had begun to discover that an advanced industrial nation is vulnerable to alarming economic fluctuations, owing to the uncoordinated nature of much business decision-making and the international complications of the trade cycle. New competitors had also emerged as other nations – particularly Germany and the USA - industrialized rapidly. The British Empire still looked secure, but the competition for new trading outlets was increasing dramatically. At the same time as doubts were beginning to be felt about the UK's economic vulnerability, working people were increasingly organizing in trade unions to try to secure, or guarantee, their share of the progress. The political price of economic failure was being raised and thus new initiatives to preserve the unity of the nation were required.

The Boer War, a rather inglorious episode in British imperial history, had considerable significance for social policy. In general, it led to a concern to examine what was wrong with *Great* Britain that she should have been unable to fight effectively against apparently fragile opposition. In particular, politicians, in this age when Britain's imperial success was believed to have been based on racial superiority, sought to examine why so many volunteers to fight had been found to be unfit to do so. At the turn of the century one in three adults died in the workhouse, a hospital or asylum and as historians report, Britain's imperial prowess was rather sullied by the revelation that however terrible the living conditions reported in Africa and Asia, equally bad and worse could be found in any British town. A third of the military recruits were too thin, too small or too ill to see active service and in 1904 an Interdepartmental Committee on Physical Deterioration reported its findings.

The committee's report urged the establishment of a school medical service and the provision of school meals within the public education system. Both these measures were adopted by the Liberals and implemented soon after they came to power in 1906. In combination with the 1908 Children Act, which made the neglect of children's health illegal, it is clear that as the workers and soldiers of tomorrow, children were one of the initial targets of developing state intervention. As future workers and voters (the franchise had been considerably widened in 1867 and 1884 – the latter having a much greater impact on working class enfranchisement), children's primary education had already become a matter for state concern from the 1870s, and by the 1890s elementary education for 5–10 year olds had become both compulsory and largely free. In addition to education, child mortality was also a cause for governmental alarm, and policy to address this allowed the expansion of both state and voluntary welfare services including health visiting and the provision of milk for babies. These two services continue today with the 2007 'Healthy Start' initiative (see www.healthystart.nhs.uk/) being the most significant overhaul of food-related welfare provision since the Second World War. Interestingly this too has been prompted by concerns with children's health, most recently the personal and NHS costs of obesity.

The dominant view amongst the governing classes in the last part of the nineteenth century was that state involvement in dealing with social issues and problems should be kept to a minimum. Middle class concern about the conditions of the poorer classes, stimulated by worries about their impact upon the better off (the spread of disease and the rise in crime for example), was particularly channelled into charitable activity. There was a substantial growth of voluntary organizations concerned to rescue children, improve housing conditions, 'teach' the poor how to manage their family lives and even to offer cash relief. Many middle class women, still shut out from most opportunities for formal employment, involved themselves in this charitable activity. As a result of this work, or middle class 'cultural assault' on the working class as Derek Fraser (2002) describes it, some of the more prosperous people became more aware of the reality of working class life. For some this generated a commitment to more radical government action. But this increased awareness of social problems also led to efforts to try to ensure that charitable work was better organized, and more able to effectively distinguish the so-called 'deserving' from the 'undeserving'.

What did capture the public imagination around the turn of the century were the reported findings of studies of poverty. As mentioned above, Henry Mayhew and others had been publishing accounts of poverty and the labouring classes throughout the latter part of the nineteenth century but these had largely been descriptive and sometimes sensationalist articles designed to appeal to Victorian curiosity. The real catalyst to action and the first properly social scientific study of poverty in Britain, using survey methods and detailed gathering of evidence was that conducted by Charles Booth, published in 17 volumes as the *Life and Labour of the People of London*. Booth's study inspired Seebohm Rowntree to undertake his more famous study in York, with more refined definitions and measurements of poverty, which was published in 1901. Rowntree's study was influential in many ways from its impact on the manner in which benefit levels are calculated to this day, to its recognition of the social and structural determinants of poverty to its specific findings on the cyclical effects of poverty over the lifecourse and the prevalence of the low waged amongst the poor. As Rowntree concluded:

> That in this land of abounding wealth, during a time of perhaps unexampled prosperity, probably more than one-fourth of the population are living in poverty, is a fact which may well cause great searchings of heart. There is surely need for a greater concentration of thought by the nation upon the well-being of its own people, for no civilization can be sound or stable which has at its base this mass of stunted human life. (1901, p. 304)

Both Booth and Rowntree had emphasized the importance of environment in explaining the incidence of poverty, highlighting the roles of poor housing conditions leading to ill-health and lack of employment. In the latter part of the nineteenth century issues of public health had begun to come to the fore as urbanization increased the potential for the spread of infectious diseases, scientific advance identified the main links between insanitary conditions and disease and politicians recognized the threat to industry presented by epidemics. Local government agencies took some steps to tackle public health problems through the construction of sewers and supplies of clean(er) water, but real progress did not come until central government gave local authorities powers to act effectively, and also required them to take such action.

Developments in medicine began, in the late nineteenth century, to render inadequate the traditional Poor Law approach to the care of the sick. Alongside the development of Poor Law hospitals, many voluntary hospitals, assisted by charitable funds that enabled them to provide cheap or free services to the poor, were founded, or grew in strength from their earlier origins. The local authorities were also given powers to establish hospitals to fulfil their duties to contain infectious diseases, and to care for mentally ill people. Medical care outside the hospitals grew in importance in the second half of the century, becoming more than the prerogative of the rich. This was partly a Poor Law development, partly the extension of the services of the voluntary hospitals, and partly an aspect of the growth of insurance against misfortune widely practised by the more prosperous of the working classes. In all, a mixed package of health care measures was evolving. This complex mixture, dominated by a powerful medical profession firmly established during the nineteenth century, posed problems for subsequent attempts to rationalize the health services, and therefore influenced the shape the National Health Service (NHS) eventually achieved.

Before they lost office, the Conservatives also responded to the growing evidence on the extent of poverty, and the inadequacies of existing measures, by setting up a Royal Commission on the Poor Laws and Relief of Distress in 1905. The report of this body, which did not appear until 1909, contains a most thorough discussion of social policy at that time. There was both a majority and a minority report. The former represented the views of the influential and in many senses reactionary 'Charity Organization Society', advocating administrative changes and an expanded role for the voluntary sector, while the latter, providing a well-argued critique of the workhouse system, reflected the conclusions drawn from Booth's research and developed by Beatrice Webb, his Fabian Socialist cousin and a member of the commission. However, without waiting for the Royal Commission, the Liberal government decided to promote two pieces of legislation that significantly modified the role of the Poor Law in the provision of social security: the Old Age Pensions Act of 1908 and the National Insurance Act of 1911. Learning from policy in Bismarck's Germany, the liberal government hoped that the provision of a national minimum income for workers, funded through their own social insurance contributions would lessen the appeal of the more redistributive systems associated with socialist ideas and suppress both revolution and the costs of social security. For pensions on the other hand, Lloyd George, the chancellor with responsibility for the design of the schemes (and some would argue the true founder of the welfare state), adopted the model developed in New Zealand which was not contributory but funded from taxation and means-tested. This period of Liberal reforms to social policy has such significance for current welfare arrangements because the details of state and individual obligations and the roles of the various social partners and professional groups that were thrashed out in the debates and meetings of the time have resonated throughout the twentieth century, shaping the social security and health services we receive today. The record of political machinations and the wealth of personalities engaged in social policy design at the turn of the nineteenth century makes fascinating and entertaining reading (see for example Barker, 1984; Jones 1994). Here we can only summarize the key themes which are central to an understanding of what came after the Liberal reforms.

The old age pension was promoted as a godsend for the elderly poor but when it was introduced in 1909 less than 500,000 people, mainly women, qualified for it. The pension, based on a personal rather than household means-test, was paid to all those over 70, which, at a time when life expectancy was around 48 years for men and 52 years for women might explain why take up was less than might have been imagined. In one sense the pension was merely an extension of the outdoor relief paid to older paupers in many parishes, and it did succeed in keeping them out of the workhouse, but other categories of pauper were excluded from its benefits including 'criminals, lunatics and loafers' (Barker, 1984, p. 70). 'Aliens' were also excluded in much the same way that asylum-seekers are excluded from the benefit system today. It was not so much the scope or generosity of the pension scheme which represented a radical break with the past but the fact that it heralded the introduction of collectivist principles to welfare provision in a society where ability to pay had previously determined health and social security. Nevertheless, despite the promise of collectivism, the spirit of the Poor Law can still be identified in the means-tested Pension Credit which is intended to alleviate pensioner poverty within the current benefit structure.

The National Insurance Act introduced compulsory insurance cover for both unemployment and sickness for the 'respectable' working class – mainly men in a limited number of strategically important trades such as ship-building, construction and engineering. The costs of the scheme were met through contributions from employees, employers and the state, and in adopting the insurance principle as the foundation of the system of funding, Lloyd George created a precedent for British social security which is unlikely to be revoked in the near future. In fact Lloyd George was not convinced that this was the best option and his vision of social security was of a tax-funded and far more redistributive model. However, at the time political expediency meant that tax levels would not cover the cost of social risks other than age and the attraction of contractual, contributory social insurance in terms of the avoidance of stigma won the day. The national insurance scheme provided both flat-rate cash benefits in times of unemployment and sickness, but also the right to medical treatment from a 'panel' doctor reimbursed by the state. This model of primary health care persists within the GP services provided through the NHS. Women's contributions and benefit payments were set at a lower rate than those of men but with the inclusion of maternity benefit for all insured and paid directly to women, the scheme clearly provided significant improvement in the material welfare of women and children. The payment of flat-rate rather than earnings-related benefits contrasts with the social insurance schemes developed in other European countries around this time which allowed much greater involvement of trades unions and thus much more occupational hierarchy. With the extension of social insurance to a pension scheme in 1925, the contributory principle has endured in British social policy despite its incongruity with contemporary patterns and forms of employment and its failure to deliver the quality of benefits required to eradicate the need for means-testing.

In 1909 Lloyd George published a budget statement that set the scene for the progress of state intervention in social welfare. However, although the budget of

1909 was radical in its use of progressive and increasingly direct taxation (of income), the revenue raised being intended to finance further welfare measures for children and unemployment, Lloyd George's universalist tendencies were somewhat curtailed in the face of war and cold economics. What was established was essentially an embryonic welfare state for male breadwinners, with a strong influence on what was to come. These developments occurred against a background of a rising volume of political controversy within the UK (emergent political movements on the Left, the women's campaign for votes and the conflict over the future of Ireland). A more dramatic tipping of the balance than actually occurred in the next few years might have been expected. In practice many of the new social policies of this period and the years to follow did little to disrupt the *status quo*; indeed, many must be seen as designed to preserve it.

In World War One, the UK experienced conscription for the first time, and the mobilization not only of the whole male work force but also of many women, to assist the war effort. The war economy produced many domestic shortages. Initially, the government was reluctant to impose controls and rationing, but its desire to curb wage rises and industrial unrest forced it to intervene. In general then, the role of the state advanced considerably during the war. Civil servants learned to carry out, and members of the public came to expect, government policies in areas of life never before influenced by state action. This was the general impact of war on public policy. Its specific impact on social policy was more limited. The imposition of controls on private rents in 1915 was a rare, but significant, example of social policy innovation in this period.

However, during and at the end of the war, the government made many promises for a better future. Even before the war ended, an Education Act was passed which recognized the case for state support for free education up to the age of fourteen. At the end of the war Lloyd George promised 'homes fit for heroes', and one of the first pieces of post-war legislation was a Housing Act that provided government subsidies to local authorities to build houses 'for the working classes'. This Act, known as the Addison Act after its sponsor, the Minister of Health, while not the first legislation to allow local authority house building, was the first to subsidize it. It effectively initiated a programme of council-house building that continued, albeit subject to regular modification as governments changed the subsidy arrangements, until the late 1970s. After the Addison Act, both of the minority Labour governments, in power in 1924 and in 1929–31, extended the local authority house-building programme by means of further subsidies. In the 1930s, there was a shift in housing policy, with the government encouraging local authorities to put their emphasis in house provision on clearing the slums. The strict rent control, introduced in the war to protect private tenants, was partly lifted during the inter-war period. However, with this, as with council-house building, no real attempt was made – until the 1980s – to turn back the clock on processes that were ultimately to transform totally the character of the UK's housing market.

While the quality and quantity of housing seemed to be soluble problems, the problem of unemployment raised an entirely different set of issues. The provisions of the Poor Law were not designed to deal with the kind of cyclical unemployment which is associated with industrial trade patterns or the problem of casual labour and consequent low and intermittent earnings, and neither did it recognize that unemployment could be caused by the structure of industrial employment rather than the decisions of individuals. The introduction of labour exchanges via the 1908 Act put into operation a young William Beveridge's ideas regarding the efficient working of the labour market where the buyers and sellers of labour could rely on a single location of transaction to meet their needs for work and workers, thus reducing the incidence of frictional unemployment (the gap between jobs). The exchanges were also set up with administrative responsibility for the cash payments made in respect of unemployment. From these 'offices of hope (and despair)', as they were described by one commentator in 1910, the Employment Service evolved, and despite some restructuring under the Conservative governments of Thatcher and Major, the creation of Jobcentre Plus by Labour has returned the system to a one-stop-shop for work and benefits although perhaps not reflecting the 'obligation of the state to find labour or sustenance' (Barker, 1984, p. 74) that Lloyd George had in mind.

The problem of unemployment has yet to be solved however, and there is little in current welfare-to-work policies and ideas of a 'hand up not a hand out' that was not tried out in the period between the setting up of labour exchanges and the Second World War (see Box 2.4). Following the First World War, the government had mismanaged the discharge of servicemen back into civilian life, and unemployment had risen rapidly. Then the economy picked up and the problem abated, but this proved to be a temporary respite and, by 1921, registered unemployment was over two million including 14 per cent of insured workers. The rate remained over a million throughout the inter-war period, falling back a little in the middle 1920s but then rising steeply in 1930. By 1931, it was over two million again, and by 1932 nearly a quarter of the insured were unemployed (see Box 2.4).

Although the first Labour governments were elected in 1924 and again in 1929, they failed to adopt a radical stance and in the inter-war years, governments of all persuasions were mostly concerned with reducing the escalating costs of benefits for the unemployed. The social insurance system was not designed to have more claimants than contributors and the 1920s and 1930s saw a whole raft (more than 15 acts in the 1920s alone) of piecemeal unemployment legislation increasing contribution rates, restricting entitlement to benefits, reducing the amounts payable and reinforcing the principle of less eligibility through the much criticized 'genuinely seeking work' tests. In yet another attempt to centralize the administration of means-tested poor relief to the unemployed, and thus keep costs low, the 1934 Unemployment Act set up the Unemployment Assistance Board. The UAB provided a model that enabled central government to take over the functions of the Poor Law agencies and gradually over the period to 1941 the board took on responsibility for most other means-tested cash payments. The 1934 act introduced the household means test (abolished in 1941) which led to the break-up of many families as a strategy for financial survival and survives in folk memory as symbolic of the kind of policing of 'need' that involved inspectors making intrusive home visits to assess the assets and income of households. The act also lowered the age at which the national insurance system would be joined (14 – school leaving age) but maintained 16 as the age at which

Box 2.4   Unemployment: some problems and solutions

In the 1930s, as now, there were regional variations in the levels of unemployment. In some areas such as Jarrow (famous for the 'Jarrow march' when the town's unemployed marched to London in protest at their circumstances) the rate was over two thirds of the working population. The depression years in the 20s and 30s were characterized by extreme hardship resulting from unemployment, and witnessed many strikes and mass protests, many organized by the National Unemployed Workers Movement. Homelessness also increased at this time as families were evicted through non-payment of rent and ex-servicemen continued to travel the country in search of a livelihood. Hunger was also prevalent as unemployed people and their families were unable to secure adequate nutrition on the rates of benefit available. There were many debates and submissions to the UAB around this issue, and disputes between the British Medical Association and other campaigning groups around the calorific requirements for an optimum diet rather than mere sustenance with evidence gathered that unemployed families were unable to obtain even this.

Schemes to alleviate unemployment in the 1920s:
- local relief schemes run by the Ministry of Transport and the Unemployed Grants Committee
- facilitation of emigration to the dominions (the Empire Settlement Act)
- transfers from depressed areas, particularly mining areas, to more prosperous areas (32,000 people in 1929 and 30,000 in 1930)
- junior employment centres (later to become Junior Instruction Centres)
- government training centres, primarily for skilled trades from 1925 onwards
- instructional centres
- training for women under the ministry's Central Committee on Women's Training and Employment, initially for domestic service but later extended to other vocations.

Source: Price (2000, p. 68)

insured workers could claim benefits, while reclassifying 14–15 year olds as non-dependents. Thus the right to benefit was removed from a substantial proportion of young people. The Conservative government used exactly the same strategy in the 1986 Social Security Act when benefit entitlement was removed from 16–17 year olds.

One of the more extreme solutions to unemployment was the establishment of labour camps or 'transfer instructional centres', 'opened up in rural areas to "recondition" or "harden" men from depressed areas' (Price, 2000, p. 76) and prepare them for employment through training in road building and excavation, while living in basic accommodation (often tents) with subsistence rations and an allowance rather than a wage. Opened in 1929, David Price reports that by 1933 over half of those who had attended had been placed in employment once their reconditioning sojourn was over, in his view a positive achievement. The quality and security of this employment is not known as public relief works had been scaled down, but the experiences in the camps do not suggest such a positive view of their utility (Humphries and Gordon, 1994). None of the employment and social security policies adequately addressed the fundamental problem of a lack of work however, and it was only with the onset of war in 1939 that the situation changed. The government was much more ready to mobilize all the nation's resources, especially people, in the Second World War than it had been in the First World War. Regulation and rationing were not adopted reluctantly, as previously, but as measures essential to the war effort. Politically, at least after Churchill replaced Chamberlain as Prime Minister in 1940, the nation was more united. The Labour Party regained its self-confidence, shattered by having being deserted by its leaders – who formed a National Government and then heavily defeated Labour in a general election in 1931. It joined the coalition government. Although Churchill sometimes appeared to be unhappy about it, planning for the peace was widely accepted as a legitimate political task during the war, and provided a source of optimism with which to boost the national morale.

Before looking at the most important example of planning for peace – the Beveridge Report – it is important to note a number of ways in which peacetime policy changes were foreshadowed by *ad hoc* wartime measures. In the last section, reference was made to the way in which the UAB, which was renamed the Assistance Board in 1940, took over various functions from the public assistance committees. In a similar way, voluntary and workhouse hospital services were also integrated during the war, under the Emergency Hospital Scheme. The evacuation of children called for the development of special services, foreshadowing developments in child care practice after the war. Rents were again strictly controlled, and empty houses were requisitioned. Price controls and food rationing, together with the full employment which followed from the enormous state investment in the war effort, also made important contributions to welfare. Food policy was at its highest point on the political agenda as, with echoes of the Boer War, children's health was prioritized and many poor children received adequate nutrition for the first time. The wartime state had many of the characteristics of the 'welfare state', which is popularly regarded as having been created after the war. Most importantly perhaps, taxation was raised and high during wartime ensuring that the public were somewhat inured to the fiscal demands of future services.

Beveridge's 'Five Giants'

The Beveridge Report was the report of a committee, chaired by one of the architects of the 1911 Insurance Act, on *Social Insurance and Allied Services* (Beveridge, 1942). The origins of the report were a need identified for the 'tidying-up' of the numerous provisions for various occupational categories and other social groups which, particularly in the view of the strengthened trade unions, required the imposition of uniformity upon social insurance and an end to administrative confusion. Beveridge however, with his previous experience in the civil service, seized his chance to influence major social reform and produced more than a dispassionate account of administrative restructuring. His commitment to a new age in welfare provision is captured in his description of the first of his three guiding principles for the report, where he states that 'a revolutionary moment in the world's history is a time for revolutions, not for patching'. The report's debt to even the more ignominious aspects of its heritage is nevertheless recognized in the later observation that 'the scheme proposed here is in some ways a revolution, but in more important ways it is a natural development from the past. It is a British revolution.' The public reaction to the report is hard to imagine today where crowds of people may queue down the streets overnight to be the first to read the latest children's novel but not the latest social security White Paper. However, historians inform us that it was a best seller, selling over 600,000 copies and that copies were airlifted and dropped over occupied France and Nazi Germany as a propaganda exercise to advertise the bright future which awaited the British people.

As for its contents, the report recommended the adoption of a compulsory contributory social security system which improved on the existing system by protecting all citizens against poverty at times of sickness or unemployment, and in old age. The new system should, it was argued, include family allowances, maternity benefits and provision for widows and orphans. The contribution principles should be insurance ones, involving the employee, the employer and the state as before, but the coverage of the scheme should be universal and therefore involve a national pooling of risks across the life-cycle, across industries and across families. This pooling of risks that we will or could all equally experience is the 'social' dimension of social insurance. Contributions and benefits would continue to be flat-rate and the latter would be paid at subsistence level. Beveridge makes reference to the findings of increasingly sophisticated social scientific surveys conducted between the wars, reiterating Rowntree's conclusions that loss of earning power and the failure of earnings to support families (rather than individuals) explained the incidence of poverty, rather than the failings of poor people themselves. Thus his report was explicit in its recommendation for the redistribution of income through both the social insurance scheme and according to the needs of families. This view was largely accepted in the post-war 'welfare settlement', although the 'truce' between capital and labour and both the benevolence attributed to the passing of associated welfare legislation and degree of consensus amongst those involved in its nativity are the subject of lively historical debate (see Page (2007) for an excellent review of this period). In his final guiding principle, Beveridge's belief in the freedom of the individual is most obviously set out in the specification of the state's obligation to the individual and vice versa, but also his view that 'the state in organizing security should not stifle incentive, opportunity, responsibility; in establishing a national minimum, it should leave room and encouragement for voluntary action by each individual to provide more than that minimum for himself and his family'. Thus as George and Wilding (1994) suggest, Beveridge was a 'reluctant collectivist' and the report represents a compromise, the content of which has provided the thin end of the more individualist wedge which has since been driven through British social provision.

The most soundbite-friendly (even in the 1940s) of Beveridge's guiding principles was that there were five 'giants' to be slain on the road to reconstruction, one of which was 'want' (poverty), the 'easiest to attack' and the subject of the majority of the report. But there were four others that required a more comprehensive set of welfare arrangements: disease (ill-health), ignorance (lack of education), squalour (poor housing) and idleness (unemployment). Hence there were a number of assumptions that the report made about the complementary arrangements necessary for the social security system to work effectively. Firstly a system of allowances for children, which, in addition to addressing the problems of poverty and family size, was expected to boost the birth rate by ensuring that low pay did not discourage larger families, while maintaining work incentives. This attempt at pro-natalist policy was not unusual in Europe in the 1940s as the effects of war were felt politically in population counts. Secondly, that there should be a comprehensive national system of health and rehabilitation services which would 'restore the capacity for work'. Lastly, that the maintenance of full employment was essential given the actuarial problems of unemployment amongst the insured experienced in the 1920s. The idea of 'full' employment, whether it exists and is achievable (or desirable) continues to be the subject of academic and political debate (see Chapter 6 for further discussion) but the centrality of paid work in the architecture of the welfare state is unquestionable.

In addition to the explicit assumptions made by Beveridge are the implicit assumptions about normal and desirable social reality and behaviour. In the arrangements for dependants and widows for example, were assumptions about marriage, the male breadwinner and women's 'duties' as wives and mothers which have left a difficult legacy for attempts to balance the interests of men and women in our own age. There were also assumptions about the meaning of 'nation' which have been and are increasingly at odds with the reality of both the UK's international relationships and ethnic identities in its constituent countries. The post-war social policy settlement was essentially a continuation of the process of creating a wage-earners welfare state. Policies for women and children treated them as essentially the 'dependants' of male workers. Little attention was paid to the enormous contributions women had made to the formal economy during the Second World War and it was presumed that they would largely withdraw from the labour force once the war was over. The 1940s may be seen as a period in which men, but not women, acquired limited 'social rights' to accompany their political rights acquired earlier in the century.

Beveridge's insurance scheme was broadly put into legislation. Family allowances were provided, for second and subsequent children in each family, by one of the last measures of the coalition government, the 1945 Family Allowances Act. Most of the rest was enacted by the post-war Labour government, though there was a crucial departure from the insurance principle in that the qualifying period for a full pension was very short. This deviation from Beveridge's plan made the scheme expensive to general taxation, and probably tended to prevent the adoption of benefit levels sufficient to provide subsistence incomes to those with no other resources and to inhibit subsequent increases to keep abreast with the cost of living.

With the passing of the 1946 National Insurance Act and the 1948 National Assistance Act, the Poor Law did cease to have effect although its ghost lives on, quite specifically, in the local assistance regulations governing homelessness and until more recently, people seeking asylum, and more generally in the continued significance of means-testing within the social security system in the UK. With regard to the slaying of the other four giants, legislation was also enacted to improve other aspects of the lives of ordinary people and their 'capacity to work'. The Education Act passed in 1944 and often identified by the name of the minister responsible, R. A. Butler, provided the framework for the education system until 1988. The Butler Act provided for universal free state secondary education, but did not specify the form it should take or rule on whether there should be selective schools. In 1948, the creation of the National Health Service provided another crucial innovation in social policy. GPs and hospital services were provided free for everyone, in a complex structure designed to unify the hospital sector, while leaving GPs as independent contractors and other community services in the control of the local authorities. This structure was achieved after hard bargaining between the minister, Aneurin Bevan, and the doctors, who were deeply suspicious of state medicine (Eckstein, 1960; Pater, 1981). The scheme was funded out of general taxation, though an element of payment for the health service remained in the NI contribution, creating a confusing illusion that this was what paid for the service. The notion of a totally free service did not last for long. Very soon, Chancellors of the Exchequer, exploiting concern that demand for services was much greater than expected, secured first small payments for spectacles and dental treatment, and then prescription charges, as ways of raising revenue.

The Labour government of 1945–51 did not alter the system of subsidizing local authority housing developed in the inter-war period, but it did, by the Housing Act of 1949, substantially extend the subsidies available. The Act formally removed the limitation confining local authority provision to housing for the 'working classes'. The government's concern throughout the late 1940s was to stimulate building to make up the deficiencies in housing stock arising from bomb damage and the wartime standstill in house building. However, post-war shortages of materials made it difficult to accelerate new building and in the decades to come there were a number of scandals surrounding the quality of cheap pre-fabricated system built constructions, not least the collapse of a high rise building, Ronan Point in 1968. The Labour government laid its emphasis on local authority housing to meet general need rather than on private building for sale, and squalour was certainly addressed through the construction of dwellings with modern sanitation despite some initial suspicion of inside toilets by new residents. Labour also involved itself, as no government ever had before, in an attempt to secure effective land-use planning and to curb land speculation. The Town and Country Planning Act of 1947 provided a grand design for this purpose, though one of limited success, which was subsequently dismantled by the Conservatives. Another crucial planning innovation, with major implications for the provision of public housing, was the New Towns Act of 1946. This provided jobs and houses in new communities for people from overcrowded cities and run-down industrial areas.

Among these widely publicized social policy reforms came another measure, with much less impact on the general public but nevertheless with important implications: the Children Act of 1948. The origins of this reform of the services for deprived children seem to have been in a child care scandal – the O'Neill case. The Children Act consolidated the existing child care legislation, and created departments in which professional social work practice would develop in child care and, in due course, in work with families. What is not so apparent in the catalogue of acts is any direct attempt to legislate for the giant of idleness with the Disabled Persons Employment Act 1944 being the only clear legislative action in this regard. Following the rash of unemployment acts in the 20s and 30s it is perhaps not surprising that governments were pleased in the post-war period to be able to push employment to the bottom of the 'to do' pile. Employment rates were high and stable and this was fortunate as the government made commitments to this in the 1944 White Paper on Employment Policy. In the decade following demobilization of the armed services there was plenty of work both in the various reconstruction projects and in the new welfare services – so much so that Britain relied very heavily on the attraction of migration from the former commonwealth colonies, particularly the Caribbean countries, to fill the jobs available. There was a commitment to the maintenance of full employment, with the Keynesian doctrine (Keynes, 1936) that budgetary management could achieve this now a point of economic orthodoxy. In the 1940s, such economic management was slightly inflationary, but this was broadly seen as a reasonable price to pay for full employment and economic growth. In retrospect, it is difficult to judge the extent to which the success of this policy, which (despite all the worries it caused at the time) was a success by comparison with the economic management disasters of either the 1920s and 1930s or the 1970s and 1980s – was due to good management, and the extent to which it was due to external and internal economic factors outside government control. Nevertheless, with no single reform or statement on employment it is easy to see why, when the heady days of post-war euphoria were over, UK policy returned, as it has done ever since, to the reinvention of the employment supply focused policies which failed to solve the problem in the past.

The 1940s were, in both war and peace, crucial years for the building of the system of social policy the UK has today. The substantial social reform programme of the 1945–51 Labour Government meant that they were the main architects. However, it has been shown that few of the innovations of this period were without precedent in the policies of earlier years, and that much of the crucial thinking about the form these new institutions should take had been done in the inter-war period. While the subsequent chapters in this book explore more contemporary developments in the key policy areas of the classic welfare state, it is important to conclude this chapter with some commentary on the fate of the giants since the introduction of the welfare reforms in the 1940s, and the significant factors shaping the more recent history of social policy in the UK.

The Welfare State after Beveridge

Broadly, the period 1951–2008 can be divided into four parts:

1   1951–64 was a period of comparatively little social policy innovation, which may be regarded as a time of consolidation or stagnation, according to one's political viewpoint.
2   1964–74 was a period of fairly intense policy change stimulated by both political parties, in which considerable difficulties were experienced in translating aspirations into practice.
3   1974–79 was a period in which rapid inflation, rising unemployment and government by the Labour Party without a parliamentary majority administered a severe shock to the political and social system, and to all who believed that there was still a need for developments in social policy.
4   1979–2008 saw reversals of the post-war developments, which, initiated by Margaret Thatcher in 1979, have largely continued under Labour governments after 1997.

Although the period between the Second World War and 1979 was broadly characterized by relative affluence and improvements in many aspects of daily life, social problems had not all melted away in the heat of post-war welfarism. As Brian Abel-Smith and Peter Townsend demonstrated in their 1965 publication *The Poor and the Poorest*, 7.5 million people remained unable to participate in the 'customary activities' of society at that time, due to lack of resources. Interestingly echoing the findings of Booth and Rowntree, a third of these people were in full-time work. Homelessness too was prevalent and 'Cathy come home' the first docudrama showing the plight of a family experiencing a calamitous downturn in their fortunes through no fault of their own, brought home to a well-off majority the existence of large holes in the welfare net. The film was watched by a quarter of the British population when it was aired in 1966 (despite most people not owning a TV) and led to the launch of Shelter, the housing campaigning organization.

The return of Labour to power between 1964 and 1970 and then again, but with scarcely a working majority, between 1974 and 1979 was seen by many pressure groups and political activists as an opportunity to deal with these issues and consolidate the welfare reforms of the 1940s. Particular objectives were the consolidation of social insurance to minimize means-testing and the achievement of comprehensive secondary education. In respect of the first of these there was limited progress. There were efforts to increase the levels of insurance benefits and to ensure adequate pensions for all. These limited measures, enacted against a background of economic difficulties that were seen as reasons for limiting public expenditure, were largely undermined by the Conservatives after 1979. The development of comprehensive education proceeded more smoothly, but (as will be shown in Chapter 9) this reform did not fulfil its egalitarian promise.

Another feature of the 1960s and 1970s – under both Labour and the Conservatives – was the beginning of a wave of efforts, which continue to this day, to secure more effective institutional arrangements for the delivery of public social services. These affected both local government and the health service. One particular change was the formulation of unified 'social services departments' (social work departments in Scotland) bringing adult and child care services together; this facilitated a period of growth for these 'Cinderella' services. It will be shown in Chapters 8 and 9 that services for adults and children have now been pulled apart again, largely because an alternative connection has become to be seen as more important: that between children's services and education. The fact is that there is no ideal formula for connecting different services, allegedly essential organizational forms for one generation can become irrelevant for another.

In this period the limitations of the post-war reforms and possibilities for further progress were acknowledged. Labour lost its big majority in 1970 and its efforts to consolidate social policies again in the mid 1970s occurred in a much less favourable economic and political environment. Hence, at the same time that doubts were being raised about Labour as the political champions of working class people and the more general success of the welfare state, alternative views from the right were beginning to gain attention. From the 1960s the Institute for Economic Affairs (now called Civitas), a free market 'think tank', has published pamphlets and essays arguing for reductions in state spending on welfare and the deregulation and introduction of market principles to public services. The IEA is only one of many policy think-tanks and although the views it promulgated were not mainstream in the 1960s, many of the policy ideas and principles have since been taken on board. Particularly influential in the 1980s (along with the *Sunday Times*) was the platform given by the IEA to Charles Murray (1990) and his 'underclass' thesis which gained far more intellectual attention and popular acceptance than merited by its social scientific credentials.

The 1970s were a time of economic turmoil with inflation, industrial unrest and a faltering of the prosperity enjoyed in the previous decade, and an opportunity for voices from the Right to say 'I told you so' in an attempt to confirm that the Right was right about the supposed damage caused by the cost and impact of welfare. So while it is tempting to attribute the change in the climate for social policy in the 1980s in the UK, to the election of the Conservative government led by a right-wing leader, Margaret Thatcher, changes had been gradually emerging before that date, and those changes were rooted as much in economic vicissitude as in ideological fervour. It was a Labour minister, Anthony Crosland, speaking in 1975, who warned local government that, as far as public spending increases were concerned, the 'party is over'.

The Thatcher years witnessed not only considerable change in the form of welfare and the balance of providers but also, and in some ways more importantly, a return to residualism as the principle underpinning state welfare. Thus reliance on the state for anything other than health and education services (and even these are bought by many where they can) has become an option of last resort and, with the echoes of the Poor Law reverberating down the centuries, the cultural significance of this should not be underestimated. While in other cultures it is a valuable aspect of the human condition, in the UK 'dependency' as Fraser and Gordon observe, 'carries strong emotive and visual associations and powerful pejorative charge' (1994, p. 4).

Despite their commitment to 'rolling back the frontiers of the state' (see Box 2.5), all the strategies of privatization, restrictions in entitlements and outright removal of

Box 2.5   Key elements of the Thatcher agenda

1   *Ideological challenge to the collectivist approach*
Media; think tanks; academic writing (especially from the US)

2   *The promotion of private welfare provision*
Health insurance (though without a direct attack on the NHS); encouragement of private and weakening of state pensions; home ownership (the sale of council houses to their occupiers transformed the role of local authority housing – a topic explored more in Chapter 9); compulsory competitive tendering for provision of public services; promotion of internal (quasi)-markets in welfare

3   *Reduce public spending*
Monetarism not Keynesian economic policy; cuts and service charges

4   *Introduce New Managerialism into public services*
Application of business principles aiming to increase 'efficiency' and 'effectiveness'

5   *Reduce the power of Local Authorities*
Centralize power over policy-making, revenue-raising and public spending; introduction of the purchaser/provider split

6   *Redefine citizenship*
Obligations to participate in the market rather than universal rights

Source: Adapted from P. Wilding, (1992) 'The British Welfare State: Thatcherism's Enduring Legacy', *Policy and Politics*, 20 (3), pp. 201–12.

some services, the Conservative governments 1979–97 only succeeded in reducing public spending in the area of housing. However, it is clear from the direction of Labour policy that the neoliberal message encompassed in New Right policies was widely received. The critique of state provision: that it is monopolistic and thus producer-led (rather than consumer-led); inefficient and bureaucratic, giving poor quality, undifferentiated services which sap the energy of consumers in relation to their expression of preferences leaving them without the motivation to act for and support themselves, seems to have been fully digested and internalized.

The Conservative governments offered 'market' solutions to the problems (real and imagined) of state provision. Doubtless there were deficiencies and unintended outcomes in welfare arrangements; service users' criticisms for example focused on the experience of services as disempowering, inadequate, inappropriate and slow. There were inadequacies in the recognition and treatment of the needs of the UK's ethnically diverse population and the operation of institutional racism was apparent long before the 1999 Macpherson Report mainstreamed this concept. Despite equality legislation enacted in the 1970s, women's social rights were still inferior to men's and inequalities of social class in education and health were persistent. These real failures of state provision are a long way from the expectations of the welfare state generated in the wake of the Beveridge Report and related legislation of the 1940s, but the supposition that they are intrinsic to state provision and thus could be remedied through privatization and a business model of welfare has not been borne out in practice.

As mentioned earlier, there has always been a mixture of public, private and voluntary social provision in the UK but from the 1980s the conservative governments undertook a wide-ranging programme of incremental privatization and marketization of social provision. 'Privatization' can mean many things, from denationalization (British Airways, British Telecom, British Gas and so on) to the contracting out of ancillary services such as hospital cleaning, catering and portering to the promotion of private insurance in respect of retirement, unemployment and ill-health, to the direct private provision of care services such as nurseries and residential homes, but as Hilary Land (2005) points out, is often as much about transferring costs and responsibilities to the family as to the market.

More broadly, and with a view to the contents of the following chapters, the change in social policy that has occurred since the 1980s is neatly captured by Zsusa Ferge's concept of the 'individualization of the social'. The acceptance and expectation of state intervention in everyday life that accompanied the warfare/welfare transformations of the 1940s, 50s and 60s was, it seems, as some historians now suggest, a blip in the conduct of relations between state and citizen. Popular myth has it that when asked to name her greatest political achievement Margaret Thatcher replied 'New Labour'. An amusing journalistic anecdote, but in policy terms we can see that there is significant continuity between the individualization of welfare which occurred under Conservative governments from 1979 and the personal 'responsibilization' strategies of Labour since 1997, both of which connect to the state of welfare before the welfare state. In the period immediately after 1997 there seemed to be suggestions that Conservative measures would be reversed. A pragmatic rather than a dogmatic approach to privatization was promised, with a strong emphasis on what would work best. The unsolved problem of the provision of satisfactory public – as opposed to private – pensions was reopened. Above all, where the Conservatives had been unwilling to acknowledge that there might be problems about poverty, the government pledged to take poverty reduction seriously. Viewed from 2008, however, while search for organizational 'fixes' to service delivery problems has become even more frenetic, in very many respects continuity is more evident than policy reversal. While the chapters on substantive policy areas in this book will only go back over past history where this is important for understanding the present, events in the history of social policy over the period since 1997 will inevitably get further attention.

Rather than providing a detailed historical account of the development of social services (see the further reading list below), this chapter has set out some of the defining moments in the evolution of welfare provision in the UK and shown how, in taking the long view, we are better able to assess what is novel, inventive and pioneering about social policy in the 2000s and to understand that despite the constellation of political, economic and social factors which shape policy at any particular time, the strands of history are intricately woven through the fabric of the welfare state.

Suggestions for Further Reading

There is a wide selection of books covering various historical periods in the development of social policy. Fraser (2002), *The Evolution of the British Welfare State*, now in its third edition is a classic historical text covering the period from the late 1700s while Kathleen Jones (2000), *The Making of Social Policy in Britain*, also in its third edition takes a more problem-focused approach to the period 1830 to the present. Harris (2004) *The Origins of the British Welfare State* provides a wide-ranging exploration of the origins of modern social policy from 1800–1945, and for the period following the Second World War Margaret Jones and Rodney Lowe (2002) *From Beveridge to Blair* examine the aims and achievements of the five key policy areas 1948–1998 while, with a journalistic eye, Timmins (1996), in *The Five Giants: a Biography of the Welfare State*, gives a lively account of the politicians and other political actors involved in shaping social policy. As mentioned in the text, Robert Page's (2007) *Revisiting the Welfare State* also provides an interesting reassessment of social policy development in the post-war period.

  The impact of the Thatcher and Major governments on social policy has provoked various accounts. The best overall sources are a collection edited by Savage, Atkinson and Robins (1994) *Public Policy in Britain* for the Thatcher period, and Dorey's edited volume *The Major Premiership* (1999). Recommended sources on the story of the Blair governments are three collections edited by Martin Powell: *New Labour: New Welfare State?* (1999), *Evaluating New Labour's Welfare Reforms* (2002) and *Modernising the Welfare State* (2008); and an edited book by Savage and Atkinson (2001) *Public Policy under Blair*. Doubtless, before long there will be an assessment of the social policy performance throughout the period of Blair Premiership. In the meantime Seldon (2007) has published an edited collection, *Blair's Britain 1997–2007*, with a number of chapters devoted to aspects of social policy.

Chapter 3
The Making of Social Policy

Introduction

This chapter deals with the social policy-making system, introducing the key institutions involved in the process in the United Kingdom (UK); Chapter 4 looks at the implementation of social policy. The two chapters must be considered together since dividing the policy processes between 'making' and 'implementation' is, in various respects, difficult. It is difficult to identify a dividing line at which 'making' can be said to be completed and 'implementation' to start. There is also a considerable amount of feedback from implementation which influences further policy making, and many policies are so skeletal that their real impact depends on the way they are interpreted at the implementation stage. In fact it is more appropriate to describe policy making as comprising both *policy formation* and implementation.

The starting point in this chapter is the ideal to which the system of government in the United Kingdom is presumed to correspond, in which policy formation is seen as the responsibility of our elected representatives, who answer to the people at elections for their stewardship of the public interest. This chapter first looks at the features of the system that correspond to this model, and at the institutions that are reputedly responsible for the policy-making process. Since 1998 the system has become more complicated because of devolution of some governmental powers to Scotland, Wales and Northern Ireland. The implications of this are considered before going on to some issues about the role of local government. After that some consideration is given to the impact of UK membership of the European Union (EU) and wider 'global' influences on social policy.

The discussion then turns to consider the various ways in which the model of representative government is modified, or perhaps even undermined, in practice. It considers how the people's will is translated into political action. It looks at the part played by pressure groups and the media in the system, and examines the case that has been made for regarding democracy as significantly undermined by 'political elites'.

The Representative Government Model

When the systems of government in the UK, the USA, most of Western Europe and much of the Commonwealth are claimed to be democratic, that proposition rests on a view that a form of representation of the people prevails in their governmental systems. Clearly, these systems do not involve direct democracy since, in complex societies, large numbers of decisions are taken by small numbers of representatives. Some countries seek to involve the people more directly, from time to time, by the use of plebiscites and referenda. The latter device has been used a little in the UK. It was used in connection with the devolution measures, the government has promised to use it before the UK joins the European monetary system (Euro) and the use of a referendum on the acceptability of the new European Union constitution is being widely advocated.

There is a further sense in which representative government is indirect. A distinction is often made between representatives and delegates. Delegates are regarded as mandated by those who elect them to support specific policies and to return to explain their subsequent decisions. British politicians have persistently rejected the view that they should be regarded as delegates, arguing instead that their duty is to make judgements for themselves in terms of their understanding of their constituents' best interests, while recognizing that they may, of course, be rejected at the next election if they become seriously out of touch with the people they represent. In this sense, they claim to be concerned with the interests of all their constituents, and not just those who voted for them. This doctrine was first expounded by Edmund Burke in the late eighteenth century. Today, of course, the importance of political parties makes it difficult for elected representatives to claim to represent all their constituents; but equally this makes it difficult for them to assume delegate roles. The presence in Parliament, and in the local councils, of party groups exerts an influence in favour of party programmes and away from a direct relationship between member and constituency. The modern modification of representative democracy is therefore to see the public as being allowed to choose from time to time between two or more broad political programmes, and being able to reject a party that has failed to carry out its promises (Schumpeter, 1950). However political parties and others also use a variety of polling techniques to test the movement of opinion.

According to the theory on which this model of democracy is based, social policies may be expected to be determined by the commitments of the political parties, and proposals for policy changes will be set out in election manifestos. The growth of the welfare state can be clearly related to the growth of democracy, with the people choosing to see their society change in this way. There are however weaknesses in this view of the policy-making process, which are explored later in this chapter. First, there is a need to identify more explicitly the institutions of government to which such an analysis must relate. Those who have previously taken courses on the constitution of the UK may wish to skip the next section.

The Central Government System

The curious feature of the constitution is that the UK has democratized institutions that were created in an undemocratic age. Most countries have systems of government that are relatively modern creations, either designed after cataclysmic political events which required the setting up of entirely new institutions, or set up to meet the needs of newly created or newly independent states. The governments of France and Germany, for example, fall into the first of these categories, and those of the USA and the Commonwealth countries into the second. The British pride themselves on having developed a system of government that has been a model for the rest of the world. The truth is that, while certainly many constitutional ideas have been borrowed from the UK, our system contains features that no one designing a system of government today would conceivably want to adopt.

In the later section on devolution it will be suggested that what happened in 1998 has further confused the whole character of the government of the UK. First, however there is a need to look at the institutions that govern the UK as a whole, bearing in mind that some of their powers have been devolved to Scotland (and to a lesser extent to Wales and Northern Ireland) but not to any separate governing body for England.

The monarchy and the House of Lords are two peculiar features of the government of the UK. Formally, the monarch has little influence on the policy-making process. The House of Lords, on the other hand, still has extensive power to scrutinize legislation, but its capacity to obstruct the will of the government has been undermined by successive Acts since 1911. It is now a curious mixture of appointed life members (peers) with a limited number of hereditary peers who have been allowed to remain. At the time of writing, after a long and convoluted series of Parliamentary debates the government is planning to legislate to make it an elected chamber. But exactly how that election system should work, and the consequences of this change for the powers of the Lords, has still not been settled. It is not proposed to complicate this discussion further by going into the issues about the limited rights and responsibilities of the monarch and the Lords.

The main legislative body, the House of Commons, is elected from over 600 constituencies (an exact number has not been quoted as regular constituency boundary changes alter it), each of which returns the candidate who gains a simple majority of votes at each election. After a general election, the monarch has the formal responsibility to ask the leader of the majority party to form a government. On most occasions, the monarch's duty is clear, but situations in which there is no party with a clear majority may complicate the task. Broadly, the expectation is that the monarch will not have to take a decision that will then prove to be a violation of the democratic process, because it will be the responsibility of whoever agrees to form a government in these circumstances to prove that he or she has adequate parliamentary support. In other words, the position of a minority government can be made untenable if all the other parties combine against it. There are, however, ambiguities in such a situation, as the lives of minority governments may be perpetuated more by a reluctance to force them to resign than by any positive commitment to their support. At the time of writing a striking illustration of this is the government of Scotland by the Nationalists, the largest single party but without a majority in the Parliament.

The newly appointed Prime Minister will form a government, giving a hundred or more governmental offices to his or her supporters. Again, the normal assumption is that these will be members of his or her own party, but exceptionally a coalition may be formed in which government offices go to other parties. All those given office will normally be, or will be expected to become, members of either the Commons or the Lords. Most will be members of the Commons (known as 'Members of Parliament' or 'MPs'). The choice of members of the government rests significantly on the preferences of the Prime Minister. However, he or she cannot disregard interests and factions within his or her own party, and will obviously give some attention to the competence of those appointed.

The most important Prime Ministerial appointments will be those of the members of Cabinet. The normal practice is to appoint a Cabinet of fifteen to twenty-five members. It will include the heads of the main departments of government, together with some members who do not have departmental responsibilities, who may be given political or co-ordinating roles. The Cabinet, chaired by the Prime Minister, is the key decision-making body within the government. Traditionally, new policy departures of any significance and new legislation need Cabinet approval, but there do seem to have been recent situations, notably during Tony Blair's period as Prime Minister, when this tradition has been ignored. Conflicts of interests between departments are generally also fought out in the Cabinet or its committees. Each Cabinet sets up a number of committees to do more detailed work. Some of these will draw on the help of non-Cabinet ministers.

The main government departments to which attention must be given in the discussion of social policy in England are the Treasury, the Department of Health, the Department for Work and Pensions, the Department for Communities and Local Government, the Department for Children, Schools and Families and the Department for Innovation, Universities and Skills. To these may be added the Department for Environment, Food and Rural Affairs inasmuch as it has responsibility for issues which affect both health in general and other aspects of welfare in the countryside.

Box 3.1   Changing of department names

As noted in the text, this occurs quite frequently, so that it can be quite difficult to keep up to date on the names and functions of departments. For example, when Gordon Brown became Prime Minister in 2007, the former Department for Education and Skills was split into the Department for Children, Schools and Families, and the Department for Innovation, Universities and Skills. Even more confusingly the department for local government in England – now the Department for Communities and Local Government – has changed many times in its history, even being known for a period in the recent past as the Office of the Deputy Prime Minister when the minister concerned also held that role.

Two other departments, the Cabinet Office and the Home Office, also play a small part. Readers must be warned that it has been the practice of governments in recent years to alter the departmental structure from time to time, ostensibly in an effort to find the best possible framework for policy co-ordination, but – it may be suggested   with less elevated political motives in mind too (see Box 3.1). Accordingly, it may be the case that, by the time this book is in your hands, departments may have new names and policy responsibilities may have been moved from one department to another.

The Prime Minister is technically the First Lord of the Treasury. This archaic title serves to remind us that, while today we regard the Chancellor of the Exchequer as the senior Treasury minister, the Prime Minister is, above all, bound to be involved in major decisions on expenditure, taxation and the management of the economy. In fact the relationship between the Prime Minister and the Chancellor of the Exchequer seems, from all the accounts provided by insiders and by informed journalists, to be enormously important for the functioning of modern government. The role of the Treasury in shaping social policy through control over expenditure has secured increasing attention in recent years (see Deakin and Parry, 1998). But in addition the arrival of tax credits as a crucial instrument of social security policy has given a more direct role to the Treasury. Tax credits are administered by an agency called Revenue and Customs, which implements policies determined by the Treasury and is answerable to that department.

Each of the departments listed above has its senior minister, the secretary of state, in the Cabinet. Again, the Prime Minister may sometimes choose to have other ministers from specific departments as Cabinet members. Each department head has the support of several junior ministers, known as ministers of state or under-secretaries, who may take on particular responsibilities for specific policy areas. Box 3.2 summarizes the departmental responsibilities of ministers.

The role of the minister who is also a Cabinet member involves a quite considerable conflict between a position as a member of the central policy co-ordination

Box 3.2   The departmental duties of ministers

- Responsible for putting forward new legislation. This is something the ambitious politician will want to do. He or she will hope to secure a job that involves the initiation of policies from the party's programme.
- The oversight of a large amount of day-to-day administration. Much of this will involve the formulation of new policies that do not require legislation, or the determination of responses to new crises within the department. It is in this kind of work that the distinction between policy formation and implementation becomes so unclear.
- Dealing with questions from MPs about the policies and activities of the department. While this may be seen primarily as a defensive kind of action, involving much routine work by civil servants who are required to produce the information required for parliamentary answers, it may also provide opportunities for publicizing new policy initiatives. Indeed, many questions are planted by friendly MPs, from the backbenches on the minister's own side, to enable activities to be advertised.
- A wide public relations role beyond Parliament. This will involve a programme of speeches, meetings and visits relating the department's activities to the world outside.

team within the government and responsibility for the protection and advancement of the interests of a department. It is personally difficult for any individual to give wholehearted attention both to departmental issues and to the main political strategy problems arising outside his or her own responsibilities. There is, likewise, a crucial problem for a rational approach to government in which strategic questions may not be best resolved by bargaining between a group of individuals all of whom have conflicting, 'tunnel vision', images dictated by departmental needs and priorities. There is a number of, still competing, ways of trying to resolve this problem. Prime Ministers have developed the Cabinet Office to help them to do this task. The Treasury's overall responsibility for public expenditure has also led them, particularly under powerful and ambitious Chancellors, to try to perform a co-ordinating role (Deakin and Parry, 1998). Members of the Cabinet without departmental responsibilities may also be expected to help in the resolution of this problem. There would seem, however, to be a continuing and inevitable conflict here.

Several references have already been made to the support of ministers by civil servants. It is self-evident that civil servants have an important role to play in implementing policy. What also needs to be emphasized is that civil servants are heavily involved in forming policy. Each major department has, at its headquarters, a group of a hundred or so civil servants, up to the top position of 'permanent secretary', who are concerned with decisions of a 'policy' kind, many of which require ministerial approval. The theory of representative government clearly requires that they be called the 'servants' of the minister, ostensibly providing information and evidence on policy alternatives but not taking policy decisions.

The British system of government involves more than a network of departments headed by ministers. Responsibility for various specific public services is hived off to a range of special agencies, though, in each case, ultimate responsibility for policy lies with one of the central departments. Students of social policy will come across a number of important examples of bodies of this kind; some with a nation-wide remit, others with local or regional responsibilities. They have grown in numbers and importance in recent years, to such an extent that a 'new public management' (Hood, 1991) system has been seen to emerge in which a formerly single civil service has been replaced by a network of different organizations with different terms of service for their employees, In central government, the 'next steps initiative', started in the 1980s, has led to the delegation of many routine governmental tasks to separate 'agencies'. While most of these remain wholly public in character, some are private organizations working under contract for the government (such as the Stationery Office Ltd. which publishes government documents). Agencies are discussed further in Chapter 4.

The discussion in this section has moved from the consideration of the composition of Parliament, and the nature of the relationship of government to Parliament, to a more detailed account of the organizations concerned with policy formation. There is a need, however, to look a little more at the role of Parliament. It has been shown that about 100 of the 600 members elected to Parliament become involved in specific government jobs. What role do the rest play in policy formation?

Primary policy formation involves the promulgation of Acts of Parliament. The overwhelming majority of these are promoted by government, and thus the initial government proposals (known as 'Bills') are prepared by civil servants within the departments. Bills then go through four stages in each House (Commons and Lords) (see Box 3.3).

Clearly, MPs without ministerial office may participate in all of these stages, and opposition members will take particular care to scrutinize and attack government

Box 3.3   Legislative stages

1   A 'first reading', which simply involves the formal presentation of the Bill.
2   A 'second reading', at which there is likely to be a large-scale debate on the basic principles of the Bill.
3   A 'committee stage', when the legislation is examined in detail (normally by a small 'standing committee' and not by the whole House).
4   A 'report stage' and 'third reading', at which the Bill that emerges from the committee is approved, but may be re-amended to undo some of the actions of the committee.

Box 3.4   Subordinate legislation

Many Acts of Parliament include clauses that allow governments to promote subsequent changes and new regulations. The idea here is that it would be a waste of Parliament's time to bring back every minor change of policy into the elaborate legislative process described in Box 3.3. An example of this is social security legislation where minor rule changes may be needed quite often. Within such legislation benefit rates are not usually specified, since these regularly need changing, so this is done through additional regulations.

To promote subordinate legislation, the government has to publish a 'statutory instrument' which is open to scrutiny by MPs. Some of these require parliamentary approval; others may be annulled if a negative resolution is passed by either House within 40 days of their initial publication. Hence, backbenchers may intervene to prevent subordinate legislation. A joint committee of the Commons and the Lords has been set up to scrutinize statutory instruments, and therefore to facilitate parliamentary review of subordinate legislation. They have, however, a mammoth task and only give detailed attention to a limited number of the statutory instruments that are put before Parliament.

action. The leading opposition party organizes a 'shadow cabinet' to provide for a considered and specialized response to the activities of the government.

In addition to Acts of Parliament, both Houses have to deal with a great deal of what is known as 'subordinate' or 'delegated' legislation (see Box 3.4).

Reference has already been made to parliamentary questions as providing an opportunity for backbench scrutiny of government actions. Members put down initial questions in advance. Many questions are answered by Ministries in writing, but those that receive oral answers may result in supplementary questions. In addition to the powers to ask questions, various parliamentary procedures provide scope for MPs to promote short debates on topics that concern them. The main opposition party is extended more specific facilities of this kind, so there are days allocated for debates on topics of its own choice.

One peculiar characteristic of the British Parliament that distinguishes it from many legislatures in other countries, and particularly from the US Congress, is the slight use made of specialized committees. The committees that consider Bills are in no way specialized; they consider new legislation in rotation regardless of subject and do not do any separate investigatory work.

There is also, however, a system of rather more specialized select committees. Perhaps the most important of these is the Public Accounts Committee, concerned to look at the way in which public money has been spent. Then, there are select committees on the work of the Parliamentary Commissioner for Administration (the 'Ombudsman'), on Statutory Instruments and on European legislation. In 1979, a system of committees was set up to concern themselves with the work of specific (or in some cases two specific) government departments. However, such is the power of the government in our system that it is doubtful whether these committees can do other than play a rather superior pressure-group role. They investigate specific topics, with the aid of specialist advisers, and have issued some influential reports, but they have no role with regard to legislation.

This account of the institutions of British central government has shown that elected representatives have a wide range of parliamentary duties. If they belong to the party that wins power they may well take on a government office of some kind. If they do not achieve office, they are still in a special relationship to government in which, while some advantages may accrue from being a member of the ruling party and having many colleagues and friends in office, there will also be disadvantages in that party allegiance implies a duty to support the government. Some of the scope for the criticism of policy that comes to opposition members is denied to government supporters. On the other hand, opposition, in a Parliament organized strictly on party lines, implies a situation in which it is very difficult to secure majority support for your own ideas.

Devolution

It has been noted that in 1998 there was devolution of government powers to Scotland, Wales and Northern Ireland. Devolution to Scotland was substantial. The main characteristics of the devolution settlement embodied in the Scotland Act 1998 are:

- A Scottish Parliament, elected by a voting system known as the 'additional member' system of proportional representation.
- The Scottish Parliament has a fixed term of four years, with provisions for exceptional dissolution and re-election.
- A Scottish Executive headed by a First Minister, appointed by the Queen following election by the Scottish Parliament. The First Minister then has powers to select other ministers.
- The functions of the Scottish Parliament are defined in terms of those powers not specifically noted in the Act as 'reserved' to the UK government. The main reserved powers are: constitutional matters, foreign affairs and the European Union, defence, economic policy, immigration and nationality, most social security policy, employment policy.
- But there is a clause that declares that the legislation does 'not affect the power of the Parliament of the UK to make laws for Scotland' (section 28, sub-section 7).
- Most of the funding for Scotland comes from a block grant but the Scottish Parliament has power to vary income tax up to 3 per cent of the rate in the UK.
- There is a procedure to ensure that the Scottish Parliament does not overstep its powers, which in effect gives ultimate veto powers to the UK government.

Hence, all the main areas of social policy other than social security and employment policy are now the responsibility of the Scottish government. However, the retention of control over economic policy and over most of the Scottish budget still gives Westminster a substantial influence over policy making even in the devolved areas of policy.

In Wales devolution is to an 'assembly' and not a 'parliament'. The main features of devolution to Wales under the Government of Wales Act 1998 can be best set out by means of a series of contrasts with the items in the list above for Scotland:

- The Assembly is elected by the same voting system as in Scotland.
- The Assembly also has a fixed term of four years, but there are no provisions for exceptional dissolution.
- There are no 'legislative functions' of the Assembly but rather the Act sets out a list of policy areas where the Secretary of State for Wales (a UK government appointee) must consider whether to devolve executive powers. They include agriculture, health, local government, social services, transport, planning, culture, the Welsh language and the environment. In practice, since the original legislation, these powers have been extensively exercised to increase the autonomy of the Assembly.
- Funding for services in Wales comes from a block grant, and there is no power to raise additional or separate taxes.
- The absence of legislative devolution means that comparatively little attention is given to a mechanism to resolve disputes with the UK Parliament; the latter clearly has the last word.

In Northern Ireland the search has been, as before, for a way of restoring the system of partial self-government, that operated between 1922 and 1974, which would satisfy both nationalists and unionists. This involved a complex negotiation process involving Eire as well. There was a need to reach a deal which comprised measures to bring violence to an end and arms under control. Negotiations towards this end that were to come to fruition in 1998 were started before Labour came to power. The crucial agreement was reached on Good Friday 1998. The implementation of this agreement proved difficult. Soon after being put in place the arrangements for the Assembly and the executive were suspended. It has only been back in operation since Spring 2007.

The constitutional aspects of the Northern Ireland agreement involve the following:

- An Assembly elected by the single transferable vote system of proportional representation.
- Election of a First Minister and a Deputy First Minister by the Assembly by a complex proposal designed to ensure that the two individuals, who hold office jointly, are broadly acceptable to both nationalist and unionist 'communities'.
- The formation of an executive by a procedure designed to ensure that it represents the main 'communities' represented in the Assembly.
- Devolution of a specific range of executive (as in Wales, not legislative) powers – principally agriculture, health, social services, economic development and the environment.

- Funding by block grant with no devolved taxation powers.
- The establishment of mechanisms to ensure that there is an active relationship between Northern Ireland and Eire, including in particular the setting up of a North–South Ministerial Council and a British–Irish council.

Mechanisms had to be set up, under all the devolution arrangements, for resolving disagreements between the UK government and the devolved governments. But these are only really important in the Scottish case, as there is no devolved legislative power to the other two countries. The key issues about disagreement resolution are three related features of the settlement already set out above: the fact that the UK still has general powers to legislate for Scotland, the long list of reserve powers about which definitional disputes are likely to arise and the fact that the UK retains veto powers and relies upon an arcane legal body, the Judicial Committee of the Privy Council, to assist with the resolution of disputes. In this situation the UK government seems able to protect its own definition of the limits to devolution, and indeed even pull them in should it want to do so. Where there is a justicable dispute – which would be about a piece of Scottish legislation (but not the other way round) then there is no autonomous 'supreme court' able to operate as the guardian of an agreement between the levels of government.

The financial settlement associated with devolution is governed by a formula which already operated prior to devolution. Until 1980 there had been no public effort to rationalize the way money was allocated between the countries. In 1980 a procedure to deal with *increments of additional expenditure* was developed which took into account population size. The new procedure was governed by what became known as the Barnett formula, after the minister who developed it in 1978.

It is argued that Scotland and Northern Ireland are over-subsidized and Wales under-subsidized, relative to England. Yet the Barnett formula – while it may change these relativities over time – was not designed to redress such inequalities. Moreover the evidence for inequalities is complicated, depending upon the stance taken about relative needs in each country. Nevertheless devolution makes much more explicit the issues about transfers between the four countries, fuelling – if the claims of over/under subsidy mentioned above are to be trusted – a sense of grievance in the proportionately lower spending countries.

It has been noted however that only Scotland has tax-varying powers, and even these are limited. But what would happen to the overall financial relationship if those powers were used? The current understanding with regard to the limited powers possessed by Scotland is that there would not be a cut in the contribution from central funds if they were used, but there is no absolute guarantee on this. While there is no doubt that a devolution measure in which the Treasury at Westminster still holds the financial reins can be easily presented as a fairly minimalist measure, it is important not to disregard the complexities inherent in financial devolution.

It is important, when looking at devolution, to give some attention to its impact upon England. There has been a considerable amount of attention recently to the question of English identity. Arguments that the arrangements after devolution are unfair to England may feed into a more atavistic English nationalism. The central issue about the implication of the devolution arrangements for England is that, in respect of a range of domestic policy issues the legislative body for Scotland has become the Scottish Parliament whilst the legislative body for England is the UK Parliament (in short 'Westminster'). Hence Scottish members of the UK Parliament can vote about domestic English issues, while most of their own domestic policy issues are reserved for their own Parliament.

This issue has been set out in terms of a contrast between Scotland and England. This is where it is at its starkest, but there are clearly more complex equivalent issues affecting the other two countries of the UK. This issue is often analysed as one about how the UK Parliament operates, leading those who dismiss its importance to argue that this can be handled by conventions about how the Scottish (or Welsh or Irish) MPs behave at Westminster. Committees dealing with legislation solely concerning one of the countries can be composed of members who only come from that country, and so on. But such an approach totally disregards the fact that to a very large extent the Westminster Parliament is subservient to the government of the day. It is generally the case that legislative decisions are made by the government and endorsed by Parliament (using its political majority to secure this).

Hence the issue about the role of the Westminster Parliament as the government of England for matters devolved to the legislature in Scotland would come to a head if there were a UK government with a narrow majority which would not be in power but for its support from Scotland. This could occur as the electoral support for the ruling Labour Party declines, since it tends to have much stronger support in Scotland than in England.

How then could this 'English question' be tackled? Is a convention about the behaviour of MPs sufficient? One step beyond that is to have a law that formally prevents Scottish MPs voting on English legislation, etc. The Conservative Party seems likely to include such a proposal in its manifesto for the next election. But that brings us back up against the scenario portrayed with reference to an election in which the balance of power amongst England MPs is different from that in the Westminster Parliament as a whole (that did occur in 1974). Surely a ban on voting in such a situation would have to mean the existence of parallel governments, dominated by different parties, one for the UK the other for England.

The simplest alternative scenario would thus involve the election of governments for all the countries including England and of another one for the UK. But that would require that problems about the comparatively fudged distinctions between the rights of the UK Parliament and the rights of the devolved governments would have to be addressed. While quite small parts of the UK (Scotland contains less than 9 per cent of the UK population, Wales just under 5 per cent and Northern Ireland just under 3 per cent) have devolution there is perhaps a case for a relatively ambiguous settlement. That would become much more contentious with the alternative, sometimes known as 'devolution all round'. There would have to be clearly entrenched rights for each government and a mechanism to resolve disputes which was not simply loaded in favour of UK government dominance. In the divided rule scenario with one party controlling the UK and another controlling England there would be a very strong clash of 'legitimacies' between the organ speaking for 100 per cent of the population and the organ speaking for 83 per cent.

'Devolution all round' thus implies the development of a form of 'federal' government. The imbalance of numbers between the 'nations' inevitably leads those in search of a federal solution to the problem to look at the case for regionalizing England. England is divided into regions for a variety of administrative purposes. Some efforts are being made to try to ensure that the administrative region used for one function is the same as those used for another. To this is then added regional consultative arrangements that have the potential to evolve into organs of government, for which direct elections may be held. But it is a big leap from an emergent regional consultative system to the formation of units for a federal system of government. The latter would involve regarding regional divisions as firm and clear cut. Collaboration across regional boundaries could become much more difficult and services (such as health and education) might become radically different on either side of those boundaries. Within UK politics such differences are often challenged. Journalists speak of 'post-code lotteries', meaning what you get depends on where you live (a more sophisticated debate on this within the social policy expresses this as an issue about 'territorial justice').

After the initial devolution measure the government explored the idea of some form of democratic devolution to English regions. But this option received a serious set back when three-quarters of the voters, in what would have been probably the best test-bed area for a regional experiment, the North-East of England, rejected it in a referendum in November 2004. In contrast though, Cornwall, an economically disadvantaged region, has a historically well-developed political movement for 'independence'.

It is contended therefore that there are elements of 'unfinished business' in respect of the devolution settlement. Inasmuch then as devolution encourages further 'nationalist' forces in any of the constituent nations of the UK, we may see further constitutional changes. In 2007 nationalist parties did well in the elections for the Scottish Parliament and the Welsh Assembly. In Scotland the Nationalist Party became the largest single party. Because of their commitment to moves towards independence the other parties refused to collaborate with them. Hence a government was formed by the Nationalists alone, despite their absence of an overall majority. At the same time, as noted above, the Conservative Party in England is making more of the anomaly under the present devolution settlement under which Scottish MPs at Westminster contribute to the making of domestic policy for England.

In the mean time the presence of separate governments means that policies may diverge. On the one hand that may be seen as a healthy development underlining local autonomy. On the other hand it generates conflicts and anomalies within a hitherto comparatively 'united' kingdom. Hence in social policy there have already been Scottish initiatives of some importance. One of those has been the rejection by Scotland of the already enacted UK measure to impose fees upon students in higher education. The other initiative involved the acceptance of the recommendation of the Royal Commission on Long Term Care (1999) that care costs (as distinguished from 'hotel costs') in residential social and nursing care should be met from the public purse. In the rest of the UK only nursing care costs are so met. In Wales the Assembly has abolished NHS prescription charges, and at the time of writing the Scottish government is expected to do this to.

Local Government

Local government in England is organized into two distinctive systems. In the metropolitan areas of London, West Midlands, South Yorkshire, Greater Manchester, Merseyside and Tyne and Wear, there is a long-established one-tier system of metropolitan districts responsible for personal social services, education and housing. After 1996, a number of further one-tier authorities came into operation. These are mostly in urbanized areas, with enlarged districts taking over powers from counties. In some cases – Avon and Cleveland, for example – county authorities disappeared altogether.

In the rest of England, there are county authorities which are responsible for education and personal social services, but also a lower tier of districts which include housing among their responsibilities. Planning responsibilities are shared between the two tiers.

Previously, there were a number of metropolitan counties, including one covering London. These were abolished in the 1980s and their powers dispersed either to districts or to *ad hoc* authorities. In 1998 the government restored an overriding Greater London Authority, with a directly elected mayor and an elected assembly. This does not have specific implications for social policy however, as the new authority is only concerned with certain conurbation wide issues such as transport and the environment.

There is also, in the counties, a third tier of parish councils, with minimal powers. While many of these are old parishes, others are towns that previously had significant powers of their own, some retaining mayors and calling themselves town councils. None of these third-tier authorities have significant social policy responsibilities, so they will not be examined further here.

The local government system of Scotland has been totally restructured; throughout that country, since April 1996, there is a one-tier system of local government. There is a similar but slightly more complicated situation in Wales, with most powers being in single-tier authorities, known either as counties or county boroughs, except that there is also a system of community councils resembling the parish councils in England.

Local government in Northern Ireland has for some time now been stripped of almost all its significant powers. It had previously been notorious in some areas for the manipulation of electoral boundaries and for the practice of religious discrimination. Health services and personal social services were brought together under four appointed boards. Education is the responsibility of three separate education and libraries boards. Public housing is the concern of the Northern Ireland Housing Executive.

National legislation defines the powers of local authorities, and may set limits to those powers. It also imposes on local government a range of duties. The relationship between central and local government in Britain is a complex one. Local government is not autonomous, but neither is it merely local administration. Some statutes impose fairly clear tasks for local authorities, but many give powers, and indicate ways in which those powers should be used, without undermining the scope for local initiative. Other Acts of Parliament merely grant local authorities powers, which they may choose whether to use. Exceptionally, a local authority may itself promote a 'private' Act to secure powers to undertake new ventures. Further discussion of the role of local government is contained in Chapter 4.

The United Kingdom in Europe

The UK's membership of the European Union (EU) (often also called the European Community (EC)) has had an impact on its constitution and on its policy making process. There are areas of the law which are now determined by the institutions of the EU, where the role of the UK Parliament is limited to one of administering implementation.

It is mainly economic activity which is subject to this European dominance. The origins of the EU lie in the aspiration to build a supra-national trading area. Other European legislation has followed from that aspiration, as explained in Box 3.5.

Hence, the evolution of the EU has led it to develop 'social policy' alongside economic and environment policy, but that policy has been principally concerned with the rights of employees and with efforts to stimulate employment through investment and training. The principal social policy interventions have been limited efforts

---

Box 3.5   How the 'commom market' aspiration of the European Union generates other European legislation

1   The presence of different regulatory systems in different countries to deal with production standards, consumer protection, environmental control and terms of employment will have an influence on competition. Countries with lower standards may have competitive advantages over those with higher ones, which the latter will want to be eliminated.
2   Economic co-operation between nations is enhanced if they enjoy broadly similar opportunities for employment and standards of living.
3   The concept of a single market embraces a single labour market, in which workers can move freely across boundaries in search of work. They will want to carry social rights with them if they do so.

to harmonize rules relating to employment and the provision of funds to help to create work and aid training programmes (Kleinman, 2002; Hantrais, 2007). The European Social Fund – not to be confused with the social fund in social security (see Chapter 5) – which sounds like a major social policy instrument, is in fact a vehicle for the subsidization of training (and to a lesser extent work creation). Compared with agricultural support, Social Fund expenditure is low, and countries receiving this money have to add matching contributions to schemes which it supports. There is, additionally, a rather larger Regional Development Fund, which certainly has 'social effects' as it is used to try to stimulate economic development in regions suffering from underdevelopment or economic decline.

Social policy has figured in the arguments about the scope of the role of the EU, in which Conservative governments in the UK have – during the 1980s and 1990s – been advocates of a limited and cautious approach. The UK secured agreement that it need not accept the 'social chapter' in the 'Maastricht Treaty' of 1992. The Labour government reversed that decision in 1997. However, it is important to recognize that the aspirations of that 'chapter' – towards a greater harmonization of social conditions and of social protection legislation – will not be easy to realize because of the continued hostility of some nations (still including the UK) to this. This topic is explored further in Chapter 6 in terms of the conflict between narrow (market) and broad (social community) views of the EU.

There is an alternative view that progress of European social policy may be accelerated by the presence in Brussels of a Directorate (DGV: Employment, Social Affairs and Equal Opportunities) which aspires to advance European social policy – which sets out goals for policy, encourages social policy experiments (the European poverty programmes) and publishes data on social conditions and social security systems. This Directorate provides a source of pressure on national governments and helps to keep social policy issues on the agenda.

This view of the potential positive effect of the impact of the EU on UK social policy is reinforced by the overall impact of the constitutional change outlined in the first paragraph of this section. King (2007) explains this as a:

> cumulative effect of, first, the supremacy of EC law, second the duty of the British courts to apply EC law and, third, the corresponding duty of the British courts to hear cases brought by British citizens under that law has been to alter the balance of power and authority in the British constitution in favour of the courts and judges as against both the government of the day and Parliament itself. (p. 98)

Readers may question what this has to do with social policy, but interestingly King goes on to cite as examples of the impact of this European Court decisions in respect of entitlements to social security benefits and pension rights. In this respect it may be suggested that the scope for the enforcement of social rights has been increased. This development is reinforced by a 'European' influence that actually comes from a body with a wider remit, whose role the UK accepted long before joining the EC, the European Court of Human Rights. This body has jurisdiction in respect of the European Convention on Human Rights, and has made several decisions with an impact upon

UK social policy, for example on the rights of mental health patients and on use of corporal punishment. The Human Rights Act of 1998 has incorporated the Convention into UK law, thereby making litigation in respect of human rights violations easier.

However, since the UK is in many respects an under-performer in social policy, by EU standards (see the further discussion of this in Chapter 11), with a relative lack of social insurance policies that give citizens' clear entitlements (see Chapter 5), it is likely, regardless of the party in power, to tend to want to impose a check upon the evolution of Union-wide social policy.

Furthermore the enlargement of the EU, with entrants from Eastern Europe, adds a further complication in this respect, since social policy is poorly developed in those nations. The admission of a range of relatively poor countries means (a) that subventions to parts of the UK from the structural funds are even rarer, and (b) that the prospects of forms of social policy harmonization are even more remote. In the struggle between the two visions of Europe – that of it as a solidaristic 'social' entity and that of it as simply a loose 'economic' union – the dominance of the latter view is ever more evident. Even in respect of the notion of an open market, consequent upon the admission of new nations (particularly Bulgaria and Romania in 2007) limitations have been put upon the free movement of labour because of fears of migration of large numbers of workers willing to accept low wages.

The Global Context

The last section has thus suggested that the impact of the EU on social policy is likely to remain limited, with a restrictive 'harmonized market' model of the union, rather than a more progressive 'social Europe' model dominant. Such a view is reinforced when it is recognized that the European Union is not the only supra-national influence upon social policy in the UK. This country is embedded, along with its European partners, in a global system in which internal policies which will impose limitations upon trade between nations are proscribed in international agreements (particularly those of the World Trade Organization).

The questions about the extent to which the global economy imposes social policy constraints are large and complex. In terms of the discussion of institutions, they can be confined to some rather specific issues about what membership of various bodies formally implies. But membership of international organizations involves (a) explicit political commitments that underpin those and (b) a recognition that the national economy (and therefore national welfare) is influenced by the role of the United Kingdom seeks to play in the world economy (see Chapter 11 for further discussion of this issue).

It can be readily identified that there is formal governmental participation in international organizations (for example the United Nations, the World Bank, the International Monetary Fund, the World Trade Organization, the Organization for Economic Co-operation, International Labour Organization and the World Health Organization). But it is hard to trace many very explicit interventions by those bodies that have a direct impact upon United Kingdom policy. However, there are questions to ask about what those organizations stand for, and who dominates them, since they may have an indirect impact. What then can be identified in respect of a number of those bodies (notably the World Bank, International Monetary Fund, World Trade Organization and Organization for Economic Co-operation and Development) is (a) a strong commitment to market based international economic activity, with national policies that prevent free competition minimised, and (b) a strong American influence which reinforces that perspective. Even then, as comparative explorations of global social policy have suggested (Deacon, 1997; George and Wilding, 2002), nations differ in their receptivity to interventions coming from these bodies. In that sense any analysis of their impact upon the United Kingdom must be related back to the willingness of our governments to shape our policies in conformity with the ideological influences coming from these sources.

However, some analysts of globalism go further to suggest that our economic dependence upon the global economy is what is the determining influence upon national policy, in which case the international organizations may be little more than the transmitters of messages we cannot ignore. The exploration of that topic requires comparative analysis that goes beyond the scope of this book (see for example, the books by Deacon and George and Wilding cited above, and also chapter 13 of Hill, 2006). All that should be said here is that there are important distinctions to be made between perspectives on this topic which suggest that global influences are irresistible (sometimes taking a form very like the predictions of historical inevitability associated with Marxist theory) and those that see them as strong influences upon what are still in various respects free political choices. As Hay has commented 'Whether the globalist thesis is "true" or not may matter far less than whether it is *deemed* to be true – or, quite possibly, just useful – by those employing it' (Hay, 2002, p. 258). In that sense there are constraints upon United Kingdom social policy which stem from political commitments to:

- international competitiveness
- the maintenance of the City of London as a key participant in world money markets
- an alliance with the United States

We will return to the some of the consequences of this when we look at United Kingdom social policy in comparative perspective in Chapter 11. These points are however by no means irrelevant to the discussion of aspects of how the political system works in the next section.

The Voice of the People?

It has already been noted that, in the UK system of government, MPs are elected in individual constituencies on the basis of a procedure in which the candidate with a simple majority is the winner. It is generally the case that the voter has to choose between two to four candidates each of whom is the representative of a specific political party, plus sometimes a range of others whom few people take seriously. In this way, electoral choice is peculiarly structured. Voters have to make their decisions on the basis of assessments of particular people, with their own special policy commitments, in relation to the more general political biases and policy commitments of their parties. The parties' intentions are of more importance than individuals' commitments. However, what the parties offer are broad packages of policies, within which voters may like some items while disliking others.

Hence the individual voter's starting point in trying to influence policy through the electoral process is a situation of limited choice in which it is general policy biases, or even more general considerations, often described as 'party images', that must govern his or her selection of an MP. Moreover, his or her vote will be taken together with large numbers of other votes, perhaps motivated by very different policy preferences. Hence, one person's voting choice might be influenced by a party's commitment to raise pensions, which leads him or her to support it despite its commitment to other policies – say increasing educational expenditure – with which he or she disagrees. Others who vote for the same party might be motivated by directly opposite considerations – a strong commitment to education, say, but no concern about pensions.

The above example was chosen to illustrate the basic underlying problem about the use of choices between representatives as a means of settling policy priorities. The reality is that party platforms are considerably more complex, with choices between desirable ends deliberately obscured. No party presents the electorate with explicit choices between widely desired ends; they generally seek to convince it that they can bring a little more of everything that is wanted, probably at less cost. Voters are forced to discriminate between the parties in terms of their general ideologies, value biases and images.

Furthermore, most voters do not really make electoral *choices*. Many vote for the same party every time they vote, and probably give little attention to the personalities or policies of specific candidates. Voters behave in ways that, as far as the collective pattern of choices is concerned, political scientists are to a large extent able to predict from their occupations, social origins and personalities. Only a minority of the electorate changes sides between elections. Indeed, many of the changes that alter the balance in power at Westminster are no more than changes between voting and non-voting, or vice versa. Research findings suggest, moreover, that the people most likely to change their votes – the floating voters – are generally the least informed within the electorate, and are thus not people who can be said to be making careful choices between policies. It is suggested, instead, that political *images* are particularly significant – the personalities of the leaders, their projections of competence and of their capacities to deal with the nation's problems. Such 'images' are largely transmitted to the public through the mass media (an issue to which we return below). An important consideration at a general election is the success or failure of the government in power in coping with the economic situation. In this sense, a verdict may be given on its policies, but only in a very general way.

Clearly, therefore, electors are not normally provided with opportunities to make clear choices about social policies, or between social policy options. There are certainly general characteristics of the parties' approaches to social policies that may help people to decide between them; and, at particular elections, ones for or against social policy may be particularly clear.

However, even that presentation of the scope for the voice of the people to be heard may be too optimistic. The very generalized perspectives described above are likely to be constrained within quite strict restraints upon the breadth of the agenda. That brings us back to the assumptions about United Kingdom political options set out in the discussion of globalism above. The leading political parties share common assumptions about limits to intervention into the economy and spending on social goals.

A general characteristic of UK elections in the last 30 years or so has been a high level of controversy over the extent to which taxation can be cut, or increased taxation avoided. After its major defeats in the 1980s the Labour Party became very wary of being seen as the party of high taxation. However, by the 2001 election all the major UK parties could be seen to be trying to balance their concerns about tax levels with concerns about the need for more spending on policy areas identified by the public as underfunded. The Labour government was able to present itself as both against taxation increases and in favour of expenditure increases on health and education, because of the budgetary surplus built up as a result of its caution over expenditure in its first term of office. The Conservative opposition on the other hand seemed to undermine its credibility by being in favour of tax cuts while at the same time not wanting to be thought to favour public service deterioration. While at the time of writing the Conservatives seem to be trying to extricate themselves from that position neither they nor the Labour Government (nor indeed the third party – the Liberal Democrats) are prepared to risk being seen as moving more than quite marginally away from current levels of taxation.

Now, of course, it may be suggested that it is popular hostility to taxation that imposes that restraint. But political elites (see further discussion below) do not just take their stances on what should be offered to the electorate from public opinion, they also contribute to the forming of that opinion. Of particular importance here is the role of the mass media in shaping the political agenda. While we would not wish to suggest we subscribe to a simple conspiracy theory that can reduce the issue to the consideration of the impact of one man, it is not without relevance that an Australian-born American citizen multi-millionaire, Rupert Murdoch, currently owns both what used (probably erroneously) to be regarded as the most authoritative newspaper (the *Times*) but also the largest mass circulation daily paper (the *Sun*) together with a substantial television network.

Beyond the issues of the overall control of the media are issues about how journalists present topics, simplifying and sensationalizing issues. They are in no sense democratically accountable. Even if their managers do not dictate their behaviour, popular accountability amounts only to a concern with what will sell newspapers. While there are papers and television channels that aim to look beyond mass circulation considerations their journalists still operate in a world in which they pay close attention to the activities and judgements of other journalists. There is thus, as studies of the media have shown (three chapters in part 3 of May et al., 2001; Franklin, 1999; Negrine, 1994), a media 'consensus' that limits the portrait of the social world and social policy provided for the public.

Beyond the 'macro-politics' like that set out in the last few paragraphs there is a complex 'micro-politics' of other issues. Many social policies are specific measures to assist quite small disadvantaged groups in the population. Policies to assist disabled people, for example, may be viewed as generally desirable and, in that sense, may have electoral appeal; but the number of people they benefit directly or indirectly is a minority in the population. Disabled people may be a relatively 'popular' minority group; but what about policies to help people who are long-term unemployed, rehabilitate criminals or provide facilities for vagrant alcoholics, for example? If there were a direct relationship between the pursuit of electoral popularity and the determination of social policies, surely minority causes would receive much less attention than they do now, and unpopular minority causes would receive no attention at all (or even more punitive responses). Opinion polls suggest that a variety of social reforms carried out in Britain – the abolition of capital punishment and the liberalization of the law relating to homosexuality, for example – were enacted in the face of popular opposition.

Other survey evidence suggests, moreover, that, while there are strong public commitments to pensions, education and the health service, other social policies which favour those most in need of help from the welfare state, such as asylum seekers, unemployed people and single parents, have little popular support (Taylor-Gooby, 1985; Edgell and Duke, 1991). In respect of these issues again, of course, the mass media play an elaborate role in influencing opinion on who is deserving and who undeserving in these respects.

There is a problem about seeing elections as involving soundings of public opinions. The victors in general elections tend to have much larger majorities at Westminster than the size of their overall vote in the country would seem to justify. Often more electors have voted against the winning party than have voted for it. There are many alternative methods of reflecting public opinion other than the traditional British 'first past the post' approach to elections. A debate about these alternatives has gained nourishment from the use of some of these for elections to the devolved governments, to the government of London and to the European Parliament, as Box 3.6 shows.

Of course, the introduction of some kind of proportional representation system does not necessarily solve the general 'political arithmetic' problem outlined above. In the Welsh Assembly the absence of an overall majority for one party has forced upon the largest group (the Labour Party in both cases) a need to compromise with some of the other parties. This was also true of the Scottish Parliament where a Labour/Liberal Democrat coalition ruled until 2007. Since then, as noted above, there is the more ambiguous situation in which the Scottish Nationalists are attempting to rule on their own without an overall majority. Where Parliamentary votes are needed, therefore, much will depend upon the disposition of the other parties in respect of the specific issue at stake. In Northern Ireland the whole system (as was noted in the section on devolution above) has been deliberately designed to force compromise between 'nationalist' and 'unionist' parties.

Box 3.6   Alternatives to 'first past the post' now used in elections in the UK

The voting systems used for the elections to the Scottish Parliament and to the Welsh Assembly involves a system in which members are elected in constituencies using the 'first past the post' system but then additional members are elected from regions on the basis of proportions, with the additional members drawn in order from lists prepared by the parties. This is known as the additional member system (AMS).

In the elections for the Greater London Assembly, the AMS system is also used. But for the election of the Mayor of London the fact that the vote was for a single person posed a choice between 'first past the post' and yet another system. What was chosen was the supplementary vote (SV) one. Under this system each elector has two votes. If one candidate receives over 50 per cent of first preference votes he or she is declared elected. If no one achieves this, the top two candidates go into a second round in which the second choices of the eliminated candidates are counted.

The system used for the Northern Ireland assembly election is the single transferable vote system (STV). This had been used there before for local government and European Parliament elections. As with the ATV system voters express preferences, but there is more than one seat per constituency and success for any one requires the achievement of a quota. Once that is attained surplus votes go to the second preference candidates and so on until all seats are filled. This system spreads votes a little towards the less extreme candidates, an effort to bridge the wide divisions in Northern Ireland.

For the European Parliament elections yet another system is used, entailing single votes for a party list in each region. Seat allocation depends upon the size of the vote for each party in relation to the quota needed for each seat (100 per cent of the total vote divided by the number of seats plus 1 representing the quota necessary for one seat). A much criticized aspect of this method is that the system allows voters no chance to express their preferences between different candidates on a party list.

Influences on Policy Making

Pressure groups

Much of the detailed analysis of the role of pressure groups in the policy-making process has been carried out in the United States. There, the political system has several characteristics that particularly facilitate the mobilization of small groups of people to influence decisions. First, power within the system is fragmented – between President and the two houses of Congress, between the federal government and the states, and between the state government and local government. Second, in that vast and diverse country, political choices are much more dictated by local interests than they are in the UK. Hence, the relationship between a congress member and his or her local electorate is much less affected by national party considerations. Third, at federal level, the parties are accordingly much less unified by political ideologies. Political actors are therefore readily influenced by small groups which can effectively threaten to have an electoral impact.

In the UK, pressure groups are probably just as much in evidence as they are in the US. A number of studies (Finer, 1958; Wootton, 1970; Jordan and Richardson, 1987) have dispelled the notion that they are of no importance in the system, but there is a need to beware of the assumption that they have as direct an impact on the political system as they do in the US. Their importance in the politics of that country has led political scientists to propound a modification of the theory of representative government in which the weakness of the individual voter, discussed in the last section, is seen as compensated by his or her membership of interest groups (Dahl, 1961). Democracy is thus seen as 'pluralist' in character with politicians engaged in continuing processes of compromise with multiple groups. Such a theory is then seen as explaining the deference of politicians to the interests of minorities; and a new and perhaps superior version of democratic theory is presented which has as its hallmark the achievement of a political consensus in which minority interests are protected.

This theory has, however, come under fire in the US. It has been pointed out that there are biases in the system that make it much easier for some interests to be heard than others, and much easier for modifications to the *status quo* to be vetoed than to be supported (see Lukes, 2005, for a discussion of this literature).

These general points about the plurality of pressure groups are worthy of our attention since they suggest important questions about the way the UK system operates. The contrasts made above between the political systems on the two sides of the Atlantic suggest that it may be much more difficult for UK pressure groups to identify points at which the political system is particularly open to influence. In individual constituencies, grievances about the established political parties have to be very deeply felt, and widely shared, to upset national electoral swings. Direct interventions in elections motivated by local issues are rare. As noted above, politicians have often been able to be singularly insensitive to local issues, and the current three or more party system further distorts the picture. It is not yet clear how much proportional representation in Scotland and Wales makes a difference.

There are similar problems for a national pressure group in persuading political parties that disregard of its case carries electoral dangers. Furthermore, any interest group able to threaten in this way probably has a special relationship with a major political party, and is acknowledged as important in that sense. Many of the most powerful of the UK pressure groups tend to have an established relationship with one or other political party. The trade unions have been the clearest example of this phenomenon. They played a key role in the original establishment of the Labour

Party. However the modern party has distanced itself from them. The other side of industry has been an important paymaster for the Conservative Party and groups such as the Confederation of British Industry and Institute of Directors have enjoyed a degree of policy influence. At the time of writing, however, business support for the Conservative Party is seriously in decline whilst the Labour Party is gaining increased funds from this source. Clearly, so long as the main political divide was one which corresponded to the division of interest between 'labour' and 'capital' its implications for pressure groups were comparatively clear. Now there are perhaps a variety of more covert influences upon policy emanating from pressure groups. To counteract these there has been a move towards a requirement of greater openness about financial contributions to political parties and individual MPs. Pressure groups have also themselves evolved to represent single issues as well as collective concerns, global questions as well as those restricted to local and national politics, and prediction of the membership and sources of support for these group is far more complex.

It is important to look more closely at the ways in which particular groups enjoy an institutionalized relationship to the political system. In particular, it is necessary to go beyond the examples of close relationships to political parties to consider whether the positions some groups enjoy in relation to the political system owe nothing to particular party allegiances.

Political elites

The power of some pressure groups can only be explained in terms of what may be called an 'insider' status within the policy-making system. This implies a further deviation from democratic theory, a system within which some individuals and groups have special status. A number of political scientists and sociologists have suggested that societies possess a political 'elite' (see Bottomore (1966) and, specifically on the UK, Urry and Wakeford (1973) and Stanworth and Giddens (1974)) and that decision makers are drawn from a narrow spectrum within a society. Traditional Marxist analyses of the social structure suggest that the political system is dominated by representatives of the bourgeoisie, the capitalist class. Modern updates of this theory have pointed out the relevance of patterns of domination based on race and gender as well (Williams, 1989). Bear in mind again here the role the media may play in determining what people and whose interests are to be seen as important.

Modern interpretations of elite theories seek to show either that key policy offices are held by people from a narrow spectrum of social origins, or that a limited number of people, characterized by close links with one another, dominate decision-making roles. For the UK, it has been shown that Cabinet ministers, senior civil servants, members of key advisory bodies and the heads of prestigious organizations tend to be drawn from a relatively narrow social class group, characterized by education at public schools and Oxbridge, and by having had parents in a similarly narrow range of upper-middle class occupations. The picture is, however, not simple, and there is evidence that the backgrounds of top decision makers have changed in recent years to embrace a slightly wider range of social origins. While, certainly, it seems plausible to suggest that, if there are people from similar social or educational backgrounds in a number of key roles, the relationships between those people will facilitate the sharing of ideas and opinions, the processes involved cannot necessarily be explained as simply as this.

What may be more important to explain the power of some of the pressure groups in the UK is the extent to which there are assumptions by governments that some kinds of consultation should occur. Such assumptions rest on several foundations. One of them is that expertise conveys the ability to help with public decision making. This is the technocratic view: that experts' opinions carry a greater weight than other people's. It is the basis on which academics sometimes secure a measure of influence in government. Similarly, some pressure groups secure attention because of their expert knowledge. In the educational and medical fields, such 'heavyweight' pressure groups abound. It has been suggested that there are a number of 'policy networks' or 'policy communities' in the various specialized policy areas, in which regular consultations occur between policy makers and representatives of pressure groups (including groups representing employees, particularly professional ones) who have been granted partial insider roles (Smith, 1993).

Another foundation on which pressure groups may secure influence is their association with traditional elite groups. Voluntary organizations believe they benefit by royal sponsorship and by the acquisition of prestigious figures as vice-presidents and supporters. Such sponsorship is not always easily earned. It is clearly helpful to have a cause that readily attracts the sympathy of influential people. It may also be important to behave in ways that are deemed respectable. This is a curious feature of this kind of pressure group activity; to some extent, the power of groups depends on their ability to forswear the more direct weapons in the pressure group armoury, to avoid mounting vociferous opinion-forming campaigns or threatening forms of direct action. The supposition, here, is based on a belief that there is an underlying elitist approach to government in the UK. A fairly narrow range of people are responsible for key decisions; some of these attain such positions through democratic representational procedures, but they co-opt others to their ranks. These other people may be individuals of shared social backgrounds, but the process of co-optation may be more haphazard. Individuals from pressure groups, or at least representing specific interests, secure entry into the ranks of those who exercise power by virtue not only of expertise but also of personal qualities, such as persistence and charm, which enable them to persuade others that they have something to contribute to public decision making. They also generally have to establish that they understand some of the unspoken rules relating to public participation: that they don't embarrass their sponsors by the use of direct tactics or indiscreet communications with the press or unseemly behaviour in committee situations. In so doing, they join that list of people who have been called on over and over again to sit on public committees and advisory bodies.

This argument, then, is that political influence may be secured in the UK without the aid of independent power. The system co-opts others to join its ranks, and pays attention to some citizens much more readily than others. In this day and age, people are rightly cynical about propositions about the power of ideas; they look around

Box 3.7   Government advisers

There are examples of people who, through the strength of their commitments and the power of their attention to detail, have secured a place in the policy-making process In the first half of this century, William Beveridge (Harris, 1977) was such an individual. In the 1980s, experienced businessmen were turned to as advisers, and one (Sir Roy Griffiths) had an important influence on the organization of the health service and on community care policy and on introducing market values to social policy more generally. His more modern equivalent seems to be a banker, Derek Wanless, who provided advice on NHS reform to Blair and Brown.

Since 1997 a new group of insiders seems to be emerging whose diverse backgrounds make them hard to classify. They seem to derive their power from close personal links with key politicians. The derisory expression 'Tony's cronies' was used about some of Blair's closest advisors; his successor Gordon Brown has however also been noted as having a small circle of close advisers. Political journalists make much of these personal networks, and in this context the role of media advisers to politicians should not be forgotten.

for other explanations and ulterior motives. Yet, in the study of social policy, the importance of individuals should not be wholly underestimated (see Box 3.7).

A great deal of pressure group activity is, of course, concerned with 'good causes'. Again, a theory of the policy-making process needs to find room for 'good causes' as well as for 'good people'. There are important questions that should not be brushed aside about the place of altruism in policy making. It is not naive to argue that politicians, or if you prefer some politicians, have commitments to ideals. It is certainly important to recognize that many politicians want to be seen as supporters of 'good causes'. Hence, pressure groups for disabled or elderly people, neglected children and so on will exert influence out of proportion to their naked power. For them, the skilful use of mass media may be important, and key contacts in positions of power will be a great help. In this sense, they aim to be co-opted into 'policy communities'.

No account of social policy making should disregard the potential influence of these 'good causes', however much there may be scope for controversy about their real power in situations where interests are in conflict. Indeed one of the frustrating phenomena many pressure groups of this kind experience is continuing assertions by politicians that they do matter, which is accompanied by minimal concrete action. It is difficult to predict the political circumstances that will favour interests of this kind. It is perhaps useful here to bear in mind the distinction often made in the study of pressure groups between 'interest' groups and 'cause' groups, though in the tactical struggle for influence each may seek to co-opt the support of the other. Interests seek to be recognized as 'good causes', and causes try to enlist the backing of more powerful 'interests'.

It has been suggested earlier that pressure groups provide a crucial qualification to the notion of a simple relationship between electors and elected. Some writers have suggested that they solve the problem of the powerlessness of the individual in relation to the political machine (Dahl, 1961; Beer, 1965). While there are many circumstances in which that is true, it seems important to acknowledge that the political system contains biases that make it much easier for some groups to secure influence than others. In addition, in the UK, there is the peculiar phenomenon of the exercise of influence by groups that, according to the crude calculations of political arithmetic, do not seem to have a power base at all. A minority who occupy powerful positions in British society are able to make choices, based neither on notions of democracy nor on calculations about who has power, but about whom they will listen to or consult.

Ministerial Power: the Role of Officials and the Influence of Outside Groups and Policy Communities

Hill (1972, 2005) has developed a typology of government styles to try to elucidate different characteristics of politician/official relationships in different political situations. Three types of political system are identified: 'ideological politics', 'administrative politics' and 'bargaining politics'.

A system of 'ideological politics' relates most clearly to the model of 'representative government'. It is one in which the traditional distinction between politics and administration is most easily made. Political parties compete to win elections by submitting distinct programmes from which the electorate can choose. Politicians instruct administrators to frame policies compatible with their mandates and commitments. The Thatcher governments stood out as examples of this phenomenon.

'Administrative politics' describes a contrasting system in which full-time officials are much more clearly dominant. The 'politics' are internal to the organizational system rather than public, hence many of the key conflicts are between departments. Ministers in central government, while formally possessing the key decision-making powers, in fact find themselves involved primarily in expounding views and defending policies generated within their departments. Politicians of the majority party without ministerial office find themselves frustratingly shut out from a decision-making process into which they are given few insights.

The concept of 'bargaining politics' was derived from examination of accounts of local politics in the US. Partly as a result of exposure to the US literature and partly because of a desire to adopt a realistic approach towards power, social and political scientists have been on the look-out for signs of a similar system in the UK. In such a system political outcomes are seen to depend on inputs of resources of power. Those who hold elected positions are not 'representatives' so much as 'brokers' bringing together coalitions of interests. Their desire for re-election forces them to adopt strategies in which they are highly sensitive to pressure groups. Some reservations about this view have already been suggested, but it was acknowledged that elements of bargaining are by no means absent from the UK scene. Bargaining politics implies a clear role for politicians which may suggest that officials will occupy subordinate positions. While this is true inasmuch as political futures are at stake, it has been suggested that in the UK, deals with quite explicit electoral implications are rare. Bargaining may therefore be more concerned with the maintenance of specific policies or particular organizational arrangements. If this is the case, it may be that officials have more to lose, or have more explicit commitments, than the politicians. Key conflicts concern relationships between departments and the outside world; ministers are expected to support the defence of departmental interests.

UK central government must be noted as a context where conflicts often appear to be of an ideological nature and where the representative model is treated as of some importance. Yet a key theme in discussions of relationships between ministers and their departments has been the extent to which politicians enter with apparent policy commitments, but become socialized into roles determined by the permanent administrators and particularly by the need for 'policy maintenance' within their department. Furthermore, a related theme to the ministerial discovery that cherished policy innovations are not administratively feasible is the recognition that vested interests and pressure groups carry a political 'clout' that had not been realized when policies were planned outside government. Policy-making outcomes may be determined by the interaction of three forces: political input (ideological politics), organizational considerations within departments (administrative politics), and external pressures (bargaining politics). Marsh and Rhodes' *Implementing Thatcherite Policies* (1992a) offers a good account of the way in which ideological politics was muted in practice in the 1980s. Conversely, Campbell and Wilson (1995) show that civil service domination was partly undermined by the tendency of the Thatcher and Major governments to advance civil servants who were prepared to offer them uncritical assistance in the pursuit of ideological goals.

Beyond these generalizations, the more detailed study of the factors that influence the way that policy is made needs to take various considerations into account. First, what kinds of policies are involved? This raises the question so far evaded in this book: What is policy? Writers on policy analysis are agreed that a policy is something more than a decision. Friend and his colleagues (Friend, Power and Yewlett, 1974, p. 40) suggest that 'policy is essentially a stance which, once articulated, contributes to the context within which a succession of future decisions will be made'. Jenkins (1978) similarly stresses the notion of interrelated decisions concerned with the selection of goals and the adoption of a course of action. Smith suggests that 'the concept of policy denotes ... deliberate choice of action or inaction, rather than the effects of interrelating forces'. He emphasizes 'inaction' and reminds us that 'attention should not focus exclusively on decisions which produce change, but must also be sensitive to those which resist change and are difficult to observe because they are not represented in the policy-making process by legislative enactment' (Smith, 1976, p. 13; see also Marsh and Rhodes, 1992b). Policy is also concerned with the setting of boundaries, whether these be related to the nature and classification of problems or the scope for action and actor involvement (Hodgson and Irving, 2007).

Policies are thus not easy to define. It is doubtful whether much can be gained by trying to achieve any greater precision than that suggested in the definitions above. It is more fruitful to look, in a concrete way, at the relevance of policies for the activity of a minister and his or her department. On appointment to office, a new minister will take over responsibility for many departmental policies. The overwhelming majority of these will be just existing ways of doing things. A good many will be enshrined in Acts of Parliament, but these will be accompanied by organizational arrangements, systems of administration and working conventions which will also help to define policy.

It is this existence of policies that determines much everyday practice in a department, and therefore provides the most crucial group of constraints for a new minister. Existing policies keep most people occupied most of the time. Innovations depend on finding opportunities for staff to work on developing new policies. They may also depend on persuading people from within the department to work to change old policies, which have hitherto been regarded as quite satisfactory. Clearly, an innovating minister has to find ways to make a vast operational organization change its ways.

What is perhaps more significant is that a new minister will also find that his or her department is developing new policies. These are not necessarily merely the left-over business from a previous administration. Many of them will derive from weaknesses in existing policies that have been recognized within the department, and that administrators are striving to correct. Some, moreover, will have their roots in changes in the world on which existing policies operate, changes that are making those policies unsuccessful or irrelevant. This group of policies or 'would-be policies' is important. The new minister may find that his or her own, or the party's, policy aspirations mesh with the policy issues on which the department are working. In such circumstances, he or she may find it comparatively easy to become, or to be seen as, an innovator. However, he or she may have to face the fact that their own view of the department's policy needs are regarded as irrelevant to the main problems being tackled within it, or even that his or her own commitments lead in quite opposite directions to those being taken by those concerned with policy innovation in the department. Popular discussions of the success or failure of ministers are often carried out in terms of their personalities and their experience. Of course, it is often possible to distinguish 'strong' and 'weak' ministers; but it must not be forgotten that the comparatively temporary incumbent of the top position of a large organization may be just lucky or unlucky – in arriving when key advisers are likely to agree that exciting innovations are necessary or, conversely, in finding that the consolidation of existing policies, or the confronting of unpleasant realities, is more important than the policy changes he or she cherishes. Box 3.8 provides an interesting, though painful to the individuals concerned, example of these phenomena.

There are various kinds of policy initiatives. Some policies have only indirect consequences for the minister's own department, particularly those whose enactment and implementation depend on another agency. Legislation which gives powers and duties to local government comes into this category. An example is legislation to protect the interests of disabled persons and their carers. While it seems to involve

Box 3.8   Personalities and policies

After the election of the Labour government in 1997 the cabinet minister for social security, Harriet Harman, was given a senior colleague of considerable relevant expertise, Frank Field, to operate as a 'minister' for social security reform. Field found it very difficult to develop an innovatory agenda against a background of expenditure restraints. Harman came under pressure from the Treasury to enact cuts already designed by the civil service. In addition it is alleged that the two found it very difficult to work together (Rawnsley, 2001). Within a year both were out of office, though much later Harman returned to become deputy leader of the Labour Party under Gordon Brown.

the development of a national policy, in practice, its dependence on local government makes it a gesture in which central government involvement is comparatively slight. Clearly, it is easier for a minister to accept this kind of legislation than to develop a policy that effectively changes the direction of a great deal of work going on *within* the department. In the above case, the policy making may be more 'symbolic' than real; ministers may hope to derive kudos without really enacting innovations.

It is also the case that modifications may be made to the administrative system, many of which do not require legislation (note the comments above about even the restructuring of government departments themselves). Such changes may be presented as designed to initiate a new response to a policy problem (underperformance in schools or health care, neglect of children), and may be easy to enact, even being seen (perhaps misleadingly) as neutral in cost terms. On the other hand, once a minister seeks to enact policies that require the expenditure of 'new money', he or she becomes engaged in what is inevitably a more difficult political exercise. Formally, the approval of the Treasury is required, probably together with the support of the Cabinet in one of its priority-setting exercises, where the minister is involved in competition with colleagues who have alternative expenditure aspirations. What this implies for the minister's relationship with civil servants is altogether more complex. The specific expenditure commitment will be, by no means, the only one the department might undertake. Hence, there will be an intra-organizational battle about the case for that particular innovation. What the outside world sees as a minister promoting a particular project is probably the end of a long process in which different groups of civil servants within the department have argued about the case for that venture as opposed to other ventures. The political negotiations between a minister and the Treasury ministers will be matched by much more elaborate negotiations between civil servants. A case that is comparatively weak when argued within the department will be faced with further problems in this tough forum, and a minister who successfully overrides objections within his or her own department may well lose in this wider battle. Students of government have, moreover, raised questions about the extent to which civil servants will fight effectively for their minister against the Treasury, in view of the prestige and power of the latter within the civil service as a whole (Heclo and Wildavsky, 1981).

In differentiating different kinds of policies, and in interpreting their implications for ministerial power, it must be recognized that some policies have implications for more than one department. A new approach to assistance with housing costs, for example, may have to be considered both by the Department for Work and Pensions, with its concern for social security policy, and the Department for Communities and Local Government with its responsibility for housing policy. The Treasury will also expect to be involved at an early stage, both because of its responsibilities for taxation and because of its concerns about overall expenditure. In addition, local government is likely to be involved. All this adds a form of complexity that greatly enhances the significance of negotiations between civil servants, and the related tendency for the maintenance of the *status quo*.

This discussion has distinguished between policies that ministers can enact with relatively slight implications for their own departments and those that require elaborate departmental involvement. It has implied that, where ideological commitments are involved, a distinction may be made between relatively easy gestures and difficult administrative battles. It may also be the case that some difficult aspects of 'bargaining politics' are involved where policy success depends on the responses of other organizations. Aspects of the development of tax credits and pensions reform has been affected by the reservations of small business about undertaking new tasks for government. The power of the doctors in health policy provides related examples. In this case, the problem comes, if not exactly within the Secretary of State's own department, at least from within public agencies. Also important for the analysis of social policy is the interplay between central government and those other organs of government, particularly local government, who have a crucial role to play in the implementation of policy, but are also themselves in certain respects policy formers.

A new minister with an overall responsibility for the health and personal social services within the Department of Health, or for education, or for housing policy will find an 'established' relationship between the department and local government or the health service with certain key characteristics. There will be a body of enacted legislation, a pattern of grants from central government, a range of procedures relating to the sanctioning of new initiatives including the taking up of loans for new capital expenditure, perhaps a pattern of inspection or policy review, and a variety of policy expectations enshrined in circulars and related messages from the centre. In a few cases, the obligations of the local authorities will be quite clear. In a rather larger number of situations, the authorities will have quite explicit duties but will not have been given detailed guidance on how to carry them out. In yet other important cases, the local authorities will regard themselves as the key policy formers; the central requirements will have been specified in such general terms that the decisions that really dictate the quality of the service given to the public are made locally. Then there will be some situations in which central government has made it very clear that the policy initiative rests with local agencies, by *permitting* activities if they so wish.

Finally, there will be a few situations in which local authorities have been almost entirely the innovators, in which they have sought to promote local acts through Parliament or in which they have interpreted general powers given to them in quite novel ways.

The new minister who wants to introduce changes into this pattern has a variety of options open, but each may involve complications wherever there is resistance to new ideas. New policies are expressed as much in ministerial statements, White Papers and circulars to the local authorities as in new statutes. In each case, the minister may be able to bolster a recommendation with indirect weapons: by control over loans and other powers to permit or limit activities, by co-operation or lack of it in situations in which joint central–local action is necessary. In the National Health Service (NHS), the control over funding also facilitates policy change from the centre.

In this section, the discussion has ranged over many of the influences on policy. Using the notion that is particularly associated with representative government, of a new minister with explicit policy commitments, attention has been given to the pressures that frustrate such commitments, or replace them by commitments derived from other sources. It has been stressed that there are strong forces in favour of the maintenance of existing policy, and that many new initiatives are, in fact, derived from concerns not so much to innovate as to correct the imperfections of existing policies.

Braybrooke and Lindblom (1963) drew attention to the extent to which the policy process is 'incremental'. That is, they were particularly concerned to attack that portrayal of the policy process which perceived it as, or able to become, a rational appraisal of all the alternative consequences of alternative policies followed by the choice of the best available. If incrementalism is perceived in these terms, there is little difficulty in understanding its applicability to social policy. As the historical chapter showed, the development of social policy has been very much a process of piling new initiatives on top of older policies, without ever clearing the ground to facilitate a fresh start. Then, as this piling-up process has proceeded, it has created new interests which future developments have to take into account. Since political values have often been at stake in conflicts over social policy, the very character of the ideological issues has precluded a cool appraisal of all the policy options.

Policy making is not a pure exercise in rational decision making. Nor is it simply the putting into practice of ideologies, or a quite incoherent process of bargaining and muddling through. Rather it is a mixture of all three, with perhaps the first least apparent and the third most in evidence.

Suggestions for Further Reading

For those who need a basic account of British politics any of the standard up-to-date textbooks will be satisfactory: Leach et al. (2006) *British Politics*, and Kavanagh et al. (2006) *British Politics* are recommended.

An account of devolution and other recent constitutional changes is provided in Jowell and Oliver (eds.) sixth edition (2007) *The Changing Constitution*. For more on local government readers should consult Stoker and Wilson (2004) *British Local*

Government into the 21st Century. On the European Union see Hantrais' (2007) *Social Policy in the European Union.* At the time of writing no one has undertaken the tricky task of charting the impact of devolution on social policy.

Hill's *The Public Policy Process* (2005; new edition due 2009), explores many of the theoretical issues about the study of policy making. Books with a focus particularly on policy making in the UK are Richards and Smith (2002) *Governance and Public Policy in the UK*, and Dorey (2005) *Policy Making in Britain.*

Chapter 4

Implementation

- Introduction
- Structures for Policy Implementation: Under Central Government
- Structures for Policy Implementation: Under Local Government
- Analysing Policy Implementation
- Issues about the Shaping of Policy
- Issues about 'Layers' in the Policy Transfer Process
- Factors Affecting the Responses of Implementation Agencies
- Horizontal Interorganizational Relationships
- The Social, Political and Economic Environment
- Conclusions
- Suggestions for Further Reading

Introduction

Why devote a chapter in a book on social policy to the study of policy implementation? What is the significance of this issue for our subject? A simple definition of implementation is that it is about what happens between policy expectations and policy results. There are several reasons why it is important. These are:

- Most importantly, what the government says will happen – even what is enshrined in the law – may not provide an accurate picture of what does happen.
- As indicated in the last chapter, the actual making of policy can be seen as involving a combination of 'formation' and 'implementation' in which there is a continuing interaction between the two and it may be the latter as much as the former that crucially determines its shape.

- Therefore concern with the ineffectiveness of policies is now recognized as requiring the asking both of questions about the character of policy and about the implementation process and the organizations responsible for implementation.

There is a widespread 'top-down' perspective from which questions emerge like: Why don't those who are expected to carry out policies do what is required of them? But that question may be turned on its head since many people concerned with policy delivery may equally ask, from their 'bottom-up' perspective: Why are we being expected to carry out policies that are inappropriate for the issues and problems we confront? Both kinds of questions are equally valid and any sound discussion of implementation needs to take into account the legitimacy of both perspectives and the realities of implementation processes in which influences from the top, bottom and indeed the middle of the system are likely to be present. To these must be added some important issues about the impact of policy process upon people who are the recipients of its outputs.

This chapter explores these issues, but first it is necessary to identify the key social policy implementation agencies

Structures for Policy Implementation: Under Central Government

This section and the next provide a brief account of the main groups of people responsible for social policy implementation in the UK. This one looks at the main policy areas where local government is generally not involved. The next looks at the role of local government. Since the organizational arrangements vary within the constituent countries of the UK, the comments in this section should be taken to apply only to England unless there is an observation to the contrary. However, in the cases of social security and employment there is a single system for Britain, and the system in Northern Ireland is in most respects a copy of that.

Social security benefits are administered by both the agency of the Treasury now called Revenue and Customs and by the Department of Work and Pensions. Revenue and Customs are responsible for tax credits, child benefit and also for the collection of National Insurance contributions. The Department for Work and Pensions are responsible for the rest of the system but work through a number of agencies, of which the most important are the Pensions Service and Jobcentre Plus.

Where once upon a time all social security was secured through applications to local offices it is only short term benefits, and in particular benefits for job seekers which require local registration and local interviews, which are administered through local offices now.

The implementation of health policy in England and Wales is devolved in a complex way. At national level, there is a National Health Service Executive. This is staffed by civil servants from the Department of Health and may, in many respects, be regarded as an extension of that department with direct accountability to the Secretary of State.

Responsibility for the provision of all services at the local level including family practitioner services comes under Primary Care Trusts. These both provide primary care services (and some community services) and commission secondary care. The latter is provided by other Trusts, which administer hospitals and some community services. These arrangements operate within a structure over which a small number of Strategic Health Authorities have an overarching responsibility. Both Health Authorities and Trusts, of all kinds, are quasi-autonomous organizations with directors (executive and non-executive) appointed by the Secretary of State, but with their own employees. Two controversial issue within health services concern:

- The extent of Trust autonomy, it will be seen in Chapter 7 that there are now Foundation Trusts with much higher levels of autonomy.
- The extent to which commissioning bodies may go outside the normal NHS provider bodies to seek services from the private sector.

Responsibility for environmental health issues and for other non-medical influences on health such as food policy lies with the Department for Environment, Food and Rural Affairs. Much of the work of this department is done through agencies, such as the Environment Agency or through local government (see the next section).

Since 2007 post-school education has been brought under the new Department for Innovation, Universities and Skills. Implementation of policy is complicated by a plethora of intervening and advisory bodies, in what Ainley shows to be a very complex and 'inherently unstable system' (Ainley, 2001, p. 474).

Higher education in Britain has required special forms of organization designed to take into account the fact that many colleges serve more than the local authority area in which they are based. For the university sector, a special intermediary body has long existed. However, the 1986 Education Act replaced the comparatively independent University Grants Committee by a more directly government controlled Funding Council.

Structures for Policy Implementation: Under Local Government

A broad outline of the local government system was set out in the previous chapter, but many aspects of the way this system works were left to be included in this chapter. The earlier discussion made it clear that the powers and duties of local government are provided in national legislation. In many respects therefore local government can be seen as 'merely' an agent of central government for implementation. Yet local authorities are elected bodies and their leaders see themselves as having electoral mandates.

Hence, the relationship between central and local government involves both partnership and conflict. Central government seeks to impose its will not merely through legislation, but also through the communication of large amounts of guidance. This may be embodied in circulars, regularly sent from central departments to local authorities, or through less formal communications from ministers, administrators and professional advisers. Central intervention will be justified in terms of national political commitments, to ensure that central policies have an impact on all localities. There is an inherent conflict between the demands of local autonomy and the principle of 'territorial justice', requiring that citizens in different geographical areas secure comparable treatment.

The Conservative governments led by Margaret Thatcher and John Major in the 1980s and 1990s, considerably curbed the powers and autonomy of local government. They imposed increased financial controls (see below), partly removed some services from local government (such as parts of the education system), increased the regulation of others and forced authorities to consider contracting out services. Labour, in power, is continuing that process, albeit with a slightly less dogmatic perspective on privatisation (DETR, 1998).

The 1999 Local Government Act established a system requiring local authorities to demonstrate that they are achieving 'best value' in the services they provide (see Box 4.1).

Efforts to secure 'best value' are required to be very much in the public domain. But in addition to general public scrutiny the government set up a system of auditing and inspection in which the responsible government departments are assisted by the Audit Commission. Hence there is a system of reporting back to central government, which has given itself powers to intervene if the evidence suggests what it regards as below standard services. In the field of education the government took powers in an earlier Education Act (1998) to replace all or parts of failing local

---

Box 4.1   Best value

A government White Paper described 'best value' as follows:

> Best value will be a duty to deliver services to clear standards – covering both cost and quality – by the most effective, economic and efficient means available. In carrying out this duty local authorities will be accountable to local people and have a responsibility to central government in its role as representative of the broader national interest. Local authorities will set those standards – covering both cost and quality – for all the services for which they are responsible. But in those areas such as education and social services where the Government has key responsibilities and commitments, the Government itself will set national standards. (DETR, 1998, para 7.2)

The 1999 Local Government Act imposes this duty on all local authorities except parish councils. Local authorities are required to establish the following for all their services:

- specific objectives and performance measures
- a programme of fundamental performance reviews
- local performance plans.

education authorities with alternatives, which might be voluntary organizations, private companies or even other local authorities. It has already used these powers. The 1999 Local Government Act means that such actions can occur in any area of local government.

Policy making in local government is the responsibility of elected members, known as councillors. These represent districts, or wards, within each authority in much the same way as MPs represent constituencies. Today, a great deal of local politics is arranged along party lines, and most councillors represent the political parties that are also found at Westminster. The politicization of local government has intensified the conflict between central and local government. This was particularly sharp in the early 1980s between radical Labour authorities and the central Conservative administration.

Until 2000 the work of councillors was organized into systems of committees. Each councillor sat on a number of these. Most business was transacted in the committees, so that the meetings of the full councils were largely rubber-stamping affairs, affording opportunities for the making of political points. These committee structures were primarily related to the various functional responsibilities of the authority for each separate activity. Now local authorities are required to form an 'executive' of some kind, responsible for effective implementation of council policy. In some cases – where that option has been chosen- this is answerable to a separately elected mayor, but in most cases this is formed from the leading members of the dominant party (or parties) with individuals taking responsibility for specific services (rather as in the central government 'ministerial' model). The idea is that a mayor or minority of councillors should take executive responsibility for decisions leaving the rest to engage in representative work. A key device to involve councillors is investigatory committees which, like Parliamentary select committees, examine issues pertinent to the operation of their authority.

Local authorities have three major sources of income: local taxes, payments for the provisions of services and government grants. The first of these was, until the mid 1980s, a system of 'rates' on property, both domestic and business.

Then the government replaced domestic rates by a tax on individuals, the community charge or 'poll tax', and centralized control over business rates. The poll tax was met by a popular reaction which contributed to the end of Margaret Thatcher's career as Prime Minister (Butler et al., 1994). After her fall, her successor sharply increased the central government grant to soften the impact of the poll tax, financing this out of an increase in value added tax. He then, in 1993, replaced the poll tax by the 'council tax'. The latter is a simplified form of the former domestic rates, with the number of adult occupants of the property partly taken into account as well as its value. These changes to local taxation involved a sharp reduction in the independence of local government (see Box 4.2).

Central government also maintains control over local authority borrowing. The trend, in recent years, has been away from a system of strict, item by item, controls to broad limitations on total borrowing. The system is currently a complex combination of these two approaches to control.

Most of the specific detail in this section describes the local government system in England. It is not possible to go into great detail here on the other countries

Box 4.2   Central control over local government expenditure

Even before the poll tax, the Conservative government had given itself 'capping' powers to prevent local authorities from raising local taxation over centrally prescribed limits. The centralization of the commercial rating system had the effect of bringing three quarters of local revenue under direct central control; and the panic reaction to reduce the impact of the poll tax, after Margaret Thatcher's fall, had the effect of pushing the centrally controlled proportion up to around 80 per cent of local government revenue. While the Labour government ended 'crude' council tax capping, it retains a 'reserve power to control excessive council tax increases' (DETR, 1998, para 5.7, p. 34). It is certainly not increasing the central funds going to local government. It retains the proceeds of the business rate, but may allow authorities the opportunity to levy supplementary rates or to give rebates (ibid., para 10.8, p. 77). On the other hand it has been prepared to accept slow increases in local expenditure. Central government is happy to see costs shift onto local government up to the point where it is perceived to be to blame for this effect.

of the UK. The systems in Scotland and Wales are broadly similar, but as indicated above local government has a much more limited role in Northern Ireland.

We turn now to those policy areas where the implementing role of local government is particularly salient.

One implementation complication for many of the policy areas discussed here is that the central department responsible for local government is the Department for Communities and Local Government. This department, together with the Treasury, deals with the main financial and legal links with local government, but has no responsibility for education, social services or environmental health policy. This exacerbates a tension, at the local level, between the demands of an integrated and corporate approach to local government and the separable service interests of heavy-spending activities. Arrangements in Scotland and Wales may be better co-ordinated.

Social services for adults are the responsibility, inasmuch as they are under public rather than voluntary control, of departments within local authorities, once called 'social services departments' but now given various names. Many local authorities have linked their management to that for other community services or housing. The increasing recognition of a need to co-ordinate social services with health services at the local level is also leading to innovations which link health services staff into care management arrangements. It may be the case that there will eventually be radical organizational changes that will move some or all adult social services into the health service. We will return to this theme in Chapter 7.

Since 1993, local authorities are required to operate, in respect of their adult care services, a purchaser/provider system in which they seek the 'best value' (see Box 4.3) service. Providers may be sections within the local authority department required to operate with some degree of managerial and, particularly, accounting autonomy. They may also be voluntary or profit-making organizations; they may also be health service Trusts. The government has been concerned that providers from outside the local authority shall have a good chance of competing for social services contracts. In the area of the provision of residential care, which was already heavily privatized, local authority direct provision is rapidly disappearing. There is a quasi-autonomous Commission (that also supervises health services) that supervises most care services, both public and private.

Many directors and senior staff in adult social services are professionally qualified social workers, but a relatively small proportion of the staff is engaged in social work. Other key workers include home helps, residential care staff and occupational therapists. Policy implementation is often influenced by the character of co-operation between these different occupational groups.

Social services for children come under the supervision of the Department for Children, Schools and Families at national level and are implemented by local authority 'education and children's departments' (again the exact titles of these departments will vary). Responsibility for the implementation of schools and other educational services for school age children also comes under these departments.

Many of the implementation issues in local authority education services concern the relationship between the authorities and the schools. While the chain image is not entirely appropriate, since varying responsibilities and degrees of autonomy are involved, and individuals in the chain may be bypassed, it is important to acknowledge that implementation may depend on a series of links: the elected members of a local authority, the chief education officer and his or her administrative staff, local authority inspectors and advisers, school governing bodies, head teachers, departmental heads within the schools, and class teachers. The examination of policy implementation in the education service raises a number of interesting questions about local authority autonomy, the role of school management and the place of professional discretion.

Since 1986 a number of Education Acts have combined the increases in central control over education authorities with measures increasing school autonomy. These have strengthened the powers of the governing bodies of local authority schools, laying down rules to determine their budgets and giving them autonomous responsibilities. They have also allowed the creation of various kinds of schools with greater levels of autonomy, extending long-standing arrangements for religious bodies to participate in the running of state financed education and allowing for businesses and other organizations a measure of control over schools in return for (generally) modest financial inputs.

While the government has claimed to be engaged in decentralization, increasing the feasibility of parent power, the weakening of local political control can equally be seen as increasing centralization (Glennerster et al., 1991). The latter impression is further reinforced by the development of the national curriculum and by the power given to an independent inspectorate (Ofsted) accountable to central government.

The way in which all the changes, briefly outlined here, work in practice is given extensive attention in Chapter 9.

The integration of education administration and children's services within local authorities is, at the time of writing, a comparably new phenomenon and it would be inappropriate to make judgements about how this is working. But it needs to be noted that this amalgamation puts together an education based administrative service, largely run by former teachers, with (as noted above) an increasingly 'arms-length' relationship with schools, with a children's service, in which qualified social workers are the dominant element, with very direct concerns to try to develop services for vulnerable children and to prevent child abuse, using both quasi-private resources (in particular foster parents, child minders and day nurseries) and directly provided care facilities. After amalgamation most of the local departments have become headed by former directors of education, but maybe in the longer run we will see social work managers moving into these roles. The child care system is now supervised by the Department for Children, Schools and Families and inspected by staff incorporated into the school inspection system.

Unitary or, in the counties, lower-tier local authorities have a wide range of specific responsibilities for environmental health issues – for example collect and process refuse, inspect shops and restaurants and have duties to deal with rats and other pests – and wider powers (operated in conjunction with health authorities – when outbreaks of infectious diseases occur.

Local authority housing in Britain is also the responsibility of the unitary or lower-tier local authorities. In Northern Ireland, protests about discrimination by local authorities led to the creation of a province-wide Housing Executive; and, in Scotland, there is an important nation-wide 'public' housing association to supplement the work of the local authorities. There is also, in England and Wales, Housing Corporation, responsible for the provision of funds for housing associations. A feature of recent government policy has been a quest for new ways of managing and financing housing. This is increasing the importance of bodies like the housing associations, financed by public money or by a combination of public and private money. The local authority controlled sector (generally called 'council housing') has substantially shrunk. In many areas the relevant local authorities no longer own houses; their responsibilities to help people in housing obtain social housing have to be fulfilled through powers to nominate to tenancy vacancies in housing associations.

The implementation of housing policy is fragmented not only because of the mixture of kinds of housing authorities but also because this is an area of social policy in which many significant decisions are made by private agencies. Since there are three main types of housing tenure- renting from a local authority or housing association ('social housing'), owner-occupation, and renting from a private landlord – and the government intervenes, or has intervened, to try to influence the quality and cost of each type, policy implementation is often a very complex matter. In studying it, attention has to be given not only to the relationship between government and the local authorities, but also to government attempts to influence the behaviour of building societies, landlords and private house builders. There are also some other public–private interactions of some significance for housing policy. For example, there have been government efforts to influence the price of land and to curb land speculation, government interventions in the money market which affect the cost of borrowing for housing, and government manipulation of the costs and benefits of various statuses in the housing market by means of taxation and social security policy.

Support for the housing costs of low-income tenants comes from housing benefit. In Britain, policy responsibility for this lies with the Department of Work and Pensions but local authorities administer the scheme. They receive direct reimbursement of most of their costs.

This section and the last one have shown that the machinery for policy implementation in the UK is complicated. Indeed it is steadily becoming more complicated. There has been a movement away from dependence on simple bureaucratic models – a single social security ministry, a hierarchically organized NHS, local authorities expected to organized departmentally – to a range of models involving contracting, cross-system partnerships and output surveillance. There has been a succession of experiments:

- new bureaucratic organizations in the 1960s and 1970s
- efforts to create market or quasi-market arrangements in the 1980s and 1990s
- a sequence of changes in the central department responsibilities
- and a confusing pragmatism in the 1990s and 2000s with emphases upon the idea that only 'what works' matters and a need for 'joined up' government together with a continued quest for new ways to control (see Newman, 2001)

Each fashion in 'governance' has left legacies behind to confuse the overall picture. This is further explored later.

Analysing Policy Implementation

While any subdivision may be arbitrary it is useful to categorize the issues about implementation into the following:

1   issues about the shaping or formation of policy
2   issues about 'layers' in the policy transfer process
3   factors affecting the responses of implementation agencies (their organization, the extent of autonomy amongst their staff etc.)
4   horizontal interorganizational relationships (relationships between parallel organizations required to collaborate in implementation)
5   the impact of the social, political and economic environment

Each of these is discussed in separate sections in the rest of this chapter, but Box 4.3 illustrates the sorts of things that might be considered under each heading in a study of implementation.

Box 4.3   Illustration of what analysis of implementation can involve

The following items which were considered in study of the implementation of government policy (Vick et al., 2006) on direct payments in social care (see Chapter 8 for a discussion of this policy):

1   Issues about the shaping or formation of policy
    • National legislation, policy and guidance

2   Issues about 'layers' in the policy transfer process
    • Central government performance monitoring
    • Inspection and regulation of local authority services

3   Factors influencing the responses of implementation agencies
    • Leadership within the local authority
    • Local political support for direct payments
    • Support from public sector trade unions
    • Training and support for front line staff.

4   Horizontal interorganizational relationships
    • Support from voluntary organizations
    • Relationships with health care organizations

5   The Impact of the wider environment
    • Demand from service users and carers
    • Availability of people to work as personal assistants (including considering local labour market conditions

Issues about the Shaping of Policy

In Chapter 3 the making of policy was portrayed mainly in terms of the production of Acts of Parliament and of regulations amplifying or modifying them. When we look at what happens when such a policy is implemented, there may be other sources which can inform us on what is to happen in practice. These may be codes of practice or briefings for implementing agencies taking various forms. Taken together all of these are likely, in order to shape a policy for implementation, to include:

• operational and procedural elements setting out how the policy is to be put into practice
• indications of the authorities to be responsible for action (specific local governments, health authorities, etc.)
• resources – that is how the costs of implementation will be met
• evaluative elements – indicating how the operation of the policy will be monitored or checked

As far as implementation is concerned a great deal will depend upon how precisely these have been dealt with in advance. In practice three things are likely to occur:

- some of these elements will not have been dealt with fully, this means that they may be settled in the course of action
- some elements will be re-negotiated, as actors concerned with implementation feed back alternatives to the original plans and these are then modified
- some elements will be explicitly ignored by implementers

There is a tendency in popular discussions of implementation for only the last of these considerations to be discussed, in terms that attribute a measure of disobedience to implementers. This can be a very misleading approach, seriously ignoring both the extent both to which it is impossible to specify all that is to be done in advance and the legitimacy of renegotiation of details as action proceeds.

Many policies will be formulated in a complex way; setting out to achieve objectives $x, x_1, x_2 \ldots$ under conditions $y, y_1, y_2, \ldots$ These complexities may well influence the implementation process. Some policies will involve vague and ambiguous specifications of objectives and conditions. These will tend to become more specific during the implementation process.

While it is possible, in the abstract, to treat policies in isolation from other policies, in practice, any new policy will be adopted in a context in which there are already many other existing policies. Some of these other policies will supply precedents for the new policy, others will supply conditions, and some may be in conflict with it. These will therefore contribute to the modification of policy as it is implemented.

Moreover there will be a number of different reasons why issues about the form taken by a policy have not been clarified in advance. First, it may be simply that those who initially formulate policy are far from clear about what they really want. The lack of clarity may be so total that it is comparatively meaningless to seek to identify a policy or to study its implementation. Some of the 'policies' of this kind derive from political aspirations to demonstrate a popularly desirable commitment.

Second, it is important to take account of the extent to which a lack of clarity about policy stems from a lack of potential consensus. Policies emerge that are not merely compromises, but also remain obscure on key points of implementation. Where this occurs, it is likely that there will be a lack of consensus among the implementers, too. Hence, wide variations in practice may emerge, together with a range of conflicts surrounding the implementation process (Box 4.4 provides an illustration).

Ambiguity arising from lack of consensus about policy goals provides opportunities for those who are opposed to their general thrust, or who wish to divert them to serve their own ends. This is the typical context for actual 'disobedience'. Bardach (1977) has developed an extensive analysis of the various 'implementation games' that may be played by those who perceive ways in which policies may be delayed, altered or deflected. While some policies contain few features that their opponents can interfere with - laying down, for example, a clear duty to provide a particular service or benefit - others, such as the Department of Health's commitment to the development of community care for mentally ill people, depend heavily on the

> ## Box 4.4   Alternative policy goals as a source of variation in implementation
>
> In Chapter 9 it will be argued that the development of the provision of care and education for children under compulsory school age has been influenced by three very different objectives – arguments for preparation for formal education, concerns to facilitate the labour market participation of mothers and concerns about the neglect of children. What has transpired is an amalgam influenced by all of these concerns. It has also been influenced by concerns to support the private provision of services for pre-school children and by desires to minimize costs. It is not surprising therefore that local arrangements vary widely, and that there are conflicts over the shape to be taken by policy in practice according to variations in views about these alternative objectives (see Liu (2001) for a study of evolution of *policy* in this field in the 1990s).

commitments of implementers, and are relatively easily diverted in other directions or even rendered ineffective.

Issues about 'Layers' in the Policy Transfer Process

As already noted, many policies are formulated by one layer in an administrative system but implemented by another. Some writers speak of one layer 'mandating' another. There is thus a 'transfer' process involved. We have noted how, in the UK, central government will generally have been involved in the policy-formulation process, but implementation is often delegated to other organizations such as local government, with the centre generally maintaining an interest in the implementation process.

This mandating process will often be accompanied by financial transactions between layers. In the UK the split between central government as a policy initiator and local government in the role of implementer produces a situation in which central intentions appear to be thwarted by local scarcities. Yet it is generally, as was shown on p. 00, central government that determines the level of local resources. In the area of social care, local authorities in the mid 1990s received some additional funds to enable them to meets costs which were previously met by central government from the social security budget. At the same time, they were subjected to centrally imposed limits on their capacity to raise local revenues. Many considered that their resources fell far short of their responsibilities under the new legislation.

The 'agencies' set up to administer central services seem, prima facie, to have clearer mandates. They are governed by framework agreements which seem to make their implementation responsibilities explicit. Yet the intrinsic difficulties in drawing a clear distinction between policy formation and implementation mean that anything

Box 4.5   Governance

The traditional view of government was linked to the notion of a single state with superordinate power over a specific territory. But there are supra-state institutions which act, to some degree as superordinate states. These include both international organizations which may seek to impose policies on nation states and organizations like the European Union which operate quite specifically as supra-national law makers. But equally within the UK, does devolution (see discussion in Chapter 3) mean that we now have four states instead of one? It is difficult to answer that question; there are (as noted) over-riding powers still held by the UK government but in practical terms there are high levels of autonomy, particularly in Scotland, much of the time.

But the world of policy is even more complicated than that. The state operates through institutions which have many features that are regarded as private rather than public. The modern manifestation of the second of these phenomena has been a deliberate shift to the delegation of what had become accepted as governmental functions. What this implies is a contract between government and a 'private' body to operate all or part of a public service. It is often presented as simply a mechanism for policy implementation with policy making still in government hands, but the delegation of a major activity, particularly a monopoly activity, tends to involve some shift of control over policy. A related phenomenon is a public/private partnership where resources are drawn both directly from publicly collected revenues and from private sources; policy control is obviously particularly likely to be shared in these circumstances.

These complications, arising both from the increasing importance of supra-state bodies and from changes within the nation state have led many contemporary writers to speak of a movement from 'government' to 'governance'. Richards and Smith thus say:

> 'Governance' is a descriptive label that is used to highlight the changing nature of the policy process in recent decades. In particular, it sensitizes us to the ever-increasing variety of terrains and actors involved in the making of public policy. (2002, p. 2)

they may do to alter the service they provide to the public may raise political concerns. Furthermore, when something goes wrong, there will be argument about whether an agency has failed to fulfil its mandate or whether that mandate was flawed In fact their apparent separation enables their executive staff to be offered as sacrifices for ministerial mistakes (see Box 5.4 on p. 116, which gives a brief history of the Child Support Agency, an organization which fell into this category).

This whole subject is made more complicated by issues about accountability and the right to control. What has happened is that discontent with older hierarchical or 'bureaucratic' models for policy implementation has led to range of experimentation with alternative models (Hood, 1991). During the 1980s and 1990s that experimentation was very influenced by a view that 'market' rather than 'hierarchy' models (Williamson, 1975) should be adopted, with services contracted out to private agencies or run by autonomous public agencies in a quasi-market relationship to a public sector 'purchaser'. That perspective has gradually been replaced by a more pragmatic stance that involves a continuing distrust of hierarchy, a conditional acceptance of market arrangements (if they work) and an interest in exploring other ways of delegating responsibility to the lowest possible level. The last named development involves, for some, a commitment to new participatory forms of democracy, involving services users in service management. We need here to introduce a concept widely used in the analysis of modern government: 'governance'. This new term has been used to try to capture the complexity of policy making and implementation systems in the modern world. Box 4.5 examines the use of this term.

Janet Newman, in her study of governance in Britain under 'new Labour', has argued that governance is 'always likely to be characterized by multiple and conflicting models' (2001, p. 39) involving tension between continuity and innovation, on one dimension, centralization and differentiation on the other. Box 4.6 sets out the four models of governance Newman derives from an exploration of this tension.

Box 4.6   Newman's four models of governance

- The self-governance model, towards devolution based on citizen or community power.
- The open-system model, towards flexibility, based on the flow of power within networks.
- The hierarchy model, towards control, based on formal authority.
- The rational goal model, towards output maximization, based on managerial power. (Ibid., p. 38)

Newman says of the Blair government:

> Labour sought to create both a new social settlement based on consensus and inclusion, and a more coercive and conditional welfare regime. It attempted to ensure the consistency and efficacy of policy delivery by setting and enforcing performance standards, while at the same time seeking to institutionalize new forms of co-steering and co-governance through partnerships and community capacity building. It sought to send out a strong and consistent set of messages from the centre, while also fostering public participation and drawing a wider range of actors into the policy process. (Ibid., pp. 163–4)

Newman's analysis thus suggests that there is a search going on for new approaches to control over implementation, characterized by conflict over the desirability of decentralization. An alternative way of looking at this is to see that there are choices to be made between alternative models for this control. Drawing upon a variety of attempts to supplement the hierarchy /market dichotomy outlined above with a third alternative involving higher levels of participation (called 'persuasion' by Lindblom, 1977 and 'community' by Colebatch and Larmour, 1993) Hill and Hupe (forthcoming revd. edn. 2009) have arrived at a typology of modes of governance involving different implementation expectations, as follows:

- 'authority': where rules are laid down in advance
- 'transaction': where certain outputs are expected, often as specified in contracts
- 'persuasion': where the essential mode of operation involves collaboration or what may be called 'co-production'.

Table 4.1 applies these models to some policy examples.

Choices between the alternatives will depend upon both the ideologies of those (at both levels) who are able to make those choices and upon considerations about the 'best' ways to organize any specific policy delivery process. The latter considerations rest upon (as suggested in Table 4.1) what is being attempted.

Table 4.1   Three kinds of governance

	Authority	Transaction	Persuasion
Core activity of government	Imposing Regulating Delivering goods and services	Creating frameworks Assessing results	Inviting participation Showing direction
Appropriate perspective on managing implementation	Enforcement	Performance	Co-production
Management via	Inputs	Outputs	Outcomes as shared results
Example of policy area	Delivery of a social security benefit where there is a clearly defined statutory right (for example: child benefit)	Operation of a straightforward service where there can be a contract that can be effectively monitored (for example: refuse collection)	Operation of a service where effective delivery depends upon experts working in a situation in which they have to be trusted to make decisions based upon specific situations (example: primary medical care)

Source: Based upon ideas set out in Hill and Hupe, 2002, chapter 7, and 2007.

Factors Affecting the Responses of Implementation Agencies

While traditional approaches to public administration involve notions of prescription of activities from legitimate policy makers to public 'servants' expected to defer to authority- within organizations as well as between - many studies of organizational behaviour suggest that there are finite limits to the prescription of subordinate behaviour. Detailed rule making is a difficult and time-consuming activity. If rules then require close supervision and control, a point may be reached where such activities are self-defeating. It is interesting to note how much manufacturing industry has moved away from what has been described as the 'Fordist' model of routine mass production work. Managerial gurus like Peters and Waterman (1982) extol the virtues of flexible forms of organization, engaging the commitments of employees and enabling them to innovate and cope with organizational change. This approach has been seen as relevant to government too (Pollitt, 1990; Butcher, 2002).

In many areas of social policy, there will be a strong element of discretion in tasks. Box 4.7, picking up theme from various parts of this chapter, identifies the main sources of this discretion.

In practice, prescriptions for policy implementation convey discretionary powers to field-level staff for reasons that are combinations of these 'sources' of discretion. Hence, an alternative way of looking at the phenomenon of discretion is to see the field official (including the teacher or social worker) as a 'street-level bureaucrat' (Lipsky, 1980). His or her job is characterized by inadequate resources for the task, by variable and often low public support for the role, and by ambiguous and often unrealizable expectations of performance. The officials' concerns are with the actual impact of specific policies on their relationships with specific individuals; these may lead to a disregard of, or failure to understand, the wider policy issues that concern those 'higher-up' in the agency. The 'street-level' role is necessarily uncertain. A modicum of professional (or semi-professional, see below) training defines the role as putting into practice a set of ideals inculcated in that training. Yet the

---

Box 4.7 Sources of discretion

1 Deliberate recognition of local autonomy
2 'Political' difficulties in resolving key policy dilemmas
3 'Logical' problems in prescribing rules for particular situations, particularly where qualitative issues are a stake
4 The inherent limits to the regulation of tasks
5 The human motivation problems which follow from trying to regulate people.

'street-level' bureaucrat is also the representative of a government agency that is itself subject to conflicting pressures. In day-to-day contact with clients and with the community at large, he or she becomes, to some degree, locked into the support of individuals and groups that may be antipathetic to the employing agency. In such a situation of role confusion and role strain, a person at the end of the line is not disposed to react to new policy initiatives from above as if he or she were a mere functionary. New policies are but factors in a whole web of demands that have to be managed; social workers and teachers are particularly likely to be in this sort of situation.

There are 'two faces' to street level bureaucracy. It may be seen as the effective adaptation of policy to the needs of the public, or it may be seen as the manipulation of positions of power to distort policy towards stigmatization, discrimination and petty tyranny. Which it is will vary according to the policy at stake, and the values and commitments of the field workers, but this will also depend on the scope accorded by the organizational control system, for this phenomenon is not necessarily independent of 'biases' built into the policy delivery system. Workers may more easily manipulate their 'system' in favour of, or against, some clients in situations where their agency grants them licence to deploy such commitments.

Consideration of discretion and of the roles of 'street-level' bureaucrats' must also involve looking at the implications of professionalism for implementation. Three interrelated points may be made about professionalism (Johnson, 1972):

1   it may entail a level of expertise that makes lay scrutiny difficult
2   professionals may be, for whatever reason, accorded a legitimate autonomy
3   professionals may acquire amounts of power and influence that enable them to determine their own activities.

These sources of professional freedom clearly have a differential impact depending on (a) the profession involved, (b) the organizational setting in which professionals work, and (c) the policies that they are required to implement. The importance of the level of expertise for professional power has led some writers to make a distinction between professions and semi-professions (Etzioni, 1969) with doctors and lawyers in the former category but social workers and teachers in the latter.

The issues about expertise are, however, complex. They interact significantly with the phenomenon of 'determinacy' - the extent to which the professional response can be pre-programmed. The more complex professional tasks are a mixture of activities which can be routinized together with situations in which they must have the capacity to respond to the unexpected (see Box 4.8)

The second point above, about autonomy, has been the subject of controversy about the impact on professional activities of organizational, and particularly public, employment. The conclusion would seem to be dictated by some of the considerations in the last paragraph. That is, in short, that 'it depends on the profession and on the organization'. On the third point, once again, a good deal depends on the nature of the policy involved.

> # Box 4.8 The balance between routine and complexity in professional tasks: doctoring as an example
>
> Much doctoring is routine - many patients present clear symptoms for which there is a predictable response or there are logical testing procedures to go through to reach a diagnosis - but a good doctor has to be able to spot the exceptional condition and react to the unexpected response to treatment. Should health care systems therefore lay down 'protocols' and monitor to ensure that standard procedures are followed? Or should they allow doctors to exercise their discretion, so that they feel they are able to respond flexibly to the unexpected? This is, of course, not an either/or matter; the problem is how to find the ideal path between the extreme positions. It is one which is a very live one for the management of the NHS; it is manifest in efforts to develop a system of 'clinical governance' to fuse professional freedom with public accountability. We return to this topic in Chapter 7.
>
> A set of similar point could have been made about teaching or social work and other public services

In a large number of situations, it is expected that professional judgement will have a considerable influence on the implementation process. Clearly explicit in many policies is an expectation of this. This applies to many decisions made in face-to-face relationships between professionals and their clients. Many of the issues involved are increasingly the subject of controversy, involving arguments about 'rules' (perhaps establishing 'rights') versus 'discretion'. Within these arguments, disputes occur about the significance of expertise and about the scope for effective limitation of discretionary power. Their effective resolution would also impose many difficult policy questions - about moral rights to choose (for example, with reference to abortion) and the best way to allocate scarce resources (for example, with regard to kidney machines) - which are, at present, partly masked by professional discretion.

There are also some important questions here, which are difficult to resolve, about the way to link together professional autonomy in dealing with an individual relationship with a client, and a policy-based concern (or 'public concern') about the way in which professionals allocate their services as a whole. Professionals have been found to be reluctant to confront priority questions; they often prefer to deal with each patient or client as an individual in need without any reference to a collective ethic which requires some degree of priority ranking. In this respect, when taken together, these separate decisions may be said to 'make' policy. A consequence of this may be lengthening waiting lists. The political response to these has been to treat waiting lists as crucial indices of services to the public (with targets enshrined in charters and published). Yet doing this does not solve the problems of competing priorities. It either forces a watering down of the service offered to all or, more likely, forces attention to be given to certain issues (like the rapidity with which patients secure a certain routine operation) at the expense of others where the quantitative indices are not available or cannot be so easily interpreted. There are also problems about the extent to which indices of this kind can be manipulated by altering procedures and recording practices rather than by improving the overall service.

Overall this section has explored the very many sources of autonomy on the part of implementing agencies. This autonomy is controversial because it occurs against a background of conflict over accountability, about the rights of various actors to exercise control - politicians at the top, organizations and professions in the middle, workers at the 'street level' and, last but not least, the public themselves as the recipients of policy outputs.

Horizontal Interorganizational Relationships

A further important complication for the operation of individual agencies is that many activities depend on the co-operation of two or more organizations. We describe these as 'horizontal' relationships since the organizations are in no sense 'accountable' to each other. The relationships between layers analysed above are complicated by deviations from the simple model in which there are single organizations at each level – a single central government department relating to a single implementing agency, or to a number of local authorities in each of a series of distinct geographical areas. Policy implementation often depends on co-operation between separate organizations where responsibility at the local level is (a) delegated to several organizations with separate territories and (b) dependent on co-ordinated action between two or more local organizations. However, in actual situations collaboration may involve both these horizontal relationships and vertical relationships between layers at the same time (for example, health and social care collaboration involves horizontal relationships at the local level which may be affected by how the Department of Health at national level deals with both local health organizations and local governments).

Many organizations are involved in a web of relationships, which vary in character and intensity according to the issue. Some activities require considerable co-operation between levels while others require very little. However, it may be misleading to lose sight of the overall pattern since the outcome of one relationship will affect responses to another. Relationships are ongoing; each will have a history that conditions reactions to any new issues. Equally, each organization will have developed its own sense of its task, mission and role in relation to others. These will affect its response to anything new.

It is widely recognized that different services to individuals need to be integrated. This issue is particularly salient in the area of health and personal social services policy. Many individuals need varying combinations of health and social care. The search for the best way to organize to make these combinations effective is explored further in Chapters 7 and 8. There are no easy answers. While various attempts have been made to create structures that do this, it is perhaps the case that what is crucial is that ways are found to encourage different professionals to work together at the 'street level' regardless of their organizational locations (see Hudson and Henwood, 2002).

The Social, Political and Economic Environment

Policies may be interpreted as responses to perceived social needs. They are evolved in an environment in which problems emerge that are deemed to require political solutions, and pressures occur for new political responses. Government is concerned with 'doing things to', 'taking things from' or 'providing things for' groups of people. Putting policies into practice involves interactions between the agencies of government and their environment.

Many policies may be seen as providing for 'outputs' that may or may not deliver what are regarded as desirable final 'outcomes'. The latter may be determined by factors other than the policy under scrutiny. Policies may seem to aim at outcomes – improving health, reducing poverty, increasing literacy, etc. – but in fact fail to do so. This may be because of environmental factors that are hard to control.

However, in looking at social policy, we must also question whether the distinction between the policy system and its environment can be easily made. The policy determinants of welfare are multiple, and sometimes unexpected; individuals' welfare is influenced by phenomena that have nothing to do with the activity of the state. The determinants of an individual's welfare can be broadly classified as depending on their own capacity to care for themselves combined with (a) market activities and relationships, (b) the behaviour of 'significant others' as providers of 'informal care' among whom family members are likely to be the most important, and (c) the role played by the state. To study welfare requires attention to all 'determinants'. Changes in the way in which welfare is provided are particularly likely to involve shifts in the roles played by these 'determinants' and shifts in the relationships between them. In other words, the process of interaction between policy system and environment is a very active one, and those interactions occur across an ambiguous, shifting boundary. Box 4.9 provides a concrete example.

Conclusions

This chapter has portrayed the implementation process as a complex one, in many respects inextricably entwined with the policy-making process. It has suggested that, in the study of social policy, it is important to give attention to implementation problems that arise directly from the way policy was formulated, but to recognize also that there is a complicated interrelationship between these and a range of inter- and intra-organizational factors. Finally, all these complications interact with a complex environment.

Box 4.9   Policy system and their environment: an example

Social care is only one element in individual care systems in which family, neighbour and purchased care are likely also to play a part. A shift in the availability of, or character of, any one of these care ingredients is likely to have an impact on the others.

The things which can change the social environment will be, for example, longer lives, changes in marriage and child-bearing practices, geographical mobility and changing views of obligations within the extended family.

Day-to-day policy implementation in the state provided sector involves the management, or indeed sometimes mismanagement, of its relationships to these other elements. Accordingly analysts of social policy have conceived of the system as a 'mixed economy of welfare' (Webb, 1985). The implementation of many contemporary policy initiatives – privatization, the limitation of social expenditure, the extension of social care – involves changing the balance between the various ingredients in the 'mixed economy of welfare'. Where government withdraws or reduces its direct contribution to welfare, it may still make an indirect contribution, for example, if the social benefits subsidize private provision; or it may have to acquire a new range of regulatory concerns about the quality of private services; or it may face increased problems in the other areas of concern, because of the new pressures placed on individuals and families. But social changes on their side alter the 'mix' too.

Relationships between the public and the organizations delivering public policies may be studied with a view to ascertaining and explaining what people actually get from the social policy system. Clearly, questions about bias in the behaviour of public officials, the mechanisms by which scarce benefits or services are rationed, the roles played by 'gatekeepers' and the problems of securing effective 'take-up' of some benefits are issues of concern for the implementation of policies. In the study of these matters, many of the issues about the motivation of implementers concern the interaction between the nature of policy, the implementation system and the characteristics of the public. Policy delivery is not easily made an 'even-handed' process; class, gender and race differences influence access to professional services; some service users are less well-informed and more easily deterred than others; and 'street-level bureaucrats' who may be regarded as highly responsive to local needs in a white neighbourhood may be seen very differently in a black one. Are these biases in the system attributable to faults in policy or faults in its implementation? The answer is very often that both may be responsible. Their interaction needs to be examined very carefully.

While we all experience the effects of the implementation process, and many of us participate in various ways in it, very few of us are involved in policy formation.

Yet, it is this policy formation, often particularly that which occurs at the highest level, that receives much more attention. It is hoped that, in considering the detailed discussions of particular areas of policy, contained in the next section of this book, readers will bear in mind the importance of the interaction between the policy formation process and the implementation process for the actual impact of social policies on the public.

Suggestions for Further Reading

Tony Butcher's *Delivering Welfare: the Governance of the Social Services* (2002) offers an overview of the organizational arrangements for social policy delivery in Britain, but is now rather dated. Hill has contributed to further discussions of the theoretical issues raised in this chapter in chapters 9 to 12 of his book *The Public Policy Process* (2005; new edition due 2009) and in a book with Peter Hupe, *Implementing Public Policy* (2009). Contributions to parts IV and V of his edited collection, *The Policy Process: a Reader* (1997), are also relevant.

A large literature is emerging on the new approaches to the management of policy delivery, and its implications for professionalism. Newman's *Modernising Governance* (2001) offers a good discussion of this.

Much information about the organization of the implementation system can be found in the websites for government departments and other public organizations. accessible via www.direct.gov.uk.

Chapter 5

Social Security

- Introduction
- The Distinctive Characteristics of the UK System of Social Security
- Contributory Benefits
- Benefits that the State Requires the Employer to Provide
- Non-contributory, Non-means-tested, Contingent Benefits
- Means-tested Benefits
- Tax Credits
- Statistics on the Benefit System
- Pension Reform
- Problems with Means-testing
- Social Security Assumptions about Family Life and Women's Roles
- Social Security Benefit Levels and Poverty
- Conclusions
- Suggestions for Further Reading

Introduction

The term 'social security' is used here to cover all the state systems of 'income support' in the UK. These fall into five categories:

1 contributory benefits
2 benefits that the state requires employers to provide
3 non-contributory benefits which are not means-tested but are contingent on the individual being in some specific category
4 means-tested benefits
5 tax credits

This chapter starts with some observations on the basic characteristics of the UK system. Then it goes on to provide brief factual accounts of the main benefits, organized in terms of the five categories outlined above. After that it proceeds to look at some key policy issues.

The responsibility for social security benefits is divided between the Department for Work and Pensions and the Treasury. The Department for Work and Pensions delivers benefits through agencies, the most important of which are Jobcentre Plus, which combines some social security responsibilities with employment services (examined in Chapter 6), the Pension Service and the Disability and Carers Service. As far as the role of the Treasury is concerned the responsible agency is Her Majesty's Revenue and Customs, which deals with child benefit and tax credits and collects insurance contributions. Housing benefit and council tax benefit is administered by the unitary, or lower-tier, local authorities, using a rule structure laid down by the Department for Work and Pensions.

The Distinctive Characteristics of the UK System of Social Security

Before examining the parts of the social security system in any detail, a discussion of the distinctive characteristics of this very muddled system, and of why they have secured their modern form, may help readers to understand it. As was made clear in Chapter 2, policy decisions at any one point in time have implications for the future, since they create expectations of benefits and costs. In the case of social security one particular kind of measure – social insurance – provides a particularly strong example of this. It involves the establishment of expectations of future benefits for citizens, and at the same time, the initiation of a flow of income for the state through contributions.

A key element in the history of social security in the UK is the establishment of a social insurance system (legislation starting in 1911 and coming to an apparent climax in the Beveridge reforms of the 1940s), which has subsequently been severely damaged but not entirely abolished. In the UK National Insurance (NI) system there is no 'funding' and investing of contributions, instead, what is paid in by current contributors is paid out towards the costs of current claims. The amounts and scope of entitlements bear little relationship to the amounts of contributions, and entitlements have been significantly eroded. Annual government income from NI contributions exceeds expenditure on contributory benefits, and the separate government contributions to the fund promised in the original legislation are no longer made.

The presence in the UK system of a safety net group of means-tested benefits, containing echoes of the Poor Law, to back up the contributory scheme is by no means peculiar to this country. What is perhaps peculiar to the UK scene is the complex overlap between the two systems. In Britain, for a variety of reasons (some discussed in Chapter 12) the contributory scheme has to be supplemented in a large number of ways.

The UK system of social security has been built up by the development of a contributory system together with a limited system of family benefits, which were conceived to minimize dependence on means-tested benefits. However, the means-tested benefits have not been reduced to the safety net role envisaged for them by Beveridge and others. Indeed, in recent years an alternative strategy has been to confine expenditure on social security, by putting the emphasis on means-tested benefits and tax credits. Since 1997 the Labour government, despite the earlier pride that a Labour government had enacted the Beveridge reforms, has set its face firmly against what had been called 'the back to Beveridge' or 'new Beveridge' approach to social security policy, on grounds of cost. Hence what was once a very lively debate had been reduced to a really rather academic one, useful for highlighting the issues but hardly part of current political controversy (its features are set out in Box 5.1).

Box 5.1   Agendas for the radical reform of social security

The 'back to Beveridge', or 'new Beveridge' approach to social security policy, sees the ideal way forward for social security policy to be a combination of the restoration of those parts of the original Beveridge social insurance edifice undermined by the Conservatives with development of new ways to put into the social insurance framework protection for those who have difficulties in building insurance entitlements (carers, part-time workers, etc.). The comparative ideal here is the strong, and largely inclusive, Swedish social insurance system with its good minimum provisions for those unable to contribute.

A variant on this approach to the reform of social security is an even more radical option, the advocacy of a 'citizen's income' or 'basic income' for all. Such a system would involve a state guaranteed minimum income paid to all citizens. Then those who secure earned incomes to supplement this state minimum would have these taxed, inevitably more heavily than is currently the case (Walter, 1988; Parker, 1989; Fitzpatrick, 1999). This would be a radical departure from our current system. What is important about this approach is that it sees both means tests with their deterrent effects and social insurance with its contribution tests as irrelevant and difficult to administer in a world in which much work is temporary, part-time and insecure. It finds little support close to the corridors of power; the strong contemporary emphasis upon employment in government policy embodies little acceptance of fears that work is insecure. There is however also a version of the basic income perspective which involves arguing for a 'participation income' for specific contingent groups such as the elderly or the sick (Atkinson, 1994). This point is relevant to the issues about pensions for those, mainly women, who have not been able to participate in the labour force at levels at which they could pay pension contributions.

Contributory Benefits

The Beveridge plan for contributory benefits (Beveridge, 1942) envisaged that these should provide the main source of protection against old age, sickness, unemployment and widowhood. The legislation of the 1940s, picking up the main pieces from earlier contributory social security schemes, attempted to provide this coverage. The few surviving contributory benefits date from that time, but – as noted above – the system of contributions, the nature of the benefits and the character of the alternative benefits available to back up the contributory system have all changed a great deal.

All employees, together with the self-employed, are required to pay NI contributions. These are calculated as a percentage of earnings, but there is a low-income threshold below which they are not required, and an income level above which additional income is not taken into account. Normally employees' contributions are deducted by employers, who also have to pay employers' NI contributions on a similar basis for those they employ.

The original NI scheme set up in the 1940s specified a clear relationship between contributions and a wide range of benefit entitlements. This is no longer the case. Therefore it is in many respects more appropriate to see contributions as simply a tax. The limited remaining contributory benefit entitlements are discussed in this section.

There is a flat-rate pension to which insurance contributors are entitled on reaching the age of 60 if they are women, 65 if they are men (the female qualifying age will be increased to 65 by a phasing-in process in the period 2010–20). The actual pension rate depends on the length of working life with full payment depending upon 44 years contributions from men and 39 from women.

This pension may be supplemented by graduated additions from the cumulative impact of two now discarded schemes (a graduated additions scheme introduced in 1961 and the State Earning Related Pensions Scheme – SERPS – introduced in 1978) together with the State Second Pension which replaced SERPS in 2002. The additions are earnings related, but with some redistribution towards those with lower incomes. Individuals who contribute to private occupational pensions may contract out of the State Second Pension (as they could from its predecessors). There is no investment of contributions in pension funds and the formulae used for calculating entitlements have been the subject of extensive amendments over the years since the respective parts of this tier were established.

The flat rate pension on its own does not provide an adequate subsistence income – as defined by the government's own policies. Moreover the additions from the various graduated schemes often do not bridge that gap either. We return to this topic later.

The employee who is unable to work on account of sickness is initially dependent on his or her employer for support. The latter is, with some exceptions, required to provide sick pay at least at the minimum levels prescribed by Parliament for 28 weeks. This is, of course, not a contributory benefit *per se*, but this scheme replaced the former NI one, and small (formerly all) employers obtain some rebate of their NI contributions in respect of sick employees.

Those who become sick when not in employment may receive a contributory benefit if they were insurance contributors for a period until shortly before, a benefit that is now called 'short-term incapacity benefit'. During this period, claimants must establish that they are unfit to return to their normal occupation.

After the first six months of sickness, anyone still unfit for work moves on to a higher rate of short-term incapacity benefit, which continues until they have been sick for a year. After a year of sickness, people may move on to long-term incapacity benefit. The rate of payment is a little higher than that of the short-term benefit.

The qualification rules for incapacity benefit are very strict. There is an elaborate 'personal capacity assessment' procedure under which ability to do work of any kind is assessed. The government's objective here is to prevent people settling down on this long-term benefit unless it is quite clear that they cannot re-enter the labour market, even with training and other forms of support (see the further discussion of this in Chapter 6).

In addition to the incapacity benefits described above, there are special, in general more generous provisions, applying to those whose incapacity for work arises from military service, an industrial accident, or a prescribed industrial disease. These will not be considered in detail here.

There is a system of statutory maternity pay, like statutory sick pay, payable for thirty-nine weeks. This must be paid by employers if their employees have been continuously with them for six months or more. This is backed up by a reduced state maternity allowance for women with recent work records who do not qualify for pay from their employers.

The benefit for unemployed people is called 'jobseeker's allowance'. As the name suggests, to qualify a person has to make a clear undertaking, signing a 'jobseeker's agreement', on the steps he or she will take to try to find work. However, contributory benefits for unemployed people have always been limited by strict previous contribution conditions, rules which disqualify a person if there is evidence that the unemployment may be to some extent their own fault, and a time limit to entitlement. With the introduction of the jobseeker's allowance, the latter was reduced to six months. After six months, or if the previous contributions and other tests are not satisfied, jobseeker's allowance is means-tested (its rules being broadly those applying to income support; see page 104). A contributory scheme for those out of work, which has initial qualifying rules and the exhaustion of entitlement after six months, leaves many in need of means-tested benefits. In particular, young new entrants to the labour force are unprotected by the contributory benefit scheme.

There is a lump-sum bereavement payment of up to £2,000 where a spouse, who has fulfilled specified NI contribution conditions, dies. There is also a bereavement allowance payable for a year to bereaved people between 45 and pension age. There are also provisions under which widows and widowers may inherit a pension entitlement. Widows and widowers also have a contributory benefit entitlement, based on their deceased spouse's contributions, to an allowance if they have children to support. This benefit is lost on remarriage or 'cohabitation'.

There are no provisions for benefits to cover the ending of marriage other than through death, or to provide for the consequences of the ending of unmarried 'partnerships' due to any cause (including death). Benefits in these cases depend on means tests.

Benefits that the State Requires the Employer to Provide

The main benefits in this category were mentioned in the discussion above, since they evolved out of the earlier insurance benefits for sickness and maternity and need to be seen as still linked to related residual benefits: these are statutory sick pay and statutory maternity pay.

In addition employers have a liability to make redundancy payments. The minimum amounts of these are determined by a formula taking into account rate of pay and length of service.

It is also appropriate to mention private pensions here inasmuch as the alternative to the State Second Pension is contribution to private schemes. There are regulations, backed up by special agencies, to supervise all private pensions. In 2001 legislation provided for new kinds of private pension schemes, to be under much stricter state supervision, known as stakeholder pensions. The government expects stakeholder pensions to be available to all but the very low paid; it requires employers to make them available to employees but does not compel people to contribute to them.

Non-contributory, Non-means-tested, Contingent Benefits

Non-contributory benefits describe those which are available regardless of whether NI contributions have been made. Child benefit, for example, is paid to the parents or guardians of all children under sixteen years of age and children between sixteen and nineteen who are still at school or are undertaking approved training programmes. The only qualifying conditions for entitlement relate to people who are subject to what the government to as 'immigration controls'.

Child benefit is paid to the parents or guardians of all children under sixteen years of age and children between sixteen and eighteen who are still at school. The only qualifying condition is a residence one.

There are some non-contributory benefits available to long-term disabled people, which must not be confused with the industrial injury disablement provision or with incapacity benefit. There is a disabled working allowance designed to contribute to extra costs, such as travel, for those of working age. There are some specific benefits for handicapped people who need extra support (these may be seen as part of the social care system and are discussed in Chapter 8). There is also an incapacity benefit entitlement for people who claim before they are twenty years old, in other words for those never able to enter the labour force and become NI contributors.

Means-tested Benefits

A comparative study of social assistance schemes described the UK as having an 'integrated safety net' built around 'income support' which is seen as 'a large, national, general programme providing an extensive safety net at or below social insurance levels' (Eardley et al., 1996, p. 169). This extensive means-testing is necessitated by the various restrictions on the availability of contributory benefits described above. It also arises because the levels of some of the contributory benefits (flat-rate pensions, short-term incapacity benefit and jobseeker's allowance) are such that claimants will often qualify for further means-tested support as well, at least in respect of housing costs. There are grounds for doubt about the extent to which that word 'integrated' in the quotation above is still appropriate. Clearly the government still expects the whole means-testing system to function in an integrated way but the development of the system of tax credits (see the next section) administered by the Revenue and Customs is making some aspects of that integration more difficult.

The main means-tested benefit is called 'income support'. Its means test is based on a simple personal allowance structure, enhanced in some cases by 'premiums'. The specific personal allowance rates are for a couple, a single person over 25 and a person between 18 and 24. There used to be age-related rates for children but the care of children is now subsumed within the Child Tax Credit scheme (see below). Then, there are different premiums for families, lone parents and disabled people. The idea throughout is that the determination of the appropriate overall entitlement for a household should be a simple, predictable process. Additions for special needs have been abolished. Rules determine how any income should be taken into account. People in full-time work (defined as doing sixteen or more hours in employment per week) are disqualified from receiving income support, but part-time workers may obtain it. To deal with this, an earnings rule is used, based on net income, which involves disregarding a small amount and then deducting the rest from any entitlement. Similar 'disregards' are used for some other kinds of income, but other state benefits are taken into account in full. There are special rules dealing with savings, disregarding small amounts, then applying a sliding scale, reducing benefits up to an upper limit at which they disqualify a person from benefit entirely.

The means-tested support for pensioners provides higher rates of benefit than the benefits for persons below pension age. It has, since 2003 been called 'pension credit'. The rules in respect of this are complicated by provisions to 'taper in' (see the further discussion of this topic below) deductions applied when people have small savings and private pensions.

The housing benefit scheme has been designed to be compatible with income support. The income support rules are used in the calculation of benefit so that anyone with a rent to pay who is at, or below, income support income level may receive housing benefit entitlement. Housing benefit provides support for rent; it does not provide support for house buying. However, owner-occupiers on income support, job-seekers allowance and pension credit may receive some help towards mortgage interest payments and other housing related costs.

The housing benefit scheme is also, in effect, extended to local taxation. Low-income council tax payers may apply for a reduction in their payments known as council tax benefit (calculated in a similar way to housing benefit).

There are complicated rules relating to the amount of housing benefit entitlement. There are provisions aimed at limiting the levels of rent covered, applied to single persons under 25 and to accommodation deemed to be either too large or too expensive. Contributions from other adults in the household (apart from the claimant's 'spouse') are also taken into account. Subject to these adjustments then, the so-determined maximum is payable to those whose incomes are at, or below, the income support or minimum income guarantee qualifying level. Similarly, for those with incomes at, or below, that level and no adult non-dependants, the council tax benefit will provide for the remission of the whole tax liability. Where incomes are above income support level, benefit tapers off proportionately, at the rate of 65 per cent for housing benefit and 20 per cent for council tax benefit.

Chapter 10 shows how housing benefit has become the main approach to the provision of housing subsidies to low-income tenants. As a system run by local authorities on behalf of the Department for Work and Pensions, it is not always well co-ordinated with the rest of the benefits system and it is administratively costly. It is also rather vulnerable to fraud, particularly in the private rented sector where there can be collusion between landlord and tenant to try to maximize benefit. The government is seeking ways to simplify the system. These may involve the introduction of formulae that extend the tendency to offer less than full support to rent payments.

Under the supplementary benefit scheme operative until 1988, there were provisions enabling single payments to be made to help people with exceptional expenditures – removal costs, furnishing, house repairs and so forth. An elaborate body of rules dealt with these entitlements. The 1986 Social Security Act swept away these single payment entitlements but, in their place, set up the social fund, administered by a specially trained group of staff. Under the fund there are two kinds of grants available as of right to people on income support: a lump sum maternity needs payment and a funeral needs payment (the amount of which depends on funeral costs). There is also provision for grants to be made from the social fund to assist with the promotion of community care. These may be available when someone needs help in establishing themselves in the community after a period of institutional care, to assist with some travelling expenses to visit relatives in hospitals and other institutions, and to improve the living conditions of defined 'vulnerable groups' in the community. Elaborate guidance is provided to social fund officers to help them to determine needs of this kind. They are expected to liaise closely about such matters with social care and health services staff, and to take into account powers these other departments may have to provide assistance in cash or kind. All other help from the social fund is by way of loans, normally repayable by weekly deductions from benefits. Again, officers have been given elaborate instructions on the circumstances in which they may provide loans. The social fund, excluding the two items of benefit as of right, is 'cash limited'. Within this budget, 30 per cent is available for community care grants and 70 per cent for loans. This means that local offices have annual budgets, and are expected to relate a set of rules about priorities to the total sum available.

One quite important means-tested benefit administered by local authorities, entitlement to free school meals, is available to children whose parents are on income support. Other means-tested benefits include education grants, relief from payment of National Health Service charges, and legal aid. Local authority social services departments also use means tests to determine charges for residential care and domiciliary services (see Chapter 8).

Tax Credits

Tax credits, Paid by Revenue and Customs consist of:

- An integrated child tax credit bringing earlier schemes – the working families tax credit, the child care tax credit, the child tax credit, the child support element in the disabled person's tax credit and the additions to means-tested benefits for children – together into a single scheme.
- A working tax credit for low income earners without children.

The development of the use of tax credits can be particularly linked to the government's concern about labour market participation. Credits are intended to increase the likelihood that returns from low income work will be higher than those from benefits for those out of work.

Although the novel feature of tax credits is that they are benefits integrated with the tax system, they are different from tax allowances, which *only* reduce tax liability and thus only benefit those with incomes high enough to pay tax. Tax credits, by contrast, allow for the possibility of tax assessment leading to benefits as opposed to payments by low earners.

Statistics on the Benefit System

Since the benefits system is now divided between those benefits that are the responsibilities of Revenue and Customs and those are administered by the Department for Work and Pensions (DWP) it is difficult to assemble a carefully related sequence of statistics on the system. According to National Statistics (2007, p. 103) the total cost of all benefits in 2005–6 was £130 billion. That included costs now coming under Customs and Revenue of £17 billion for tax credits and £10 billion for child benefit. In 2007 there were 7.5 million payments of child benefit going out, covering the entitlements for 13.3 million children. There were 5.9 million tax credit awards to households for 9.8 million children, and 0.3 million for working tax credits.

Within the share of the budget coming under DWP, 65 per cent was for benefits for men and women over pension age. In May 2007 there were 12.1 million people receiving state pensions, of which 21 per cent were getting pension credit.

That leaves 31 per cent of the DWP budget directed at adults below pension age and 4 per cent for children (note that the needs of children are generally covered by child benefit and tax credits, but of course many adults on benefits – particularly those on income support – are carers for children). Table 5.1 gives some other statistics on the distribution of the DWP non-pensioners group across the main benefits.

Pension Reform

We now turn to a number of policy issues, first pension reform. The issues about pensions policy fairly obviously divide into issues about the adequacy of pension

Table 5.1　Benefits to non-pensioner adult households, May 2007 (thousands)

Total	5237
Job-seekers allowance	837
Incapacity benefit	2643
Lone parents (on income support, with a child under 16)	766
Others on income support	167
Bereavement allowances	114
Carers	375

Source: Figures put together from various Department of Work and Pensions published statistical returns.

provision now, and the issues about provision in the future. Connected with both of these issues are questions about how costs should be borne. In relation to this almost all private pension arrangements and most approaches to public pension provisions involve contributions by current non-pensioners. In this sense issues about pensions are not just issues about the needs of the old, but also about both the future expectations and current payments to be made by the young.

It was noted above that the basic national insurance pensions provide on their own what would generally be regarded as a below-subsistence level income. The assumption made when this scheme was introduced in the 1940s was that benefits were to be at about subsistence level (though what was actually meant by this is a matter of dispute between historians). In any case it was expected that many would make private provisions to ensure that their actual incomes were above that level. It was indeed the case that this happened. But since, of course, it was primarily those in long-run well paid employment who were able to do this, significant class and gender differences in the extent of security in old age emerged. The various supplementary contributory schemes described above, culminating in the State Second Pension, partly addressed this problem. But since they have been also employment linked they have offered limited solutions. Means-tested benefits have remained crucial for the alleviation of poverty in old age.

After the election of the Labour government in 1997 pension reform was regarded as high on the political agenda. Nevertheless the government baulked at any measure that would substantially increase public expenditure. Like its Conservative predecessor it sought to increase access to private pension schemes, a measure that was in fact frustrated by difficulties in that market. But it also – as noted – reformed the state supplementary pension. However, its most significant measure was the introduction of pension credit. This has been quite appropriately described above as a means-testing measure. It built upon earlier means-testing for pensioners by lifting payments rates well above those for non-pensioners on means tests and by liberalizing the procedures for taking other incomes into account.

Then, the setting up of a committee to further investigate pension reform in 2002 promised more action. The Pensions Commission provided a very detailed initial assessment of the situation in 2004 and a carefully documented set of recommendations in 2005. In a White Paper responding to this work the government repeated the Pensions Commission's judgement that the UK system is 'the most complex in the World' (DWP, 2006, p. 13). It went on to outline some proposals for change that aim to deal with what the government sees as the key problems about the system. These are being translated into legislation initiated at the end of 2006, but with a leisurely timetable to accommodate a quite complex implementation process.

There are differences between the Pension Commission's proposals for reform and those adopted by the government. It is not particularly illuminating to go into a full comparison of the two approaches. Attention will here be upon the government's proposals as set out in the White Paper.

Understandably the White Paper starts with a defence of the existing system and of the steps taken by governments to improve it since 1997. But it then goes on to acknowledge a case for reform in terms of:

- the implications of demographic and social change
- evidence on the extent of under saving for retirement
- inequalities in the state pension system
- complexity

The Government's agenda is framed in terms of (a) the issue of under saving (which its earlier efforts to stimulate private pensions had failed to reverse) and (b) the fact that the main plank in its current policies to deal with pensioner poverty is the means-tested pension credit.

The pensions savings system proposed is, on the face of it, relatively straightforward (though we may well find that 'the devil will reside' in the future administrative details). It is a system of personal pension savings accounts to which employees will contribute 4 per cent of a band of earnings between £5000 and £33,000 a year. To these employers will add an equivalent 3 per cent. There will be an additional 1 per cent from the government, though it is acknowledged that this is merely the equivalent of basic rate tax relief which is already the minimum given to support private pension contributions. This will not be a compulsory scheme but there will be what the government calls 'automatic enrolment' from which employees will have to explicitly opt out. Employers will not be able to opt out unless their employees do so. This money will then be invested and, while the White Paper indicates that there is a need yet for further exploration of the way the personal account scheme will be managed through private sector investment companies, the aim will be to keep management costs low. There will be choices of funds, underpinned by a 'default fund' for those who do not exercise choice.

The accompanying proposals for state pensions aim to increase the numbers who qualify for them and to lead eventually to a situation where means-testing is reduced. The proposal is to reduce the qualifying period for the basic state pension so that only 30 years of contributions are needed to secure full pensions. This change is linked with improvements to the way credits of contributions operate for those caring for children and for disabled people. These measures will increase access to state pensions for people, particularly women, not able to be participate fully enough in the labour force to secure full pensions under present arrangements.

Box 5.2   The funding fallacy and demographic change

The case for the funding of future pensions either through the private market or through social insurance, is widely expounded on the grounds that otherwise societies will not be able to cope with the increase in the numbers of the elderly relative to the young. There are two reasons to question this. First, savings towards pensions are actually used by their current recipients (governments, private pension funds, etc.) as investments to contribute to current economic activity. When therefore the money is required back in the form of pensions these will be claims upon the economic activity of that future time just like taxes (see Barr, 2001, 2002). Second, inasmuch as these claims will be problematical the problem will arise because of the ratio of those in employment to those not in employment at that time. While this may be affected by the widely cited 'unfavourable' demographic ratio of older to younger people, this is not at all the same thing as that. It will depend rather both upon the nature of the economy and upon choices about economic participation made by people of all ages (see Hill, 2007, chapter 6).

It should be noted here that there has been a reluctance to abandon completely the notional contribution principle embodied in National Insurance. We find both in this and in the continued eagerness to encourage private provision, government adherence to the conventional view that contributory approaches are necessary features of pension policies. Box 5.2 suggests that it finds its conventional justification (as set out in newspaper accounts of the issue) in a fallacy about pensions, widely given sustenance in discussions of demographic change in our society. However, from the government's point of view the object is surely to try to avoid explicit tax increases.

These reforms will be limited in impact so long as the basic state pension remains well below the subsistence level guaranteed by the pension credit. So then what does the White Paper have to say about the uprating of this? In fact all that is offered is the start of a change back to uprating the basic pension in line with earnings (see Box 5.6) from 2012 (hedging even that with the weasel clause 'subject to affordability and the fiscal position'). That means an incremental year by year shift upwards that pays no attention to the long period over which the basic pension has fallen in value since that uprating principle was abandoned in 1979. Moreover since the proposal is to apply the same uprating principle to pension credit the change will do nothing to reduce the gap between the values of the two pensions.

However, to understand fully the change it is necessary to look at what is happening to, and proposed for, the State Second Pension. The government say:

> Few people are aware of it at all, and even fewer of how their entitlement to it builds. Many people are building entitlement to the State Second Pension without even being aware they are doing so. (DWP, 2006, p. 116, para 3.46)

That pension works with graduated contributions and graduated benefits subject to a minimum for the latter. Individuals in private pension schemes deemed by the government to be adequate alternatives can opt out of contributing to it. The implications of the scheme for a significant proportion of its contributors is that they will eventually acquire combined basic state pensions and state second pensions that bring their incomes over the pension credit threshold. What is now proposed are two changes, one that the scheme will evolve into one offering a flat rate pension, the other that the opt-out option will be eliminated. What this means therefore is that the White Paper holds out the prospect of evolution by about 2030 to a situation in which the combination of what will then be two flat rate contributory state pensions will amount to an income above the pension credit level for a significant number of people, thereby eventually achieving its objective of reducing dependence on the latter.

So in the face of two demands from radical critics of the UK pension system for:

- the uprating of the basic pension to above the pension credit level
- the elimination of complex social insurance qualifying rules

what is offered is:

- a very long term programme to, in effect, increase the basic pension by combining it with the State Second Pension
- some lightening of social insurance rules but no shift away from contributions, on the contrary a subtle measure to increase contributions from some people

One final aspect of the reform proposal must not be left unmentioned. The plan is that there should be upward shifts of the age at which people may qualify for the state pension, by changes of one year in each of 2024, 2034 and 2044. These of course imply public expenditure savings (fewer pensions and more contributions). Elsewhere in the White Paper there are general observations on what the government is doing and might do to encourage longer working lives on a voluntary basis. It should be noted that while the journalistic response to this change is to stress that 'people will have to work longer for the state pension' the reality is complex since such a statement disregards the issue of when we start our workforce participation and also the fact that the government are relaxing the rules relating to the numbers of years in employment for full state pension entitlement.

The underlying question here is: has all this work by the Pensions Commission and by the government resulted in a satisfactory solution to the problems with pensions in the UK? A new approach to private pension saving, in the context of evidence that many insecure and low income workers are not well placed to save for their own pensions, accompanied by a marginal and very gradual approach to improvement of the basic pension do not offer a satisfactory solution to this long running problem. The difficult issues about pensions policy are discussed more fully in Hill (2007).

Problems with Means-testing

There is an extensive literature on the problems of means-testing. Much that has been written on this subject comes from those who advocate, as an alternative, strengthening the contributory benefits system so that it becomes more universal in its coverage and provides better benefits. We have seen already some of the political objections to this approach – on grounds of cost – and noted the development of tax credits and pension credit as the officially preferred approach to social security reform.

The development of tax credits may be seen as a response to calls for the development of what was originally called 'negative income tax' (Minford, 1984). The UK 'pay-as-you-earn' (PAYE) system for the deduction of tax seemed to be the ideal vehicle for the development of a system whereby additions, rather than deductions, could be provided in some cases. However, it was for long objected that there was a problem that the basis for the assessment of tax is an annual one. Where the objective is to deal with the needs of low income people whose circumstances change frequently annual assessment is very inflexible.

The establishment of tax credits has changed the situation in the administratively simple direction of embedding tax credits in the annual assessment process, not any shift towards the more frequent assessment of tax liability. Research by Hills and his colleagues suggests that fluctuating income amongst low earners is very common. Inevitably therefore there are problems of rough justice involved in setting tax credit levels on the basis of past incomes (Hills et al., 2006). If then higher levels of credits are sought to compensate for falling income after assessment, delays in payment cause hardship. There are provisions for individuals to make initial income estimates and then secure retrospective adjustments once the tax year has finished, but this may have the ultimate result of landing people with debts to the Inland Revenue which they have difficulty in meeting out of low incomes. An examination of this topic by a Parliamentary Select Committee noted that in 2003–4 one third of all tax credit awards were overpaid (1.9 million awards at a cost of nearly £2 billion). Rules about reclaiming overpaid credits have been relaxed but the rough justice problem remains. A newspaper article (*Guardian*, 1 June 2006) reported opposition attacks on the continued inefficiency of the service, a union view that the quest for staff cuts in Revenue and Customs is part of the problem and an observation by Frank Field, a Labour MP with extensive expertise on social security benefits, that 'Tax credits are clearly the bluntest of antipoverty weapons ... the equivalent of attempting delicate keyhole surgery with a hacksaw'.

A tax credit is – in terms of the categories of benefits explored in this chapter – no more than a means-tested benefit administered through the tax system. What is involved is a maximum rate, payable to those with very low incomes which tapers off as income rises until they reach the point at which they are taxed instead.

The general case against means tests is that they confuse, deter and stigmatize those who need help. People prefer benefits to which they have clear-cut rights, and about which they can obtain unambiguous information. Those who have to claim help are often already in trouble, about which they are ashamed or for which their neighbours criticize them; to have to reveal intimate details to an official so as to obtain benefits deepens the sense of 'stigma' (see Box 5.3). The low take-up of some benefits is attributed both to this stigma and to the complexities surrounding the administration of means tests.

It is undoubtedly the case that take-up levels for means-tested benefits are lower than for many other benefits, but there are also marked variations between the various

Box 5.3   Stigma

The characteristics of a system of social support may stigmatize claimants. The very strict controls surrounding the administration of the Poor Law made application for means-tested benefits a very degrading process, and it has therefore been argued that the stigma of the Poor Law extends today to the means-tested benefits which are its successor. The existence of a distinction within the social security system between those benefits to which people have contributed (the insurance benefits) and the benefits which are non-contributory and means-tested tends to keep the concept of stigma alive within the system. This distinction reflects, and in some cases amplifies, stigmatizing distinctions within our society. As Marsden put the issue with regard to unsupported mothers 'our society defends the institution of marriage by stigmatizing them' (Marsden, 1973). A similar point may be made about the propagation of the value of work by stigmatizing the unemployed. In some respects, moreover, in an affluent and materialistic society to be poor, for whatever reason, is to feel stigmatized. With such a feeling one will he reluctant to draw attention to one's plight.

Efforts to stimulate a view that individuals have rights have, sometimes simultaneously, been counteracted by campaigns to increase the vetting of social security claims. The widespread publicity given to cases where individuals have been convicted of defrauding the social security system, political campaigns which have emphasized the number of fraudulent claims, and measures adopted to try to identify individuals who could be working but are claiming benefit have all contributed to keeping the problem of stigma alive (Deacon 1976; Golding and Middleton 1982).

means-tested ones. Data is available from the Department for Work and Pensions published estimates on the take-up rates for some benefits. There are difficulties in interpreting such data, and in identifying the seriousness of the problem since it is obviously failure to claim a large rather than a small amount that is a particularly serious problem. Piachaud suggests (in Hills, Le Grand and Piachaud, 2007, p. 209), using 2003–4 data, shortfalls in take up of between 39 and 50 per cent of the total potential caseload for income based Jobseekers Allowance, 26 and 38 per cent for Pension Credit, and 9 and 13 per cent for the benefits that preceded Child Tax Credit.

The linking of benefit entitlement with tax assessment seems to have reduced the take-up problem. On the other hand the new system puts a considerable onus upon employers to identify situations in which there may be a tax credit entitlement. It will be important, once they have settled down, that there is a fuller assessment of the take-up issues in respect of tax credits.

Take-up of some benefits is facilitated by rules that treat income support as an automatic 'passport' to them. This is most evidently the case with relief from NHS charges. However, this implies a cause for concern about the needs of those just above income support levels, together with those who, in not claiming small amounts of income support, may also be shutting themselves out from ready access to other benefits.

One particular problem with the multiplicity of means tests is that, operating together, they may create a poverty trap (or poverty plateau). This is a kind of 'tax effect' whereby an individual whose earned income rises may find that tax and NI contributions increase while benefit income decreases, together diminishing any actual gain to a very low level. The lower taper rates for the new tax credits help to deal with this problem but the housing benefit taper rate still has a strong impact. Overall Piachaud has noted that 'while the poverty trap has been eased in severity, it has been extended to yet more low-income households (Piachaud in Hills, Le Grand and Piachaud, 2007, p. 206). Quoting government estimates he suggests that more than a million and a half households experience deduction rates as incomes rise of over 60 per cent. Bear in mind that the highest comparable rate for income tax higher up the scale is only 40 per cent!

It is important to bear in mind that the poverty trap effect applies with part-time work, when either of a couple on benefits together finds work, and to temporary work. In other words, there are some complex issues about disincentives to labour market participation, which flow directly from the poverty trap effect.

The poverty trap problem must afflict any unified means-testing system. If the tapering-off effect is to be reduced, benefit receipt will logically spread further up the income distribution, adding to the cost of the scheme. In the last resort, this can only be compensated by increasing tax rates, either across the board or through altera-tions to the higher-rate bands.

A study by Alcock and Pearson (1999) shows the problem of the poverty trap may be intensified by public services for which charges are related to income. They show that this is true of a range of local authority services – social care services, charges for extra education benefits (music lessons, for example), travel passes, entry to swim-ming pools, etc. The problem can only be avoided if less targeted status considerations rather than income tests are used in determining concessions (age, for example). Alcock and Pearson also indicate the way in which rules about capital holdings may impose a similar 'savings trap'. This particularly applies to the means-testing of social care, a topic explored in Chapter 8.

The complexities associated with means-testing have necessitated the development of aid and advice services to help people secure their entitlements. Pioneers of this work, often described as 'welfare rights work', have been voluntary organizations, particularly the Child Poverty Action Group, and some local authority social ser-vices departments (Fimister, 1986). There has been an extensive controversy within social work about the extent to which that activity should include such work, with some people seeing it as essential for an effective service for clients who are very often poor, while others feel that it distorts their activities and pulls them away from 'real' social work (Becker and Silburn, 1990). Increasingly, now, such work is concentrated in voluntary agencies and advice bureaux.

Social Security Assumptions about Family Life and Women's Roles

The assumptions about family life incorporated in the Poor Law involved a household means test whereby all a household's needs and resources were taken into account and also its resources, so that adult children of a needy couple were expected to contribute to their maintenance. The contributory benefits developed in 1911 treated the insured claimant as the sole beneficiary, providing flat-rate payments at the same level, regardless of his or her family commitments. However, in the 1920s, the principle of additions to benefits, taking into account the needs of wives and children, was introduced. The improved contributory scheme developed in the 1940s carried forward this principle, while means-tested assistance shifted from a household means test to a family one. Broadly, then, UK social security policies have been developed on the assumption that the typical claimant is a married man with a non-working wife and dependent children. That is not, of course, to say that the system cannot cope with claims from single people, but that it has had difficulty in coming to terms with both female employment and multi-person families constituted other than on the basis of legal marriage. Interesting even the arrival of the possibility of gay marriage has not led to the abandonment of this. The observations here may apply to gay people too, though obviously without the gendered construction explored here.

Until the 1970s, married women were required to pay lower contributions and to receive lower benefits than men. While this anomaly was then eliminated, it continues to have consequences for pension entitlements. In any case other anomalies remain. Married women cannot claim contributory benefit increases in respect of dependent husbands. The continuation of provisions for non-employed wives to be treated as 'dependants' for whom husbands can claim additions to benefits implies that the return which an employed woman receives on her contributions may, in some cases, be worth only the difference between the full pension or benefit and the addition for a non-working wife. In other words, there are difficulties in securing a fair balance in a scheme that tries, on the one hand, to make provision for dependent wives and, on the other, to enable the married woman to be a contributor and claimant in her own right.

The position with regard to means-tested benefits is even more complicated when men and women live together, and perhaps have children, but are not married. A family means test requires judgements to be made about whether a family situation exists. Generally, this is straightforward; claimants agree with official interpretations of their situations. Indeed, it is to the advantage of a male claimant living with a non-employed 'wife' and children (even if they are not his) to claim them as his family. However, difficulties arise when claimants, usually female, wish to be treated as independent, but find that the social security and housing benefit authorities regard them as the 'wives' of male friends. The government tried to develop a definition of 'living together as man and wife' which distinguishes stable relationships from more casual ones, but difficulties and disagreements still occur. The issue here, which, also applies to widow's or widower's benefits, arises from the family-based approach to benefits. While it would be possible to treat unmarried 'couples' differently from married ones, the only fair way to avoid problems of this kind is to cease to make assumptions about family patterns of support, and instead have a structure of *individual* entitlements.

A related issue concerns the treatment of single-parent families, most of which are, of course, headed by women. The UK treatment of this group has been relatively generous, by comparison with other countries. Income support has been available. Mothers have not been required to become labour market participants until their children reach sixteen years of age (but see in Chapter 6, the discussion of impending changes to this). Absent fathers have been expected to make contributions, though the system has found it difficult to secure these because of the extent to which the fathers are low-income men with commitments to new families.

Charles Murray's (1984) tirade against the single-headed household in the USA was taken up in the UK. Politicians began to attribute the growth in single parent-hood to the availability of benefits and housing. This stimulated a debate, reaching beyond the ranks of the extreme Right, about (a) work opportunities for single parents and (b) contributions from absent parents. Attention to the first issue involves encouraging single parents without children under five to seek employment; as noted above this is examined in Chapter 6.

As far as the second issue is concerned, the Conservative government decided in 1990 to tackle the issue of contributions from absent parents by means of a comprehensive, formula driven scheme to replace both the assessments made as part of the administration of the existing means-tested benefits and the assessments made by the courts in determining maintenance on the breakdown of a relationship. It enacted the Child Support Act in 1991, setting up an agency to administer it. That legislation ran into severe implementation problems. Further legislation in 1995 and 2000 tried to sort these out, but there were still difficulties (Box 5.4 sets out the main features of this story). After commissioning a review of the whole system the government decided, at the end of 2006, to have another go at reform. From 2008 the Child Support Agency is to be replaced by a public body to be called the Child Maintenance and Enforcement Commission. While this change has some of the flavour of a government ploy to deal with an inefficient administrative arrangement by changing its name, other aspects of the proposal suggest that, to some extent, the government is abandoning the comprehensive approach adopted in 1991. It says that the legislation will 'empower and incentivize parents to make private arrangements where possible'. It then goes on to a series of ways to strengthen enforcement of maintenance obligations. Hence it may be assumed that, instead of a formula driven system ostensibly applying to all, the emphasis will be primarily upon securing money to reduce or prevent social security income support dependence. This seems to take the system back to something like the procedures within the social security legislation that were used before 1991. The arrangements to collect child support for parents with care responsibilities not on income support seem to be being abandoned. At the same time however another crucial problem from the past is being more effectively addressed: 'all parents with care in receipt of benefit can keep the first £10 of child maintenance paid without it affecting their benefit'. There is clearly more detailed work to be done on this new measure.

Box 5.4   Efforts to reform child support

There were four main objections to the 1991 legislation:

1   That it was retrospective in effect – agreements, including court settlements, made in the past were overturned (a particular problem here was the over-turning of agreements in which the absent parent relinquished an interest in a house in return for a lower maintenance expectation).

2   That where the absent parent had obligations to a second family, these were given relatively low weight in the calculations.

3   That the parent with care of the child had nothing to gain from collaborat-ing with the agency if she (it is nearly always she in this situation) was on income support, since everything collected went to reimburse the state; a special problem here was the expectation of co-operation in the supply of information unless there are strong reasons to protect a woman from fur-ther indirect dealings with the father of her child.

4   That the operation of a rigid formula was unfair when there are regular contacts with the absent parent and a variety of connected expenses.

The enforcement of the Act was not helped by the income targets imposed on the agency and a programme of work which meant that it started with families on 'income support' and had incentives to tackle the easier cases (that was, the more compliant absent parents).

In 1995, the government brought in amending legislation. It bowed to a vociferous male lobby. It did not change the basic principles of the Act, but it did give the agency some limited leeway to modify its application in rela-tion to the points made in (1), (2) and (4) above. However, there were still difficulties. Further amending legislation in 2000 simplified the formula for the determination of liabilities. It also gave attention to point (3) above by allowing parents with care to retain some proportion of the contribution from the other parent, even when they are on state benefits. But still there were administrative problems, hence the further wave of reform outlined in the text.

Social Security Benefit Levels and Poverty

Clearly, it is important in assessing a system of social security to look not merely at the structure of the system but also at the level of benefits provided by it. In the UK, debate about the social security system has been dominated by concerns about the levels of benefits relative to income levels that are deemed needed to prevent poverty. In this sense there has been, ever since the Beveridge report, a concern to assess ben-efits in terms of their minimal adequacy not in terms of the replacement incomes they offer. Hence, a great deal of debate about poverty is concerned not about the contributory benefits as such, but about the means-tested benefit levels and about the people and families whose incomes fall below those levels.

It is thus obviously important to look at benefit levels in terms of their impact upon poverty. Given the extent to which UK social security legislation – unlike that in the United States – has involved efforts to ensure that anyone without other means of support should get benefits, this implies that much of the debate about poverty in the UK can be seen to be a debate about the adequacy of the benefits available. However, there are two important considerations to bear in mind about the relationship between social security and poverty:

(1) Social security should not only be seen as a policy designed to prevent poverty. There are various arguments for social security policies as mechanisms to share or spread incomes. Benefits may be evaluated in terms of the extent to which they offer individuals inc.ome replacements, as percentages of their original incomes. They may also be evaluated as mechanisms to spread resources between people, since there are a variety of justifications for ensuring that incomes are not simply derived from earnings. The question here is whether we should see redistribution by methods other than market ones as only justifiable in order to prevent poverty, or whether we consider that there are other justifications for state interventions to influence income distributions.

(2) It is important to see social security as only one of a range of phenomena that influences income distribution and has an impact upon the incidence of poverty. Analytically it is often appropriate to see it – alongside taxation – as operating *after* other influences upon income distribution. But, whilst market forces are likely to be a key influence upon incomes *before* tax and social security they will not be the only ones. Public policies influencing and regulating market behaviour may also be very important. As far as the prevention of poverty is concerned, measures to influence what people are paid (minimum wage laws, equal opportunities legislation, etc.) may be important. So may job creation measures. We will return to these issues in Chapter 6.

There are various ways to approach the analysis of poverty. In the first half of the twentieth century there were studies which attempted to relate poverty to an absolute standard, based on the cost of providing a basic minimum of necessities. Towards the end of that century this approach was shown to be unsatisfactory. One particular researcher, Peter Townsend, led the way in showing that poverty is a meaningful concept only when individual standards of living are related to those widely taken for granted in a society (Townsend, 1979, 1993). The UK bare minimum could certainly equate with a good absolute standard of living for poor people in the less developed countries of the world. At the same time, views about what is necessary for an adequate way of life change over time. These changes are related to developments in living standards within the nation as a whole. When the national assistance scales – which today, much updated for inflation, form the basis for the income support scales – were first set, in 1948, television was not even available, and few households had refrigerators, washing machines or central heating systems. If a definition of the poverty level is to take into account these considerations, the key questions are, for example: to what extent should those on the official poverty line have incomes that make it difficult for them to share the way of life of the majority of the people? Or, alternatively, how large should the gap be between the incomes of those on the poverty line and average incomes?

Townsend pioneered an approach to the study of poverty which looked at deprivation in terms of the inability to afford a life style taken for granted by others. He persuasively made a case for regarding large numbers of UK people, including both people dependent on social security and many on low wages, as living in poverty (Townsend, 1979). A more recent study (Gordon and Pantazis, 1997) lends support to Townsend's argument. They demonstrate the extent to which low-income people lack things which, according to public opinion surveys, are regarded as necessities. This approach helps to uncover the wider implications of having low incomes, and some additional dimensions of this are set out in Box 5.5.

> **Box 5.5   How an approach to the understanding of poverty that recognizes that some people may not be able to participate in activities and a way of life taken for granted by others highlights other significant problems**
>
> People with low incomes may have difficulties that will not be self-evident from a simple examination of their resources. If you can only afford cheap housing this is likely to be poor quality housing that is more costly to heat and keep in a good state of repair. If you live in an area where many people have low incomes the best – and ironically the cheapest – shops may be inaccessible. The cost of transport to places where shops, entertainment facilities, even work and education, is more available may make further inroads into your slender income. Moreover if you cannot afford a car you will be dependent upon limited and unreliable public transport. All these considerations will apply to poor people living in urban areas where deprived people are concentrated. But they may also apply to the isolated poor, in rural areas. Hence it is likely that poor people will get less value than others for each pound they spend and will find that their low income has 'knock on' effects upon their life-styles.
>
> While a common sense response to some of those problems would seem to be to make free or cheap facilities available to the poor this has the consequence of intensifying the problems about means-testing discussed above, particularly the poverty trap. An alternative approach involves forms of territorial targeting of specific services – giving deliberate attention to the improvement of services in areas where deprived people live. This has been seen as a good non-discriminatory approach to deprivation. The drawback is that these measures are indirect and may not readily benefit those most in need. The phenomenon of rural poverty, where people are isolated and may often be located in areas where much of the rest of the population are prosperous, is particularly intractable in this respect (see Cahill, 2002, ch. 6).

Table 5.2 Poverty lines and benefits available April 2005 (housing costs assumed to have been covered)

	Poverty line (60% of median income) £	Benefits available £	Poverty gap
Couple aged 65, no children	193	88.15	54.4
Couple aged 25, one four-year-old child	228	148.13	35.1
Single person aged 25, one four-year-old child	141	116.18	17.7
Couple aged 70	193	167.05	13.5

Source: Figures taken from CPAG (2005).

While a sensitive official approach to the measurement of deprivation is desirable it is expensive to have a regular sequence of precisely targeted studies of the kind developed by Townsend. An alternative is income surveys that explore the incidence of incomes that are significantly below average income levels. Taking their cue from deprivation studies such surveys can arrive at regular estimates of the numbers likely to lack necessities. In the UK since 1979 there have been regular surveys that enable estimates to be made of the numbers of households with incomes below a specified percentage of the average income level. These surveys also offer some information on the household types with low incomes.

Commonly used indices of poverty are then numbers of individuals living in households with incomes either 50 or 60 per cent below average incomes. Table 5.2 then picks up the general point made above that the UK debate is mostly about the level of benefits by relating the poverty yardsticks for some notional households to the incomes provided by the benefits available. What this indicates is that short of income additional to benefits for such individuals an effective government anti-poverty strategy requires percentage benefit rate increases that substantially surpass the increases in median incomes. This is a costly proposition for governments which has only occurred in respect of the pension credit, making the gap for pensioners (as shown in Table 5.2), rather slighter than that for other groups.

Otherwise poverty reduction depends upon changes in the circumstances of poor people which bring with them incomes other than state benefits that lift them over the identified thresholds. That of course supports statements that work is the best route out of poverty, but quite aside from the feasibility of this there is still a snag (identified above): the poverty trap. This means that 'work and welfare' strategies require assessment of the ways in which benefits like tax credits kick in as incomes rise (a topic more easily tackled within government or academic modelling exercises than by means of individuals trying to make strategic choices about their best options).

In a short account of data on poverty in the UK it is not possible to go into the range of technical questions that arise in relation to this survey data: about the impact of differential housing costs, the impact of household size upon deprivation and the implications of changes over time within households. Readers should consult the writings on poverty recommended at the end of this chapter for discussions of

Table 5.3 Incidence of poverty (individuals in households with income below 60% of median income after housing costs in the UK 2005/6)

Household type	Number of people in poverty	Proportion of people in group at risk of poverty (%)	Proportion of household type in poverty (%)
Children	3.8 million	30	30
Of which:			
• Couple with children		23	58
• Lone parent		50	42
Working age adults	7.2 million	20	20
Of which:			
• Single person without children		24	36
• Couple without children		12	20
Pensioners	1.8 million	17	17
Pensioner couple		16	55
Single pensioner		19	45

Source: DWP, *Households Below Average Income* (HBAI) 1994/5–2005/6 various tables 4.5–6.5.

these issues. Table 5.3 provides data on the incidence of poverty for various house-hold types. As is often the case with data of this kind, delays in their production means that these figures are a bit dated. But it is unlikely (for reasons suggested above) that the basic picture will have changed very much.

In many respects the key questions about social security policy concern not so much the setting of levels in the abstract as the need for, or the amount of, benefit increases. Pressure groups regularly draw politicians' attention to the ways in which, over a period of time, those whom they represent are losing ground. Two important alternative kinds of yardsticks are used for these judgements: indices of earnings and indices of prices. The plural form is used in both instances since there have been extensive arguments about the best ways of calculating these. In particular, it has been argued that a price index for the poor should be rather different from a more general one, since the poor spend their incomes in rather different ways. Box 5.6 provides an account of the recent history of benefit uprating rules.

The relationship between social security incomes and low wages is important, and this is discussed further in the next chapter. But as well as a concern about the relationship between benefits and other incomes, there is also a concern about relativities within the benefit system. The income support scheme rules make assumptions about the extent to which a couple may live more cheaply than a single person, about the extra needs of elderly and disabled people, about the different costs of children at various ages, and about the lower needs of single adults under 25. Some of these judgements are clearly controversial. In particular, the low-income support rate for

Box 5.6   Benefit uprating rules

Before 1973, there was no statutory requirement for government to take specific notice of wages or price movements in determining benefit levels. *Ad hoc* political judgements governed up-rating decisions. However, there was a tendency, over time, for the relationship between short-term benefit rates and wage rates to remain roughly the same (Barr, 1981). In the Social Security Act of 1973, the Conservatives provided a statutory link between benefits and prices. In 1975, an amendment to the Social Security Act committed the Labour Government to up-rating long-term benefits in line with prices or earnings, whichever was greater, and most short-term benefits in line with prices. Heavy price inflation in the late 1970s did produce some relative gains to social security recipients. In 1979, the Conservatives amended the statutory requirement so that long-term benefits were to be linked only to prices. Also, short-term benefits might be increased by up to 5 per cent less than the inflation rate. These rules related only to the contributory benefits but, in most cases, means-tested benefit rates have been up-rated on a similar basis. The changes after 1979 led to a serious fall in the value of all benefits relative to average wages. Since 1997 the Labour government has shown little general inclination to rectify this position, except in respect to pension credit. The latter was discussed above, where it was noted that the government has announced an ultimate undertaking to restore basic pension uprating rules to the position established in 1975.

single under-25s, and the particularly harsh treatment of sixteen- to eighteen-year-olds who have left school, seem to be related to an assumption that such people can live with their parents, and not form separate households. The assumptions about the costs of children made by the rules have also been challenged as unrealistic regarding the costs of teenage children. It seems fair to suggest that considerations of the evidence on actual costs have been mixed, in the determination of some of these rules, with views about who are the most deserving among the poor.

We see then that there is a wide range of complicated issues about benefit levels and about their role in the eradication of poverty. In this discussion actual benefit rates are not cited. These are changed every year, hence it would be confusing to cite them in a textbook designed to last for several years. Students who want to go into issues about these rates in more detail will need to turn to some of the sources cited in the recommendations for further reading.

Conclusions

This chapter has shown that the UK social security has diverged markedly from the model expected after the implementation of the Beveridge Report, in which a social insurance system (NI) was expected to be the dominant element, supported by a shrinking social assistance safety net and some private provision. Instead means-testing has become more and more important for the incomes of the poor, whilst the better off have generally looked to private pensions to provide security in their old age.

The replacement of the Department of Social Security by the Department for Work and Pensions in 2001 underlined the Labour government's social security reform strategy – a strong emphasis upon work (and therefore on work-supporting benefits like the tax credits) for those under pension age, and some further privatization of the pensions system. In this context not only have the 'universalist' expectations of many on the Left been disappointed but serious concerns about the effectiveness of the system remain. Issues about this have been highlighted here with reference to problems about securing an effective framework of pensions for all, deficiencies in the means-testing approach to benefit provision, unsatisfactory features about the treatment of women and evidence that the poverty is still widespread in the UK.

Suggestions for Further Reading

The most up-to-date textbook on social security policy is Jane Millar's edited volume *Understanding Social Security* (2003). A new edition of this is in preparation. Walker's *Social Security and Welfare* (2005) explores how the social security system works using much material from the UK but looking abroad too.

A good overview of many of the issues discussed here is Alcock's *Understanding Poverty* (third edition, 2006). A good source on the issues about poverty and bene-fits is Lister, *Poverty* (2004). David Piachaud charts the impact of social security developments in his work, and his essay in Hills, Le Grand and Piachaud (2007) *Making Social Policy Work* is recommended.

The issues about pension reform are examined in Hill (2007), *Pensions*.

The Child Poverty Action Group (CPAG) annual handbooks on means-tested and contributory benefits are the key sources for details, including benefit rates, which change at least annually (and have not therefore been quoted here). CPAG pam-phlets are useful critical sources of information on the system. Other good, general, up-to-date sources are CPAG's journal *Poverty* and a journal called *Benefits*. The Child Poverty Action group's website is www.cpag.org.uk.

The Department for Work and Pensions has a website which, in addition to pro-viding most of the key publications, offers advice to claimants and job seekers at www.dwp.gov.uk.

Chapter 6
Employment Policy

- Introduction
- Alternative Approaches to Employment Policy
- The Evolution of the UK Approach to Employment Policy
- The Impact upon the UK of European Union Membership
- The Main Employment Policy Measures
- Training
- Encouraging/Enforcing Labour Market Participation
- Reducing Unemployment or Stimulating Employment?
- Government Regulation of Work Conditions and Job Security
- Employment and Social Policy: a European Future?
- Conclusions
- Suggestions for Further Reading

Introduction

Employment policy will be likely to involve attempts to influence:

1 the overall level of labour market participation
2 the characteristics of work
3 the nature of the supply of labour
4 the demand for labour

This implies that while studying employment policy will involve examining the operation of specific government interventions, these concerns must be seen to be embedded in much wider considerations: on the one hand about the role of the government in the management of the economy as a while, on the other about the relationship of all social policy provisions ('welfare') to work. This chapter, whilst not aiming *either* to explore government management of the economy in great detail *or* to cut across the specific concerns of other chapters of this book, does examine questions about the overall orientation of the UK governments to the promotion and management of employment.

Hence this chapter has the dual function of examining policies relating to job placement, training and employment protection and dealing with some wider issues. It has been placed immediately after the chapter on social security not simply because the same government department now administers that and employment policy but also because there are some important issues about the relationship between social security policy and the management of the labour market.

Alternative Approaches to Employment Policy

In considering the role of the government in relation to the management of the labour market, two extreme political positions may be contrasted. One sees the preservation of a market-based economic system as the main priority, and requires social policy to do as little as possible to interfere with the market. The other gives primacy to social goals and requires that market forces must be managed, and in certain cases eliminated, to ensure those goals are realized. If the former position is adopted, market forces impacting on individuals' prospects of finding and retaining work are to be left alone, the only concern is that those state interventions in society that are deemed to be unavoidable have a minimal impact on the labour market. The characteristic social policy of such a regime is a 'Poor Law' (see Chapter 2) to provide social aid in exceptional circumstances but designed to ensure that it has no adverse effect on labour market participation. By contrast the other extreme position sees the management of the labour market (and other markets) for social ends to be a perfectly legitimate concern, and it therefore regards employment policy as a central concern of public social policy.

The actual political discourse, of course, lies between these polar positions. Hence, there are employment policies, which have social effects, to be studied. There are also issues to be considered about the employment effects of other social policies (particularly social security policies). However, it is also the case that there is considerable controversy about those effects, which needs to be seen in the context of different views about the extent to which the labour market can (or should) be subject to manipulation by governments. Comparative social policy analysis has suggested that governments differ significantly in this respect (see the exploration of this topic in Chapter 11). The UK is put by comparative theorists into the group of nations whose governments have (at least since the late 1970s) been broadly in favour of maximizing market freedom. Yet, as a member of the EU, it is confronted by nations that have favoured the alternative models. Furthermore, within the EU, attempts are being made to develop active labour market policies, with social goals, despite different social security policies that cannot easily be harmonized. Hence, ever since the UK joined the EEC (now called the EU), there has been a political debate about the shape of employment policy, and the UK has had to respond to measures from that community which may have an impact on the working of the labour market.

There is a developing debate about the most appropriate response to what are seen as increasingly significant 'global' market forces. One side in that debate argues that the only way a nation can compete in the global economy is to adopt labour market deregulation, lowering wages and related employment costs. The other side either disputes the power of the so-called global forces or argues that a large economic bloc like the EU can resist or influence those forces. An in-between position involves the suggestion that an efficient highly trained labour force can enable a nation to compete without at the same time necessarily lowering wages. It will be shown that some of the UK's employment policy responses are premised on the possibility of this 'middle' course.

In the context of these wide considerations, we can now go back to the four specific issues identified in the introduction. First, government interventions may aim both to increase and to decrease the overall level of labour market participation. The Poor Law approach (see Chapter 2) clearly aimed to maximize participation. Conversely, the introduction of pensions and sickness benefits may be seen as enabling some people to withdraw from having to try to participate. However, many other policies influence participation. Women have been explicitly excluded from some forms of labour market participation in the past, whereas more recently efforts have been made to counter discrimination against women and to encourage them to enter the labour force. Education policies may offer opportunities for young people which keep them temporarily out of the labour force. Finally, emigration and immigration policies will have effects on the size of the labour force (see Chapter 12 for further discussion of this last issue).

Second, Governments may regulate work – influencing its hours, conditions and rates of pay, i.e. the characteristics of work. They may also enact measures which influence the security of work. More indirectly they may influence the conditions under which employers and employees are able to bargain about these issues, through rules about trade unions and collective bargaining.

The first point above dealt with the quantity of labour; the third one particularly concerns what may be called the 'quality' of labour. Government education and training policies affect the nature of the supply of labour, and so may measures designed to influence attitudes to work. In this category are also included measures (job centres, etc.) which influence the rates at which employees and employers make contracts (inasmuch as these do not affect the level of labour market participation *per se* but rather its working). Immigration policies may also be relevant here.

Fourth, governments influence the demand for labour in many different ways. Attention in discussions of employment policy tends to be focused on explicit job creation measures, or explicit 'Keynesian' demand creating economic policies but, in reality, work may be created by many government initiatives (sometimes without this being a specific intention). In this sense, many social policy innovations – to increase the availability of health or social care or education or to increase the supply of houses – will have employment-creating effects. So, of course, will a decision to wage war.

All of these themes occur in UK employment policy, but there has been a tendency for 1 and 3 to be more evident than the other two. For an understanding of contemporary policy there is a need to explore the way in which policy stances have evolved over quite a long period, with varying emphasis on the four themes. This is done in the next section.

The Evolution of the UK Approach to Employment Policy

Nineteenth-century governments paid little attention to managing the labour market, but they did adopt measures both to maximize the participation of adult males in the labour force and to restrict the participation of women and children. Alongside, and sometimes part of the latter measures, were efforts to control working conditions.

In the early twentieth century, UK governments gradually came to reject the view that the economy, and accordingly the labour market, should be left to work 'naturally'. At the end of the nineteenth century, adherents of 'classical' economic theory began to acknowledge that it was perhaps necessary for government to play a role in assisting the market system to operate more smoothly. In particular, the problems of adjustment to changing economic situations in the short run began to be regarded as sufficiently serious to justify intervention. One such problem concerned the linking of 'sellers' of labour with 'buyers'. To this end, after 1909, systems of labour exchanges were created.

Around the beginning of the twentieth century, attention was given to the existence of various 'sweated trades' in which marginal workers, often including large numbers of women, were exploited. A measure of protection was enacted for workers in the 1909 Trade Boards Act, and in moves towards the establishment of minimum wages in some industries during the First World War. These might have been steps towards much greater regulation of employment. However, a bigger concern of the male-dominated working class movement was to give greater legal protection to trade unions and for these to be the main protectors of wage levels and conditions of employment through negotiated agreements with employers. A voluntary approach to employment regulation became dominant.

Between the two World Wars, continuing evidence that the economy could not readily absorb all who wanted work kept the issue of unemployment on the political agenda. There were strong pressures that forced the erratic development of income maintenance measures for the unemployed but government employment policies evolved very little. A few limited job-creation and training schemes were developed, but economic orthodoxy was against the heavy public expenditure on the creation of work that, by the middle of the 1930s, began to characterize the policy response in the USA. Only as preparation for war began to alleviate unemployment did official thinking begin to come to terms with its structural character. This change of approach is primarily associated with the Keynesian revolution in economic thinking that linked unemployment with under consumption and urged governments to spend, and, if necessary, to unbalance budgets, to pull out of a recession. The primary policy response required was, in this case, a macro-economic one, rather than a form of employment policy *per se*. However, at the same time, the special problems of certain regions, particularly those where employment had depended on declining heavy industries, also began to be recognized.

As indicated above, the two World Wars could be seen as massive labour demand creation schemes! Indeed, so strong was the need for labour that measures were adopted to draw new participants, particularly women, into the labour force.

The unexpected low unemployment from 1945 to 1970 enabled UK governments to continue to adopt a comparatively passive stance on employment policies. The trade unions were broadly satisfied with inaction on employment policy; full employment offered the ideal context for the continuation of male working-class advancement by way of collective action. The employment situation, initially at least, did not favour female interests. An expectation that the high female labour market participation of the wartime period would come to an end was reinforced by neglect of attention to the prevention of discrimination against women and an absence of child care provisions.

Full employment led, in the 1950s and 1960s, to official acceptance of the recruitment of labour from the countries of the former British Empire. Public employers, including the health service, sought workers from these countries. There were racist campaigns against open entry to the UK from the Caribbean and the Indian subcontinent, and controlling legislation was enacted (a sequence of measures starting with one in 1962). These control measures used need for labour as a crucial test for the grant of an entry permit.

In 1970, the incoming Conservative government, led by Edward Heath, decided to restructure the public employment service as part of its effort to make public administration more dynamic. A consultative document *People and Jobs* (Department of Employment, 1971) declared that the employment service needed to be modernized. The employment exchanges were too identified with a limited service to the unemployed. The government was influenced by German and Swedish concepts of 'active manpower policy', in which the employment service was seen as playing a crucial role in preserving full employment without high inflation. In practice, the UK's employment policy initiatives of the early 1970s were brought into operation in a context not just of high inflation but also of rapidly rising unemployment. The modernized employment services had to operate in an economy about which many economists had abandoned the 'Keynesian' belief that there is a direct, simple relationship between unemployment and inflation. 'Active manpower policy' was rendered comparatively irrelevant, and measures to deal with unemployment continued to dominate.

On coming to power in 1979, the Thatcher government inherited various special measures to deal with the problem of unemployment from its Labour predecessors. Its initial inclination was to curb these activities as part of its general attack on public expenditure. The main employment policies of the government involved an emphasis on reintroducing the full rigours of the marketplace into the labour market. A succession of measures weakened trade unions. At the same time the government was eager to reduce the impact of the meagre employment protection measures still on the statute book, such as the wage regulation which had survived since 1909 for a small number of trades.

It is difficult to separate the impact of Thatcherite measures designed to free the working of the labour market from the changes in the labour market that had already started to occur in the 1970s. It seems likely that the former accelerated the rate at which the latter took effect. It is not appropriate here to go further into these issues. What is relevant, however, is that Margaret Thatcher's government soon decided that they could not entirely discard the special measures developed in the late 1970s. It quickly came to realize that the special programmes, particularly those for the young unemployed, offered the cheapest way of providing a response to the problem of growing unemployment. So, in fact, the early 1980s saw a growth of expenditure on special training schemes and temporary job-creation measures (Moon and Richardson, 1985). Since then, programmes of assistance to unemployed people and training have gone through a large number of changes. Students will find even quite recent books misleading on detailed schemes, and if they try to trace the changes over recent years, they will be bewildered by the 'alphabet soup' of different schemes each often identified only by its initials.

In the early 1990s, the Conservative government's approach to job-creation and training measures became one in which the needs of the existing economic system were stressed, and control was firmly in the hands of private sector employers. There was a strong emphasis on the training of the young. For older, long-term unemployed people, there were special programmes, with an increasing requirement of activities as a condition of financial support (even if these do not readily help the individual back into the regular labour market). Conservative governments blew hot and cold about the desirability of measures of this last kind. One influence was the considerable sums the government was being forced, by the high level of unemployment, to spend on benefits. It spent with great reluctance, and increasingly found ways to reduce benefits and prevent individual access to such help.

Since 1997 the Labour government has placed a strong emphasis on employment policy but, in many respects, there is a high level of continuity with the policies of its predecessor. The examination of the history of employment policy suggests that Labour might have been expected to adopt a stance of stressing job creation measures and strengthening the trade union role as the protector of the work-force. That has been rejected as very much an 'old Labour' strategy. Alternatively, Labour might have adopted some of the initiatives of the 1970s again and given them a more distinctly 'continental' European twist, with an emphasis on increasing employment security. That too has been rejected, with the partial exception of the acceptance of a need for a minimum wage. Instead the emphasis has been very much on measures to improve and increase the supply of labour. Labour's 1997 election manifesto emphasized its supply-side programme on youth unemployment and said:

> Labour's welfare-to-work programme will attack unemployment and break the spiral of escalating spending on social security.

Typical examples of this emphasis are given in the Green Paper on Welfare Reform (Department of Social Security, 1998, p. 31):

> The Government's commitment to expand significantly the range of help available therefore alters the contract with those who are capable of work. It is the Government's responsibility to promote work opportunities and to help people take advantage of them. It is the responsibility of those who can take them up to do so.

We thus see here supply side measures that, by putting pressure upon people to seek work – perhaps for less money than they want or received before they became unemployed – reduce the cost of labour. These have been accompanied by the tax credits, discussed in the last chapter, which subsidize low wages. There are also related training measures that are expected to derive their supply side effects by increasing the efficiency of this low paid labour.

To sum up, the UK moved from a situation in which little was done to try to plan to prevent unemployment in the 1930s, through an era when regional policies were quite prominent, but generally the health of the labour market seemed to make planning unnecessary, between 1945 and 1971, into a brief phase when it was recognized that part of the UK's economic problem stemmed from the lack of an 'active labour market policy'. The rise of unemployment from 1975 onwards then 'hijacked' active labour market policy, concentrating efforts on special measures for the unemployed. Responses to the problem of unemployment preoccupied the system from then on, but since 1997 (in a situation of falling unemployment) the government have added to that an increasing concern to encourage labour market participation even by those not previously defined as unemployed.

The Impact upon the UK of European Union Membership

It was noted above that the development of an interest in active labour market policy coincided with the commencement of UK membership of the EEC. We will return at the end of the chapter to explore further the observations above about differences between UK and continental European attitudes to the management of employment. But what does need to be inserted before going on to the main employment policy measures is a brief discussion of the quite specific way in which European Union policy impacts upon UK employment policy.

It was noted in Chapter 3 that the principal social policy interventions emanating from the European Union have been limited efforts to harmonize rules relating to employment and the provision of funds to help to create work and aid training programmes. It needs to be noted that, in practice, the European Union has no resources of its own. Its budget is acquired by levies upon the member states. Consequently it is small, little over one per cent of European GDP. Historically it has been heavily oriented to agricultural support. While that has come down proportionately in recent years in favour of other sorts of support policies, this change has been heavily influenced by the enlargement of the community, involving the admission of nations with a much stronger claim to support for their economies that has the UK. Nevertheless, the UK still secures some benefits with an impact upon employment from the European Regional Development Fund and from the European Social Fund. The latter provides help towards the relief of long-term unemployment, youth unemployment and the problems of the 'socially excluded' (see Box 6.1)

The politics of European Union expenditure is complicated. While efforts are being made to channel funds to those in greatest need it is inappropriate to see this as simply a process in which wise people in Brussels make rational expenditure decisions.

Box 6.1   The European Social Fund

A report celebrating 50 years of the European Social Fund (European Commission *Social Agenda* issue 15, September 2007) outlines the plans for the Fund during the period 2007–13. Support is to be focused under four priorities: 'adaptability, access to employment, inclusion and human capital'. The budget for the whole period is to be 347,410 million Euros (at current prices; a Euro is about three-quarters of a pound). The UK share is expected to be 10,613 million Euros, that is about 3 per cent of the total.

National governments try to maximize what they get back from what they pay in. Arguments about the structural funds are therefore influenced by how the distribution of agricultural subsidies works out. Beyond that governments stress national needs that the Structural and Cohesion Funds should consider. Moreover it is generally the case that where grants are made, matching contributions are expected from the receiving country. All this adds up to saying that there is a small budget from which the UK, as a relatively well-off member of the EU, cannot expect to get very much.

However, the presence of the EU Funds described here does have an impact upon the orientation of national policy. In relation to support for unemployment people the EU's priorities influence national policies because they offer the possibility of some supplementary funding. Hence the emphases upon youth training and upon support for long-term unemployed people in the EU's priorities have been reflected in the UK. Similarly the fact that the EU identifies regions in need of some support tends to steer expenditure towards those parts of the UK where unemployment is high. This is however a complex matter since it is quite difficult to detect the impact of a small external addition to a much larger national budget. The real impact of Structural Fund additions in Wales has been the subject of dispute between the UK government and the Welsh Assembly.

Since the EU is a relatively small direct spender it will try to influence policy by the way it directs its grants. But probably more significant for the influence of the EU upon the UK is the stance it takes in relation to employment regulation. This subject is explored further in a later section.

The Main Employment Policy Measures

The UK's employment policies are the responsibility of the Department for Work and Pensions. Local services for job seekers are managed by an Agency which integrates employment services with benefit administration (for all able bodied adults) called Job Centre Plus.

'Job centres' are the modern successors to the labour exchanges which were set up in 1908 to do just what their name suggests, to link employers seeking workers with employees. In the 1970s, job centres were seen as replacing the large institutional exchanges with modern shop-front offices in commercial and shopping centres. There was an emphasis on self-service, individuals being able to select jobs from open-display advertisements, turning to staff only when advice was necessary. The aim as expressed in 1971 was to counter the problem that 'the Service is regarded by many workers and employers as a service for the unemployed' (Department of Employment, 1971, p. 5). The hopes for this approach were dashed, however, by the rise in unemployment. The 1990s saw an explicit acceptance by the government that this is precisely who the service is for. Accordingly, a visitor from the 1930s would find the modern job centre a puzzling place: on the one hand, all the apparatus of modern consumerism – a pleasant office, courteous staff, ample explanatory material – and on the other, a battery of questions and controls which would seem remarkably familiar.

Labour, in 1997, made the development of the existing measures to get people into work central to its social policy programme. It expressed its commitment in terms of the setting up of a 'New Deal' in 1998. This was expressed in fact as a number of New Deals (official material seems to switch freely between the singular and plural version here) (see Box 6.2).

It may be questioned whether it is appropriate to continue to use 'new' to describe policies after 10 years, nevertheless in January 2008 the government issued a report celebrating 10 years of success and setting out its continuing commitment to the objectives of the New Deal. We come back below to some comments on difficulties in evaluating the policy. While much that was proclaimed as 'new' involved continuation of initiatives by its Conservative predecessors, what has been evident has been the thorough review of the circumstances of unemployed people by personal advisers and a strong emphasis on the enhancement of skills, backed up by an emphasis on getting personal commitments from unemployed people themselves (with some strengthening of the long-existing sanctions to enforce this, see the further discussion below).

It should be noted from Box 6.5 that the Labour government started the New Deal with an emphasis upon young people:

> Crucially there is no longer any option of simply remaining on unemployment benefits indefinitely. NDYP ensured for the first time that every young person claiming JSA over a long period had to participate in meaningful activity designed to improve their chances of getting a job. (DWP, 2008, p. 4)

Box 6.2   The new deals

- New Deal for Young People (NDYP) (1998)
- New Deal 25 Plus (1998)
- New Deal for Lone Parents (NDLP) (1998)
- New Deal for Partners (1999)
- New Deal 50 Plus (2000)
- New Deal for Disabled People (NDDP) (2001)

The government specifically pledged to give a quarter of a million young people (aged between 18 and 24) six months in either work or training.

In Chapter 5, it was shown that the state financial support for unemployed people is provided by the jobseeker's allowance. To qualify, a person has to make a clear undertaking, signing a jobseeker's agreement, on the steps he or she will take to try to find work. Even for those who have been contributing to the national insurance (NI) scheme, jobseeker's allowance is means-tested after six months. Benefit may also be stopped or reduced if individuals are found to have lost employment unnecessarily or to have failed to take employment opportunities.

The job centres play a central role in the surveillance of the behaviour of the unemployed. The initial jobseeker's agreement is subject to regular review. Particular attention is paid to those who have been out of work for six months or more. At the reviews, the individual's efforts to find work are examined, and a variety of other options are explored. In their literature the government refers to a variety of alternative strategies applied at this stage, according to the characteristics of the job seeker.

The job seeker who is aged between 18 and 24 will, after six months of unemployment, experience extensive consultation from a 'personal adviser' who may, alongside normal employment opportunities, consider referral to subsidized work, work in the voluntary sector, work with a specially set up 'environmental task force' or full-time education and training. Job seekers over 25 experience similar intensive examination of their situations, with referral to subsidized employment their main alternative to normal employment.

The consultation or advice in these programmes may involve a requirement to attend a seminar or training course (there has been a variety of jargon names for these, which change from time to time: 'jobplan', 'workwise', 'restart', etc.) where attention will be on job search strategies and personal attributes and attitudes.

Training

Inasmuch as employment policies involve training, particularly training for younger people, then departments responsible for education also participate in the policies this chapter is concerned with. In July 2007 the restructuring of government in England involved (as noted in Chapter 3) the splitting of education policy, with post-school education being brought under a new department called the Department for Innovation, Universities and Skills. While at the time of writing it is difficult to identify how exactly the work of this new department is developing it is significant that in defining its role it has identified raising 'participation and attainment by young people and adults in post-16 education and learning' and tackling 'the skills gap amongst adults, particularly equipping people with basic literacy and numeracy'. In fact, well before the setting up of this new department the field of further education had been identified as a complex maze of interacting agencies (see Ainley, 2001).

A wide range of organizations, both private and public, have been commissioned to provide training for work. The Learning and Skills Council plays a key role in the development of training in England (there are equivalent bodies in the other countries). They direct the work of a network of local Learning and Skills Councils. It has also been involved in setting up a distinct range of qualifications, National Vocational Qualifications.

While adults of all ages take advantage of training opportunities, either as a direct result of interventions by Job Centres or as a personal initiative, there has been a particular emphasis on the training of younger people. A primary target has been those who terminate their full-time education at the minimum age. In England this is true of about 24 per cent of 16 year olds. Over half of these then went into some form of further training or employer based learning (National Statistics, 2007, p. 29). A key element in the system of training for this group is what as are called 'modern apprenticeships'. These divide into schemes involving attachment to an employer, where modest wages are provided and college based ('programme led apprenticeships') courses, for which means-tested education maintenance allowances are available.

Beyond 18 there are many people undertaking some further education (probably over 5 million in the UK as a whole), with a strong bias in the system towards those in the younger age groups. The available statistics on this are confusing – not surprisingly given the wide range of types and lengths of training and the mixture of full-time and part-time – so no statistics are included here.

As far as training programmes directly orientated to unemployed people are concerned there is a wide range of schemes – provided by private employers, voluntary organizations and public bodies – offering a mixture of work experience and training. The achievement of qualifications is strongly emphasized. But, these schemes vary enormously in quality, from elaborate skill training at one extreme to what are little more than 'make work' schemes for lower-ability young people in high-unemployment areas at the other. The better the local demand for young workers, the better the quality of the schemes, in terms of both the training they offer and the real labour market opportunities they lead on to.

The development of policy in this area has been affected by one historical characteristic of the transition from education to work in the UK. By contrast with some of the continental European nations (particularly Germany) training for work had been seen very much as matter to be left to employers. For much manual work (and indeed for many middle class professions too, though the terminology was different) training on the job, often by means of 'apprenticeships' had been the norm. The collapse of large scale industrial employment seriously undermined this system. Therefore three points must be recognized:

- The UK has (by contrast with most of continental Europe) a very high proportion of young people ending their full-time education and training at the age of sixteen.
- The UK used to have a strong pattern of apprenticeship into skilled work in industry, which has now collapsed.
- Before the rise of unemployment in the mid-1970s, the labour market for young people was a thriving one; it has now more or less disappeared.

Youth training may be seen as a necessary means of filling a vacuum in the UK education and training system, but it has also contributed to the creation of that vacuum by undermining the incentives to employers to provide work or training for young people at their own expense. The state now pays for most of this, through youth training.

Encouraging/Enforcing Labour Market Participation

There has been extensive controversy about the impact of the social security system on the behaviour of the unemployed. The relationship between social security incomes and low wages is clearly important. Several studies of poverty have related incomes to the level provided by the main means-tested scheme. Apart from drawing attention to numbers falling below it because of a failure to claim benefits, they have shown that there is a significant group who fall below that standard because of low wages. There are alternatives ways of responding to it. One is to concentrate on raising wage levels. The introduction by the government of a minimum wage in 1999 was a modest move in this direction. But other than this, the government has been reluctant to do anything that would push up direct wage costs. The oldest additional solution to this problem was the introduction of universal benefits designed to subsidize families, enabling questions about what families need to be separated from issues about wage levels. In the UK the introduction of Family Allowance in 1944, (now in an enhanced form called Child Benefit) is an example of this response. However, the universal entitlement to Child Benefit – and the high costs involved in uprating it – led governments instead to consider means-tests that would subsidize wages (something that, after the abolition of the Speenhamland system of wage subsidy under the Poor Law back in 1834, was long considered unacceptable). Hence, the UK has seen in modern times the introduction of various forms of means-tested wage subsidy, culminating in the Tax Credit discussed in the last chapter.

The developments described in the last paragraph have largely undermined a widespread objection to generous benefits for unemployed people, that they deterred work participation. There is still undoubtedly a relatively small gap between the benefits paid to some workless people and the wages paid for low-skilled work. The deterrent effect of this will depend first on the actual costs of going to work, second on individual views of the psychological costs and benefits of work, and third on the benefits still obtainable when in work (where much may depend upon knowledge of those benefits and capacity to work out their likely impact).

However, politicians remain sensitive to the belief that benefits deter labour market participation. That accordingly influences government decisions on increases in the short-term benefits. One relatively small group who have been singled out for attention are childless wives of men who claim the jobseeker's allowance. They have been required to register for work, and a special advice programme has been developed for them. But more significant is the way attention has thus transferred away from concern about the now very low levels of benefit offered by Job Seekers Allowance to two other issues: the support of single parents and benefits for disabled people.

The New Deal for Lone Parents is designed to help lone parents into work. This arose to fulfil a pledge in Labour's 1997 election manifesto:

> Today the main connection between unemployed lone parents and the state is their benefits. Most lone parents want to work, but are given no help to find it.... Once the youngest child is in the second term of full-time school, lone parents will be offered advice by a proactive Employment Service to develop a package of job search, training and after-school care to help them off benefit.

There has been a gradual stepping up of the pressure towards labour market participation under this scheme. What started as a voluntary advice programme (designed to explore work and training opportunities and inform about in-work cash benefits) shifted to compulsion to attend work-focused interviews once the youngest children were 14 years old or more. But further pressure upon lone parents is promised, moving away from the long-standing view in the UK (contrast the United States where some of the ideas for the revised approach come) that single parents with school age children should not be compelled to go into employment. The Government proposes that lone parents will have to actively seek employment once their youngest child is 12 or over, from October 2008, and to go on tightening the system so that one year later all with the youngest child over 11 will have to seek employment and two years later this will apply to all where the youngest child is over 10.

In a society of high labour market participation by women, the government has had some justification – in the light of the high poverty levels amongst single parents (see Chapter 5, p. 120) – in seeing work participation as a way forward for this group of people. But the issues are complex. Clearly in principle the stress upon increasing the contributions from absent (generally male – though this issues does arise a little the other way round) parents is also part of the key to the solution of this problem (see Chapter 5). More important is the availability of low-cost child care arrangements (discussed further in Chapter 9). The New Deal programme has given some attention to this, as has the development of Child Tax Credit though the remaining issues here are about the low wages available to the women who seek work, together with the fact that much of that work is – or has to be – part-time.

The issues about disabled people are also complex, but in rather different ways. Benefits for disabled people are very much better – and potentially more secure – than those for unemployed people. There was, during the last years of the last century a massive increase in the numbers of people claiming incapacity benefits. Since then the numbers have fallen (see Table 6.1), but the government considers they could fall much more. Any good welfare rights adviser will suggest – if these is a choice – securing such benefits rather than registering as unemployed. More curiously, there was a period in the 1980s when government officials explicitly encouraged people to opt for sickness and disability based benefits rather than register as unemployed, as part of government efforts to reduce the perceived size of the unemployment problem.

But the last two observations do not alone explain the rise in the numbers of people claiming incapacity benefits. This is by no means an issue for the UK alone, as a

Table 6.1   Numbers claiming incapacity benefit

	2002–3	2003–4	2004–5	2006–7
Numbers (thousands)	852	829	818	777

Source: National Statistics, 2007, table 8.9, p. 106.

similar phenomenon has been identified in other countries in Western Europe. It may been seen also as an aspect of ageing across these societies, but there is a converse trend that people are getting fitter and living longer. It must also be seen as a feature of the structural change that has occurred as large scale industrial employment has declined. But this should not be regarded as a sufficient explanation on its own. It has various dimensions. Certainly the decline of mining and heavy industry forced out of work many people (mainly male) approaching the end of their working life and carrying injuries and health problems that were a product of their earlier work environments. While they might be expected to be competitors for newer lighter forms of work, they had other competitors – better educated, more willing to be flexible and (here we come to a controversial issue) perhaps willing to accept lower rates of pay. But these effects might be expected to be short run: the prematurely retired would soon reach the official retirement age. The questions are now also about the extent to which there are choices being made by employees with health problems about what work they can do and by employers about who they will take on. Certainly the government's two-pronged attack on this issue makes these assumptions.

There is a 'New Deal for Disabled People' on offer to people on disability benefits as well as those registered as unemployed. Measures for disabled workers have evolved considerably in recent years. As far back as the Second World War a specialized advice service was set up for disabled workers. This measure was supported by a quota. The Disability Discrimination Act of 1995 replaced the quota with procedures for the prevention of discrimination against disabled workers. These include a requirement that employers should make 'reasonable' adjustments to premises to overcome the disadvantages of disabled people. It is hard, so far, to assess the impact of the changes under the 1995 Act. The quota was poorly enforced, but the new law requires action against discrimination to be activated by disabled people themselves. This may be very difficult to do. It is difficult to assess whether there has been discrimination in a context of stiff competition for jobs.

Whilst, as noted above, in the 1980s the government tolerated and partly encouraged a situation in which people with disabilities were able to leave the unemployment register and receive the long-term, higher-rated invalidity benefit, in the 1990s, they became concerned about the cost of supporting this group. In 1995, invalidity benefit was replaced by incapacity benefit, with a much stricter test of fitness for work. The Labour government then followed up on that measure by further reducing the availability of incapacity benefit and by developing the arrangements for interviews with an employment adviser to explore work possibilities. At the time of writing the struggle to further make inroads into the numbers of claimants of incapacity benefit continue. The government promises the following measures:

- That instead of going onto incapacity benefit new and repeat claimants will go on to a benefit called 'Employment and Support Allowance.
- Existing claimants of Incapacity Benefit 'will have access to' the 'pathways to work' programme offered by Job Centre. Obviously there are alternative views about the extent an expression like 'will have access to' implies compulsion.
- In the assessment of benefit claims the existing 'personal capacity assessment' will be replaced by a 'work capacity' one (DWP, 2007, p. 13).

Reducing Unemployment or Stimulating Employment?

As noted above, the government claims that its employment policies have had a massive impact upon unemployment: 'Unemployment has fallen in every region of the country; and record numbers of people are in work – over 2.8 million more people in employment now than in 1997' (DWP, 2008, p. 6). In the Prime Minister's preface to the document making that claim he says 'more than 1.8 million people have been helped into jobs by the new deals' (Ibid., p. 2).

The evidence on the fall in the unemployment rate between 1997 and 2007 is unequivocal (see Box 6.3). The issues about the employment rate, by contrast, are

Box 6.3   Unemployment

Statistics featuring the first quarter of each year – generally the lowest point in the annual cycle – (thousands).

1997	1998	1999	2000	2001	2002	2003	2004	2005	2006	2007
2050	1810	1775	1682	1472	1512	1523	1433	1413	1602	1705

The source of these statistics is web site material from the employment statistics series maintained by National Statistics. It is based upon a regular labour force survey. This is important; the alternative is the count of people registering as unemployed which can be very misleading, since administrative procedures to influence this can have a big impact. However, even labour force survey data is challengeable. People are asked whether they are actively seeking employment. This may lead to over counting, inasmuch as respondents may want to create a favourable impression upon interviewers. It may also – in our view more probably – lead to undercounting, particularly when jobs are scarce, inasmuch as there will be numbers of 'discouraged' potential workers who are not actively seeking employment since they see no point in looking for something they consider they are unlikely to find. This consideration will be particularly applicable to those with plenty of other 'work' to do, notably female parents.

complex. But then the claim that the government's employment policies (as opposed to other policies, or economic factors that are outside their control) have had a direct influence upon employment is particularly difficult to evaluate. We look at these topics in succession below.

The unemployment levels of today are still high by comparison with the 1950s and 1960s. Moreover, as Box 6.3 shows, the upturn of the middle 2000s gives some cause for concern about the future. Moreover, when the impact of unemployment is considered there remain traditional inequalities between regions, classes and ethnic groups.

Comparison of unemployment levels is made notoriously difficult by the different ways these are measured (see the note in Box 6.3). The new concerns about stimulating labour force participation confuses the issue of unemployment still further by identifying a group of people who clearly choose to remain outside the labour force, some of whom the government think should be within it. It has been shown above that in the UK in early 2007 about 1.7 million people were unemployed. Yet at the same time there were about 7.9 million people between 16 and the retirement age who were not economically active. That 7.9 consisted of 3.2 million men and 4.7 million women. A more detailed breakdown of these figures would reveal, alongside the 'incapacitated' group, identified above, a comparatively small element in the total, two large groups:

- people (nearly all female) not participating because of family responsibilities
- students.

We see therefore that there is a very large element in the population, much larger than the number who are formally counted as unemployed, many of whom may enter the labour force in conditions of high labour demand (particularly if the government is seeking to encourage labour force participation). In fact, from the two groups – parents and students – we have identified as major elements amongst the economically inactive we recognize that there will be large numbers classified as 'active' because in part-time work. There are some similar issues that could be addressed here about people who are past retirement age who may participate in the labour force, and whose participation will be affected by the presence of absence of employment opportunities.

Data about labour force participation has been discussed at some length partly because of the way policies to stimulate participation are very much on the current agenda. But it was also introduced because there is – on the part of politicians and journalists – much misleading talk about labour shortages. This kind of talk shifts dramatically, according to fashions, from expressions of worries about the emergence of a world in which there will be a permanent lack of work (many examples of this could be found in the 1980s) to concerns about a lack of people to do the necessary work to support an ageing population (this is the 'demographic time bomb' perspective set out regularly from the 1990s onward). In fact, as the data above show there is a great deal of scope for variation in the size of the labour force according to the demand for labour. At the same time there is still little known about the factors that lead to long-term shifts in that demand.

If so many issues about choice in relation to market opportunities can affect the statistics on employment and unemployment, what does this tell us about the effectiveness of government employment policies? What contemporary policies have done is to concentrate very much on the *supply* side of the labour force. The UK government has been prepared to countenance measures which will have the effect of increasing the pool of people seeking work. It has boldly characterized its own efforts in these terms (Department of Social Security, 1998, p. 23):

> The Government's aim is to rebuild the welfare state around work. The skills and energies of the workforce are the UK's biggest economic asset. And for both individuals and families, paid work is the most secure means of averting poverty and dependence except, of course, for those who are retired or so sick or disabled, or so heavily engaged in caring activities, that they cannot realistically support themselves.

An even stronger sound-bite on this is provided by the Prime Minister for the Ten-year report on the New Deal:

> In the old days the problem may have been unemployment, but in the next decades it will be employability. If in the old days lack of jobs demanded priority action, in the new world it is lack of skills. (DWP, 2008, p. 2)

That very bold statement begs a variety of questions. At worst it introduces a new form of the long-used stigmatizing statements that blame the 'victims' for their unemployment. At least, it is always difficult to separate the impact of specific schemes from other influences. Of course, given that experience of unemployment is concentrated amongst low skilled workers the emphasis in the New Deals (particularly that for the young) upon training is to be welcomed. However, in evaluating the real effect of such measures, there is a need to be aware of the phenomenon of 'positional competition' (Hirsch, 1977). If good job opportunities are in short supply the effect of additional training may be merely to increase the qualifications needed to get into such jobs. If that happens additional training for the weakest competitors for those jobs may do very little to enhance their job prospects. Furthermore while enhancing skills levels is widely seen as desirable to increase the competitiveness of the nation as a whole, if what actually happens is that an increasing number of jobs are able to recruit overqualified new employees much of that effect may be dissipated.

In contrast to that emphasis on skills it will be evident, from some of the discussion in Chapter 5 and in this one, that a driving force for current efforts to increase labour force participation is the government concern to reduce benefit dependency. But there are obvious difficulties about trying to drive single mothers or disabled people into the labour force if there is a lack of work for all who want it. Clearly, contemporary official thinking on this subject is that this is not the case, and that UK economic development can be stimulated by encouraging labour force participation. There are two alternative expectations here. One goes back to the longstanding view that the market works best if public policies stimulate demand for work and drive down wages. The other rests upon a view that demographic changes are leading towards shortages of workers. There are some very complex economic questions that lie behind both those propositions.

The very high premium placed upon employment in contemporary policy is open to four objections. First, it may be challenged as placing paid work on a pedestal, above all other means of sharing resources in society. That is a philosophical issue, which will not be examined here. Second, it disregards the very large amount of unpaid work carried out, particularly within the household and most of it by women. Third, it presumes that the problems of supplying enough employment, for all who are to be forced to need it, can be solved. Fourth, and closely related to that second point, is that it seems to be silent on the quality of employment opportunities on offer. If the government's initiatives increase the volume of employment available, what kind of work will that be? And fifth, who will get the work opportunities, and to what extent will labour market segmentation be enhanced in which the poorest quality work is performed by women and people from ethnic minorities?

A more gloomy assessment of this approach is based on the extent to which employment growth in the UK, as opposed to economic growth (these are issues that are not necessarily linked), has involved low-paid insecure and often part-time work. Dex and McCulloch (1995) estimated that around half of all women and a quarter of all men were in what may be called 'non-standard work' contracts, i.e. part-time work, temporary work or self-employment. However, a much higher proportion of new work may be of that kind (Cousins 1999; Dickens, Gregg and Wadsworth, 2003).

Many people, including the previous Prime Minister, Tony Blair, tell us we have to learn to live in a world in which working lives need to be more flexible. The crucial problem here is, as Wheelock (1999) suggests, whether we are on the 'high road' or the 'low road' to flexibility in the labour market. The low road means that:

> Global competition and the structural shift to services put downward pressure on the wages of the unskilled, wages which are already at the lowest end of the market. (pp. 79–80)

The high road on the other hand:

> relies upon employment based on sophisticated technology and innovation to keep abreast of international competition. Those employed in this sector – in high tech industries such as petrochemicals, computing, biotechnology etc. – must be highly trained. They must be prepared to be 'functionally flexible' in the sense that they undertake a range of tasks and learn how to do new ones. (p. 80)

In fact, analyses of divisions in labour markets (Piore and Sabel, 1984; Goos and Manning, 2003) suggest that while a lucky minority may be on the 'high road', the majority, and particularly those people who are likely to have to apply for benefits and to use state services to help them in the labour market, are on the low road.

These divisions are also global divisions of labour. The optimistic view about the quality of the labour supply in the UK also rests upon a view that in international competition global economic forces, placing the richer nations at a disadvantage, will be resisted because *our* economy is one in which highly skilled people provide 'value added' in terms of the provision of quality goods and services. It would go beyond the scope of this book to chase this argument through fully (it is examined a bit in another book by one of the authors, Hill, 2007, chapters 5 and 13). But there is one aspect of this that merits attention: that is the extent to which evidence on labour migration provides signs that the internal divisions in the labour market indicate the impact of globalism in a very different way. This theme is addressed in Chapter 12.

Government Regulation of Work Conditions and Job Security

It was noted in the introduction that another approach to employment policy, comparatively neglected by UK governments involves the regulation of work, influencing its character and its security. A closely related topic concerns the role of government as an influence upon the conditions under which employers and employees are able to bargain about these issues, through rules about trade unions and collective bargaining. While the general stance adopted in the UK has been to see the work contract as a private deal between employer and employee in a free labour 'market', since the middle of the nineteenth century employment regulation has not been entirely absent in the UK. Moreover modern concerns about discrimination and the influence of membership of the European Union have both had some significant impact upon employment policy. It is therefore appropriate to look briefly at these issues, where government social policy involves not the provision of benefits or services but rather the regulation of private activities.

The earliest regulatory legislation was measures to prevent or restrict the employment of women and children, enacted in the middle of the nineteenth century. While from one perspective this legislation can be seen as designed to prevent exploitation of the vulnerable, from another it is recognizable as having the effect of protecting adult males from competition. Today most of the measures affecting female labour market participation have disappeared but limitations on child employment remain. To some extent men also gained indirect benefits from the early regulation, inasmuch as downward pressure on the hours of women and children had an impact on those of men.

A crucial related question, on the political agenda from the middle of the nineteenth century onward, concerned the right of collective organizations – trade unions – to bargain on behalf of employees. The history of this issue is a convoluted one, beyond the concerns of this book, in which the main concerns of the trade unions, and the political labour movement, was to secure legal protection for bargaining rights. What this implied, therefore, was that the UK followed a very different road to many continental European countries where government became a crucial party to bargains between employees and employers, participating in and protecting the terms of agreements reached. To use a sporting analogy, in the continental model of industrial relations the government is often a player, in the UK one it is at best a referee, and in fact often a reluctant one (or even one biased in favour of employers).

What has followed from this approach is that where the UK government has intervened it has been to influence the terms under which employers and employees arrive at contracts of employment – determining what it sees as good employment practice in respect of working conditions and the way in which workers are hired or fired (more the latter than the former). In this respect an important government role has been to provide special 'courts' to settle disputes between individual employees and employers. These 'courts' comprise the Employment Tribunals (formerly Industrial Tribunals) set up in 1964 and the Employment Appeal Tribunal set up in 1975 to handle appeals, principally those coming from the Employment Tribunals. These organizations originally had quite a minor role in respect of training matters, they became more important after the enactment of rights to redundancy payments in 1965. But their role particularly advanced after the enactment of legislation to deal with 'unfair dismissal', the Industrial Relations Act of 1971, and their work has further increased as a consequence of anti-discrimination legislation.

The emergence of legislation to curb discrimination in employment should be seen against this backcloth of government reluctance to be involved in more than a passive way in the protection of employment rights. The first measure directed against racial discrimination in employment, an Act passed in 1968, was very weak. In 1975 a measure to combat sexual discrimination in employment was passed and a year later the legislation against racial discrimination was strengthened. These measures set up government-supported bodies to help to enforce the law, the Equal Opportunities Commission and the Commission for Racial Equality, which combined with the Disability Rights Commission in 2007 to form the Equality and Human Rights Commission (EHRC). The Equal Pay Act of 1970, updated by an amendment Act in 1984, also contributes to the reduction of discrimination against women in the labour market. Significantly in its approach to the prevention of racial discrimination the government initially drew a clear line between race and religion, to avoid dealing with the widespread religious discrimination in Northern Ireland. Subsequently Fair Employment Acts specific to Northern Ireland were passed in 1976 and 1989 to try tackle that problem. At the time of writing, however, issues about religious discrimination seem to be emerging on the overall UK political agenda. Finally amongst the battery of anti-discrimination measures it is important to note the Disability Discrimination Act of 1995 and the Disability Rights Commission Act of 1999 which together establish a framework rather like those for combating racial and sexual discrimination to deal with discrimination against disabled people. At the time of writing concerns about discrimination against older workers are also emerging on the political agenda and are addressed explicitly in the work of the EHRC.

There is thus now a group of legislative measures, with supporting enforcement bodies, which extend government intervention into the labour contract – curbing unfair selection practices, harassment at work and unfair dismissal – on behalf of the various groups that may be the victims of discrimination. But the process of rooting out deep-seated discriminatory practices is not an easy one. Reforming legislation has been brought in slowly and reluctantly, the enforcement bodies are still poorly funded and elimination of discrimination largely depends upon individual actions through the tribunal system. At the time of writing an extensive attack has developed against gender discrimination. But significantly it has chosen the softest target first, discrimination by public bodies. An extensive number of cases of this kind are being considered by Employment Tribunals.

One of the key driving forces towards measures to attack discrimination in employment in the UK has been initiatives emerging from the European Union and decisions by the European Court of Justice. It has been noted that European Union social policy consists primarily of a range of measures in the field of employment and that probably the primary impact of the European Union has arisen from efforts to harmonize employment conditions across the member nations. These efforts stem particularly from the fact that with the creation of a single market comes a need to ensure that – through the maintenance of inferior labour conditions – particular nations cannot compete unfairly with others. In this respect the relatively unregulated UK labour market has been viewed with some concern. Accompanying that overall economic concern has been the fact that within the notion of the single market is the idea that free movement of labour should be possible. That leads on to a trade union concern about the rights of workers who move to work in other member states.

The issues about the relationship between the UK's approach to labour market regulation and that of the rest of the Community came to a head in connection the establishment of the Community Charter of the Fundamental Social Rights of Workers (often called simply 'the Social Charter') in 1989 and the negotiations about the Maastricht Treaty of 1993. That Treaty, crucial for the steps towards monetary union, contained a 'social chapter' endorsing most of the aspirations of the Social Charter. The UK government negotiated an arrangement under which the 'social chapter' should not apply to them. But that did not eliminate the general pressure towards increased recognition of workers' rights. On coming to power in 1997 Labour accepted the 'social chapter'.

Some recent developments flowing from European Union social policy have been:

- Rights to parental leave to care for sick children (though significantly this does not mean a right to paid leave).
- A right to paternity leave.
- Limitations upon working time – particularly a measure requiring the working week to be limited to 48 hours.
- Extension of employment protection rights to part-time workers and temporary workers (though it should be noted that the UK government is resisting some of this).

In addition to these more formal policy influences originating in the EU, the Labour government's concern to improve 'work–life balance' has also been influenced by both the work–family reconciliation debates which have developed in the EU since the early 1990s, and the policy prescriptions emerging from the Organization for Economic Cooperation and development (OECD) and set out country by country in their 'Babies and Bosses' series of publications. Work–life balance policy is clearly

Box 6.4   Work–life related policy developments

- Working time directive
- Part-time work directive
- National child care strategy
- National strategy for carers
- Parental leave directive
- Time-off for dependents (Employment Relations Act 1999)
- Work–life balance initiative (2000)
- Parents' right to ask for flexible working arrangements (Employment Act 2001 effective from 2003, for carers effective from 2007)
- Extensions to maternity leave and pay; paid adoption leave and two weeks paid paternity leave (Employment Act 2001 effective from 2003)

(Adapted from Dex, 2002, pp. 7–8)

part of the wider employment strategy aimed at ensuring maximum participation in the labour force, including participation by parents (for which read mothers). At present it is constituted by a range of different measures and legislation (set out in Box 6.4), and includes the parent's and carer's right to ask for flexible working hours. However, although work–life balance may suit government aims for employment policy, it is also an important step forwards in terms of the recognition of the social value of non-employment related activities for parents and non-parents alike.

Finally it is important to mention one recent piece of legislation affecting employment which is not a response to European legislation, the National Minimum Wage Act of 1998. This specifies a minimum hourly rate for workers. The implementation of this measure is supervised by an appointed body, the Low Pay Commission. That body makes recommendations from time to time on the need to upgrade the minimum wage; there is no automatic inflation linking process. The minimum wage in 2008 is only £5.52 an hour (£4.60 for people aged 18–21 and £3.40 for under 18s).

Employment and Social Policy: a European Future?

This chapter has explored the determination of recent UK governments to stress the role of work in relation to social policy. It took strong symbolic form in the creation of a Department for Work and Pensions in 2001. That new departmental title seems to tell us that unless we are pensioners, and thus allowed to be out of the work force, our social security must be linked to labour market participation. The government's slogan in the first line of the summary of the Green Paper on Welfare Reform (Department of Social Security, 1998) was 'work for those who can and security for those who cannot'.

To what extent does contemporary UK government policy prompt a rethink not just about employment policy but also about what social policy is all about? It is useful to link that question to the issue about the relationship between UK social policy and European social policy. To do so uncovers some paradoxes. On the face of it making a strong link between social security and work brings UK thinking more into line with European approaches to social policy. A textbook on European social policy suggests that:

> In the British empiricist tradition, social policy is identified closely with the collective provision of social services ... Elsewhere in Europe, the term 'social policy' has been identified more with institutions and relations pertaining to the labour market, and in particular with the rights of workers and the framework for agreements between employers, unions and government – the social partners. (Kleinman, 2002, p. 1)

But there are three different glosses that can be put on a statement like that:

1   As Kleinman shows very clearly in his book, issues about employment have dominated thinking about social policy in the European Community precisely because that community is primarily aiming at the creation of a single market in which economic institutions are shared between the constituent nations. In those circumstances, as noted above, issues about employment conditions are bound to be dominant.
2   Equally, as also mentioned above, if the notion of the relationship between workers and employers is a compact between them, setting out conditions for social protection guaranteed by government (sometimes described as a 'corporatist' social order) then this will be much more central for social policy than is the case in the UK.
3   This leads then to a third point, that in most of the continental European countries a key ingredient of this social compact has been a social insurance system guaranteeing much better income replacement rates outside work than the UK's social security system. Furthermore in many cases this social insurance deal extends to health care (and recently, in the German and Luxembourg cases, even to social care). In such circumstances the link between work and social security rights is much more explicit than in the UK case.

What the three points made above add up to is a suggestion that the UK perspective on social policy is changing to resemble the European one only in respect of the first of the three considerations set out above. If, in the UK case, work is the key to 'security', we are individuals in the market place *unaided* by constitutionally incorporated trade unions and required to buy pensions and other sources of future security.

But that brings us to what is identified as a crucial issue about where the European Union is going. Kleinman's analysis of this topic identifies the European Social Charter as the high point of the aspiration towards a Europe of shared collective social policy. Behind that Charter were people, in particular French socialists, with a vision of a European-wide society where social standards could be raised through collective action, bringing the laggard countries up to the standards of the leaders. But, in Kleinman's view, an even more important force in the development of European policy came from those who saw the achievement of monetary union as involving the establishment of an economic regime in which there would be strict controls over inflation and measures that prevented government use of deficit spending to solve social problems. It was in other words a 'monetarist' vision of strict fiscal control, to operate effectively in the global economy as opposed to a Keynesian vision of a European society in which active economic policies could be adopted to combat unemployment.

Kleinman's prediction of the development path for Europe is reinforced by the new aspiration to enlarge the community. The inclusion of former Communist bloc countries in Eastern Europe could make the achievement of rising social policy standards even more difficult. Additionally one of the strongest European defenders of a positive role for social policy in raising social standards, France, acquired in 2007 a new President with a much more neo-liberal stance on this. The UK's similar stance, coupled with the widespread public ambivalence about the European Union, suggests that the European Union is at best a marginal influence on UK employment policy.

Conclusions

This chapter began by setting the issues about employment policy in their wider social policy context and by emphasizing the wide range of ways in which governments may develop policies. Attention was drawn to the fact that employment policies may concern:

- the overall level of labour market participation
- the characteristics of work
- the nature of the supply of labour
- the demand for labour

It was then shown that these concerns have all appeared from time to time in UK employment policy but that the overall stance has been relatively *laissez-faire*, doing little to intervene directly in the labour market, leaving influences on labour demand to a combination of comparatively accidental effects stemming from other policy decisions and treating unemployment as an issue to be tackled largely through income maintenance policies. Then, the rise of unemployment in the 1970s was met by revitalized public agencies committed to 'active' employment policy. Initially, this led to exploration of the development of job-creation measures, but these measures were undermined by a reluctance to compete with the 'regular' labour market. This led to a concentration on intervention in the labour market on behalf of specific groups of the unemployed. Such intervention has a strong 'supply side' emphasis, the concern being with 'what is wrong with' the victims of unemployment, rather than on deficient demand. Workers who are either more highly skilled or more willing to work for very low rewards are seen as less likely to be unemployed. Concentration on these issues is expected to reduce unemployment. There are good grounds for believing that the enormous emphasis on the future of welfare as lying in labour market participation by all who can do so involves a sophisticated political exercise at 'blaming the victims', who are perceived as making insufficient efforts to secure skills and/or paid work.

Suggestions for Further Reading

A key source is Dickens, Gregg and Wadsworth's edited volume *The Labour Market under New Labour: the State of Working Britain* (2003).

There have been a large number of books on unemployment, but few have dealt with the measures for unemployed people in any depth. Two quite old books which nevertheless sets out the issues about unemployment and policies for the unemployed very well is Sinfield's *What Unemployment Means* (1981) and White's *Against Unemployment* (1991). Dex's *Families and Work in the Twenty-First Century* (2003) is an important source on many of the issues government policies in respect of female employment.

Pitt's *Employment Law* (6th edn. 2007) is recommended on some of the issues about employment regulation. Hantrais' *Social Policy in the European Union* (2007) recommended at the end of Chapter 3 is a valuable source on the issues about the EU explored here.

The Department for Work and Pensions has a website www.dwp.gov.uk. European Union publications can be located via www.europa.eu.int/index_en.htm.

A site that is a good source for recent studies of employment issues is that of the Institute for Employment Studies www.employment-studies.co.uk.

Chapter 7
Health Policy

Introduction

Inevitably, examination of the role and organization of the UK National Health Service (NHS) will be a central part of this chapter on health policy. But it is important to bear in mind that the health of the nation will be influenced by many factors either outside the remit of the NHS or given little attention by that organization. The NHS has been criticized as a 'national illness service', and while governments have attempted to address that problem it is inevitably the case that it is the treatment of identified health problems that is the central preoccupation of state health policy.

This chapter therefore starts with issues about the organizational arrangements for the delivery of NHS services. The exploration of these goes to the heart of contemporary controversy about the National Health Service (NHS), leading on to issues of accountability and the financing of the service. Except where it is essential to explain the current system, readers will be spared a detailed account of the succession of structural changes experienced by the health service since the 1980s.

Governments continually respond to health service problems – service inadequacies and hard to control costs – with structural changes. Yet, many of the concerns about need and rationing, and about the extent to which the service deals effectively with health inequalities, which the later parts of the chapter explore, have to be seen in the context of the changing organizational complexity of the NHS. Conversely, some of the continuing search for the best organizational structure is motivated by a view that this is the key to solving problems of equity. Sceptics may argue that this search for an organizational 'fix' cannot solve a basic underlying problem of under-funding, but the political imperative to seek to provide a good health service at the lowest possible cost inevitably links these two issues together.

The Organization and Management of the National Health Service

The ingredients of the NHS are hospitals, the family or primary care practitioners (doctors, dentists, pharmacists and opticians operating outside the hospitals), and other community-based services (community nursing, health visiting and preventive medicine).

The Secretary of State for Health is responsible for the NHS in England, while in Wales, Scotland and Northern Ireland it is the responsibility of the devolved govern-ments. The detailed description to be provided below is for England alone. The system in Wales is broadly similar. So is it in Northern Ireland, except that in that country health care and social services are integrated. But the Scottish system is a much more integrated one in which Health Boards plan services, manage the hospital system and directly commission general practitioner services.

Hence this section deals only with England. The Secretary of State is assisted by a policy board, which he or she chairs. Then, to deal with operational matters, there is a management board chaired by a chief executive. While this seems to involve a departure from the normal top civil service control structure towards a system which mimics that of a private company, the NHS executive is not a separate agency like the Benefits Agency.

In England, below the NHS executive there are, since 2006, ten Strategic Health Authorities. These have three functions:

- creating a coherent strategic framework
- agreeing annual performance agreements and performance management
- building capacity and supporting performance improvement (Department of Health, 2002)

In addition to the Strategic Health Authorities there are a variety of executive agencies which the Department of Health web site describes as 'arms length bodies' to carry out specific functions: 'inspection and regulation, setting and improving standards and pro-moting public welfare across the entire health and social care system'. Of key impor-tance is the Healthcare Commission which provides an independent scrutiny of clinical governance arrangements in England and Wales. But there is also a variety of agencies with specific functions that the government has decided are most appropriately centralized such as the blood transfusion service (for an account of all these bodies and their varied administrative arrangements see Talbot-Smith and Pollock, 2006, chapter 2).

The next tier below the Strategic Health Authorities is a network of 152 Primary Care Trusts (PCTs). It is their responsibility to secure primary care for the people in their area through contracts with general practitioners and with dentists. They have to make contracts with GPs that allow for this. The PCTs commission secondary care from hospitals, etc. for the patients in their areas. However, the government is seeking to develop ways in which GPs can take on this role. PCTs are also responsible for the oversight of other primary services, from opticians and pharmacists.

The main sources of 'secondary' care services are also called Trusts; organizations responsible for hospitals and other services. There are also Trusts set up specifically to manage ambulance services.

Within the ranks of the hospital Trusts there are what are known as Foundation Trusts, with more autonomy than others. The Department of Health allows high performing hospital Trusts to apply for a greater measure of autonomy. The management of these NHS Foundation Trusts is vested in local people, selected by a complex process from local volunteers. This measure has been attacked as widening rather than reducing the variations in standards within the NHS. It seems unfortunate to see measures to increase autonomy and the capacity to raise extra funds as a reward for good performance, when the pressing need is to raise the standards amongst the poor performers (Pollock, 2004). However, the government has responded that its aim is to eventually enable all provider Trusts to be Foundation Trusts, once it is satisfied that they can maintain adequate standards.

The main providers of primary care remain general medical practitioners (GPs) (see the comments below on dentists, pharmacists and opticians) operating under the contracts provided by the PCTs. Broadly speaking, GPs are free to decide how they will organize their practices, and are free to accept or reject patients. For the patients on their lists they have obligations to provide services (though controversially now not outside normal working hours; the PCTs have to set up contracts with special out of hours services for this). They used to be paid primarily on a 'capitation' basis, so much for each patient on their list, plus an allowance for practice expenses and special payments for various exceptional tasks undertaken. Now there are elaborate contracts rolling together these elements with amounts for the cost of the secondary care which the GPs need to commission.

A note is appropriate here on the use of the concepts of 'contracting' and 'commissioning' in the discussion above. A contract suggests a legally enforceable agreement where breach may lead to action through the courts. Where both parties are public bodies this is not the case. So the strict sense of the term contracts only applies to arrangements with private providers (and the new more independent 'foundation trusts). Otherwise it is perhaps more appropriate to speak of 'commissioning', though this will involve very specific obligations on both sides.

This role of GPs as commissioners of secondary care services is a relatively new one, reached after a variety of experiments with different ways of organizing the relationship between the two tiers. Box 7.1 provides a very abbreviated account

Box 7.1   Contracts and commissioning: an outline of recent history

Some of the issues about the current relationship between primary and secondary care services, and thus that between the two types of Trusts can be better understood if we take a brief excursion back into the reorganization carried out by the Conservatives in the early 1990s. This reorganization split purchasing of services from their provision. The health authorities were purchasers, but only exceptionally direct providers. What this meant was that the health authorities were required to enter into specific contracts to secure the services needed for the patients in their area. The providers which were engaged in this way did not necessarily need to be in the health authority's geographical patch. The providers were organized into 'Trusts'. These Trusts remain the key elements in the secondary care service. Providers can however be private organizations.

The changes made then created what was often described as an 'internal market' or 'quasi-market' system of purchasers of services and providers. This arrangement generated considerable controversy. The case for the internal market was that the separation of purchasers and providers helped to undermine the tendency for those who provide services to exaggerate their value and hide their inefficient aspects. Bureaucratic allocation procedures had been replaced by a system of contracts, giving purchasers the capacity to make choices between providers and to change them if they did not deliver what was required.

The system that actually developed did not measure up to the aspirations of the market advocates. Political and managerial interventions sought to allay some of the anxieties expressed by the opponents of the internal market. It proved to be very much a managed market, with its potential effects on some hospitals and some services damped down (Le Grand et al., 1998).

When Labour came to power it declared, at the outset, that it wanted to end the 'internal market'. However, in changes enacted in 1999, it accepted the idea of a purchaser/ provider split but set out to operate it in a way which would have more stability. It also accepted the idea of GP involvement in secondary care purchase, but was unhappy about the way in which this had been developed as a 'GP fundholder' system operated in parallel with the health authority purchase arrangements. It therefore initiated a process under which PCTs would commission services for their area. But then it shifted ground again, returning to something that has much in common with the fundholder system, with the GP practices as the budget holders overall under PCT supervision.

of the twists and turns of policy since the early 1990s on the organization of the purchaser/provider relationship between primary and secondary care.

Patient Access to Health Services

Access of patients to the health service, except in emergencies, is by way of the primary care practitioners. These practitioners are thus the 'gate keepers' of the service, making judgements about when referral to the more specialized secondary services is appropriate. Direct self-referral is accepted in the event of accidents and emergencies. This tends to increase, therefore, when primary care services are slow to react (notably outside the office hours of primary care providers) or when waiting lists for hospital consultations impose unacceptable delays.

Governments have been at pains to develop mechanisms by which patients can exercise choices in respect of secondary services. The theory is that when referral to secondary care is required patients should be able to secure information about the alternatives available to them (including information on the performance ratings of hospitals and consultants). They should also be able to affect the timing of their own operations (a topic on which more is said below). To increase the feasibility of these objectives the government has ruled that in certain circumstances operations may be commissioned from the private health sector (this sector is discussed further later).

There are three essential problems about the choice agenda:

*   Much hospital admission occurs in circumstances in which there is not time for the exercise of an informed choice. This is obviously the case when admissions are the direct result of accident and emergencies, but also applies when swift action is needed in situations in which life-threatening conditions are identified.
*   With many chronic health problems (for example: heart disease, asthma and many other chest conditions) continuity of care is important, ideally with strong working relationships between primary and secondary care practitioners. While there may be times when 'shopping around' for the best care is appropriate, most of the time stable relationships between practitioners will be important.
*   For many people either their geographical location or their dependence upon the use of public transport for themselves or their relatives (bear in mind that a high proportion of those admitted to hospital are elderly) means that there is no real choice of alternative providers.

The choice model seems to rest on a concept of the patient as a relatively fit, well-informed person exploring the case for cold surgery; a realistic model perhaps in the minds of healthy academics (Le Grand, 2007 in Hills, Le Grand and Piachaud, chapter 7) but hardly appropriate for many NHS patients most in need of care.

It is an inevitable feature of a managed and non-marketized service that difficulties will arise about swiftly matching supply to demand. The main manifestation of an emergent problem of this kind will be the development of a queue, or waiting list. If that queue then persists there are grounds for regarding the service, or part of it, as under-resourced. This issue has been a consistent source of concern for governments for a long while. At various times in the recent past government have adopted policies directed at reducing specific waiting lists through systems of incentives and penalties to provider Trusts. There are, however, problems about a political emphasis on waiting list reduction. Waiting lists are, in many respects, merely a function of administrative practice. There is an easy way to shorten waiting lists, by refraining from putting people on them. Another approach is to terminate an initial wait by a consultation, but that does not necessarily lead immediately on to effective treatment. Using waiting lists as a general index of unmet need will not take into account the fact that some needs are more serious than others. It may be desirable that some people are kept waiting for minor surgery in the interests of securing more rapid responses to life-threatening conditions. Simply concentrating effort on shortening waiting lists may distort the overall service provided.

The government has been concerned about the growth of self-referral to hospitals and the difficulties some people have in securing access to general practitioner services. They have established an organization called 'NHS Direct' to enable people to telephone for medical advice from a team of nurses, who may in emergency be able to activate other services.

Once under hospital care, individuals may be treated as in-patients or out patients. The general notion here is of a hospital-based service for problems that are beyond either the expertise or resources of GPs and other primary care staff. However, the lines are sometimes blurred. Modern health centres can often provide services that are elsewhere provided by hospitals. GPs may undertake minor surgical procedures. The strong emphasis upon the provision of services as cheaply as possible means that governments have encouraged this development. Moreover, even when people are treated in hospital stays are nowadays very short, with many minor operations being carried out without an overnight stay.

Patients have a free choice of dentists and opticians, whom they approach direct. Opticians are paid on a fee-for-service basis. Until recently this was the system for dentistry too. However, there were problems about the setting of a system of remuneration that was administratively straightforward and could be supervised without detailed surveillance of day-to-day activities, while at the same time rewarding most adequately the best practice. Hence the government shifted to a system of contracts in 2005. At the time of writing early indications suggest that since these reforms the supply of NHS dentists has reduced and that there has been an expansion of private insurance in this area. Hence choice is not a characteristic of dental treatment if you are on a low income.

When patients are in hospital necessary drugs will be dispensed there. Outside hospitals prescriptions for medicines normally have to be taken to pharmacists working in private shops, who are remunerated for this work. Exceptionally, in rural areas where shops are hard to access, doctors' surgeries are allowed to provide medicines.

Charges cover much of the cost of spectacles and dental treatment and part of the cost of the supply of drugs and medical appliances. Prescription charges do not have to be paid by hospital in-patients or by children, pregnant women and elderly people. There are means tests that enable low-income people to secure remission of charges. The Welsh Assembly has abolished these charges in their country and the Scottish government plans to follow their example. In the cases of dentistry and optical services these charges are sufficiently high now to mean that those who have to pay the full charges enjoy little benefit from the NHS. Opticians have always been largely private practitioners mixing private with NHS subsidized work, but now this is also the case with much dentistry.

Patients may receive a range of community health services. These include community nursing services, maternity clinics, preventive services offered by doctors and health visitors and measures to prevent the spread of infectious diseases. These are sometimes run by separate Trusts, sometimes organized as part of the work of hospital-based Trusts and sometimes organized by GPs. Box 7.2 gives an example of the thrust of contemporary services towards prevention. There is a particular need

Box 7.2 Community based and 'personalized' preventative services

In the 2004 White Paper *Choosing Health* the government was concerned to demonstrate that the measures laid out were designed in response to public consultation around the levels of state intervention necessitated by public health issues and the priorities in this area of policy. The changes in the approach to public health policy were stated to reflect a shift away from 'top down', paternalistic interference in peoples health behaviour and a better understanding of consumer choice and individual freedom which did not neglect or ignore health inequalities. With its three underpinning principles of 'informed choice', 'personalization' and 'working together' the measures included in the White Paper, such as more trustworthy information for consumers, support for parents to make 'healthy choices' and corporate social responsibility are intended to achieve improvements in the areas of diet and exercise, smoking rates and the effects of passive smoking, sexual health, alcohol consumption and mental health. Many of the provisions identified are area-based initiatives targeted on communities which score highly on indicators of deprivation.

In addition to localized measures to improve public health, other forms of support available nationally are also intended to achieve these aims. Aiming for an improvement in the rate of smoking cessation for example, GPs are able to refer patients to 'Stop smoking clinics' run in local health centres and hospitals which provide individual and group counselling sessions and free prescriptions for aids such as nicotine patches. The short-term success of these programmes is relatively high, but long-term success is more difficult to measure. One of the important elements of the government's

Box 7.2 *(cont'd)*

concern with smoking is child health and this is also a feature of another national policy introduced in 2006, the 'Healthy Start Scheme' which is the twenty-first century version of the welfare food scheme introduced in the 1940s. This is a means-tested voucher scheme that provides help towards the costs of purchasing fruit, vegetables and milk and infant formula milk for parents on low incomes. In 2008 the vouchers were worth £2.80 per week per child under 4 years with an extra voucher for each child under one year. While the vouchers are accepted by many retailers, the problem of stigma (see Chapter 5) associated with schemes such as this is likely to affect take-up, and in fact, a similar scheme for food vouchers introduced for asylum seekers in the 1990s was soon abandoned. Moreover, the governments intention to move away from public health as something that is 'done to the population, for their own good, by impersonal and distant forces in Whitehall' (DoH, 2004, p. 1) seems to have been discarded in this case.

for these services to work closely with local authorities. There are clear overlaps between their concerns and those of social care services authorities (we return to this in Chapter 8, pp. 188–90). Education authorities and schools have concerns about health services for children. There is also a need for liaison with local government services to deal with environmental hazards and community health services.

The Financing of the National Health Service

The NHS is financed out of national taxation. In 2007–8, in England, it is estimated that it will have cost about £90 billion (HM Treasury, 2007). Fifty-eight per cent of the expenditure is on hospital services, 28 per cent on family health services (mainstream primary care) and 12 per cent on community health services. Government expenditure on the NHS in the UK as a whole was 7.1 per cent of GDP in 2005–6 and is expected to be 7.8 per cent of GDP in 2007–8.

Nearly three-quarters of its expenditure is on hospital and community health services, much of the rest on family health services.

Throughout its history, the growth of the cost of the health service to the Exchequer has been a matter of political concern. Demographic changes affecting need, technological changes affecting the quality of treatment, and rising staff costs mean that the cost of the NHS increases without there necessarily being any improvement in the service it provides. Attempts have been made to estimate how much expenditure has to grow each year merely to maintain a consistent level of services to the public. A conservative estimate puts it at 2 per cent, but many suggest that it is nearer 4 or 5 per cent (see the discussion of this difficult, controversial subject in Glennerster and Hills, 1998, chapter 4 and Glennerster, 2003, chapter 4). This is important as part of the explanation of why both the public and NHS practitioners regularly complain about falling standards, supported by concrete evidence from increasing waiting lists for operations, while governments claim they are spending more, in real terms, than ever before on the health service.

Public investment in new hospitals and other health care facilities is kept under strict control by central government, with the Treasury eager to ensure that public sector debt is kept down. The Conservatives developed a device to try to deal with the lack of investment which followed from this control. It allowed Trusts to bring forward, for approval, plans for privately financed developments. What this implied was the new capital investment by the private sector providing facilities then leased to the NHS. In addition support services such as portering, catering and cleaning (but not professional services), might also be leased. Such ventures would be interested in linking other money-making activities with hospital building, for example the inclusion of shops within a hospital complex. Objectors to this 'private finance initiative' were concerned that health policy priorities might be distorted by these ventures, and even that this might be the 'thin end of a wedge' that would lead to health service privatization. Perhaps a more cogent concern still was that this approach to capital underfunding merely shifted costs forward, since health service budgets would become increasingly encumbered by leasing commitments. It might have been expected that a new Labour government would abandon the private finance initiative. This has been far from the case. Its commitment to continue to keep down public sector borrowing coupled with its desire to be seen as the party of health service development has led it to approve many new ventures under the initiative.

At the 1997 election the Labour Party committed itself to maintaining the levels of spending on public services that had been set by their Conservative predecessors. They continued to expect deficiencies in health services to be met by greater efficiency and set a variety of targets for reducing waiting times. Gradually it became evident that under-funding had to be addressed. Glennerster portrays the change of attitude as coming in the following way:

> It was the flu epidemic of Christmas 1999 that triggered an explosion that was really inevitable at some point. Blair presumably saw this. His pledge to raise UK health spending to that of the rest of Europe in January 2000 was highly significant as are the detailed plans for spending the increment that followed in July 2000. (Glennerster, 2001, p. 401)

The detailed plans Glennerster mentions were both a comprehensive spending review by the Chancellor providing for a 27.3 per cent cash increase over three years and a document called *The NHS Plan* (Department of Health, 2000) which set out in detail a range of ways the new money would be spent (including particularly marked improvements in staffing levels), a variety of performance targets and new endeavours to increase efficiency. The restructuring described above represents aspects of the latter, being seen in the plan as 'redesigning' to ensure the enforcement of 'national standards combined with far greater local autonomy', objectives, that in the context of a very prescriptive plan, may be contradictory. The Secretary of State made clear his commitment to breaking down barriers to service efficiency including, controversially, using resources from the private sector where necessary 'to provide NHS patients with the operations they need' (ibid., p. 15).

The commitment to increased spending on the NHS was an important pledge in the general election of 2001. One key event during the campaign was a confrontation about inadequate cancer care, which clearly embarrassed the Prime Minister. The opposition warned that the spending increases could not come without tax increases yet such was the public recognition of the need for NHS improvements that this did no apparent electoral damage to the Labour Party. In the budget of 2002 the Chancellor made a further commitment to continuing the increases in NHS funding. To do this he raised National Insurance contributions (a further indication of the way governments see that as simply another tax, see p. 101). He linked this with some measures of further reform of the mechanisms to control the operation of the NHS, a topic to which we now turn.

Hence since 2002 there have been quite substantial increases in NHS funding. The figures above of expenditure at 7.8 per cent of GDP represent a substantial growth from 5.4 per cent of GDP in 1996–7. In Table 7.1 UK spending is compared with a number of other countries. Our public spending compares unfavourably with that in France, Germany and Sweden. But we appear as a country in which, apparently, people do not spend massively to make up for public services inadequacies.

Despite the recent increases in health service expenditure, in 2006–7 the newspapers were full of stories about hospitals facing budgetary problems and about proposed service cuts. There are competing explanations for this. It may be that expenditure still does not match the level of health problems, in the context of an ageing population. Other explanations include:

- The extent to which in an area of provision where professional services represent a high proportion of the costs, and those professions can to some extent influence their own deployment, it is inevitable that a significant proposition of any new

Table 7.1   UK health expenditure as a % of GDP compared with that in other countries (based on OECD data for 2004)

Countries	Public health expenditure	Private health expenditure
UK	7.1	1.2
Canada	6.9	3.0
Germany	8.5	2.4
France	8.3	2.3
Japan	6.5	1.5
Netherlands	5.7	3.5
Sweden	7.7	1.4
United States	6.9	8.5
OECD countries average	6.4	2.5

Source: OECD (2007) table HE2.1.

funds will go into raising the rewards accruing to those staff. Indeed since one of the concerns has been with staff shortages – particularly in nursing – pay increases are amongst the devices required to address the NHS's problems.

- In the context of a situation in which health service provision is changing, with the length of hospitals stays falling and more and more services being provided in the community, a shift of actual arrangements will be difficult. Inefficiencies will arise as delays occur in closing facilities, and of course the public will be more aware of the services they are losing than of those they are gaining.
- To ensure that resources are used efficiently, and to manage service change, the funding of services is being shifted to one in which attention is given to the actual costs of specific items of care (including operations) and resources are being made available on the basis of the specific expectation of need for those items. This generates a situation in which higher cost providers are being squeezed (whether legitimately or not is of course a matter for debate from case to case).

If the items in that list sound like a defence of the government that is not the intention. The politics of NHS finance involves a continual tension between centralized efforts to rationalize the whole system, balancing resources and need across the country (a topic to which we return below) and local political demands (see Box 7.3). What are, from a national perspective, health service rationalizations are from a local point of view often attacks on cherished services (even sometimes hospital closures) that will be hotly fought by local politicians. Whether or not the NHS is still relatively under-funded it is important to recognize that there are complex change processes going on that need attention before we jump to the simple conclusion that every local funding crisis is simply a manifestation of under-funding. In any case the politics of the NHS will always be a politics of competing priorities for the use of resources that are not infinite.

Box 7.3　Hospital reorganization

Students may want to examine battles over these issues in the area where they live, and the arguments used on both sides. Both of the authors are aware of disputes across 2006–8 in their areas. In the Chesterfield area there are battles about a planned rationalization of maternity services which would see them disappear altogether from one cottage hospital in Matlock which serves many villages in west Derbyshire, pressure for home births in outlying rural areas and midwives on call for huge geographical areas. A similar conflict is occurring on the south coast which will leave a big gap in hospital maternity services between Brighton and Hastings. In that area also planned closures of accident and emergency services have also been the subject of a bitter dispute, potentially subjecting accident victims to long journeys on busy roads into Brighton or Worthing from the smaller towns in their vicinity, including the county town of Chichester.

Management and Professional Accountability

All over the world, health services have largely been set up on terms dictated by doctors (this is often described as being 'provider led'). Doctors have been closely involved in the politics of the creation of state health care systems, often securing organizational arrangements that suited them as a profession. They have acquired high financial rewards and they have secured positions of power from which to influence the day-to-day running of services. In doing all this, they have defined good health, health care needs and the responsibilities of health services in ways which put them in a central and indispensable role (Friedson, 1970; Moran and Wood, 1993). As people and politicians have begun to demand more control over health services, and as it has become increasingly recognized that it is difficult to control the costs of 'provider led' services, so efforts to curb medical power have assumed a central place on health policy reform agendas.

Until the 1980s, the managerial arrangements for the NHS could have been described as broadly 'collegial': that is, the various professionals within the service were represented in the management structure. Then, after 1983, each administrative unit was required to appoint a general manager, on a fixed-term contract. Many of these general managers were already health service administrators, but there were appointments from outside and, in a few cases, senior professionals, particularly doctors, but occasionally nurses, received these posts. These managers were accountable to the relevant appointed authorities. Then, under the changes enacted in 1990, the health authorities were restructured to comprise up to five 'executive members', to include the chief executive and the finance director, and five non-executive members (including a non-executive chairperson). Non-executive members were appointed by the secretary of state. Trusts are required to have similar management structures.

However, it is necessary to look beyond these 'board room' levels to examine the main issues about the roles of doctors and managers Hospital doctors have traditionally exercised a considerable degree of autonomy. Crucial for this is the concept of clinical freedom, which can be effectively extended from a right to determine the treatment of individual patients to a right to plan the pattern of care as a whole. The managerial arrangements adopted in the 1990s, and the significance of the contracting system for patterns of work, have been seen by some to threaten that freedom (Harrison and Pollitt, 1994). It is difficult to say how significant that threat is, since much depends on the internal management arrangements made within the Trusts. There is a requirement to have a medical member of the hospital Trust executive. This may place one doctor in a strong position; but alternatively, he or she may be seen merely as a figurehead to represent the consultant group as a whole, without disturbing individual autonomy.

Hospital consultants may be part-time appointees, who combine private practice with NHS work. Junior hospital doctors, below consultant status, are organized in consultant-led teams. Most of them are in short-term appointments, which are seen as building blocks of trainee experience leading to consultant status. There are problems of relatively low pay, heavy duties and insecurity for junior doctors, enhanced by difficulties in advancing to consultancies.

At the same time the funding of hospital work has become governed by the use of a system of 'payment for results' in which model costs have been identified and used for reimbursement for 'health resource groups' (HRGs). Hence Trusts will be aware of circumstances in which the activities of their medical staff incur costs out of line with these norms.

The government sees the involvement of doctors in the managerial and monitoring arrangements for the service rather than the imposition of hierarchical controls as crucial for increasing public accountability of doctors, and other professional staff. Key aspects of its strategy are:

- to involve Trusts in the shaping of their local Health Improvement Programmes
- to ensure that explicit quality standards are set in local agreements
- to involve professional staff in the design of service agreements
- to develop a system of 'clinical governance'

The concept of 'clinical governance' (see also Box 7.4) requires that the processes that are currently used in the NHS to try to improve the quality of clinical work are integrated with quality planning for the Trusts (and ultimately the NHS) as a whole. An earlier measure was a requirement that systems of 'clinical audit' should be set up in each Trust to review clinical work, but this was criticized as being a private review process within the medical profession, which individual doctors do not always take seriously and for which there is no system of external accountability. Now this

Box 7.4   Clinical governance

Clinical governance is another attempt by government to bring about significant shifts in the way that medical staff conceive of their work and hence bring about substantial change in relations within clinical settings. For it to be successful there will need to be major investments in information systems, and programmes to increase clinical effectiveness. The government describe it as 'a partnership between the Government and the clinical professions. In that partnership, the Government does what only the Government can do and the professions do what only they can do' (Department of Health, 1998a, para 1.13). It goes on to argue (para 3.9): 'Clinical governance requires partnerships within health care teams, between health professionals (including academic staff) and managers, between individuals and the organizations in which they work and between the NHS, patients and the public.'

Sceptics may feel that this is merely another attempt by the government to convince the public that it has clinical autonomy under control. However, it does seem to involve a much more explicit attempt to integrate professional accountability with managerial accountability in the NHS.

is tied in much more to the system of clinical governance. There are also requirements that better use should be made of what the profession calls 'evidence-based
practice', with wider dissemination of new examples of good practice. A National
Institute for Health and Clinical Excellence has been set up to provide an independent
scrutiny of clinical governance arrangements in England and Wales, to promote clinical effectiveness and to produce and to disseminate clinical guidelines.

In 1999 the government established the Commission for Health Improvement to
provide an independent scrutiny of clinical governance arrangements in England and
Wales. This body, managed by an appointed board, was set up to carry out a rolling
programme of reviews of quality of patient care in every health authority and Trust.
It was also expected to conduct studies of specific parts of the health service's work
and responds to requests for investigations of services that are causing concern. In
2004 it had its remit widened to include an additional range of inspection duties and
a key role in the investigation of complaints and became the Commission for Health
Care Audit and Inspection (generally called the Healthcare Commission).

This section has explored some of the efforts being made to deal with the extent
to which it has been seen as problematical that the NHS tends to be 'provider led'.
Central to this activity has been a search by governments of ways to provide better
value for the public whilst minimizing increases in costs. But perhaps they have
expected too much; perhaps the central problem is that the UK has an underfunded
health service.

Need and the Rationing of the Health Service

The main medical services provided by British health service are, broadly speaking,
free and universally available. The general issues raised by the absence of a price
mechanism to convert needs into effective demands will be discussed in the next
chapter (pp. 190–3). One of the political preoccupations ever since the founding of
the NHS has been the difficulty about how to respond to need.

There seem to be two crucial problems that were given insufficient attention by
those, in the 1940s, who forecasted a decline in need for health services once the
NHS was in place. One is that everyone whose life is saved, lives on to become ill
again. More precisely, increases in life expectancy bring with them the likelihood of
increased work for the service in dealing with chronic illnesses. Such illness is concentrated amongst older people. Over-65s were only about 11 per cent of the population in 1951; they now constitute about 14 per cent of the population. Over 3 per
cent of the population are over 80. The growth in the proportion of older people has
temporarily stopped, but will start again just after 2010, as the post-Second World
War baby boom population begins to reach 65. However it is important not to exaggerate the implications of this; the fact that older people are living longer is an indicator that they are healthier and most critical health care episodes are concentrated
at the very end of life, at whatever age that occurs.

The other problem in predicting need for health services arises from difficulties in
defining need. There is a growing understanding that the relationship between having

a medical need and seeking medical attention is complex and obscure. Individuals may experience considerable suffering from a condition that manifests no pathological abnormality. Conversely, they may have serious medical problems, yet experience little suffering. Perhaps more significantly in quantitative terms, minor deviations from 'good health' are tolerated by many people for long periods of time without medical attention being sought. This applies, for example, to problems like indigestion, recurrent headaches and skin complaints. It is important to recognize that 'Illness is the subjective state which is experienced by an individual, a feeling of ill-being. Disease is a pathological condition recognized by indications agreed among biomedical practitioners' (Stacey, 1988, p. 171).

The definitions of illness provided by 'biomedical practitioners' are no more valid than people's subjective judgements. They are subject to variation over time and between 'experts', and are conditional on the dominant paradigms in medical knowledge. They are, however, crucial in influencing demand for health services. This is the sense in which there may be a problem for health services about 'producer'-determined demand, deriving from 'biomedical practitioners' claims to competence and, in some circumstances, their tendency – encouraged by public faith in medicine – to 'medicalize' social problems.

There is a choice between the policy conclusions to be drawn from these findings. One is that a great deal more should be spent on the health service, and, in particular, that many more efforts should be made to screen for unidentified illness in the population at large. The quite opposite view is that the fact that many people manage without medical treatment for many complaints suggests that those who do 'bother' doctors with similar problems should be encouraged to become more self-reliant and to make more use of self-medication. A less extreme version of this view suggests that, since medical resources are clearly limited, it is important to control access to the services in such a way that the more serious complaints are treated, while doctors are not overburdened with the trivial. The development of NHS Direct (see p. 153) is a step towards the examination of the idea that access to health services may be channelled, and implicitly controlled, in other ways. Increasing attention is being given, as with NHS Direct, to the use of nurses rather than doctors as 'gatekeepers' for the service as a whole, engaging in initial diagnosis and authorized to provide or prescribe various medicines and treatments.

Another issue on the agenda is the exclusion of some kinds of treatments from the NHS; for example, one much-debated example is the treatment of infertility. There are also issues about the use of medicines that are being given attention, limiting use of expensive drugs when there are cheaper equivalents or their therapeutic properties are not regarded as having been clearly established.

There have been suggestions that there are ways of controlling demand by pushing the responsibility for it back to the patients. This provides one argument for the exploration of the case for 'cost sharing' charging systems to control demands on the service. One possibility that has been debated is the introduction of 'hotel charges' for hospital stays. The problem with this is that stays are becoming shorter. The administrative costs of billing and collecting charges for the many very short stays would be considerable. Further complications would be introduced if, as with prescriptions, some patients were not required to pay. Similarly, considerations apply to another idea: flat rate charges for consultations with GPs.

A case for health service charges is also argued in terms of the desirability of choice and competition. This case has been made most cogently in the USA by Friedson (1970), who sees the power of the consumer as enhanced by a relationship with the doctor in which he or she has the capacity to 'hire or fire'. In Friedson's view, the British model of health service organization places individuals in a very weak position in dealing with doctors, and provides the community at large with an absence of weapons for bargaining with a medical profession that would not be so united were doctors in competition with each other.

The fundamental point in favour of a free service is that charges may deter people from seeking necessary help. This is particularly likely to be the case with people on low incomes. Moreover, one of the effects of ill health is naturally to reduce income and to increase other costs. Clearly also, while in other areas of life people may be expected to make choices between different ways of spending money, serious illness leaves little choice. Individuals will bankrupt themselves to save their lives and those of their loved ones.

Where much of the health service is still 'in the marketplace', as, for example, in the USA, the issues are rarely actually quite as stark as these. There are two reasons why not. One is that many people insure themselves against sickness. The other is that a 'safety net' means-tested medical system exists for the poor. Arguments in favour of a free service must therefore deal with the weaknesses of these two alternative forms of provision.

The key problems with private insurance schemes are that they will not insure the 'bad risks'; they often exclude some conditions (especially preventable ones – for example, pregnancy); and they may collapse. These schemes may reduce the powers of doctors, making them dependent on the patronage of the insurance agencies; but the latter often encounter the same problems of provider-determined need as the British system has been alleged to suffer from. Moreover, they do not necessarily curb trivial demands, since subscribers may be determined to obtain their money's worth. In the 1980s, the case for an insurance-based approach to health care re-emerged on the British political agenda. Private insurance schemes had grown rapidly, facilitating the growth of private hospitals. Debate developed, therefore, about the extension of such schemes nation-wide. Those advocating such an approach argue that individuals should be required to insure themselves privately, and that the state should underwrite such schemes and make special means-tested provision for those for whom they cannot cater. This approach was given serious attention by the Conservatives in their review of policy before their 1990 changes to the system. The creation of a tier of potentially autonomous providers (the Trusts) opened the way for such a development.

The problems with a means-tested health service are the requirement of a test of means before treatment, the likelihood of situations in which individuals will have to abandon resources - or wait to 'hit the bottom' - before they can ask for treatment, and the probability that (as was the case in the UK when such a system operated) two classes of health service will result. In the last resort, as implied above, the case for a free service is not that it helps to distribute resources from the rich to the poor, but that it enables the healthy to support the sick. If it is believed, on the other hand, that it is in the interests of the evolution of society that the 'weak should go to the wall', it will of course be comparatively easy to take an alternative view.

Whilst arguments for a shift towards a system of wholly or partly private health insurance are now less widely heard in the UK, another idea that has gained ground as a response to the problem of under-funding has been that the NHS should be specifically funded out of a health tax (Le Grand, 2001). It is suggested that whilst people are resistant to general tax rises they may accept them when they see them as clearly linked to service improvement. The problem with this argument is that it would then encourage those who have private insurance or purchase private health care to argue that they should not pay the tax, thereby opening the door to a greater drift towards privatization and a two-tier health system. Also, if there is a case for earmarked funding for health then why not for other public services, such as education, opening up a lot more complicated issues about the relationship between taxation and public spending.

Hence the debate about the level of funding needed to sustain a satisfactory NHS runs on. As noted above, at the time of writing the injection of new money has been quite considerable. Whether it is enough remains to be seen. Meanwhile improvements to the service as a consequence of that new money may be quite slow to emerge. Inasmuch as staff shortages are a central part of the problem, it will take a long while to see a change since many of the key people, this is particularly true of doctors, take a long while to train. At the same time, cynics argue that much of the new money may simply contribute to pay increases for the current staff, without necessarily increasing recruitment.

Equality of Treatment: the Impact of the Private Sector

In the atmosphere of concern about rising health service costs and advocacy of privatization by the Right, there is considerable concern in Britain about two related issues: the most appropriate relationship between the health service and the residual private medical sector, and the extent to which the health service provides equality of treatment to all the population.

These two issues are related, since the diversion of medical resources into a private sector, largely accessible only to the better off, reduces the resources available to other sectors of the population. However, the defenders of private medicine argue that the resources involved are, in a sense, extra ones, which would not necessarily be diverted into public medicine in an entirely nationalized sector. Particular bones of contention, however, have been not so much the right of the private sector to exist, as the support that sector receives from a variety of special links with the health service.

It is difficult to achieve a precise estimate of the size of the private sector. Around 7 million people in the UK have private health insurance (National Statistics, 2002, p. 143), but this does not mean they will be not also be users of the public sector.

Box 7.5 The erosion of free health care?

As noted in the text the government's view is that private resources and private providers can strengthen the service provided by the NHS. Alongside the argument as to whether this is actually the case, since private services are not necessarily cheaper and phenomena like the private finance initiative is pushing up health costs in the long run, is a more complex argument about the ultimate impact of these developments. The government takes a stance in various public services that so long as the state is paying the provider can be anyone. The challenge to that logic is that if an extensive network of private providers builds up (including foreign providers like the big American health care companies) they will be able to dictate terms to the purchasers. A stronger private network of providers would be better able than they are now to sell private services. In a context then of a mix of public and private services it would be easy for a government to shift to means-testing, only paying for those unable to get private insurance or pay for themselves. Not only is it the case that the United States offers such a model, so also does the UK's own social care system.

Most people use public sector GPs, using insurance to secure themselves easier access to secondary services.

Both GPs and consultants are able to take on private patients as well as health service ones, and NHS Trusts may offer private services for patients from home or abroad. The private finance initiative, discussed on page 156, may further encourage this. Similarly it has been noted (see p. 152) that the government is encouraging the purchase of services from private providers as a way of reducing pressure on public services. While the government argues that this is just enabling the NHS to obtain services - at lower cost or where public providers are unavailable - such arrangements may implicitly subsidize the private sector, and may be the thin end of a wedge leading to the transformation of the free health service (Pollock, 2004). Box 7.5 explains how such a process might occur.

NHS resources have always tended to support private medicine. Hardly anyone in the UK uses only the private sector. What most typically happens is that people with private insurance use NHS GPs, then when secondary services are regarded as unsatisfactory or cannot be easily accessed (there is a 'queue' for scarce beds) they secure referrals to the private sector. That sector specializes in 'cold surgery'; it is not equipped to deal with emergencies or with some of the most complicated and/or life threatening situations. Private hospitals are able to turn to the public sector (since after all every citizen has a right to NHS services) when they encounter problems beyond their resources or emergencies in the course of their work.

The way in which doctors with both public and private work distribute their time between the two may also result in subsidy to the latter, in that they may neglect

NHS duties to enhance fee earning. There is a substantial hidden subsidy from public to private medicine because doctors are trained in the NHS, and much medical research is publicly funded.

To sum up, the growth of private insurance raises the question of the overall impact on the state service of alternative ones. Is there scope here for desirable competition? Is it a valuable addition to consumer choice, enabling people who are so inclined to pay a little extra for a superior service? Or does it threaten the basic service, and reduce its capacity to meet the needs of all?

Equality of Treatment: Inequalities in Health and Medical Treatment

The health service's capacity to meet need has been subjected to extensive scrutiny. Epidemiological studies of the differential impact of mortality and morbidity have been of importance here. These show considerable differences in the experience of ill health between different regions of the country, between different social classes and between different ethnic groups (Townsend et al., 1988; Acheson, 1998). More challengingly for the NHS, as mortality rates have declined overall, these differences have not decreased; indeed, in many cases, they have increased. Particular attention has been given to what is termed 'premature' mortality. While this applies throughout life it can be most clearly identified in the first year of life, in relation to infant mortality rates. Table 7.2 shows two things: (1) a social class differential in respect of infant mortality (2) evidence that, despite the fall in mortality over time, the differential is widening rather than narrowing.

There is similarly evidence of health disadvantages amongst minority ethnic groups. One very disturbing statistic reported by *The NHS Plan* (Department of Health, 2000) is that 'children of women born in Pakistan are twice as likely to die in their first year of life than children of women born in the UK' (p. 108). Such indices in many respects reflect socio-economic differences between ethnic groups, but there are also issues about the quality of service minorities receive. A report on *The Future of Multi-Ethnic Britain* speaks of a 'striking paradox':

Table 7.2   Death in the first year of life by social class 1978–9 and 2001

Social class	Rate 1978–9	Rate 2001
I	9.8	3.6
II	10.1	3.6
III (non manual)	11.1	4.5
III (manual)	12.4	5.0
IV	13.6	6.1
V	17.2	7.2
Other	23.3	7.1
Ratio V/I	1.8	2.0

Source: Flaherty, Veit-Wilson and Dornan, CPAG, 2004, table 4.1, p. 125, drawing on a mixture of government data sources.

The NHS depends, and for several decades has depended, on the contributions of Asian, black and Irish doctors, nurses, managers and ancillary staff. At the same time, patterns of mortality and morbidity are more serious in Asian, black and Irish communities than in the population as a whole, and there is much insensitivity in the NHS to the distinctive experiences, situations and requirements of these communities. (Parekh, 2000, p. xix)

Regional differences will also to a large extent reflect social class differences. Inequalities of health have been found between different localities, down to quite small areas. Such work has shown differences which it is possible to correlate with other indices of deprivation (including environmental factors) (Thomas and Dorling, 2007).

The policy questions this evidence raises obviously concern the extent to which these differentials are attributable to differences in the availability of health services. But it must also be asked, inasmuch as they are attributable to other factors (low income, poor housing and so on), to what extent can better health services offset these disadvantages?

A government committee, chaired by a former Chief Medical Officer (Acheson, 1998) in their examination of these issues, suggest that the key questions that remain are about the extent to which sufficient services are available to those groups particularly likely to have poor health. They note (ibid., p. 112):

Access to effective primary care is influenced by several supply factors: the geographical distribution and availability of primary care staff, the range and quality of primary care facilities, levels of training, education and recruitment of primary care staff, cultural sensitivity, timing and organization of services to the communities served, distance and the affordability of safe means of transport.

The Acheson committee argue that many deprived areas have difficulty in recruiting GPs and other primary care staff, and that there are many poorly equipped primary care practices in deprived areas, particularly in parts of inner London (Acheson, p. 116). In *The NHS Plan* (Department of Health, 2000, p. 107) the government points out that primary care service inequities have been excluded from attention in the formulae governing NHS resource allocation (see the discussion below):

Instead, the Medical Practices Committee (MPC) has sought to ensure the fair distribution of GPs across the NHS, with only limited success. For example there are 50 per cent more GPs in Kingston and Richmond or Oxfordshire than there are in Barnsley or Sunderland after adjusting for the age and needs of their respective populations.

They promise action to deal with this, seeing it as one of the issues to be tackled with the abolition of the MPC and the setting up of a new Medical Education Standards Board.

Overall the Acheson committee suggest (p. 112) that 'Communities most at risk of ill health tend to experience the least satisfactory access to the full range of preventative services, the so-called – "inverse care law" '. They suggest that evidence on secondary services is more difficult to interpret, indicating a need for better monitoring (p. 112), but they also note continuing inequalities in the allocation of funds for hospital and community health services. This emphasis is echoed by *The NHS Plan* (Department of Health, 2000, p. 107).

Back in 1974, the government set up a Resource Allocation Working Party (RAWP) to develop a formula to facilitate comparisons between the resource needs of different regions. This used population estimates, weighted to take into account differential mortality, and different utilization rates based on differences in the age and the structure of the population. Allocation of new money to the then existing 'regions' was based on the RAWP formula, and allocations by regions to districts were based on similar principles. This proved a difficult, controversial exercise in light of the inadequacy of the statistics available, the difficulties in relating such data to needs, and the uncertainty about the relationship between costs and effectiveness. The 1990 changes brought the RAWP procedure to an end; some of the problems that it had had to deal with in relation to 'flows' of patients across boundaries were solved by the contracting procedure. The allocation of money to health authorities was then based on population numbers weighted to take into account some of the considerations about differential needs.

While the new world of contracts and decentralized budgets changed the allocation process the issue remains a live one. The considerations embodied in RAWP remain relevant and affect current allocations to PCTs and GP practices, with implicit 'knock on' implications for secondary care.

While efforts to tackle some of the problems of 'territorial injustice' that have beset the NHS since its foundation have been widely welcomed, there are some other issues about the availability of services that require attention. As suggested in the references to the Acheson report quoted above, social class differentials in the use of health services suggest that efforts need to be made not only to ensure that adequate resources are available in underprivileged areas, but also to facilitate access to the use of those resources by all in need. This raises policy questions about the siting of surgeries and hospitals, the arrangements made by doctors to enable patients to secure appointments, the extent of the use of health service personnel – such as health visitors – who actively seek out those in need of health care, the extent of health education, and the significance of screening services.

Finally, these questions lead on to the other question raised: the extent to which there might be an expectation that health services should be better in some areas, or for some people, to help to compensate for other social disadvantages. Alternatively, to what extent should the concept of a state health service embrace a responsibility to point out how other social factors contribute to ill health? The Acheson report, as a product of an independent enquiry commissioned by the Secretary of State for Health, is an important step forward in indicating the wide policy agenda that has to be addressed if health inequalities are to be reduced. The issues considered in Chapter 5 on the growth of poverty, and the slow progress being made in efforts to reverse that trend are clearly enormously relevant here. So are the issues about the prevention of unemployment considered in Chapter 6. The same is true of the incidence of homelessness and poor housing to be considered in Chapter 10. Other aspects of this topic are explored further in the next section.

Health Policy or Illness Policy?

At the very beginning of this chapter it was stated that it is important to bear in mind that the health of the nation will be influenced by many factors which may not be given attention by the NHS. Reference was made to the criticism of the NHS as a 'national illness service'. In *The NHS Plan* (Department of Health, 2000, chapter 13) this issue is examined, stressing the government's concerns about inequalities in health and its commitment to the prevention of ill health. It is fair to say that these issues have been given increased attention by the NHS in recent years. GPs have been encouraged to provide health checks for their patients and develop health advice programmes.

There are a number of interrelated approaches to the prevention of ill health, many of them going beyond the simple questions about the provision of health services. Ever since it was recognized that uncontrolled effluents from domestic and industrial premises could be a cause of ill health there have been governmental responses to these problems. In the nineteenth century local authorities were pioneers of measures to improve the environment, their efforts reinforced by a range of public health legislation. When direct responsibilities for health services were taken away from local government, a process finally completed in 1974, a split system was developed to deal with public health issues. Local authorities remained responsible for inspection, data collection and basic preventative action against public health nuisances, and were able to draw upon the services of medical public health specialists employed by the health authorities. The environmental health officers of the unitary and lower-tier local authorities remain the lynchpins of the system, with powers to inspect shops and restaurants, regulate markets, take preventative actions against the spread of infections and deal with effluents from some industrial processes. At the same time the more complex forms of pollution from industry and agriculture are regulated by central government through agencies answerable to the Department for Environment, Food and Rural Affairs, in particular the Environment Agency and the Food Standards Agency. There is a large and complex body of legislation dealing with these issues, which cannot be examined in any detail here. Nowadays the European Union also plays a key role in the advancement of the environmental health agenda. The approach to these issues in the UK obviously requires collaboration between central and local government and the NHS. Characteristically it involves a combination of powers to deal swiftly with the most obvious abuses and a rather more cautious, often essentially educative, approach to emergent problems. The system is often seen as too slow, and too ready to see the point of view of the producer.

In many respects the traditional approach to public health was to see it as only concerned with serious dangers. A liberal ideology saw many matters of consumption to be matters for free choice. Note, for example, the slow and still limited official responses to evidence on health hazards from smoking and drinking. A recognition of the nation's economic dependence upon manufacturing and commerce inhibited drastic action. In any case the health of the nation steadily improved over the twentieth century. There are good grounds for regarding growing national prosperity as more important for health improvement that medical development (McKeown, 1980). It is only over the past twenty to thirty years that many of the more subtle and complex dangers to human health have begun to be recognized. Health improvement has been seen to be less than it could have been. Unexpected health hazards have emerged, from pesticides or from food additives for example. Accordingly a 'green' agenda has emerged, challenging complacency about the institutions ostensibly there to protect us, and showing the need to improve capacity to identify risks for current and future generations. That agenda recognizes both the need for individual action in respect of consumption choices and for official action to curb health hazards and to try to modify behaviour (Huby, 1998; Cahill, 2002).

Governments have responded to the public health implications of this new agenda with a combination of tightened regulation, increased recognition of a role for the NHS in relation to health improvement, and an emphasis upon health education. It is very difficult to measure the impact of government interventions, while some regulatory measures have been adopted much government action has consisted of providing information and advice, and making health checks easier to obtain from GPs. Yet life-style options are influenced by income and environment, constraining choices. They may also be influenced by the practices of the food and drink industry, the additives they use and the things their advertisements promote. Other aspects of our living and working environments may be quite outside our control. It may be argued that governments could embrace more boldly their regulatory responsibilities to help to protect our health. Box 7.6 illustrates an initiative of this kind, highlighting some of the contradictions in this policy area.

The Representation and Protection of the Public

When the formation of the NHS was debated in the years before 1948, many doctors made clear their opposition to local government control. While some community services were kept within local government between 1948 and 1974, the main forms chosen for the local control of the health service were hybrid organizations in which ministerial appointees served alongside local authority nominees. Since 1991, the arrangements for direct local government representation on health service governing bodies have disappeared. Elected public representation is therefore only at the national government level.

The choice agenda sees the public as able to influence policy through choice (and the privatization agenda goes even further in seeing markets as the best policy influence device). The separation of commissioning and providing could facilitate the development of a new approach to the issue of democratic control. However the decision by the government to give the commissioning role to GP practices under

Box 7.6   Public health and consumer choice – the case of school dinners

Since the airing of a series of programmes following a TV chef's attempts to influence the content of school dinners in 2005, the content and cost of food provided in schools in the UK has been the subject of intense debate leading to an injection of government funding and several publications by the (then) Department for Education and Skills (DfES) and OFSTED and the setting up of the School Food Trust to improve the quality of provision. Criticisms of school meals identified problems with facilities such as the lack of kitchens in many small primary schools, poor general canteen facilities and a reduction in lunch breaks which do not allow sufficient time for the delivery and consumption of meals. In addition, questions were raised as to the poor nutritional content of meals and unimaginative approach to school catering. In 2006 and 2007, provisions for the banning of 'junk food' in schools and the restriction of menus were introduced. Falling levels of school meals take-up were reported for 2005–7 (School Food Trust, 2007) which may be partly due to adverse publicity or, as some have suggested, an unwillingness on the part of children to change their eating habits. However, the cost of school meals has also been increasing year on year, and there is parental concern over value for money. On average less than one third of the amount paid per primary school child is actually spent on ingredients, but at the same time the School Food Trust report that due to food and labour cost increases, meals provision is not a profitable activity and is mostly subsidized by local authorities and schools themselves. In the immediate period following the regulatory changes, the revenue of one catering company was affected to the extent that its parent company withdrew from many schools contracts and a developing problem is that the introduction of new standards has resulted in catering companies failing to re-tender for schools contracts despite their value (one of the largest in England is for £9m) citing them as 'unprofitable'. What this case illustrates is the clash of policy objectives that the government needs to reconcile – the fall-out from a programme of contracting-out of public services which relies on private companies' perceptions of profitability set against both public health and child welfare aims.

the supervision of the unelected PCTs means that suggestions that there could be democratic control of commissioning have been ignored.

There is clearly an issue here about the feasibility of other ways of involving the public in health policy making and implementation in addition to simple participation in national politics. Between 1974 and 2005 there was one institutional device

Box 7.7   Community health councils

An interesting innovation in 1974 was the setting up of locally based community health councils (CHCs) to enable the public viewpoint to be expressed. However, the status of these bodies was that of officially recognized and subsidized pressure groups, with rights to make representations and to seek information. Such power as they had primarily rested on their capacity to embarrass health authorities. Even in relation to this weapon, they had an awkward choice to make, between seeking a close day-to-day working relationship, which might inhibit its use, and remaining more aloof, but thereby losing opportunities to secure information and to make informal representations. They also had difficult choices to make between concentration on individual grievances, the passing on of views of all kinds from the local groups which formed their 'constituency', and the development of a carefully documented, informed critique of the service. Their low resources exacerbated these choice problems.

CHCs were not themselves representative bodies in any of the senses in which that term is used in democratic theory. Half their members were appointed by local authorities, one-sixth by the Department of Health; the remainder were elected by relevant voluntary organizations (by means of rather haphazard election processes which did nothing to ensure that they were representative of the patients in their areas).

There does, however, seem to be good grounds for arguing that the relatively simple system for patient consultation and support is being replaced by very complex arrangements that may baffle patients.

to do this: local Community Health Councils. Box 7.7 describes these now defunct organizations. While they were always modestly funded weak organizations there are grounds for doubts whether what has replaced them is any better.

There are complicated arrangements for the consultation of the public. There is a central Commission for Patient and Public Involvement in Health and a requirement that every Trust should set up a Patients' Forum. There are separate arrangements to assist people with complaints, a Patients Advocacy and Liaison Service. Complaints against health service Trusts have to be formally investigated, using a new procedure organized by the Healthcare Commission.

Finally local governments are given a small role - as sorts of quasi-official pressure groups. 'Scrutiny committees' formed from the ranks of elected members may investigate local health issues.

For many members of the public, what matters more than representation is protection from abuse and malpractice, and the chance to be heard when dissatisfied with the service provided. Apart from the general opportunities to make representations, which apply to all the public services, there are, for the health service, a number of special procedures available. Practitioners and hospitals may be sued for negligence, and professional malpractice may result in debarment from practice by the relevant professional organization.

Conclusions

Long ago, an American student of the NHS (Lindsey, 1962), described it as 'something magnificent in scope and breathtaking in its implications'. He went on to say (p. 474):

> In the light of past accomplishments and future goals, the Health Service cannot very well be excluded from any list of notable achievements of the twentieth century. So much has it become a part of the British way of life, it is difficult for the average Englishman to imagine what it would be like without those services that have contributed so much to his physical and mental well-being.

That expresses rather well the peculiar mixture of utopian expectations and of taking the service for granted that gives a slightly exaggerated quality to UK discussions of policy issues in the health service.

We have expectations of the service that often go quite beyond any capacity to deliver results. We oscillate wildly, therefore, between pride in our system and disquiet about its waiting lists and overcrowded wards. We put doctors on a pedestal as the experts who dominate the system, and we are angry about their arrogant presumptions. We demand more and more from the service, and we worry that we are perhaps becoming a nation of hypochondriacs who can too easily make demands on it. These mixed emotions colour the reactions of both politicians and the public to the main policy dilemmas that inevitably confront the service.

Undoubtedly, a public approach to medicine involving disproportionate expectations about its capacity to solve the problems of suffering and death lies at the root of some of our difficulties in putting health policies in context and coming to terms with the strengths and weaknesses of our health service. There are signs, however, that a 'demystification of medicine' is beginning to occur. This is helping us to assess, much more realistically, decisions about the allocation of resources between the hospital service and the community services, and between the health service and other public policies. Some of these issues have been considered in this chapter.

We are beginning to ask whether we have not so far been too ready to delegate decisions involving moral questions as well as medical questions to professional practitioners. We are beginning to achieve a better understanding of the extent to which many of the determinants of the health of the nation have little to do with the quality and nature of its clinical medical services. Yet the debate about these issues is inevitably conducted in the shadow of concerns about the continuing rise of health care costs. Questions about what the NHS cannot, and should not have to, be considered in a context dominated by questions about what the NHS can afford to do.

It is all too easy to pillory the NHS for its shortcomings. Of course it is in need of improvement, but it remains a surviving monument to its socialist founder, Aneurin Bevan, who said 'A free health service is a triumphant example of the superiority of collective action and public initiative applied to a segment of society where commercial principles are seen at their worst' (1952, p. 85). That 'superiority' can only be sustained if the NHS is adequately funded. Contemporary Labour politicians have tended to brush aside anxieties about the various ways privatization is occurring, arguing that it is a *publicly funded* system that is no longer dogmatic about the need for *public providers*. Yet the strengthening of private providers, and the increasing compromising of the autonomy of public ones through the contracting out of services and the Public Finance Initiative, can be seen as the thin end of a wedge. These developments make it easier for the advocates of private health care to try to move the system in a hybrid direction of a kind like the social care system to be described in the next chapter.

Suggestions for Further Reading

The are several textbooks on health policy. One long-lasting one is Ham's *Health Policy in Britain* (5th edn. 2005). A more recent one is a contribution to the series the Policy Press publish for the Social Policy Association, Baggott's *Understanding Health Policy* (2007). A very detailed account of the institutional arrangements for the NHS, with an emphasis on recent changes is provided by Talbot-Smith and Pollock (2006) *The New NHS: a Guide*.

The Government *NHS Plan* (Department of Health, 2000) is a good source for many of the recent developments, but this is another policy area where it is important to follow matters by consulting the official website (www.doh.gov.uk). The website of Kings Fund (www.kingsfund.org.uk.) is also a useful source for discussions of contemporary health policy issues.

Issues about finance and performance are well examined in the relevant chapter of Glennerster (2003) *Understanding the Finance of Welfare*. The Acheson Report on *Inequalities and Health* (1998) is a vital source on the evidence about health inequalities. Stacey's (1988) *The Sociology of Health and Healing* exploration of the wider sociological issues which need to be taken into account in any evaluation of health policy is still very relevant.

Chapter 8
Social Care for Adults

Introduction

In earlier versions of this book, there was a chapter on the personal social services in which both adult and child care services were discussed. These services were combined as the responsibility of the social services *departments* in England and Wales (social work departments in Scotland). In 2003, a Green Paper was published by the government that made it quite clear that it expected education and child protection policy to be brought together at local level in England. It announced that it proposed to require local authorities to create posts of Director of Children's Services 'accountable for local authority education and children's social services'. Legislation to enact this proposal was completed in 2004. This left adult social services as a separate element within the duties of local government. The government did not prescribe how local authorities should deal with this situation, and actual organization arrangements for these services now vary. In some places there are distinct adult social care departments, in others this work is combined with other local government functions, including in some cases the education and children's service.

Furthermore there are in some areas Care Trusts (not to be confused with the Primary Care Trusts discussed in the last chapter) in which some or all social care for adults is linked together with community based health care activities in a jointly managed organization (this development will be discussed further on pp. 189–90).

Expressions like social care and social services are vague and ambiguous, so it is therefore appropriate to say a word here about what is meant by social care for adults. It is perhaps best explained in terms of what it is not about. In all sorts of situations we need caring services from others. Mostly we secure that care from family, friends or by way of a private purchase. But in cases where exceptional amounts of care, or forms of care beyond the capacities of families and friends, are needed then public provided and/or funded care may be available. As we will see, when we examine forms of care in more detail, the 'need' for exceptional care is accepted on account of some form of disability (with a particular – but not sole – emphasis on disability arising in old age). Issues about defining this need will be explored at various points in this chapter, and it will be shown that two tests of need are nearly always applied: one relating to the extent of disability, the other (also described as a 'test of means') relating to whether those in need of care have resources available to pay for the care themselves. In addition, in relation to this second test of need the availability of support from family or friends may, implicitly if not explicitly, be taken into account. Beyond these issues lie some wider policy questions of importance, about the extent to which needs for care can be met without isolating people from 'normal' life in the community.

Policy for social care is, at the central government level, the responsibility of the Department of Health in England, and the respective devolved authorities in Wales, Scotland and Northern Ireland. This division of responsibility, accompanied by some legal differences in Scotland, make the assembly of statistical material for the UK difficult. In this chapter most of the statistics quoted will be for England only.

Except in Northern Ireland, where it is integrated with health services under Health and Social Services Boards, the provision of social care is the responsibility of local government. Local authorities are experiencing increasing regulation of their social care work by central government.

An Overview of Social Care Services

One way of classifying the social care system is in terms of contributions to the needs of specific groups in the population: older people, people with physical impairments and disabilities, people with mental health problems, people with learning difficulties, and children. An alternative classification is in terms of kinds of services: residential care, day care and services in the homes of recipients. Table 8.1 sets out social care expenditure in England in terms of amounts spent on the different groups, while Table 8.2 shows the divisions within the expenditure on the four groups in terms of services.

These tables highlight how over half of all expenditure is to meet the needs of older people and how it is then residential provision for this group that accounts for over half of that expenditure.

It should be noted that services for adults are sometimes called 'community care', and that this title is used regardless of whether the care is residential or domiciliary.

Table 8.1   Social care expenditure on adults in England 2005–6

Care group	Expenditure (£millions)	% of total
Older people	6850	57
Physically disabled people	1300	11
Learning disabled people	2960	24
Mentally ill people	1010	8
Total	12120	

Source: Figures calculated from Department of Health (2007).

This was the conventional terminology at the time the National Health Service and Community Care Act of 1990 Act was passed, but it is falling out of use with the generic expression 'adult social care' being preferred. The White Paper which preceded the 1990 Act started by saying:

> Community care means providing the services and support which people who are affected by problems of ageing, mental illness, mental handicap or physical or sensory disability need to be able to live in their own homes, or in 'homely' settings in the community. (HMSO, 1989, para 1.1)

The fact that the last part of that definition includes 'homely settings in the community' and that it has long been the aspiration that all adult social care institutions should be 'homely' means that this definition embraces all care except that provided by hospitals.

It is reasonable also to ask what is implied by 'services and support' in that definition. There are two points about this: at the margins, health and social care services tasks may be difficult to distinguish, and it is certainly widely recognized that effective care depends on close liaison between the providers of health care and the providers of social care. These issues are taken up later in this chapter; see pp. 188–90.

The second problem embedded in the reference to 'services and support' is that it is not clear who is to provide or pay for this. An outsider reading that definition may jump to the incorrect conclusion that it is the state which is the sole provider and carrier of the costs of community or social care. That is very definitely not the case.

Table 8.2   Percentages of total social care expenditure on different services (percentages read across)

Care group	Assessment and care management	Residential provision	Day and domiciliary provision
Older people	11	55	34
Physically disabled people	17	26	56
Learning disabled people	7	53	40
Mentally ill people	28	36	36

Source: Figures calculated from Department of Health (2007).

> ## Box 8.1   Impact of means-testing of social care services
>
> Means tests take into account both income and assets. An independent report on the care system for older people neatly summarized the impact of means-testing of care services as follows:
>
> > Under the means-tested system, the eligibility rules lead to a stratification of people into three groups:
> > - individuals with low wealth, who qualify for state support and receive benchmark levels of care
> > - individuals with high means, who are able to secure high levels of services by funding their own care
> > - individuals between the two groups, a significant proportion of whom struggle to pay for their own care, and as a result do not receive enough formal support.
>
> (Kings Fund, 2006, p. xxxii)

As already noted, anyone who seeks any form of care has to go through rigorous tests of *need* and *means* before help is available from the public sector. Many who are clearly 'affected by problems of ageing, mental illness, etc.' (as in the above definition) fail those tests and have either to go without services and support, or pay for them or receive them from their family and neighbours. The thresholds used in tests of need are inevitably influenced by the levels of resources available (see Box 8.1). There will be further discussion below of both of these issues.

Social care authorities have a wide range of responsibilities for the social care of adults. In 1948, when it was finally abolished with the passing of the National Assistance Act, local authorities inherited residential care responsibilities from the provisions of the Poor Law. To these were added a range of domiciliary services, as it became recognized that care concerns might be better met in this way rather than by admission to an institution. The restructuring of both social services and health services in the early 1970s brought further developments: the evolution of services outside health service institutions for mentally ill people and adults with learning difficulties, and the aspiration to use skilled social work services effectively in the care of adults.

In the early 1980s, while the public residential care sector was continuing to contract and hospitals were increasingly reluctant to become involved in long-term care, the number of private, voluntary residential care facilities began to increase rapidly. This growth in independent (that is, both private and voluntary) care was stimulated by an increase in availability of social security benefits to enable people (in particular, older people) to pay independent home charges. This came about during the early 1980s as a result of the relaxing of some of the rules relating to the means-testing of applicants from private residential homes by the social security authority. To keep the story short, this can only in retrospect be described as a 'mistake'; the Conservative government led by Margaret Thatcher, which had as was shown in Chapter 2 to have a strong commitment to privatization thought it a good idea to subsidize private care but did not accurately forecast the implications of this for the social security budget.

The growth of private residential care was uneven. In some areas, it dramatically reduced the demand for local authority care; in others, its impact was quite slight. An Audit Commission report on this issue in 1986 described this growth as a 'perverse effect of social security policies', distorting efforts to create the right balance between care inside and outside institutions. People might be given social security subsidies for residential care in circumstances in which social services authorities would not regard them as in need of such care. The social security authorities were not concerned with this issue; they merely carried out a test of means. This development increased regional inequalities. The greatest growth of independent care was in the south and west of England, particularly in seaside areas.

An odd situation had thus developed by the end of the 1980s, to which it was necessary for the government to give attention. Local authorities had been seeking to extend forms of care outside institutions. The local authority burden had been reduced, relatively, by the growth of an independent sector. Yet this was a substantial charge on the social security budget, unconstrained by public authorities' concerns regarding the importance of maintaining people in their own homes and confining the use of residential places to the most needy. The government's response to this was contained in its White Paper, entitled *Caring for People* (HMSO, 1989), and legislation was enacted in 1990 to try to deal with the situation. What was decided was that local authorities should be responsible for assessing need for care (for all who sought publicly supported care), and should then either provide or purchase that care. Hence, they would be responsible for determining whether residential care was necessary or, alternatively, whether some form of domiciliary care should be provided (or, of course, nothing), and also for determining who should be the provider. At the same time the government enacted controls designed to make purchase from private (or voluntary sector) providers rather than direct local authority provision the option likely to be chosen.

This transferring of responsibility was a complicated process. It involved mechanisms to shift resources from the social security budget to local authority social services budgets over a period of time, leaving arrangements for people already in independent care undisturbed. The new system came into full force in April 1993.

This account of events has laid a strong emphasis on the anomaly that developed because of the social security subsidy of the independent care system. The government's concern to reform the system of care stemmed particularly from the problem it had in controlling the growth of social security expenditure on independent care for older people. However, the case for reform was expressed in wider terms, which suggested that there was a need for the rationalization of social care as a whole. It was proposed that there were problems about the boundaries between health and social care to be resolved. It was argued that there was a need for better planning, to maximize care in the community and participant involvement in decision making. It was even suggested, though there is little evidence that what was enacted achieves this, that there was a need for the system to be more responsive to the wishes of the consumer. This political desire to inject consumer choice into what critics were suggesting were unresponsive and inefficient public services coincided with the demands of service users, particularly within the disability rights movement, for greater autonomy in the design and operation of their care. Hence, it was possible for practitioners to try to seize on the 'community care reforms' as an opportunity to give those in need of care and their carers a better deal, and the appearance of an uneasy alliance between government and campaigners around the theme of choice paved the way for further shifts in policy.

All this occurred against a background of a growth in the numbers of those in need of social care (particularly among older people), a search for economies in the health service which contributed to reducing that system's contribution to care, and a central attack on local government expenditure. The specific proposals for change were laced with new pro-market language. Social care authorities were to become 'purchasers', making contracts for the supply of services with 'providers' ideally (from the government's point of view) from the private and voluntary sectors but, if not, then from separate units in their own authority. The government's aim was to increase the role of the independent sector. Not surprisingly, therefore, the process of change was a complex one.

Residential Care: a More Detailed Examination

Official statistics indicate that in March 2006 there were, in England, 259,000 people supported by local authorities in residential and nursing places for older people and other adults in need of care (Department of Health, 2007). However, the term 'support' in the second statement will, in many cases in practice, mean 'partly supported', because all these places were means-tested. Residents are required to contribute to their care costs from their income and capital. It is estimated that the number of people who are paying the full costs without local authority help, in the whole of the UK, is around 120,000 with probably about 100,000 of these in England (Kings Fund, 2006, p. 97). That means that the proportion currently unsupported by local authorities is a little over 25 per cent.

About 10 per cent of the local authority supported places were in local authority homes. The rest were in independent homes. These independent institutions have contracts with local authorities to take people who are judged by a social care authority to be in need of care. Many of these homes will contain a mix of local authority supported residents and people paying for themselves.

The registration and regular inspection of all care homes and nursing homes, including those owned by local authorities is the responsibility of an independent body. This is the Commission for Health Care Audit and Inspection, mentioned in the last chapter as having a supervisory role in respect of the NHS. There was a separate body for social care inspection but with effect from 2008 its responsibilities are subsumed within the Commission for Health Care Audit and Inspection.

Note the distinction above between 'residential' (sometimes called 'care') homes and nursing homes. The latter offer high levels of support for those needing intensive nursing care and were formerly the responsibility of health authorities. About 28 per cent of residents cited above are in nursing homes. All of these are within the independent sector. The support of residents, who are unable to meet the full charges themselves, in these homes, is now the responsibility of the local authorities and the distinction between the two types of homes is increasingly blurred. Some homes are explicitly recognized as 'dual purpose' and a significant proportion of the residents of care homes are in need of some nursing care. In the old public sector, before the community care legislation, there had been a problem about maintaining a distinction between the population of local authority homes and the patients of the overburdened geriatric wards of hospitals. Long-stay hospitals have now largely disappeared, being replaced by independent sector nursing homes as far as older people are concerned and by a variety of forms of community care for those with disabilities, those who are mentally ill or who have severe learning difficulties.

A Royal Commission on Long Term Care set up to examine options for a sustainable system of funding of long-term care reported in March 1999. Its central concern was the arrangements made to pay for residential care. The main problem about much of the care system, particularly the arrangements for residential care, is that the means tests force large numbers to contribute substantial sums towards their own costs. This is a particular problem as far as residential care is concerned, where home charges may absorb large parts of the savings of older people. Where an owner-occupied house has been left on entry to residential care, its sale will be expected to contribute to these charges. There is therefore resentment that assets which a next generation expected to inherit may be used up to meet care costs. This problem has risen on the political agenda as more and more people survive into very old age, with a significant percentage of them becoming severely dependent. The issue has been further highlighted by the fact that whereas, in the past, many highly dependent older people occupied free beds in NHS hospitals, they are now expected instead to seek the social care which these charging rules apply.

The Royal Commission recommended:

> The costs of long-term care should be split between living costs, housing costs and personal care. Personal care should be available after assessment, according to need: the rest should be subject to a co-payment according to means. (Royal Commission on Long Term Care, 1999, p. xvii)

It justified this split in terms of the fact that it is the personal care that is the additional element, inasmuch as people being cared for in their own homes expect to meet normal living and housing costs. They were obviously forced by this logic to argue that the more intensive forms of domiciliary care should be free too.

In support of its recommendation, the Royal Commission is critical of some of the exaggerations of the future burden of care. They argue that the risk of long-term care is appropriately covered by some kind of 'risk pooling' but that private insurance cannot deliver at an acceptable cost and that (p. xvii):

> A hypothecated *unfunded* social insurance fund would not be appropriate for the UK system. A *prefunded* scheme would constitute a significant lifetime burden for young people and could create an uncertain and inappropriate call on future consumption.

That last comment seems justifiable in the British context, where the NHS is tax funded and the NI system has largely collapsed. Hence the Royal Commission offers a classic justification for a universalist approach (p. xvii):

> The most efficient way of pooling risk, giving the best value to the nation as a whole, is through services underwritten by general taxation, based on need rather than wealth.

The Royal Commission were not unanimous. Two members appended a note of dissent, arguing against the central proposal. The government's response was to draw a distinction within personal care between social care and nursing care, making only the latter free. Clearly the government's response was influenced by the cost of the Royal Commission's proposal. Yet failure to enact it leaves very high costs for many old people. Means and asset tests remain therefore still very significant in relation to residential care, with strong incentives to hide or pass on assets. It may be doubted whether a satisfactory distinction can be drawn between nursing care and social care when people are so disabled as to need residential care. There is considerable pressure on the government to try to get it to think again on this issue. In this respect pressure groups have been encouraged by the fact that the government of Scotland has accepted the Royal Commission's recommendation.

The numbers of older people with private occupational pensions or with owner-occupied houses, or of course both, is growing. Hence amongst those seeking residential care there is an increasing number who will 'fail' local authority means tests. It is hard to be sure of the exact numbers of people in this situation already within residential homes, the figures above suggest it is around 25 per cent though other estimates make it nearer one third (Kings Fund, 2006, p. xxiv). At the margins there are anomalies and hard cases. Some people successfully pass on assets before means tests are applied to them.

The adoption of the Scottish solution in England is advocated by many. Alternatives that are being debated include the development of some kind of public care insurance, such as exists in Germany. But in a country without health insurance that would be politically difficult to introduce, being seen as simply another way to tax people. An independent review of this topic, commissioned by an influential independent health and social care support organization and chaired by Sir Derek Wanless – a banker who had earlier advised the government on health care costs-, reported on this issue and came out with an elaborate alternative to the Royal Commission proposal which involves the matching of private spending with contributions from public funds (the Kings Fund, 2006).

There are already some social benefits available to hep to support handicapped people, which are not means-tested. There are also a disability living allowance and attendance allowance. These are set at various rates depending on the extent of need for care by another person. There is a range of detailed rules confining the availability of these benefits to people who cannot perform many basic personal tasks themselves. In 2004–5 the costs of these benefits (in the UK) amounted to £3.7 billion (Kings Fund, 2006, p. xxiv). There is also a benefit available for carers who are not gainfully employed and have to devote a substantial amount of time to the care of someone disabled. This is invalid care allowance, and its rate of pay is low. While these currently only support a very modest proportion of care costs – if residential or intensive home care is needed – they could be extended.

The sticking point for the government is of course the cost of the solutions mentioned above. It must then be recognized that any proposal for a shift away from means-testing implies increased subsidy to the (relatively) better off. But, on the other hand, it is clearly the case that the burden of care costs falls in a very haphazard and largely unpredictable way. Social survey data suggest that residential care is a very unpopular option. Most of us hope to remain in our own homes and then of course die in our beds with minor health complications, but of course the reality is that many experience serious physical and mental health problems at the end of their lives which make this an unrealizable aspiration. Particularly salient here are the problems associated with Alzheimer's disease in which mental faculties become seriously disturbed. Whilst in the UK today there is still a great deal of caring done by family members, few houses are occupied by multi-generation families and many people have no close relatives to whom they can turn for help.

Care Outside Residential Homes

The whole discussion of the issues about paying for residential care, discussed in a separate section for presentational reasons here, cannot be disconnected from the issues about care outside those homes. We have seen how government policies to contain the rising costs of residential care have involved efforts to ensure that cheaper alternatives are considered. We have also noted the widespread public preference for care at home. The current statistical trends indicate that, despite demographic change, there is little growth in residential care. It looks as though a shift towards other kinds of care is occurring. In the period before the 1990 legislation the development of procedures to ration domiciliary services was haphazard. Since then local authorities have been encouraged to use both rigorous tests of need and means tests to ration domiciliary care, with a view to reducing the need for residential care. In particular they have been encouraged to adopt strict but consistent definitions of need categories. The consequence of this is the withdrawal of limited services to those in lower need categories in favour of intensive domiciliary care for those in higher categories.

This is a source of resentment, and is argued to be counter-productive inasmuch as lower levels of support may be designed to prevent forms of health deterioration that will take people into higher need categories. There are clearly some difficult issues here about the most effective use of limited resources by local authorities.

Social care authorities organize, or purchase from independent providers, a variety of day care services. For older people, there may be day centres where people can go for company, social activities, occupational therapy, perhaps cheap midday meals, and perhaps some aid or advice. Similar facilities are often provided for people with disabilities. For younger people with disabilities, and particularly for people with learning difficulties, there are centres where company and therapy may be accompanied by productive activities. In some cases, these are more or less sheltered workshops, doing commercially sponsored work and paying wages to employees (see Box 8.2) There are some difficult distinctions to be drawn here between sheltered work, therapy, and provision for some daytime life outside the home. Under the community care legislation, the government's expectation is that local authorities will become more flexible about the range of help they provide 'in the community' and, of course, that they will make use of an increasingly wide range of non-statutory providers.

Box 8.2   Remploy: the rise and fall of supported employment

Remploy is an employment service for people with disabilities and health conditions which provides a range of employment, support and training programmes, more recently in local branches which have begun to operate as a mixture of employment exchange and careers service. Remploy was originally set up as a company by Ernest Bevin, the then Minister of Labour, in 1945 following the 1944 Disabled Persons (Employment) Act, and had registered factories providing direct employment in the manufacture of furniture, motor industry supplies and other products.

In 2007 the management of Remploy released a proposal for 'modernization' which included the closure of 32, and merger of 11 of 83 factories nationwide, along with a number of other cost-cutting measures. Although under trade union pressure the plans have been modified (17 proposed closures rather than 32) it is clear that this last bastion of state supported direct employment is eroding rapidly. Its role and business activities have evolved and it is now presented as helping people into mainstream employment through provision of skills training and other 'employability' measures, as well as advising employers on the recruitment and retention of employees with disabilities. The history and future of Remploy is very much bound up with changes in the politics of welfare, but its development also reflects change in the attitudes towards and treatment of disability in society.

In a sample week in 2006 about 3.7 million 'contact hours' of support were provided by local authorities in England to about 346,000 households. At the same time 29 per cent of those households received 'intensive home care' (over 10 hours a week). The trend towards greater emphasis on services for those needing intensive care has been noted above.

Of course, people may purchase their own domestic help unaided by a local authority, and where services are inadequate, the gap is likely to be filled by large amounts of unpaid work by relatives and neighbours.

Local authorities may also support the provision of meals, taken to people in their own homes. These 'meals on wheels' services are often provided through a voluntary or private organization. Again, the extent of coverage varies widely from area to area, from, at one extreme, a 'token' meal a week to, at the other, the provision of a comprehensive, seven days a week service. Local authorities may set charges for this service, and the extent to which they subsidize it is variable.

Local authorities provide a range of other 'benefits in kind' to assist with the care of people within the community. The Chronically Sick and Disabled Persons Act of 1970 suggests a wide range of services that local authorities may offer. Despite the emphasis in that Act on local authority duties, the word 'may' in the last sentence is appropriate. There are wide variations in the adequacy of the help provided. Authorities may provide, and pay the rental costs of, telephones; they may adapt houses to meet the needs of disabled people; and they are able to provide a variety of aids to daily living. They tend, however, to impose budgetary limits that ration quite severely the money available for such benefits. However, the Disabled Persons (Services, Consultation and Representation) Act of 1986 increases the rights of disabled people to be informed about provisions and consulted about their needs. Additionally, the Carers (Recognition and Services) Act of 1995 is designed to facilitate the consultation of carers, and attention to their needs.

The administration of these diverse mixes of services is the responsibility of social care authorities. The purchaser–provider split means that the purchaser role in social care authorities has to be undertaken by 'care managers', who assess needs and commission services from the available providers.

Direct Payments and Personal Budgets

The discussion in the last section has deliberately left out one form of support outside residential settings: direct payments. This approach to social care, although currently at a comparatively low level, needs to be examined in a separate section since it is at the centre of new government initiatives in social care. What is involved are new policies designed to facilitate choice by means of systems in which authorities determine how much cash should be spent on care and individuals choose, or participate in the making of choices on, how to spend it.

Local authorities have been formally allowed to make direct payments to some social care recipients since 1996 legislation. What is meant here is payment of cash – on a one off or regular basis – to enable individuals to purchase their own

Table 8.3   Numbers of direct payments recipients in England as at 30 September

	Older People	People with learning disabilities	People with physical impairments	People with sensory impairments	People who use mental health services	Carers	Total
2001	537	353	4274	100	61	21	5346
2002	1032	736	5459	159	132	95	7613
2003	1899	1337	6944	207	229	957	11573
2004	4365	2354	9285	448	520	2327	19299
2005	7566	3803	12460	748	1136	3438	29141

Source: Figures assembled from Department of Health returns in Vick et al., 2006.

care. The 1996 legislation followed from what were previously isolated practices in parts of England and Scotland of providing indirect payments to service users through a third party, such as a voluntary organization, to purchase personal assistance. Subsequent changes to the legislation opened up access to direct payments to all deemed entitled to social care. Direct payments must now be offered to everyone assessed as needing social care, however in practice take-up so far remains quite low. Table 8.3 gives some figures on this, and an indication of the growth of direct payments. If you bear in mind the statistic quoted above of 346,000 households getting home help services you have some idea of the small scale of this development.

Since implementation, the largest group of direct payment users has consistently been non-elderly people with a physical disability. As far as the other potential recipient groups are concerned there have been issues to consider about capacity to and willingness to negotiate direct payments arrangements. Initiatives to deal with this problem involve the use of other people as 'agents' for the recipient, but this only partly deals with the problem.

Direct payments give greater control over their lives to people assessed as needing social care or support, but they also raise many challenges. Individuals – other than those receiving simple one off payments for specific facilities or activities – are likely to have to become employers (with the responsibilities to have regard to employment law and to make tax and social insurance payments). There are issues too about choice of employees in these situations, with a need for safeguards against securing inappropriate people who may exploit the vulnerable situations of their employers. Local authorities and voluntary organization 'agents' may assist with these issues, but the arrangements need to be quite complex. There is an issue about the extent to which family members can be employees in this situation. In similar schemes in some other countries – notably the Netherlands and Austria – this is quite possible. Initially it was impossible in the UK scheme, now local authorities have discretion to accept arrangements in which relatives take on this role in some circumstances. This opens up a range of new issues, in a situation in which at the moment relatives do a great deal of caring for nothing, about the formalization and monetization of a family caring relationship.

> ## Box 8.3   Personal budgets: the 2006 White Paper's plans (Department of Health, 2006)
>
> 4.31 Direct payments only cover local authority social care budgets, but individual budgets will bring together separate funds from a variety of agencies including local authority social services, community equipment, Access to Work, independent living funds, disabled facilities grants and the Supporting People programme.
>
> 4.32 Individuals who are eligible for these funds will then have a single transparent sum allocated to them in their name and held on their behalf, rather like a bank account. They can choose to take this money out either in the form of a direct payment in cash, as provision of services, or as a mixture of both cash and services, up to the value of their total budget. This will offer the individual much more flexibility to choose services which are more tailored to their specific needs.
>
> This idea is being piloted in a sample of local authorities.

The government is committed to moving ahead on this issue, but dependent upon local authorities who are the implementing organizations, many of which have been cautious about direct payments and reluctant to espouse situations in which such developments may undermine their existing services. A 2006 White Paper sets out the aspiration to extend the direct payments idea with 'personal budgets' (see Box 8.3).

It needs to be noted that both with direct payments and personal budgets means-testing procedures continue (hence payments/budgets may only be part of the actual cost of what is needed). Also, as mentioned earlier, there are some social security benefits that assist with social care. Taking the long view, this mix of approaches may need rationalizing further, particularly if there are new initiatives in respect of government support for social care, both within and outside institutions.

While actually developing a system in which most social care recipients may be able to secure money to make their own choices of care may be difficult, the important thing about the debate around this subject is that it brings out strongly the importance of 'empowerment' in this field of social policy. The fact that the system is so strongly regulated through means tests highlights the division between those who purchase their own care and those who secure it through an application to a public authority. Direct payments seem to get away from that, though of course the means test remains salient. There are other approaches to empowerment, through greater consultation about services and how they are delivered. But it requires imagination to get beyond the traditional model of social care recipients as vulnerable people for whom other people have to make the decisions (as splendidly sent up in the title of a radio programme called 'Does he take sugar'). Box 8.4 sets out a useful model for thinking about these issues.

Box 8.4   Empowerment: 'exit, choice or loyalty'

An American monograph by Hirschman (1970) explores the options available to consumers (in both public and private systems) as being 'exit, voice or loyalty'. This approach sees the 'market' option as involving 'exit': if we do not like what one supplier offers we go to someone else. Traditional public services can be said to often depend upon 'loyalty': we accept what we are given and are grateful for it. There are good reasons, explored further later in Box 8.6, for seeing the exit option as hard to exercise in some situations. Once a person chooses a residential home, they want to settle down and make it as far as possible a real 'home', but using the exit option when all is not well imposes substantial 'costs' (using that notion in a broad sense as well as in the narrow economic sense). But that makes all the more important the issues about 'voice', about getting one's views and opinions heard.

While this trilogy is emphasized here, it should be seen as similarly important for education and health services, and for social housing.

The Relationship between Personal Social Care and the Health Service

In many respects, the concerns of the health service and those of the social care authorities overlap. People are likely to need mixtures of health care and social care. Increasingly, the NHS is trying to limit its care to what may be described as 'treatment'. Where possible, also, in-patient treatment is being replaced by out-patient treatment. Hospital stays are becoming shorter, the aim being to send patients 'home' as soon as high inputs of specialized treatment are no longer necessary. Mentally ill people are hospitalized as little as possible. It is broadly accepted that there is only very exceptionally a case for hospital care for those with severe learning difficulties. In general, there is a concern to maximize care 'within the community' rather than in hospitals. This is of course not just recognition of the failings of institutional care; as far as the government is concerned cost considerations are important.

Many people are in receipt of a combination of health treatment from GPs and community-based nursing staff, on the one hand, and social care, on the other. Deficiencies on either side may have to be made up by extra services on the other.

The discharge of patients from hospital in itself has substantial implications for social care provision. It is important that social support services are readily available at this stage. Hence day-to-day co-ordination between the two services is crucial.

In this context, there is a special problem when residential, including nursing home, care may be necessary. As was noted in the discussion about the Royal Commission on Long-Term Care (see pp. 181–2) hospital care is still free, whereas residential care deemed necessary by social services authorities is not. The increasing unwillingness of the health service to keep people in hospital is creating situations in which people are discovering that they have to pay substantial amounts for social care in situations in which, in the past, they might have expected free hospital care. Furthermore the supply of residential care, and the local authority budgets to support such care, is limited. The consequence is the unnecessary retention of people in hospital, thereby limiting the capacity of the health service to respond to emergent need. The government has had to recognize that one of the responses needed to deal with the lack of hospital beds is enhanced funding for local authorities. But it has also tried to deal with the situation by developing a system in which local authorities are effectively 'fined' if people who should be entitled to local authority support remain in hospital because of failures to put such support into operation.

The importance of the overlap between health and social services has long been recognized (here this embraces child care as well as adult care, though the changed institutional structure means that the latter need considering separately – as we will do in the next chapter) At the service planning level, the Department of Health has led the way by emphasizing the need to look at the health service and personal social services together. Within individual localities, they have encouraged the development of formal joint planning activities. A particular stimulus to this has been provided by 'joint financing'. Money from the health service budget is made available to help to finance projects within the social care authorities that can be considered to meet needs that might otherwise have to be met by the health service. In the long run, social care authorities are expected to take over the full cost of these ventures. After the 1990 changes to both health and social care services this topic was given more intensive attention.

In the ferment after the 1990 Act, collaboration between the health service and the local authority social services was given a new impetus. Then after the election of the Labour government in 1997 the White Paper *The New NHS* (Department of Health, 1997), made a commitment to consulting on ways to encourage further joint working between health and social services. A later ministerial commitment, set out in the foreword of *Partnership in Action* (Department of Health, 1998b) expressed the view that 'all too often when people have complex needs spanning both health and social care good quality services are sacrificed for sterile arguments about boundaries'.

Partnership in Action set out a range of proposals to enhance joint working, required at three levels: strategic planning, service commissioning, and service provision. The Health Act 1999 was then enacted to make joint working easier through arrangements whereby health and social services authorities can:

- operate 'pooled budgets' (putting a proportion of their funds into a mutually accessible joint budget to enable more integrated care)
- have 'lead commissioning' arrangements with one authority transferring funds to the other, which can then take responsibility for purchasing both health and social care
- integrate provision so that one service providing organization can provide both health and social care

This flexibility was designed to allow National Health Service organizations greater freedom to provide social care and allow social services authorities to provide some community health services on behalf of the National Health Service. These new measures were to be accompanied by a new statutory duty of partnership on all local bodies in the health service, and on local authorities to work together to promote the well being of their local communities.

It should also be noted that as Primary Care Trusts were developed, local authorities were given formal positions to ensure that local policy making was co-ordinated and they were involved in health care commissioning. One direction in which all this could be leading is the shift of adult care services out of local government into the NHS. While official statements deny this intention there is a distinct shift in this direction, perhaps enhanced by the development noted at the beginning of this chapter of separation of adult social care from child care in some local authorities. Also significant is the development in some areas of Care Trusts (bear in mind the note above that these are not the same as Primary Care Trusts). These are explicit joint bodies delivering social care 'under delegated authority from local councils' and thus 'able to commission and deliver primary and community healthcare as well as social care for older people and other client groups' (Department of Health, 2000, p. 73). The development of these has been slow, and most are specific to the needs of particular groups of people - people with mental illnesses, people with learning difficulties or older people.

Hudson and Henwood (2002) provide a good overview of these developments suggesting that despite the fact that *Partnership in Action* rejected structural change as the solution to these boundary issues this now seems to be the way that the system is moving. Drawing on evidence from Northern Ireland, where there are combined Health and Social Services Boards, they argue that this is not the best way forward, the issues about collaboration are essentially about behaviour at the 'street-level' and are not necessarily solved by large structures.

Needs and Priorities

The increased recognition in the 1980s of the limited funds available for public services and the relationship between this and the growing need for social care (see Box 8.5) have sharpened concern to find ways of balancing the respective contributions to what is called the 'mixed economy of welfare'. While this is sometimes presented as a new issue, social care has always above all been about care within the family and to some extent the community. This is often described as 'informal care'. It is very hard to estimate its scale; after all we all give or receive care from time to time. It has been estimated that there are 5.8 million carers in England, mostly providing care for older people (Kings Fund, 2006, p. xxv). Many of these carers will be older people themselves and many will be caring for a spouse or partner. In addition to this informal care there is:

- care which is bought
- care which is provided by voluntary and charitable agencies
- and care which is provided by public agencies

Box 8.5   The growth in the need for social care

The ageing of the population is the main source of the growth in the need for social care (as the numbers in need of care below pension age is falling). Estimates of this growth are complicated. It is important not to use the simple demographic evidence that the numbers of older people (and indeed very old people) is growing, since there is good reason to expect that the health conditions of future generations of older people will be better than is the case at present. The realization of that expectation, of course, depends upon the development of preventative health measures.

Using a 'no change scenario' the Kings Fund's commission estimated an increase of people over 65 from 8,457 thousand in 2005 to 11,961 thousand in 2025. Within those figures they estimated an increase in 'disabled' (their definition and terminology) people from 888 thousand (10.26%) to 1,446 thousand (12.09%). But their alternative 'improved population health scenario', based on expert estimates of the impact of current measures, suggested – obviously – a bigger population of 12,168 thousand over 65, within which they expected 1,366 (11.22%) thousand 'disabled' people. (Kings Fund, 2006, pp. 40–1)

What is perhaps new is acceptance that the contribution from the last source is inherently limited – hence the development of a lively debate about the roles of the other forms of care. An important part of that debate concerns the search for ways of defining need, recognizing the limitation of approaches to this derived from economics using pricing mechanisms (see Box 8.6) and identifying how public agencies should respond to it.

Box 8.6   Need and pricing mechanisms

Economists have a distinctive approach to this issue. Instead of attempting to tackle the concept of 'need', they emphasize the concept of demand, which they define as a willingness to buy at a given price. This approach emphasizes the price mechanism as a means of adjusting services to demands. If there is a high demand for a particular thing, then this will be reflected in a willingness to pay higher prices. Higher rewards will attract more suppliers, and may ultimately bring down the price. Always, however, equilibrium is maintained in which supply and demand are balanced by the price mechanism.

(cont'd)

Box 8.6   *(cont'd)*

To what extent does this offer a solution to the problem of needs in the social services? Clearly, it does not if the local authority is the only supplier of a particular service or the controller of access to that service. Equally it does not if that authority is the funder of the service for low-income people without the resources to purchase it themselves. Conditions of monopoly or near monopoly then exist, in which, in theory, the supplier can determine the price, and those unable to pay must go without. The attempt to identify real needs regardless of ability to pay is the hallmark of the public service here. Rationing according to the capacity to pay is quite widely regarded as an inferior way of distributing many such services. The price mechanism solution is also inappropriate where it is arguable that people who need particular services are either unlikely to recognize the need or to translate it into an effective, money-backed demand. Social care services for people who are mentally ill fall into this category. There remain, however, services like the home care service that are provided both by the statutory authorities and by the private market. In some sense, the need for these services can be regarded as fairly limitless - most of us would like our domestic chores to be done by someone else. The price mechanism seems to offer a basis for distinguishing absolute need from effective demand, and of allowing for the existence, side by side, of a public and a private sector.

The use of the price mechanism may be fair enough in theory, but what happens to those with high needs, in some absolute sense, but a low capacity to pay? There are two possible answers to this objection to the use of the price mechanism. One is that social affairs should be arranged in such a way that what are really income maintenance problems do not have to be solved by the provision of subsidized services. This is an attractive argument, but one that matches poorly the real world. The other is that means-tests should be devised to enable cheaper services to be given in some cases. The trouble with this latter solution is that it can cope with situations in which only a minority has to be helped outside the marketplace, but it quite destroys the market concept when it has to be widespread. The reality is that for many of the personal social services (including the home care service) some more fundamental way of defining need is required: a minority can buy the services on the open market; but there remains a large group who appear to need them free or at a reduced price, only some of whom actually receive them. The problem remains of determining how much the service should expand to meet the unmet needs.

Box 8.6 examines the market approach to need, first because it has significant advocates, and second because it offers a firm approach to the problem of defining need where others are more difficult. The alternative is the ascertainment of some more absolute way of determining need. In some cases this does not seem too problematic; in relation to some diseases, for example, there may be a finite group whom it is generally agreed are in need of treatment. In other cases, however, the problem is one of making a distinction between 'absolute need' and some more limited concept. While we may all contend that we *need* our houses cleaned to free us for other activities, it may be argued that most of us are still physically capable of doing this work while others are not. Those it will be argued are the ones really in need. But, is this a disagreement about needs or about priorities?

For social care, then, the determination of needs is complicated first by the fact that the authorities do not have the sole responsibility to meet certain kinds of needs, and second because their views of needs must be determined by their views of priorities. With an ageing population and limited funding growth the level at which need is being recognized is getting steadily more stringent. A system known as 'Fair Access to Care' requires local authorities to classify people's needs in categories: low, moderate, substantial and critical. The relationship between the resources available and the extent of demand then determines where authorities operate the cut-off point. Henwood and Hudson found, in a study for the Commission for Social Care Inspection, that over two-thirds of authorities were setting the entry point to services at the 'substantial' level and that some were only providing services for those in the critical category (Henwood and Hudson, 2008). This leaves many people whose capacity to cope, and avoid moving up to the critical level, is limited, with no public support at all.

Theoretically, the purchaser–provider split in social care requires the care managers to take decisions about need, based on some of the ideal considerations set out above. They must then commission the services they regard as appropriate. At that stage, means-testing is likely to occur. However, it is doubtful whether this split system operates in this way in reality. Henwood and Hudson observed, on the basis of the study quoted above:

> At best, councils in our study conceded that people funding their own care could ask for an assessment of their needs, 'but it is not encouraged'. At worst, self-funders are highly vulnerable, isolated and at risk of being 'fast-tracked' into residential care, equipped with little information or advice to use in making life changing decisions. (Henwood and Hudson, 2008)

Conclusions

The responsibilities of the care authorities involve a wide range of activities.

This mixture of activities has grown rapidly. The growth is perceived with quite considerable anxiety by the public, since most of the activities were hitherto undertaken outside the statutory sector, within the family and the community. One interpretation of this growth is that public services can now be provided to help to strengthen family and community life. If this view is taken, then residential care replaces the neglect of the isolated old, and domiciliary care supports the maintenance of home life, and so on. However, there is an alternative view, that the growth in these services is itself an index of social pathology, that people are not coping so well with aspects of life that in the past were of little concern to public services. This ambivalence is compounded by widespread uncertainty about what social care authorities and a deep uncertainty about the circumstances under which help may be sought from the various specific services.

Social care services in Britain are going through an intense period of change, which it is difficult to portray accurately. Government surveillance is increasing. Best value indicators (see p. 79) specify objectives for social care in local government. An increasing range of specific grants are adding to the capacity of the centre to prescribe local responses. Inspection of services is becoming more rigorous, and the government has made it very clear that it will not hesitate to use legislation that enables it to take social care functions away from local government where it is dissatisfied with performance.

Different authorities are changing at different rates. The shift initiated by the 1990 legislation towards increased private provision (under local authority contracts) is continuing. But then more recently the government's commitment to enhancing individual autonomy through direct payments and personal budgets is generating further change. At the time of writing local authorities are still working through the changes that separated adult services from children's services, and the pull of adult care services towards the NHS continues. There is still a great deal of uncertainty in this area of social policy.

Suggestions for Further Reading

Means, Richards and Smith's *Community Care: Policy and Practice* (2008) is particularly recommended. The Kings Fund review mentioned in the text (2006) offers a good review of the debate about the costs of care services. Two essays on issues about empowerment, choice and control which are recommended are: Knapp in Hills, LeGrand and Piachaud (2007) *Making Social Policy Work* and Rumney in Clarke, Maltby and Kennett (2007) *Social Policy Review*.

For social services in England the Department of Health web site (www.doh.gov.uk) is a key source for current policy. Readers may also find the web site for the Joseph Rowntree Foundation (www.jrf.org.uk.) useful, since that is an organization that funds social care research and has an active dissemination policy.

Chapter 9
Education and Children

Introduction

While much of this chapter deals with education, it has been decided to include discussion of all the issues about child care in this chapter in the light of the overlap between issues about pre-school child care and pre-school education, and the fact that the government has brought education and child care policy in England under integrated departments at national and local government levels. On the other hand the organization of the book has not entirely followed another change in the system of government for England: the splitting of responsibility for higher and further education from the responsibility for schools; whilst issues about training were discussed in the chapter on employment (6) this chapter contains some discussion of higher education.

In Scotland, Wales and Northern Ireland, education is the responsibility of the devolved governments. In England, the relevant central government department for schools is (since summer 2007) the Department for Children, Schools and Families.

At local level these services come within the responsibilities of the top-tier or single tier local authorities. Further and higher education comes under the Department of Innovation, Universities and Skills.

The state's role in education is a dual one; it is the major provider of education, and has also assumed a responsibility to supervise education and child care in the sectors for which it is not directly responsible. Historically, the public sector has been seen as involving a partnership between central and local government, yet recent years have seen a shift towards much greater dominance by the centre and a readiness to reduce the role of, or even discard, local government as a partner. Issues about the changing nature of the central–local relationship in respect of the control of education will arise at many points in this chapter.

The Organization and Management of the State School System

Public education in state schools in the UK is free. Even from the Right, there has been little challenge to that principle. There have been some attempts on the Right to make a case for education vouchers, which could be cashed at both state and private schools. Only in the area of nursery schooling has this movement had some success. There was an explicit scheme until the fall of the Conservative government in 1997, and now the fact that funding is available for both public and approved private places in nursery education may be regarded as an implicit scheme.

The majority of schools are, as has long been the case, the responsibility of local government in the UK. In England they come under the counties, the metropolitan and other single-tier districts, and the London boroughs. However, legislation forces local authorities to fund schools on the basis of a centrally determined formula and to delegate significant management responsibilities to the schools' own governing bodies.

There has long been a group of schools partly under local education authority control and partly independent, that is schools linked to faith groups. The greater part of these are Church of England schools, but there is also a substantial number of Roman Catholic schools. There is a small number of Jewish schools and recently a number of other faith groups have added to this list: Greek Orthodox Christians, Muslims and Sikhs. While most of the funding for these schools comes from the state the religious bodies pay a small proportion of the costs. Local authorities are involved in the management arrangements for these schools.

A variety of other schools which are only partly under local government control have emerged in recent years. Under the 1988 Education Act, the Conservative government made it possible for schools to be directly funded by central government, through funding agencies. They might apply (with the agreement of a majority of parents) to apply to become 'grant-maintained'. In the School Standards and Framework Act of 1998 the Labour government abolished this grant maintained status for schools. Instead these schools have been allowed to apply to become 'foundation' schools under the overall supervision of their relevant local authority but with a status which enables them to retain special arrangements for their government and a substantial measure of autonomous control over their land and property. Another kind of school deriving from another Conservative innovation, partly privatized City Technology Colleges, was also allowed to survive. But since then the government has developed other kinds of quasi-independent schools: City Academies and Trust Schools. These, like City Technology Colleges, have modest inputs from non-governmental sources and a measure of management autonomy. They are seen as widening school choice, at secondary level, and encouraging educational innovation. We will return to issues about these in the course of this chapter.

Furthermore, alongside the encouragement of new kinds of schools the overall government of the local authority system has been changed. There has been what has been described as a 'hollowing out process' (Bache, 2002) in which power has been taken away from local government both through more central control and by central legislation that shifts powers from local authorities to school governing bodies Bache highlights two features of this 'hollowing out':

- First, the complex formulae governing the funding of education which central government modified in ways which force increasing proportions of the money going to local government to be passed on in predetermined ways to the schools.
- Second, the scrutiny of the performance of local authorities as managers of the school system which include powers – that have been used – to take functions away from them. This may involve both taking the management of specific schools out of local authority hands, and taking away the management of the whole education service. In both of these cases funding arrangements are unchanged; in other words the costs fall upon local authority budgets.

While the state system has remained intact, various forms of what may be called 'quasi-marketization' have occurred. Funding depends on pupil numbers. Inasmuch as this interacts with parental choice (and how much this really applies depends upon geography) it has an impact upon school success or failure. The publication of test results for individual schools can then further influence this process.

A separate, but logically connected development has been government encouragement of local authority maintained secondary schools to become 'specialist schools', offering the full curriculum but aiming to be centres of excellence in specific subjects. This is another topic to which we will return below.

The system can be identified as involving three sectors: pre-school education, primary education and secondary education. In most cases, these sectors can be identified respectively with the education of children under five, between five and eleven, and between eleven and the school-leaving age of sixteen (with many pupils continuing at school until eighteen). However, some authorities have developed systems that deviate from the strict break between primary and secondary education at 11-plus. These have generally introduced an intermediate, middle-school system, for children in two or three of the year bands between nine and thirteen years old. Another innovation has been the introduction of 'sixth form colleges' for the over-sixteens. The educational arrangements for those over the minimum school-leaving age are further complicated by the fact that further education colleges offer both practical and academic courses for people in the sixteen to eighteen age brackets.

The arrangement for the starting of compulsory education at the age of five differentiates Britain from many other countries, which do not make it compulsory until six or seven. However, the concomitant has been that public pre-school education was, until recently, ill-developed. This began to change in the 1990s, so that now nearly all children in the UK aged three and four secure some (generally not full-time) pre-school education, which as mentioned above, is funded by but not necessarily provided by the state.

Until the 1980s there was limited government regulation of primary schools. A diverse range of local practice emerged, relatively lightly supervised by national and local inspectors. The gradual elimination of selection at 11-plus clearly contributed to this freedom. However, in the late 1970s and early 1980s voices began to be raised questioning whether this largely professionally driven innovation had gone too far. There was a growing concern about levels of literacy and numeracy, with responsibility for their alleged inadequacy sometimes attributed to liberal regimes in primary schools. Increased controls, involving a national curriculum, testing and more rigorous inspection under the 1988 Education Act, were a response to this concern. These developments are discussed further on pp. 209–10. Diversity ceased to be celebrated and there were pressures against the more extreme examples of informality. Under the Labour government, this reversal has been continued, with quite explicit central prescriptions about the amounts of time to be devoted to formal teaching designed to increase literacy and numeracy and even recommendations about amounts of homework to be done by children.

In the 1960s and the 1970s comprehensive secondary schools gradually replaced the bipartite or tripartite system envisaged at the time of the passing of the 1944 Education Act. By 1979, the development of comprehensive education was nearing completion. The Labour government had, in the 1976 Education Act, required local authorities to develop plans for comprehensivization. A minority of authorities were holding out on this. On coming to power, the Conservatives repealed this law; this had the effect of stemming the tide, but not reversing it. In the mid-1990s, the Conservative government encouraged a partial return to selectivity, mainly by enabling schools to reserve a small proportion of their places for pupils with identified higher abilities in general or in specific subjects. Labour, on return to power, in 1997, decided not to revert to its 1970s' stance of pushing through to total comprehensivization, without reference to local opinion. On the other hand, in a move characteristic of its stance on the powers of local government, it did not simply leave the veto power in the hands of elected local authorities but decided instead that pro-comprehensive campaigners should be able (if they could secure the signatures of 20 per cent of eligible parents) to secure local ballots of parents on the issue, in the areas where selection was still in use. At the same time the government encouraged a variety of forms of school specialization (this is where the variations in school types listed above is particularly important) that partly undermines the comprehensive principle. This will be discussed further below (see pp. 210–13).

The importance of examinations towards the end of the school years has always meant that, in many respects, the comprehensive schools had to have ability divisions and different programmes of instruction within them. Extensions in testing (see p. 209) throughout the education system, accompanied by the publication of results in ways that can influence parental choice of schools, further encourage the opening up of those divisions within schools.

Higher and Further Education

Higher education and further education are outside local authority control. Higher education involves a network of quasi-autonomous universities and related bodies funded and supervised through funding councils. A Learning and Schools Council in England and a National Council for Education and Training in Wales have responsibility for both further education and to some extent also for post-16 education in schools. They direct the work of a network of local Learning and Skills Councils.

The concepts of further and higher education embrace a number of different activities: vocational education, further academic education (both of a kind provided generally in schools and at higher levels) and non-vocational adult education. There are about two and a half million students in higher education in the United Kingdom (Table 9.1 gives further information on these figures). This is estimated to now mean that between 40 and 50 per cent of the population leaving school go on to higher education.

In the Higher Education Act 2004 the government made radical changes to the system of funding for higher education in England and Wales. These changes did not apply to Scotland, as the government there was not willing to accept the proposal to charge students fees. The fees involved are a minimum of £1,100 a year for an undergraduate course (these may be raised higher in due course). Universities may vary the current standard fee of £1,100 up to £3,000 or down to nothing. The fees for students for low income families are paid by the government up to the £1,100 level, and cash has been made available to universities to provide additional bursaries for students in difficulties. Any university that proposes to charge more than the standard fee will be required to have an 'Access Agreement' approved by an Access Regulator, committing it to facilitate the take up of places by students from disadvantaged groups. The adoption of the higher rate has been very widespread. Students

Table 9.1   Students in higher education 2004–5 (thousands)

	Full time	Part time	Total
Undergraduates	1229	725	1954
Postgraduates	227	311	538

Nearly 60% of undergraduates and about 53% of postgraduates are female.
About 240,000 students are from overseas.
Source: National Statistics 2007, table 3.8 p. 30 and commentary on p. 31.

can have loans to enable them to pay these fees (and their maintenance costs) which they do not have to repay until their incomes are above £15,000 a year. The government has re-introduced a means-tested grant for students from low-income families.

The White Paper proposing these changes argues that higher education in the UK has been under funded, but that any case for increased funding had to be made against the claims of other under funded public services. Thus, rejecting the straightforward but expensive option of a simple increase in tax funded expenditure, it argued that there should be a greater contribution from those whose incomes will be enhanced by higher education. A widely canvassed approach to this had been the establishment of a graduate tax (see Barr in Hills, Le Grand and Piachaud, 2007, for a discussion of the difference between the measure enacted and his proposals for this). While this might have raised more in the long run the government's view was that the impact of this upon the current funding situation would have been slight. The shift away from up front fees and the increase in the loan repayment threshold represent the government's compromise moves in this direction. They may be seen as involving a shift in the costs of higher education from parents to students themselves, inasmuch as repayment of loans is delayed until students begin to earn. But the low threshold of £15,000 a year income at which repayment begins means that heavy costs are imposed upon students at a time when they are starting out on independent life.

Post-graduate education is subsidized for some through grants, most of them from the government subsidized research councils. There is considerable competition for these; consequently, many students (or their parents) are paying for post-graduate education. Some further, non-vocational education has to be paid for by students, but generally the fees are subsidized.

Child Care

It was noted at the beginning of this chapter, that what were hitherto officially seen as social services for children are now linked with education. Hence attention to that topic in this chapter.

Child care policy may be seen as about:

- Care which will supplement (or even exceptionally replace) the care provided by parents.
- Care for children who are exceptionally vulnerable because of their own health problems or disabilities.
- Educational activities for children that will prepare them for the compulsory education system.
- Care to facilitate labour market participation on the part of the parents, including additional care for children already attending full-time education.

These may be seen as involving both regulatory roles and provider roles, but their exact manifestations will be affected by:

- The institutional locations of closely related services, in particular: mainstream education, health care and services to support labour market participation.
- Alternative views of the extent to which these activities should under normal circumstances be the responsibility of parents – making their own provisions or purchasing services in the market.

A distinction tends to be drawn between the issues about child protection (the first two items in the introductory list above) and those about either supplementary education or child care to assist parental labour market participation. We leave the specific topic of child protection for consideration in the next section.

Justifications for child care as a form of supplementary education are based upon a view that what is provided by the regular education system does not start soon enough or is not enough. Then, if the regular education system is provided free by the state, surely there is a case for this education to be free too? An argument against that view will be that it is an inessential extra, in that sense it may be regarded as much like post-school education. In practice we find an official view being taken which stands somewhere between those two positions: that there is a case for some subsidized pre-school education for all which may be 'topped up' by means of additional purchases.

The issues about child care to assist labour market participation are of course linked with issues about the encouragement of the latter. The central issue is of course labour market participation by women. Closely connected with this is the issue about such participation by single parents, most of whom are women. Those who regard this as unnecessary, or simply a matter of private choice, will equally see child care provision as a private matter. If on the contrary it is seen as every parent's right then there will be a case for state provision of child care. But even here it may be regarded as a matter for attention by employers rather than the state. Again, there is a middle position, which sees a need to subsidize child care to facilitate employment where the rewards from work are low. At the same time the issues about labour market participation by single parents are very bound up, as was shown in Chapter 6, with the fact that the alternative may be another cost for the state (a social security benefit).

The reason for this long prelude is that the arguments for and against public child care provisions in the UK, and about which part of the government system should pay for anything provided, have been complex precisely because of the alternative positions taken in relation to the three justifications outlined above. The Second World War saw the development of subsidized child care provisions to facilitate female employment. After the war there was a dramatic decline in this, the dominant view was that labour market participation by mothers was not desirable. The publicly subsidized child care system shrank to a small local authority provided sector, seen as an essential supplement to the child protection system. Then there was a growth of provision by the education system, 'nursery education' for under 5s. In the 1960s and 1970s developing interest in compensatory education stimulated that growth, particularly in deprived areas. Evidence suggested that pre-school education might offset disadvantages that were contributing to educational under-achievement

(Halsey, 1972). Later demand grew for pre-school education for all and a wide range of private nursery schools and play groups emerged. In the 1990s the government developed a voucher system that would extend subsidy to all pre-school education. Labour repealed this at the end of the decade in favour of the extension of public provision, but then in fact developed a not-dissimilar approach to the subsidy of private providers. But alongside the growth of pre-school education more and more parents were making arrangements for pre-school (and after school) care to facilitate labour market participation by mothers. The state recognized this as a phenomenon in need of regulation through a registration system but was reluctant to subsidize it.

Some new money has been put into public provisions, particularly in deprived areas. In these there has been strong emphasis upon the setting up of partnerships of statutory and voluntary organizations. Notable here has been Sure Start: the funding of local partnerships in deprived areas to improve the early learning experiences of pre-school children, improve child care and offer a range of support to parents. By 2006 this provided 1,000 local facilities, catering for 800,000 children.

The end result of the developments described above is a confusing mixture of activities with a confusing pattern of state support. In the UK today 64 per cent of children aged three and four are attending nursery schools, but many on a part-time basis, but then a further 35 per cent are attending what are described as 'non-school education settings in the private and voluntary sector, such as local playgroups' (National Statistics, 2007, p. 26). So in effect almost all children aged three or four are in some kind of provision, at least part-time. All education in state schools is free. But levels of provision of full-time state pre-school education have historically been low. Since 1998 all four years olds have been entitled to a publicly funded early education place and since 2004 this entitlement has been extended to three years olds. A funded place only guarantees a minimum of 12.5 hours per week for 33 weeks a year, and not all parents take it up. These funded places may be in state or independent schools.

A different set of statistics can be found on day care places. In the UK about 20 per cent of children aged 0–3 have 'access to licensed services' (OECD, 2006, p. 416). This means a mix of services: private child minders, play groups and day nurseries. There is only a very small amount of public provision, this is used by local authorities as a resource for the child protection system. In 2005 in England there were 11,800 day care providers (National Statistics, 2007, p. 27). There were also about 250,000 places provided by registered child minders (Ibid., p. 26). Local authorities paid for only about 1 per cent of these places.

Local authorities subsidize the places in the day nurseries they own; while they may impose charges, in practice the resources of the vulnerable families who are being supported in this way will be low and charges are unlikely. Otherwise the only public subsidy for child care (as opposed to pre-school education) comes by way of an element in the child tax credit.

There is a requirement for all child minders and day nurseries to be registered by the local authority, which has a duty to approve arrangements and inspect from time to time. Undoubtedly there are some child minding arrangements that have not been registered, particularly where family members and friends undertake this care, but there is here now a well established local authority role which – given the numbers quoted – will be a not inconsiderable task. The costs of this activity and the costs of the limited number of local authority places in nurseries and child minding arrangements fall upon the normal budgets of local authorities.

While this may be confusing to the reader, what is even more important is that it is confusing to a parent who wants to make satisfactory care arrangements for a child. What this is likely to involve is a progression through from child-minding arrangements to some nursery education by the age of three (which has to be supplemented by continuing child-minding to cover all working hours and school holidays) and then on to a similar hodgepodge of measures (child-minding, after school clubs, holiday play schemes) for the early school years. Very little of the non-education provision gets public subsidy.

Child Protection

A distinction may be made between the issues about 'child protection' and those about 'child care in general'. This distinction is made because it is appropriate to separate the issues about the specific measures that may be brought into operation in respect of the relatively small number of children who are seen as 'at risk' of ill-treatment, neglect or abuse and the wider issues about child care policy which may be applicable to all children. In theory of course, the child protection system protects all children; in practice most children and their parents will have no encounters with any part of that system. It is hard to provide precise figures to back up this distinction, but it has been estimated that perhaps about 600,000 children in England (5 per cent of the child population) may be in need of some attention from the child protection system (Department of Health, 1995). Figures quoted below will show that fewer children than this are actually directly affected by child protection measures at any one time.

Whether it is desirable to make the distinction between child protection policy and other child care policy is a matter for debate. It may be argued that much more public policy attention should be given to the welfare of all or most children, and in particular that it is undesirable to have special measures that focus upon a limited number of ill-functioning families whilst disregarding the many problems of child poverty and deprivation. It is also sometimes contended that child protection policies are too intrusive, stigmatizing and controlling the lives of many families who do not need this intervention. Nevertheless it does seem important to recognize that on the one hand the child protection system is not a 'child care' system affecting most families and that on the other there are some policies in respect of child care in general, particularly with regard to pre-school children, which are much wider in their impact.

The Children Act of 1989 (and a Scottish Act passed in 1995) consolidated previous legislation on the protection of children. Later Acts have further developed these measures. The complex legal framework in these Acts tries to ensure that children are protected while at the same time recognizing that public interventions into family life should be kept as low as possible. It carries forward a long-standing concern to minimize the likelihood of the removal of children from their family of origin. The legislation identifies a wide range of ways in which authorities may spend money to try to avoid taking children into direct care.

Social workers in the child care authorities have a crucial role to play in situations in which evidence comes to light that children may be at risk of ill treatment, abuse or neglect. Their authorities are required to maintain 'child protection registers' of children 'at risk' and develop 'child protection plans' to offer appropriate supportive services to these children and their families. There were about 28,000 children on these registers in England in 2005, that is, about 25 children per 10,000 children in the population (DFES, 2007, key points, p. 2). Only a small proportion of children at risk are taken away from their families.

The most draconian powers available to child care workers are those which enable them to activate procedures under which children may be 'looked after'. The rather confusing expression 'looked after' is now used to describe situations in which children are taken into the 'legal' care of a local authority. To avoid ambiguity it will be put in inverted commas in this discussion. Children become formally 'looked after' when their parents are unable to care for them or are providing care that is deemed to be placing the child seriously 'at risk'. Decisions on this are the responsibility of the courts, but most action to 'look after' children will have been initiated by social workers in the child care authorities. Once a child is 'looked after', the local authority will seek to ensure a settled future for him or her. In some cases, this will mean return to parental care under supervision. Where this is not possible, foster care is widely used. Institutional care is likely to be regarded as a temporary expedient in many cases, while the situation is assessed and longer-term plans are made.

There were about 60,000 'looked after' children in England in March 2007 (DFES/National Statistics, table 1, 2007) Of these, 71 per cent were boarded out with foster parents, 4 per cent placed prior to adoption (we come back to that below) 9 per cent were 'placed' with their own parents, and there were 6 per cent 'other placements' (generally with a friend or relative). Only about 11 per cent were in some kind of institutionalized care. There has been a slight tendency for the number of 'looked after' children to increase in recent years, but the proportion in institutional care has remained stable.

Among the children who may be deemed to be in need of this form of statutory care is a group of generally older children who are considered to be out of parental control. Under the 1969 Children and Young Persons Act, local authorities acquired increased responsibilities for the care of children brought before the courts for delinquent acts. The object of this legislation was to move away from labelling young offenders as criminals, and to make the issue for decision by the juvenile courts one about responsibility for care rather than punishment for crime. Child care authorities may now have to undertake the 'supervision' of such children, or they may be given legal custody of them. They may fulfil the parental responsibilities entailed in a variety of ways, including the supervision of a child within a residential institution. The former remand homes and approved schools became specially staffed 'community homes' under this legislation. Since many local authorities do not possess the residential resources to fulfil responsibilities of this kind on their own and, in particular, lack the necessary range of resources, which must include (exceptionally) a 'secure' institution, regional planning committees have been set up to facilitate the use of homes by authorities other than those responsible for their management.

Where the responsibilities of local authorities to 'look after' children are discharged through the use of foster parents, payment will be made, and the arrangements will be supervised by social workers. Some 'looked after' children may eventually be legally adopted into another family. Child care authorities have responsibilities to organize and supervise adoption procedures, but these may sometimes be sub-contracted to private agencies. Box 9.1 sets out some data on adoptions and comments on this issue.

There has been considerable attention to the long-run implications in which, in effect, parental responsibilities are in the hands of public authorities. This is particularly a problem for those children taken into institutions, but may also apply in respect of foster care (where parent/ child type relationships may not be established, particularly when there are moves between different foster homes). Research shows that looked after children underperform in the education system. Perhaps the fact that child care and education services are now combined will help to ensure more attention is given to this issue. But then there are problems to be addressed about transitions from education to work, where looked after children may abruptly shift into independence, without the parental support that others generally have over a transition period. Local authorities have powers to give some support across this period, but by comparison with youngsters in 'normal' families this is likely to be slight.

In many cases, prevention of child abuse or neglect requires activities other than the formal institution of legal procedures to transfer formal responsibility for the care of children. Social workers have a number of ways in which they may try to do this.

Box 9.1 Adoption

It is important to bear in mind how low the level of adoptions is in Britain today; there were just 3,300 in England in 2005–6 compared with 21,000 in 1969–70 (DFES/ National Statistics, 2007, notes).

A little over half of all children adopted were 'looked after' prior to adoption. The government is putting pressure on local authorities to try to ensure that they consider the possibility of adoption when they are 'looking after' children. But, there is a need to be sceptical about suggestions that there are large numbers of unwanted young children that could be adopted. As was shown above, many children are in care in ordinary homes. Many are away from the care of their parents for relatively short periods. More than half of 'looked after' children are over ten years of age (ibid.).

They may themselves try to offer support to families – visiting regularly, making suggestions about how to deal with stresses in the household, listening and counselling, and generally responding to cries for help from families under pressure. In doing this, they may be able to mobilize resources: domestic help, day care for children, grants or loans, help in kind. They may also try to secure help for the family from other statutory organizations: for example, better housing or attention to educational or health problems. There may also be voluntary organizations that they can mobilize to help: providing charitable help in cash or kind.

In recent years, there has been a succession of very disturbing incidents. Children have been seriously ill treated and even killed by parents or step-parents. Typically these cases do not come 'out of the blue'. The families have been known to child care authorities beforehand and the case for the removal of the children has been considered. Child care authorities have been criticized for a lack of decisive action, but there has also been criticism of them for over-reacting. Furthermore, there have also been worrying cases that have come to light in which children have been abused while 'looked after'. In sum, while various public inquiries and central government have, from time to time, been very critical of child care authorities, there are no easy formulae to guide them on when to act and when not to act.

The changes to the policy-making and administrative arrangements for child care in England, taking these services in to the Department for Children, Schools and Families and integrating them with education at the local level have been seen as influenced by one of the investigations of failure in the child protection system. A report by a former Chief Inspector of Social Services, Lord Laming, argued that a lack of attention to child care in general leads to child protection failure (Laming Report, 2003). In Chapter 7 we took a sceptical view of a government tendency to see structural change as an appropriate response to policy failure in the health service. A similar comment is appropriate here. In Chapter 2 we noted that this reform puts together an education based administrative service with an increasingly 'arms-length' relationship with schools with a child protection orientated children's service. The issue here surely centres around the relationship between overall pre-school and out of school child care provision and child protection, not the relationship of both to the education system. Since Lord Laming was a former civil service 'insider' one cannot help wondering whether there were not other motives for this large structural shift. However, what is clear is that Laming's report contributed to bringing the issue of the relationship between overall child care and child protection higher up the policy agenda. The structural changes were accompanied by a wider batch of measures to tackle this issue. Soon after the Laming Report the government published a Green Paper (DFES, 2003) that led on to a Children's Act in 2004 and other administrative measures. That Green Paper, *Every Child Matters*, is seen as a seminal document for modern child care policy (see Churchill, chapter 5 in Clarke, Maltby and Kennett, 2007). Its key points are set in Box 9.2.

At the same time as the connections between child care and the education system has been on the agenda, so too has been that between the former and the health care system. The challenge to government aspirations to manage the interactions between services is choices have to be made about which bits to put together within

> **Box 9.2   *Every Child Matters***
>
> This Green Paper defines child well-being in terms of five objectives:
> - health
> - safety
> - contribution to society
> - enjoyment and achievements
> - economic well-being
>
> As well as leading on to the Children Act 2004 and the changing of departmental responsibilities, it generated a range of initiatives by various government departments. Churchill (2007, pp. 102–3) specifies the following 'key dimensions of change':
>
>> a shift towards outcome-led, integrated, responsive and preventative services; improved vertical and horizontal service accountability; more joined-up working; and better workforce retention, recruitment and performance.
>
> It is difficult for the outsider to assess developments of this kind, hard to specify concrete gains and hard to summarize in a generic textbook like this.

departmental structures. The key development on the child care/health care frontier has been experiments with Children's Trusts within specific local authority areas. These seem to contradict the other institutional changes, but in this case the aim is to facilitate collaboration and joint working across the services.

Control over the Education System

It was shown, earlier in this chapter, that where control over the school system in the UK used to be described as a 'partnership' between central and local government, it is now the case that the former is quite clearly dominant. It is not perhaps surprising that this is now the case. Since central government exercises strict control over local government expenditure, the fact that education accounts for around half of this expenditure inevitably puts it in the spotlight. Furthermore, politicians at national level take a great interest in the way education is organized and conducted. The development of comprehensive education was an issue that fundamentally divided the parties. Governments have also felt it important to take stands on such matters as literacy, the core content of the curriculum and the role of nursery education. Concern about 'failing schools' has led to a willingness to replace local authority control in some cases.

The uneasy relationship between central and local government is not the only area in which there is a power struggle within the UK educational system. At the local level, the running of the system involves a number of different groups which are contending for influence or protecting their prerogatives.

Schools are required to have governing bodies. These are required to consist of parents, teachers, co-opted members and local education authority nominees. As pointed out above, these bodies are now responsible for delegated budgets partly guaranteed by the central government. They have significant control over appointments.

An issue which has received considerable attention has been parental choice of schools for their children. While there were high pupil–teacher ratios and pressure on school numbers in many parts of the country, the scope for parental choice was fairly limited. As school rolls have fallen, though, the situation has changed. In urban areas, in particular, variations in the popularity of schools have often become very clear. In the Education Act of 1980, the government tried to provide parents with some measure of choice over schools. Local authorities are required to give information which will help parents to choose schools, and there is an appeal procedure available for those whose wishes are not granted. Parental choice seems to be operating as a curb on innovation by teachers; it may also be helping to determine where cuts will be made. Inasmuch as choice is more likely to be exercised by middle-class parents, it may be enhancing the tendency for there to be a hierarchy of schools, under the influence of geographical location. We return to that topic below.

In the schools themselves, head teachers expect a considerable measure of freedom in determining how their school is run and the way in which subjects are taught. They operate, of course, in consultation with their teachers, but vary extensively in the degree to which they allow staff participation in decision making. In the last resort, however, the class teacher clearly has some autonomy in determining his or her input, and relationship to pupils.

However, contemporary political developments have influenced these relationships. The next section will look at the ways in which central control over the curriculum has increased. That has been accompanied by the elaboration of the long-standing system of school inspection, now run by a quasi-autonomous agency - the Office for Standards in Education (Ofsted) - which regularly produces reports, some of which are highly critical both of the way schools are managed and of the effectiveness of individual teachers. On top of this, now, teachers have been put even more directly under the government spotlight. The government has been developing a new career structure for teachers involving a rigorous appraisal and assessment system and a salary structure that gives extra rewards for good teachers. Contemporary sociological analyses of the education system see the cumulative impact of these as involving changes to the way the teaching role is perceived - by teachers, pupils and the public – that may be described as changing educational 'discourse' (see Box 9.3).

The further and higher education systems have experienced parallel developments under the supervision of their funding councils. In higher education, the expectation that staff will be researchers as well as teachers has involved the development of a 'research assessment exercise' in which research and publications are assessed by an expert panel drawn from within the profession. Part of the funding formula for universities and colleges is based on this exercise.

Box 9.3   The 'remaking' of teaching

Ball (2008, p. 147) argues as result of the many changes to the way the teaching task is structured and controlled:

> teachers have been remade within policy, and their work and the meaning of teaching have been discursively re-articulated. This has been brought about by the introduction of new forms of preparation, new work practices and new workers into the classroom and the use of a new language through which teachers talk about what they do and are talked about, think about themselves and one another and are measured and appraised, and paid, in relation to their performance.

Ball's analysis is contained within a broader examination of the many new forces – managerial and economic - upon the education system. An obviously related topic is the way in which the roles of head-teachers have been changed too.

All of the education system has experienced the development of a control system in which the activities of teachers are increasingly under scrutiny. Under the Conservatives, there was some attempt to make the crucial control devices market-based. The success or failure of schools and colleges were to depend on their success in attracting students (and, in higher education, research funds). The Labour government seems less happy with the use of such devices, but we therefore see, instead, further prescriptions about how activities should be carried out and the strengthening of methods of checking that the instructions given are followed. In the next section, this theme is explored further, with reference to the national curriculum.

The Government and the Curriculum

The 1988 Act introduced a requirement that a national curriculum should be developed for use in state financed schools in England and Wales. It initially applied to all state supported schools, but oddly recent legislation to allow the setting up of quasi-independent Trust Schools exempt them from this requirement. That curriculum has been elaborated since the original legislation, and it is kept under review. Its elements are set out in Box 9.4.

Linked to the curriculum is the testing of children at 'key stages': seven, eleven, and fourteen years of age. The testing system involves the setting of attainment targets, and is carried out under the supervision of a central curriculum and assessment body. This testing supplements the longer-standing arrangements for examinations at the end of the school years, between 16 and 18.

These measures represent a marked departure from the philosophy of the 1944 Education Act, which left most education under local government control and issues

Box 9.4   The national curriculum

Three core subjects: English, Maths and Science (plus Welsh in Welsh-speaking areas).

Seven foundation subjects: History, Geography, Design and Technology, Information and Communications Technology, Music, Art and Design, Physical Education, Citizenship and another modern language. The last two only apply to over-11s.

There is also a requirement to provide a programme of religious education, which reflects the 'dominance' of Christianity in Britain.

about the determination of the curriculum largely in the hands of teachers, operating with an eye on the entrance requirements of higher education and the expectations of employers.

A comment is appropriate here about religion in the curriculum. A British Social Attitudes survey showed that only 60 per cent of the population claimed to belong to a specific religion, with 55 per cent being Christian (quoted in National Statistics, 2002, p. 220). A much lower percentage actually practices their religion through regular attendance at a place of worship. It may seem strange that the state education system should take on a role as the propagator of religious belief. Historically the arrangements for religion in schools originated from a compromise between the government and the religious bodies in the 1940s, providing both for religion in state schools and the possibility of participation by religious bodies in the provision schools given state funding.

A feature of education policy under Labour governments since 1997 is that it has been happy to reinforce religious participation in the provision of publicly funded education. Where before most 'single faith' schools were Anglican or Roman Catholic, with a very small number of Jewish schools, now Muslim and Sikh schools have been set up. Furthermore, there have also been some schools set up by smaller Christian groups. At the time of writing controversy has developed about teaching that challenges evolutionary theory in biology at a City Technology College run by a fundamentalist Christian group. But perhaps a more serious worry about the encouragement of diversity in religious participation in education is that it may undermine efforts to eliminate discrimination and racism. We will return to this theme.

Diversity and Selectivity in the Education System

Results of the statutory tests required by the National Curriculum are published, providing data on the 'achievements' of individual schools in a form which encourages their presentation by the media in 'league tables'. Since much educational attainment is determined by factors outside the control of the schools, these can be very misleading (see Box 9.6). Some schools may be securing a considerable 'value-added' element in enhancing the achievements of children. Others may be doing very little for pupils who, by virtue of their socio-economic backgrounds, are likely to score well in tests in any case. Schools in the former group may be unfairly perceived as achieving little, while those in the latter group win unwarranted esteem. These comparisons encourage schools to try to recruit pupils with a high academic potential. To be fair, efforts are being made to include 'value added' data, taking into account social backgrounds as well as progress between tests, but the methodology is complex and it is probably still the crude results that are given the most attention: as Warmington and Murphy put it, coverage of this by the media is 'predictable, simplistic, ritualistic' (2004, p. 290).

Sociological studies of education have suggested that as pupils approach school-leaving age, there are many factors, often beyond the control of the schools, that contribute to divisions between school-oriented 'academic' pupils and an anti-school group who increasingly see their education as irrelevant and who drop out of participation in all school activities (Ford, 1969; Willis, 1977). A relevant concern in secondary education, therefore, is not so much the fate of the brighter pupils - the comprehensive schools have been eager to 'prove themselves' by doing justice to the needs of this group – as the difficulties entailed in providing a relevant education for those at the other end of the ability range. There are related problems here, of course, of absenteeism and delinquency. Box 9.5 highlights contemporary concerns about this issue.

Box 9.5   Arguments about extending education for those who get little benefit from the system

In January 2008 the government introduced a bill to force all young people in England to stay in education or training until the age of 18. The government argued that making teenagers stay on is seen as essential to improving people's skills amid growing global competition.

But critics argued that the government needs to make the curriculum more interesting to tempt young people to stay on. The education charity Edge argued that the government will need to overhaul the curriculum if the bill has any chance of succeeding, welcoming the measure as a brave attempt to solve the problem of under-achievement but saying:

> the bill will be condemned to failure unless the government tackles the reasons why young people drop out in the first place. For some young people, a curriculum based on the traditional timetable of academic subjects continues to be the best option. They respond well to learning by listening and reading. However, many young people are bored and uninspired by education pre-16. A third of young people drop out because they think it's boring and irrelevant.

http://news.bbc.co.uk/1/hi/programmes/bbc_parliament/7186730.stm

Overall, this issue concerns the relationship of the education system to the needs of underprivileged groups in our society – for example, low-skilled workers and some ethnic minorities. Since, moreover, such groups are located in specific areas, there is a geographical dimension to this problem. One of the arguments advanced in favour of the comprehensive school is that it is able to take all the children of a limited geographical community. But suppose such a 'community' is manifestly not truly 'comprehensive', and, worse still, suppose atypical residents in that community take steps to educate their children elsewhere, then new distinctions arise between schools. This is a significant problem for comprehensive secondary education in Britain.

This problem has been intensified by government efforts to ensure that parents have maximum opportunities to choose schools for their children. Where choices are available there are distinct social differences in the extent to which these are exercised. Such choices will be influenced by the extent to which parents seek appropriate information and explore options. Then capacity to take up options that entail travel away from the most accessible school will be influenced by family resources, particularly the availability of cars and the capacity to meet transportation costs. The result is that that more choice is actually leading to more segregation, in terms of social class and ethnic origin (Burgess et al., 2006).

The Conservative governments of the 1980s and 1990s seemed prepared to disregard these issues in favour of an approach to education which emphasized the raising of standards through competition between schools. The rhetoric of the Labour politicians suggests a commitment to changing this. In its 1997 manifesto, Labour argued that 'far too many children are denied the opportunity to succeed', spoke of 'zero tolerance of underperformance' and said 'no matter where a school is, Labour will not tolerate under-achievement'. Labour has given a high priority to education. It headlined the education section in its 'annual report' for 1997–8 (HMSO, 1998, p. 30):

> The Government's aim is to build a world-class education system by taking excellence wherever it is found and spreading it widely. We want every school to be a good school so that parents know that wherever they send their children they will get a decent education.

The underlying question here is whether a search for 'excellence' throughout the education system, with a strong emphasis on standards, can be sustained without, in the process, creating winners and losers. In the last analysis, an education system channels people towards the limited opportunities that exist in the wider society. In aiming to raise education standards for all, the government has an obvious political need to reassure parents whose children are already benefiting from the best the system has to offer that the process is one, to borrow other words from the Labour manifesto, of 'levelling up, not levelling down'.

Yet any emphasis on reducing educational disadvantage must imply, in a race that all cannot win, advancing some at the expense of others. Perhaps a shift of attention away from crude competition between schools, in which those with the right social catchment areas must inevitably win, towards a more egalitarian system is occurring, under the camouflage of an 'all can win' rhetoric designed to reassure anxious middle-class parents.

Doubts about the reality of the government's egalitarianism are however reinforced by its willingness to allow greater diversity in schools, particularly secondary schools, and its willingness to countenance the reintroduction of some forms of selection. Conservative legislation in 1993 allowed schools to become 'specialist' and practice limited forms of selection. It was argued that this implied specialization in technology (as in the city technology colleges) or in the arts or sports. Labour's 1998 legislation permitted specialist schools to admit up to 10 per cent of children on the basis of aptitude. By September 2006 82 per cent of all secondary schools, covering about two-thirds of all pupils, were specialist schools. Since specializing to establish a centre of excellent in specific subjects brings with it additional funds for the school, the pressure to go in this direction has been very strong. Overall, Tomlinson concludes:

> The Conservatives promised *Choice and Diversity*, New Labour promised *Diversity and Excellence*. The reality was that structural differentiation was ensuring a hierarchical pecking order of schools, which unsurprisingly, given the history of English schooling, continued to mirror the social class structure. (Tomlinson, 2001, p. 99)

Yet the government continues to see increasing the range of choices of schools as a solution to educational inequalities. Their most recent additions to the complex educational 'pantheon' – Academies and Trust Schools – have been targeted at socially deprived areas. But is seems odd to address the issue in this way in the face of the evidence on how choice works in the system as a whole. The issues about policies to combat educational disadvantage are explored further in the next three sections.

Education and the Disadvantaged

In the last section the Labour government's commitment to education improvement for all was quoted, but reservations were expressed about how this is being translated into action. In fairness it is important to acknowledge other aspects of the government's strategy. Key measures toward the improvement of education, with an eye on educational disadvantage include:

- the establishment of Education Action Zones in deprived areas, where public/private partnerships have been set up to try to secure additional investment and to encourage innovation;
- setting improvement targets for schools and assuming government powers to intervene in failing schools (including the power to impose an alternative management system, as described above);
- new investments to reduce class sizes;
- as noted above, targeting new school initiatives at disadvantaged areas.

The discussion in the last section highlighted the role education plays in relation to the distribution of occupational opportunities in our society. On the Left, there has traditionally been considerable concern about the extent to which education contributes to upward mobility. There are two versions of this preoccupation. One of these involves a commitment to equality of opportunity, and therefore a demand that all able children of whatever social background should have access to educational openings. The other is a concern about equality in a more absolute sense. A naïve version of this places faith in the possibility of an education system that can help to create a more equal society. A more sophisticated approach recognizes that education cannot be, by itself, an engine of social change, but stresses that it must play a part by ensuring that children are not socially segregated and that schools attempt to compensate for other sources of inequality.

These issues have been explored in relation to gender, socio-economic status (or social class) and ethnicity. This section will concentrate on the first of two of these. The next section explores some of the issues about ethnicity. As far as gender is concerned, most explicit discrimination against females has now disappeared. In fact, there is now a female majority in higher education (see Table 9.1). There have nevertheless been concerns about the extent to which there is within the education system a 'hidden curriculum' which socializes males and females differently – inculcating separate gender roles and influencing the subjects chosen in the later years in schools and in universities. This may have indirect implications for women's treatment in the labour force, where inequality is still very evident.

Male underachievement has begun to secure attention, with suggestions that the culture of primary schools is largely feminine. This is a complex subject which will not be explored further here. It is perhaps symptomatic of continued male dominance in society that, as soon as most discrimination against females has been eliminated, concern about male underachievement is leading to calls for explicit interventions!

As far as the issues about socio-economic class are concerned, 'equality of opportunity' is a slogan that finds quite wide political support. Differential educational opportunity and achievement have been extensively studied by sociologists and psychologists (see Box 9.6).

As far as social class disadvantages are concerned, there are limits to the extent to which this issue can be fully met, if only because of the extent to which it implies a conflict with the objective of facilitating social mobility through education. If a key concern of education is to prepare children to operate in a middle-class world, even perhaps to join that world, then it may not be particularly functional for it to be concerned to relate to working-class culture. There is a great dilemma here, which is relevant to the alienation of some children from an education system in which they are becoming the 'failures'. You cannot eliminate the concept of failure as long as you have the objective of enabling some to 'succeed' through the education system. It may be desirable to eliminate the more invidious aspects of competition within the system – to recognize, for example, that progress relative to ability may be as important as the easy success of the advantaged and talented - but notions of achievement, and consequently non-achievement, are fundamental to the role of education in our kind of society.

Box 9.6 Research evidence on the determinants of educational achievement

The evidence accumulated by research in the 1950s and early 1960s (Floud et al., 1956; Jackson and Marsden, 1962; Douglas, 1964) was used in making the case for comprehensive education and for the abandonment of streaming. Later, attention shifted to those problems of underachievement in the education system that cannot be directly attributed to the way that system is structured. Two particular themes were emphasized: the significance of home background for educational success and the extent to which the 'culture' of the school system is alien to some children.

It has been shown that poverty and poor housing conditions militate against educational success (Douglas, 1964; Central Advisory Council for Education, 1967). There is little the education system can do about these problems, but it can try to compensate for them with extra efforts to help deprived children. Home backgrounds are relevant in another sense, too. There are wide variations in the extent to which parents help with the education of their children. Such help takes many forms, involving not only the more obvious forms of encouragement and the provision of books and study facilities, but also a great deal of implicit 'teaching' through interaction with children. The latter starts when babies are very tiny, and one of its most significant ingredients is the learning of language. The children who are most deprived in these respects are often those who are also most deprived in a material sense. However, parental educational levels and abilities are also relevant. There is a variety of practical ways in which the education system may help to compensate for these less straightforwardly material disadvantages, both before and after children reach compulsory school age (Halsey, 1972).

The issue with regard to the culture of the schools is a more difficult one. In part, the problem is one of identification of the needs and special interests of children whose backgrounds differ from that of the white educated middle-class whose needs have dominated the values of the system. There is a variety of ways in which stories, educational situations and examples can be devised that seem relevant to these children. Hence there is ample scope for change here.

While the key research findings date from a long while ago, the situation remains very much the same. Ennals (2004) documents the continued class divide.

Tomlinson (2001, p. 160) quotes research by Killeen et al. (1999) showing young people's views of education to be very instrumental, with 'qualifications ... a paper currency that could be exchanged for work opportunities' and a low opinion of vocational courses. At the time of writing the government is trying to address issues about the relevance of education for under-achievers by giving more attention to vocationally relevant courses in secondary schools. They face a dilemma that there is an inherent conflict between this objective and a truly comprehensive approach to education.

The idea of attempting to compensate for disadvantage by providing special resources for the schools in some areas was suggested in a report of the Plowden committee (Central Advisory Council for Education, 1967). Many of the measures adopted did no more than attempt to redress the imbalance of educational resources between run-down inner-city areas, where the schools were old and facilities were limited, and newer suburban areas. Additional money was made available for capital projects and current expenditure in areas where there were high levels of deprivation. In addition, the government provided for extra teachers, above the normal quotas, and special additional allowances for teachers in those areas. Areas were designated on the basis of statistics on the socio-economic status of parents, the extent of absence of housing amenities, proportions of children receiving free school meals, and proportion of schoolchildren with serious linguistic difficulties. In 1998 this was replaced by an 'ethnic minority achievement grant'.

The Education Action Zones, listed above as one of the post-1997 policies, involve a return to interventions of this kind. They are expected to involve a range of innovations and experiments including the development of specialist centres and the employment of teachers with special roles, family literacy schemes and literacy summer schools and the exploration of new forms of work-related learning. The government has expressed a willingness to adapt the national curriculum to meet specific local needs. The sums of public money going into these zones are quite slight, but the government is seeking partnership arrangements with local firms and other organizations to try to increase the resources available.

Education and Minority Ethnic Groups

It is important to bear in mind that the pattern of migration to the UK has been such that there are now few children who were not born in the UK. Of course there will be some, particularly the children of recent migrants from Eastern Europe, for whom there will be issues about reception into a strange system and intensive language training will be an issue. But the main issues about the education of ethnic minorities are about the treatment of children of migrants. Related to this are issues about the incidence of discrimination based upon skin colour or cultural differences. Most of the parents of these UK-born children of migrants come from the Asian sub-continent, the Caribbean and Africa. There is thus a substantial non-white school population, concentrated in urban areas.

The Parekh report (2000) summarizes the evidence on the educational performance of ethnic minority children as showing that children of Afro-Caribbean parents start school 'at much the same standard as the national average' but have fallen behind by the age of 10, pupils with Indian parents achieve above the national average and those with Pakistani and Bangladeshi parents achieve below average but 'steadily close the gap between themselves and others in the course of their education' (2000, p. 146).

In the period when many non-white children were themselves immigrants, the system saw their language problems and cultural differences as the main issue. While there are still children for whom this is true, many children are encouraged by parents to make the most of educational opportunities, and many have made remarkable progress within the UK system. They may face problems, however, in coming to terms with strong contrasts between patterns of home life and those of school life.

Some Asian groups have begun either to make demands for new developments in the education system in tune with their cultural needs (e.g. appropriate religious education and courses in Asian languages) or to call for separate state-subsidized schools for their children. It has been noted above that the government has been prepared to respond to this demand (see p. 196). There is a particular difficulty here about the extent to which the demand for separate educational arrangements comes from Islamic groups (see Box 9.7).

Box 9.7   The education of children from Islamic families

Given the longstanding special provision within the UK education system for schools for specific Christian denominational groups, and for Jewish children, there seems to be a strong case for state support for schools set up by Islamic groups. That case is reinforced by the extent to which children from Islamic backgrounds encounter prejudice, and the extent to which there are strong Christian traditions running through the culture of this country. That case has been further strengthened by the extent to which much contemporary international conflict is between the Judeo-Christian world and the Islamic one. Terrorism involving fundamentalist Muslims contributed further to popular views of that divide.

Yet it is precisely this cultural division that presents us with a reason to question the encouragement of cultural divisions by divisions in the educational system. A look across to Northern Ireland, where a division in education along religious lines has many of the characteristics of a division along cultural lines, and contributes to the division of that community, provides evidence for doubt about this model of education for a culturally diverse society. Such misgivings are reinforced by the extent to which there has also been interest in independence from white parents eager to minimize the Asian influence on certain schools.

But, as noted above, it would be actively discriminatory to refuse to allow some kinds of 'faith schools' where others have for long had official support. A radical alternative could be – in an otherwise increasingly secular society – to eliminate state support for faith schools of any kind.

At one time in the late 1960s and early 1970s, a number of education authorities bussed children to other areas, to try to prevent certain schools from having high concentrations of Asian children. Since this bussing was a one-way process, applied only to Asians, it was rightly abandoned as discriminatory. Now, the imposition of rules about regard for parental choice means that local authorities cannot even manipulate catchment areas in the interests of any kind of ethnic 'balance'. Parental choices may enhance tendencies towards segregation.

Caribbean immigrants came from a society in which European cultural models have a strong influence, and are reinforced through the education process. It is precisely this bias in British African-Caribbean society, and in African American society, that has been attacked by those concerned about the development of black consciousness. It is argued that this dominance of a white cultural model contributes to the maintenance of a subordinate self-image. Black leaders in Britain have become deeply concerned about the underachievement of children of West Indian origin. They attribute this to a variety of factors, but see the white ethnic and cultural bias in the education system as reinforcing other aspects of disadvantage.

Hence, while the education system continues to see the issues regarding non-white children as issues about their characteristics, it may alternatively be suggested that the central issue is its ethnic and cultural assumptions, the phenomenon described as 'institutional racism'. An official committee, chaired by Lord Swann, reported on its 'Inquiry into the Education of Children from Ethnic Minority Groups' in 1985. In a brief guide to the report, Lord Swann, while not using the expression 'institutional racism', made it very clear that the issue of society and the education system's response was of central importance in explaining the problem of underachievement by non-whites. He argued (Department of Education and Science, 1985, p. 9):

> on the evidence so far there is at least a dual problem. On the one hand, society must not, through prejudice and discrimination, increase the social and economic deprivation of ethnic minority families. On the other, schools must respond with greater sensitivity, and without any trace of prejudice, to the needs of ethnic minority children.

Lord Swann saw the latter as to be achieved through the concept of 'Education for All'. This meant that (p. 10):

> [t]he fundamental change needed is a recognition that the problem facing the educational system is not just how to educate the children of ethnic minorities, but how to educate all children. Britain has long been an ethnically diverse society, and is now, mainly because of her imperial past, much more obviously one. All pupils must be brought to an understanding of what is entailed if such a society is to become a fair and harmonious entity.

A later report by the Office for Standards in Education (Ofsted, 1999) indicated the need for continued attention to 'institutional racism' in schools. It spoke of a lack of attention to explicit strategies to attack these issues and of an absence of monitoring.

Clearly, the central issues now concern the culture of the education system. There is a need to tackle the biases in the system through the encouragement of culturally relevant studies, and action to combat ethnocentric biases in the curriculum. This last problem about the education of black children is very closely linked with the issue of the place which disadvantaged white children find themselves occupying within the system – as discussed in the previous section – and with the quite concrete disadvantages of children from lower-income homes. Inasmuch as black entrants to Britain have generally been forced to accept many of the poorest jobs and worst housing, children find that the 'inferior' stereotype of the black person seems to be reinforced by their, and their parents', experience. Moreover, the fact that many black parents have themselves experienced educational disadvantage means that, like comparable lower-class white parents, they are ill-equipped to help their children to tackle the education system.

There is a web of reinforcing disadvantages here. In a context of general progress in tackling racial disadvantage in the education system some of the most intractable problems occur where disadvantages of class and race (and even perhaps gender, inasmuch as black boys from poor backgrounds are particularly salient under-performers) come together. Ball argues that, in respect of these issues there is a 'history of policy avoidance' (2008, p. 172). That may seem a harsh judgement. It seems to be particularly based upon two important points. One is that official attention to issues about ethnic disadvantage has been sporadic, fuelled by panics based upon investigations of specific incidents – riots and official mishandling of murders and other incidents that highlight prejudice and discrimination (the Stephen Lawrence case in particular). The other is that the very high emphasis upon satisfying the demands of the white middle class within the education system has led to the paradoxical result that, where upwardly mobile people from ethnic minorities have assimilated well to the demands of the system there have been significant achievements but others have been left behind by an uncomprehending system (see also Gillborn, 1998, 2005, on this). We come in the next section to another symptom of the latter: exclusions from schools.

Many of the points made here are relevant to other policy areas. In particular, the chapter on the personal social services might have discussed some of the issues about the inadequacies of services for minorities. Similarly, the chapter on the health service could have dealt more with the extent to which there is an ethnic dimension to inequalities in health, and explored some of the communication difficulties which arise when white health professionals pay insufficient regard to cultural and language problems. Lack of space prevented those discussions; it has been interposed here because of the particular salience of the issue for education. Readers are urged to think about the relevance of the points made here for those other policy areas. We will return to this subject in Chapter 12.

Special Education and Other Welfare Measures

The education of children with disabilities requires the system to develop certain special resources. However, the trend is to try to integrate children with special educational needs as far as possible into the ordinary system. There is a significant group of children in each authority who are classified as experiencing 'learning difficulties', as a result of the possession of various kinds of physical or intellectual disabilities. It is important to bear in mind that this is a diverse group. The expression 'learning difficulties' – adopted to try to avoid pejorative language – rather masks this. There will be children with physical impairments, including two groups with distinct needs stemming from sight or hearing difficulties. There are many forms of intellectual disability. At the one extreme there is dyslexia, at the other forms of brain damage or brain malfunction that make even the most elementary tasks difficult. There are also various kinds of behavioural difficulties that may interfere with learning. It is also important to bear in mind that many of the most intractable difficulties arise where pupils manifest more than one of these problems.

All these children are required to be carefully tested, and a 'statement' has to be prepared setting out their needs. Parents have a right of appeal to an independent tribunal if they are dissatisfied with the statement. On the basis of the statement, children with learning difficulties will either secure some extra teaching or support in an ordinary school (for which school budgets are enhanced) or be sent to a school where there are special facilities and staffing arrangements. There is a variety of special schools. In most authorities, there are separate ones designed for children with 'moderate' or 'severe' learning difficulties. There are also some specialized schools, run by private or voluntary bodies, at which local authorities may buy places. But there is a strong emphasis upon efforts to integrate as many children with learning difficulties as possible into mainstream schools.

There are a number of non-teaching activities that make contributions to the overall performance of the education system. Schools may provide meals and milk to children. The former may be available free to pupils whose parents are on income support. The extent to which they should be subsidized for others has been something of a political football, and extensive cuts have been made to these services. Means-tested grants may also be available towards the cost of school clothing, and towards support of pupils in the sixteen to eighteen age group who are still at school.

The welfare of schoolchildren is also given attention through the school health service and the education welfare service. Historically, the main concern of this service has been truancy. Today, its objectives have been widened to embrace a whole range of problems that may affect educational performance. In this, it has the support of child guidance services.

There are growing concerns about the tendency for schools to use their formal powers to exclude disruptive children. This seems to have been encouraged by the development of competition between schools encouraged by parental choice and the publication of performance data. In 2004–5 there were 9,400 permanent exclusions of children from schools. Such children may be found places in other schools, or they may be provided with special educational arrangements outside schools. Disturbing aspects of exclusion policies include the fact that exclusion rates for boys are nearly four times those of girls and the fact that children from families of all or part Caribbean origin are more likely to be excluded than others.

Conclusions

The state system of education had roots in a mid-nineteenth-century concern with the training of an effective workforce able to operate in an increasingly complex industrial system and society. Its growth has been inextricably entwined with the development of a democratic society. The original view that the newly enfranchised should be literate has been answered by a belief on the part of the electorate that education holds the key to social advancement. Such a view is certainly encouraged by the enormous emphasis put on education by the political parties. This may be, in part, an illusion. The opportunity structure is determined by the economy and by the political system. Increased education does not, in itself, increase the supply of 'top jobs'; it merely increases the competition for them. The fact that educational qualifications are widely used as a basis for discrimination between applicants for jobs emphasizes the link between education and social and economic advancement, regardless of whether those jobs require education at the level, or of the kind, possessed by those deemed best suited to fill them. Hence, the nature of the education system and the opportunities it provides are of central political importance in the UK.

As job opportunities for young people diminished in the UK in the 1980s and 1990s, a debate about the role of the education system was stimulated. This was linked to a long-standing controversy about the extent to which the UK's economic underachievement can be attributed to defects in the education system – insufficient emphasis on science and engineering, high esteem for a cultural education that has no immediate practical use, and so on. This is a complex issue, involving propositions which are difficult to test empirically. What it does involve is a tendency to assign too much importance to the role of the education system, disregarding the extent to which it has to respond to social and political demands on it. More immediately, this debate seems to encourage a tendency to attribute the shortage of jobs not to deficiencies in the demand for labour but to inadequacies in the supply of labour - to see the education system as failing the youth of this country. This flies in the face of the evidence that competition for jobs is stimulating 'qualification inflation', that the qualifications needed for many jobs are being increased because of the stiff competition for them. It is leading, however, to an ever-increasing demand for vocationally relevant education (particularly for the vast majority of publicly educated boys and girls unlikely to move easily into elite jobs).

The emphasis in political rhetoric about education as a preparation for work – both in discussions of individual underachievement and in evaluations of the role of the education system as a contributor to global economic competition – exacerbates the difficulties about developing an egalitarian education that can offer a preparation for life for all children.

This chapter has devoted quite a lot of attention to issues about the relationship between education and social class (and the relationship between that and ethnicity and gender as alternative concerns). Government rhetoric suggests a great concern about educational inequality, yet this is contradicted by concerns about performance and about choice which suggest that above all our politicians do not want to fail parents who expect the education system to help them pass their economic advantages on to their children. This chapter has not looked at the rather minor regulatory role the state plays in respect of the private sector. Yet that sector casts a shadow over public policy. Ball quotes one Labour secretary of state, Charles Clarke who confided in journalists that 'There is a significant chunk ... who go private because they feel despairing about the quality of education. They are the people we are after' (Ball, 2008, p. 93).

Education has become perhaps more politicized than ever before. Government are now very clearly unwilling to leave education to the educationalists, or to delegate responsibility for education policy to local authorities or the governors of schools and colleges.

Suggestions for Further Reading

Tomlinson's *Education in a Post-welfare Society* (2nd edn. 2005) provides an excellent more or less up to date account of this area of policy. Ball (2008) *The Education Debate* complements this with a critical examination of the contemporary developments.

There is a lack of policy, as opposed to practice, orientated books on children's policy. Churchill's essay in the *Social Policy Review* (Clarke, Maltby and Kennett, 2007) offers a good short account of developments. Liu (2001) *The Autonomous State of Childcare* provides an exploration of the complex evolution of child care and nursery school policy.

Much of the sociological literature on social class and education is now very dated, but a formidable modern overview of this subject is available in Halsey et al. (1997) *Education, Culture, Economy and Society*. The Parekh Report (2000) explores the issues about education and ethnicity, among other policy issues. Gillborn's *Race, Ethnicity and Education* (1992) is a rather older examination of these issues, but his articles cited in the text (1998, 2005) provide updates.

The official website for the Department of Children, Schools and Families in England is www.dcsf.gov.uk.

Chapter 10

Housing

Introduction

In the UK in 2005, the housing stock comprised about 26 million dwellings. 18.4 million of these were owner occupied, the remainder rented. The rented housing comprised 2.8 million rented from local authorities, 2.2 million rented from registered social landlords and 2.8 million rented privately (National Statistics, 2007, p. 132).

As a concern of social policy, a narrow view could be taken about housing, seeing the only concern to be about public interventions to try to ensure that all can secure affordable housing. Alternatively, a wider view is taken here, noting that governments have long been concerned about the quantity and quality of housing available to all, and have in recent years been very committed to protecting the advantages secured by owner occupiers regardless of their income. In other words, as we will see, there are many interventions into the housing market that have *social effects*, protecting individuals and conferring advantages (or even disadvantages). What is more it will be shown that, in order to understand the housing situation today, an historical view has to be taken, since past interventions into the system continue to have effects. That fact is, of course, a reflection of the fact that houses last for a long while and that housing construction, purchasing and rental decisions made a long way in the past continue to have considerable implications for individuals and families long after they were made.

Hence it will be shown in this chapter that public policies have influenced and continue to influence all the housing sectors, if not directly through public provision, then indirectly through subsidies, controls and rent support. The government departments directly responsible for housing policy have undergone many changes of structure and name over the years; at the time of writing the responsible department for England is the Department for Communities and Local Government. In the other countries of the UK, housing policy is one of the devolved responsibilities.

We start this chapter therefore with a brief historical overview, then proceed to explore key points about each of the housing sectors and finally look at some specific topics about housing problems.

How the Housing System Acquired its Present Shape

In Table 10.1 some statistics are provided to show how the housing system in the UK has changed over the past 100 years. At the time of the First World War, most people rented from private landlords. In the inter-war period the two other sectors grew, but the private sector was still dominant in 1945. After that however the situation was transformed both by the growth of owner occupation and by the development of social housing. After 1979 however, while the decline of the private sector continued a little there was a dramatic shift from social housing to owner occupation. This was attributable both to policies that encouraged the latter but curbed the growth of the former, and to the 'right to buy' legislation that enabled social housing tenants to purchase their homes at favourable rates. There was another development between 1979 and 2005 that Table 10.1 does not reveal. Whilst in 1979 all but about 7 per cent of all social tenancies were local authority ones (widely called 'council housing) by 2005, as noted above, approaching half were rented from 'registered social landlords' (generally 'housing associations'). This change is still occurring (and is discussed further below). Hence, now it is appropriate to talk about a 'social housing' sector distinguishable from privately rented housing, consisting of rented housing under a mixture of local authority and housing association ownership.

Table 10.1 Estimates of housing tenure in the UK: an historical picture (percentages)

	Social tenancies	Owner occupied homes	Private tenancies
1914	Less than 1%	10	89
1945	12	26	62
1961	27	43	31
1979	32	55	13
2005	19	71	11

Source: These figures are approximate; the figures up to 1979 are ones for Britain rather than the UK, taken from Mullins and Murie (2006), p. 36; the 2005 figures are from National Statistics (2007), chapter 10.

Hence, it may be suggested that the history of housing in the UK since the beginning of the twentieth century can be divided into three phases:

- the dominance of private renting, gradually brought to an end across a long period from the First World War through to the 1960s
- a brief period – roughly the 1960s and 1970s – when it looked as if the system was moving simply to one in which most people were either to be owner occupiers or tenants of local authorities
- a shift since 1979 in which, while the importance of owner occupation continues to grow, the pattern in respect of renting has been changed through the shift from local authorities to housing associations as social landlords and the checking of the decline in private renting

Government policies, as we shall see, have been important influences on these shifts. Since the 1950s political parties have explicitly recognized increases in the provision of houses, regardless of the sector to which they belong, as matters which they will seek ways to support, and for which they will claim credit. While, through much of the second half of the twentieth century, differences may be detected between the parties in respect of commitment to the increase of the public sector, that is no longer the case. Now, as Murie puts it 'housing policy in Britain has home ownership at its heart' (Murie in Clarke, Maltby and Kennett (eds.) 2007, p. 49). Hence protecting and strengthening the owner occupied sector is seen not only as an important political objective but also, more controversially, as a core element in improving housing for all.

As far as the rented sector is concerned, the growth of social housing – from the 1920s to the 1970s - depended upon government subsidies to local authorities. Then from the 1970s onward, while subsidies for social housing development did not altogether disappear, there has been a shift away from subsidies *housing* to subsidizing tenants, in other words targeting subsidy through means tested housing benefits. This has facilitated changes in ownership of rented housing, since such benefits may subsidize the rent payments of tenants of private as well as public landlords. This shift has also made social housing a much less favourable deal for better off tenants, encouraging their movement into owner occupation (with of course the government policies giving tenants a subsidized 'right to buy' from social landlords further encouragement to this). To understand housing policy, there is a need to look at issues about all the housing sectors. There are complex interactions between them; a change in one sector has implications for others.

The Social Housing Sector

As already noted, the effective growth of the social housing sector dates from the enactment of legislation after the First World War to enable local authorities to receive central government subsidies towards the provision of housing 'for the working classes'. A long succession of subsequent Acts of Parliament elaborated this initiative, encouraging both the building of large estates designed to meet basic housing needs and the adoption of substantial slum clearance schemes. This sector became the main provider of houses for those unable to buy their own.

The history of the subsidy system developed in this sector is complicated. There is a need to look at it briefly so as to understand the contemporary situation. For many years the government used, but regularly changed, a system whereby local authorities secured a fixed sum per dwelling annually over a fixed period of years. In the 1960s, the Labour government adopted a new approach, without terminating the older subsidies, whereby percentage subsidies were paid, effectively to subsidize the rate at which authorities borrowed money. However, in the 1972 Housing Finance Act, the Conservatives sought to sweep away all the continuing older systems of subsidy. The objective was to move to a system in which general-purpose subsidies would eventually be eliminated. They recognized the need to continue to subsidize certain particularly expensive forms of development, in particular slum clearance. They also acknowledged a case for subsidizing low-income tenants by requiring authorities to operate benefit schemes (originally called 'rent rebates') which received an element of national subsidy. Otherwise, they expected local authorities to move towards balanced housing budgets by raising rents. A national system of 'fair rents', at higher levels than existing rents, was to be developed, which might leave some authorities, those whose housing commitments were particularly costly, with deficits, but these would be met partly out of central government grants. However, most authorities were expected to reach a position at which general subsidies would be unnecessary, and some would achieve surpluses.

This new scheme was designed to be phased in gradually. In fact its progress was complicated by the fact that the Conservatives lost power in 1974. Labour developed a modified version of the Conservative policy, which we need not go into here. On return to power in 1979 the Conservatives continued the shift towards so called 'fair rents', phasing out subsidies and preventing authorities using other local funds to subsidize tenants. They used general guidelines to determine how much each authority should expect to earn from rents.

Thus, during the 1980s and 1990s, large numbers of local authorities ceased to be entitled to a subsidy from central government, other than contributions to pay the cost of rent rebates (later called housing benefit). Under the arrangements described above, rents could still be subsidized from local resources (at that time, the 'rate fund'), but only a few authorities did this. At the other extreme, an increasing number of authorities were making contributions to the rate fund from rents; that is, council tenants not on housing benefit were subsidizing rate-payers! Legislation in 1989 forced local authorities to eliminate these exchanges between housing accounts and their general accounts. This measure was widely described as 'ring-fencing' the housing revenue accounts. Local authorities were forced to raise rents to replace local contributions.

In 2002 the new Labour administration took this form of control further, but using a new approach designed not to mimic the market through so called 'fair rents' but rather to set rent levels in terms of principles of 'affordability'. Target rents were set for local authority area taking into account – on the one side – the size, location and value of the house or flat and - on the other- average earnings in the area. This is much more directly interventionist. Local authorities do not, however, have simply to implement the formula. Rather they are expected to phase it in, when seeking rent increases. Failure to comply will have an adverse effect on any subsidy they get. The consequences of this policy are complicated. The ease of compliance with it will depend upon the existing rent structure in an area (dependent upon the complex past history of subsidy). Where that structure is seriously out of line with the new policy rent increases may be required that seem unjust to some existing rent payers, radically changing the proportions of income they have to pay in rent. In effect, whilst the past differentials within local authority rent schemes were a product of the complex history of housing subsidy (varying according to when developments occurred in each area) the new ones are dictated by a central government view of what should be appropriate.

The policy was rendered more complicated by two opposing aims – the government took the opportunity to introduce a 0.5 per cent top-up to the inflation rate used for rents over the phasing period to engineer 'harmonization' between local authority and other social housing provider rent levels; and fearful of the political impact of very significant rent increases, an 'annual affordability limit' for individual properties was introduced, thus capping the yearly increase, and as a by-product making it more difficult for authorities to successfully implement the policy.

Of course, however, what people actually pay may be affected by whether or not their incomes are low enough for them to be entitled to subsidy from housing benefit, a topic to which we return below.

Since 1979 governments – both Conservative and Labour – have systematically run down the amount of local authority building. In the late 1970s, local authorities in the UK built a little over 100,000 dwellings each year. In the early 1980s, it was down to a little over 30,000 a year and, in the 1990s it dropped to a very low figure indeed. It has remained negligible. However, since the 1990s new building by registered social landlords has been encouraged a little. In 2005–6 there were 214,000 new dwellings built for the social housing sector, but hardly any of them were for local authorities.

The changes in public housing policy in the 1980s, towards the reduction of subsidies and the restriction of new building, need to be seen together with the government's stimulation of the sale of council houses. This involved first, sale of houses to their occupiers and then, later, measures to try to shift ownership of estates from local authorities to either private or housing association landlords. Initially these measures had limited success, as the idea that tenants might want to choose alternative landlords proved to be wrong. However, the strict controls over local rent setting and the continuation of limitations on the availability of capital for new building by local authorities have had two effects. One has been the growth of the hitherto small housing-association sector, because it has had relatively greater freedom to raise loans for building and rehabilitation work than local government. The other has been the exploration by local authorities of the case for voluntary transfer of their stock to a housing association so as to achieve greater managerial freedom, in particular the freedom to raise money for building and repairs. This latter development is involving not only housing stock transfers to existing housing associations, but also the setting-up of new associations, often formed from the staff of the local authority housing departments. There are provisions to seek tenants' support for these changes, and in some areas tenants have been resistant to moving from local authority landlords. However this process has been directly encouraged by the government inasmuch as capital funds for stock improvement have been made conditional upon transfers to housing associations.

Housing associations in England may receive grants and subsidies from the government through the Housing Corporation. There is a similar, separate body in Wales. In Scotland, Scottish Homes functions both as a lender of government money and as a direct housing provider. In Northern Ireland (where, incidentally, local authority housing functions have been transferred to a single Housing Executive directly responsible to the government), there is no intermediary body for housing associations.

While since the 1980s housing associations have been able to borrow at government subsidized rates more easily than local government, inhibitions on publicly supported capital projects have led to curbs on the resources going through the Housing Corporation and related bodies. Housing associations are able to borrow money on the open market more easily than local government without government permission. Loans from central government have to some extent been replaced in this way, but with inevitable consequences for the rents charged to tenants.

Housing associations vary widely in size, scope and character. Some differ little in their characteristics from private companies; these have grown in size recently, absorbing some smaller associations along the way. Others have distinct charitable aims and objects, and many are specifically local in their coverage. A small number are co-operatives.

The post-1997 Labour government might have been expected to be interested in reversing the trend away from social housing. However, the first new Minister responsible for housing, Hilary Armstrong (1998), had this to say in a presentation of the principles that were to govern the new housing policy:

> I am agnostic about the ownership of housing - local authorities or housing associations; public or private sector - and want to move away from the ideological baggage that comes with that issue. What is important is not, primarily, who delivers. It is what works that counts.

The policy shift, firmly away from local government and with only comparatively weak support of the alternative social housing sector, has clearly been influenced by a view that owner-occupation is the ideal for as many as possible. Mullins and Murie sum up the situation saying: 'The policy is fundamentally residual: committed to raising the quality of the housing service but not to altering its residual status' (2006, p. 86). We return later to explore further the view that public housing is now regarded as 'residual', as Murie has said elsewhere: 'a welfare sector catering for low-income and benefit-dependent people, elderly people and people looking for short-term accommodation until they were able to move on to owner occupation elsewhere'

(Murie, 2007, p. 52). That remark is in the past tense, characterizing the impact of the period of Conservative rule between 1989 and 1997, but Murie goes on to show that Labour has done nothing to change this situation.

Owner-occupation

It has already been suggested that the examination of housing policy raises difficulties for any distinction between social policy and other areas of public policy. It might be imagined that the private market for owner-occupied houses had very little to do with social policy or indeed with government interventions in society. However, as noted above, such an impression can be readily corrected by examining the attention that housing has been given in the policies of the major parties in the years since the Second World War. A central issue in the general elections of 1950 and 1951 was the performance of the Labour government in 'building' houses, and the claim of the Conservative Opposition to be able to 'build' more houses. The argument was about the building of houses in general, not just building by public authorities. The Conservatives came to power in 1951 committed to 'building' 300,000 houses a year, but many of these were to be built by private enterprise for owner-occupation. Indeed, the Conservatives increasingly encouraged the development of this sector during the 1950s. The continuity here between Conservative and Labour governments in modern times has already been noted.

But then, how do public policies influence the owner-occupied housing sector? What used to be of central importance was the large public subsidy that was given to owner-occupiers through the fact that interest payments on mortgage loans attracted relief from the income tax system. This was phased out during the 1990s, but had by then played a crucial role in stimulating the very high levels of owner occupation we have in the UK. Although we should note here also that there are differences in the share of tenures within the constituent countries of the UK: Scotland for example has a higher proportion of social housing tenants while private renting has represented a higher share in England and owner occupation has traditionally been more important in Wales and Northern Ireland.

It has not been only through tax relief that the government has influenced opportunities for individuals to secure owner-occupied housing. In the period immediately after the Second World War, the government maintained a tight control over building through control over access to building supplies. As it relaxed these controls, it stimulated private building. Then, in the 1950s, as it began to reduce the amount of local authority building, it thereby encouraged a shift of resources into building for sale. During that period of management of a full-employment economy along Keynesian lines, the government came to realize that one of the ways in which it could most easily influence the economic climate was by influencing the demand for new building. While the direct controls of the immediate post-war period have long since gone, there remain a series of factors that influence the scale of building of houses for sale: the extent to which alternative – particularly public sector – opportunities exist for the building industry, the availability of credit – particularly cheap

Box 10.1   The Barker Review, *Delivering Stability: Securing our Future Housing Needs: Final Report* **(Barker, 2004)**

This review commissioned by the government from economist Kate Barker suggests that current levels of house building are inadequate to meet current and future needs and that there need to be an increase in the building of private sector houses of between 70–120,000 a year. Central to achieving this goal has to be an increase in the availability of land, hence a central focus is upon weaknesses in planning policy. Changes to regional and local planning policy are therefore recommended. Attention is given to the issues about the affordability of new houses and increasing land availability and reducing the cost of land – whilst ensuring that developers cannot simply appropriate this gain- is seen as important

credit – for building enterprises and land speculators, the availability of mortgage funds for home-buyers, and the availability of land. Box 10.1 gives a brief account of a report commissioned by the government, published in 2004, on housing supply. This report, which the government broadly accepted, expressed concerns about the supply of housing but recommended solutions that were essentially about how the private market might be influenced.

It is difficult to estimate rates of change in housing need and the relationship between that and any change in housing supply. The Barker report was not the only one to indicate a need for more homes. A Joseph Rowntree Foundation report more conservatively estimated that about 210,000 new homes are needed in England each year, and noted that over the period 1997–2002 only an average of 154,000 has been provided. This led them to warn that by 2022 there would be a shortfall of 1.1 million (Joseph Rowntree Foundation, 2002). We should perhaps note, in passing, that there is an alternative 'green perspective' on this issue, that suggests that it is not necessarily desirable to encourage separate household formation on this scale, since the more housing arrangements are shared the less the consumption of expendable resources and the contribution to pollution, Nevertheless, to return to the conventional view, the whole issue of household formation is complicated by population movements within the country (see also Chapter 12) reducing housing pressure in some areas where jobs are scarce and increasing it elsewhere (for example in London and South East England). What is clear however is that leaving both the movement of people and the allocation of houses largely to market forces seems to be generating a new housing crisis in parts of the UK. At least the local and regional implications of this, highlighted by Barker, were taken seriously.

The big growth in owner-occupation at the end of the twentieth century was heavily influenced by changes in the supply of money to enable people to buy houses. Until the 1980s, the main suppliers of finance for house purchase were the building societies. These were comparatively cautious financial institutions, whose activities grew slowly. Their origins lay in nineteenth-century self-help and charitable ventures. They depended for their operation on being able to attract money from small investors to lend to house-buyers.

Once the proportion of the population with their own houses was high enough, government encouragement of home ownership naturally entailed a concern to open opportunities for borrowing money to those who were regarded by the building societies as 'bad risks'. Hence, there was governmental pressure on these 'private' organizations to lend to more 'marginal' people or for more 'marginal' properties.

During the 1980s, the government deregulated the financial market. Restrictions on building societies' activities were removed, and other lenders, including banks, discovered opportunities to move into the domestic mortgage business. Developments occurred that today make building societies and banks more or less indistinguishable.

In the late 1980s there was a boom period when lenders saw the housing market as an ideal source of profits. Mortgages were sold aggressively, and the customary caution about the creditworthiness of borrowers was abandoned. This further fuelled the boom to which it was a response: owner-occupation expanded, and house prices rose rapidly. This boom, pushing house prices well beyond the overall rate of inflation, eventually collapsed in the recession at the end of the decade. House prices started to fall; the housing market became exceptionally static; and, with rising unemployment, many recent borrowers were soon in difficulties with their mortgage repayments.

During the 1990s the housing market recovered a little. The effect of the phasing out of mortgage tax relief and caution about the events of the late 1980s seemed for a while to have inhibited the development of another boom. Then at the beginning of this century another housing boom became established. An additional feature of this boom has been new investments in housing-to-let, stimulated by cheap money for those who want to borrow and the low (or negative) returns on money invested elsewhere.

The upward trend in house prices in many areas, and particularly in London, made it increasingly difficult for people wanting to occupy property for the first time to become owner occupiers. This occurred in a context in which, as shown above, the supply of social housing has fallen. People who would, in the second half of the twentieth century, have expected to buy houses relatively early in their 'housing careers' – police, teachers, civil servants, etc. – find it difficult to do so, particularly in the London area. A measure of this problem is supplied by data on house prices. In 2005 the average home price in the UK was about £184 thousand. In England it was £193 thousand, in South East England it was £233 thousand and in London £266 thousand (National Statistics, 2007, p. 140). Of course an average can be a very misleading statistic, and the key issue here is about new entry to owner-occupation. The average price paid by a first time buyer in 2005 was £141 thousand, a figure that was nearly four times the annual incomes of those buyers (ibid., p. 141). It was moreover about six times the average income of full-time workers.

But in looking at these figures it is important to look at the rates of change in house prices. The source for the average prices quoted in the last paragraph notes a 5.6 percentage change (more than double the ordinary rate of inflation) between

2004 and 2005. However the longer run change was much greater; average prices in 2005 were 275 per cent of those in 1997! And this is across a period in which government had been proud of its control over inflation.

At the time of writing another check has emerged to the upward movement of housing prices. How substantial it will be remains to be seen. It has been greeted by the media as a problem. What we see in this is a tendency to take for granted the growth of owner-occupiers' house prices, as an investment more productive and safer than any other available. Housing is a source of widespread capital gains, particularly desirable if there is low growth with other forms of investments. This means that very large amounts of the housing assets of the nation are held by those fortunate enough to have got onto the owner-occupation ladder at the time when this form of housing was growing very rapidly in the second half of the twentieth century.

There are some important questions for social policy about the emergence of these large scale capital gains. They are the main source of capital growth for many middle class people, and the extension of owner occupation suggests that such gains may extend a long way down the social scale. Murie suggests that 'asset ownership has been identified as a key part of the government's welfare policy' (Murie, 2007, p. 62), noting also the establishment of the 'child trust fund scheme' under which an endowment £250 is provided for every child (plus a further £250 if the family is on a high rate of child tax credit) to which other investments may be added. The latter is insignificant alongside some of the capital gains from housing, but is indicative of a new emphasis in social policy.

Murie goes on from his observation of this development to suggest that we are moving towards an 'asset based welfare state' in which release of assets may be encouraged for various purposes. He notes the way in which assets are taken into account in care policy (a topic that was explored in Chapter 8). He might also have observed the ways the Pensions Commission (2004, 2005) explored assets release as a contribution to income in old age (whilst rejecting the case for taking it into account in pension policy). But there are alternative contradictory signs, notably the rapid government response to a Conservative attack on inheritance tax: raising the threshold so that it will rarely have an impact where owner-occupied housing is the main source of transmitted wealth.

The fact is that the issues about the unlocking of assets are very complicated. Greater longevity means that many transfers between generations occur very late in the lives of beneficiaries. The incidence of a need for the unlocking of assets to pay for care is very haphazard, depending upon the extent to which self-care or spouse-care is impossible in old age. Moreover, just as individuals can find ways to evade inheritance tax so too can they hide assets from care means-testing.

There are good grounds for suggesting that much more important than the encouragement of asset accumulation, is the need to address the way in which rising house prices have made access to owner-occupation ever more difficult and more expensive. A period in which house price inflation falls below general inflation, and above all below average wage growth is surely to be welcomed as providing some reversal of that trend.

Of course a reversal of a trend may produce casualties. Those on the house price 'escalator' have an interest in its maintenance and certainly in the avoidance of the 'negative equity' situation which was described above as temporarily arising at the end of the 1980s. Those who face problems in such situations will be those who are heavily mortgaged whose incomes fall at the same time as the fall in house prices (particularly if they get into a situation of 'negative equity' in which they find their debt is greater than the potential sale price of the houses). Moreover, people who, on account of a fall in income, actually have to default on their mortgages lose the benefit of their earlier sacrifices. The government has however encouraged lenders to develop codes of practice and insurance policies that would prevent the rapid dispossession of people who became unemployed, but nevertheless, at the time of writing, the rate of house repossessions has begun to increase. There are also issues here about how the social security and housing benefit system works. Owner-occupiers cannot get housing benefit. Owner-occupiers who claim income support or job-seekers allowance can get limited help with housing costs (the rules are complex and delays are imposed on access to this). There could be measures that extend benefits. In this area government concerns about owner-occupiers are offset by desires not to make benefit receipt more attractive!

However, certain special problems – that can be addressed by various kinds of 'rescue packages' – should not divert attention from the case for the ending of the runaway price inflation outlined above. To have house prices rising faster than either prices or wages distorts the housing market, increasing the wealth gap between those on and those not on the house price escalator. Murie's critique of the government's stress on asset accumulation as a welfare policy suggests:

- is that it is wildly optimistic to expect that growth of owner occupation can extend much further down the income scale
- that the growing gap between those who can and those who cannot get on a potentially profitable (see Box 10.2) owner-occupation 'ladder' makes a serious contribution to the growth of inequality (we return to this in the discussion of 'residualization' below).

Furthermore there are questions that need attention, but are beyond the scope of this book, about the long run dangers in having an economy in which investment in housing is seen as much safer than any other form of investment.

However, the government seems determined to try to increase home ownership, and even to address the housing needs of lower income people in this way. The concept of 'affordability' now used in the assessment of appropriate rent levels in the social housing sector is now also being used in relation to owner-occupation. Lund (2006, p. 92) notes, in the context of evidence that the average age of first time buyers is increasing (from 29 in 1974 to 34 in 2001), that the term 'affordable' is 'being used to draw attention to financial barriers to owner-occupation ... Home-ownership affordability indicators have been developed to highlight the impact of housing market changes on potential first-time buyers.'

The solution to this problem being developed by the government is the initiation of a variety of 'shared equity' schemes in which individuals part buy/ part rent homes

Box 10.2   Is owner-occupation necessarily always a 'ladder' to asset accumulation?

We qualified the statement about asset accumulation above with the expression 'potentially profitable'. It is important to recognize that all owner occupied houses are not of high quality, and that certainly those who buy out of desperation to secure a home (notably new migrants) may acquire sub-standard houses. Such houses may impose high costs on their owners and may not inflate in value.

Moreover, the discussion of prices above has been about averages. At the same time as there is this potentially unstable boom there are places where low demand for housing leads to falls in prices, in relative and sometimes actual terms. The problems that follow from this include a danger that people find it hard to move in search of work, the neglect of housing maintenance and, at worst, the abandonment of houses. Such trends have then effects upon the way an area is perceived, adding an additional twist to the downward spiral, particularly in areas where the stock is a mixture of owned and rented houses. (Bright, 2001; Martin, 2002)

at the outset, with the option to buy out the rent element in the future. This has been particularly developed for 'key workers' – public sector workers on comparatively low incomes in London and the South-East. In this respect then we see a sort of coming together of owner-occupation and social housing around the affordability concept. Clearly a great deal will depend, first, upon how widely this idea can be extended and, second, upon whether it contributes to a new form of asset accumulation. Much will depend upon the extent to which the asset accumulation part of the deal works well, and upon the subsequent incomes of those who benefit from these schemes.

The Private Rented Sector

It has been noted that the private rented sector provides about 11 per cent of the accommodation in the UK as a whole. As noted earlier this sector has declined to that level from one in which it housed most of the population at the beginning of the twentieth century. In fact its lowest point seems to have been in the early 1990s after which it rose a little in importance.

There was a political, but now rather academic, argument about the original decline. Was it inevitable, as better outlets for investment opened up? Or was it produced by government-imposed controls? From 1916 onwards, there were rent controls of various kinds, applied with varying degrees of stringency. Controversy raged over the protection of private tenants from both eviction and high rents. Between 1965 and 1988, the fair rent principle was adopted for the regulation of most forms of private tenure. This represented a political compromise based on a comparatively nonsensical formula according to which rent officers were expected to assume that properties were let in a market in which there was no scarcity. The reality was that rents were determined by a system of comparisons at levels some way below what the market might be expected to bear. At the same time, many landlords sought to evade the rent controls altogether by legal devices such as the granting of a 'licence to occupy' rather than a tenancy. The 1988 Housing Act effectively abandoned rent control, apart from various rather complex measures of protection for tenants with agreements dating from earlier rent control regimes. In the last section the attractiveness of housing as an investment was discussed. Together with the lightening of controls over the activities private landlords that attraction seems to have contributed to the slight recent growth of this sector.

Excluding temporary residents of an area, among whom students figure as a significant group, the superior advantage of owning means that many private tenants will tend to be low-income earners and recipients of social security benefits. To enable them to pay market rents, the government has had to allow them access to the housing benefit scheme. However, the problem with this scheme is that receipt of benefit removes any incentive to the renter to behave like a free market participant. The cost of the rent falls on the state. To cope with this problem for the social security budget, a complex procedure has been adopted requiring rent officers to rule whether rents should be regarded as excessive for benefit purposes and the unlucky hapless tenant to find the balance, rather than central government. In addition the 'single room rent rule' restricts housing benefit payments to single persons under 25. In other words, a special system of benefit control has replaced rent control. The government also launched a scheme, as an experiment in 2003, that took this issue further. In a limited number of 'pathfinder' areas it fixed housing benefit levels at limits, related to average rents in the area, and decreed that payments to claimants should be based on those limits. It was found the landlords were reluctant to take tenants on these terms and the scheme has been abandoned for the time being.

The private rented sector is unevenly distributed across the country. In some areas, particularly in the north, there are still old, poor-quality houses occupied by elderly tenants who have been in them for many years. With this property, the main public concern has been about conditions. Elsewhere, the private sector may have rather different characteristics. In London, in particular, but also in many other big cities, much of this accommodation is in the form of flats created out of large old houses. These areas tend to accommodate people whom local authorities do not see as their responsibility (or at least place very low on their scales of priorities): in particular, newcomers to the area and the young single. The decline in the rate at which social housing is provided (discussed above) intensifies the pressure on this sector. As other housing problems have been solved, the gap between the good housing conditions of the majority and the often very poor conditions experienced in this part of the private sector has become increasingly evident. But by contrast to these examples, we have also noted the growth of the purchase of houses, sometimes new houses, by people who aim to profit from the combination of rental income and capital growth. The national data suggest that there have been some overall improvements in the quality of the private sector. While it is acknowledged that the government has encouraged efforts to eliminate slum dwellings in this sector, developments like the last-named may be contributing to this, but not of course doing anything to improve things in that part of the market which most disadvantaged people can access. The private sector is now rather diverse.

Homelessness

The exact meaning of homelessness is a matter of dispute, just as is the case with poverty (see Chapter 5, pp. 117–19). There is in particular a distinction to be made between literally 'on the streets' (the expression 'roofless' is sometimes used for this) and so inadequately housed, on a temporary or permanent basis, that securing another home is vital. Lund provides a good discussion of alternative definitions and of the evidence available on this topic (2007, chapter 6). He notes:

> If homelessness is construed as rough sleeping then the small numbers of rough sleepers can be interpreted to be a result of their disturbed personal biographies. If a broader definition is accepted, including for example, those in insecure and unfit accommodation, then the larger numbers involved may indicate a shortage of housing as the cause of homelessness. (ibid., p, 119)

In contemporary policy in the UK a broader definition is accepted, but that does not mean that it is accepted that 'shortage of housing' is the sole cause of the problem. In any case, who suffers from that shortage will be determined by a wide range of factors, including of course 'disturbed personal biographies'. There is an important issue here about the extent to which a 'blame culture' inhibits an effective response to the problem.

Homelessness needs to be seen as a consequence of a combination of a lack of supply of sound low cost accommodation with mobility in search of work in the overcrowded south and with family breakdown. It also has causes outside the direct control of housing policy, in the unwillingness of the social security system to pay adequate benefits to some groups (in particular, the young). Finally, it must be noted that many among the homeless are in need of health and social care, to assist with problems of mental illness, alcoholism and drug abuse, and that community care policy, particularly since the 1990s has contributed to the current situation.

In 1977, the Housing (Homeless Persons) Act imposed a duty on local housing authorities to provide accommodation for homeless persons in certain 'priority' groups. These priority groups were, broadly, families with children or elderly or sick persons, together with those made homeless by disasters such as flood or fire. However, authorities did not have to help families who were deemed to have become homeless 'intentionally'. This controversial provision was added to the Act by an amendment, and used to justify refusal of help to someone who has been evicted for not paying rent. The 1977 Act made it mandatory for an authority to give temporary help, and for more permanent help to be given where a homeless person had a (carefully defined) local connection (see Chapter 2 for discussion of the historical context of this restriction on eligibility for assistance). It was implicit in the Act that the homeless should be rehoused, except on a very temporary basis, in permanent homes, and not herded into inadequate accommodation. Thus they were in competition with those being rehoused by the housing departments from their waiting lists. In practice, many authorities, particularly in London, used poor-quality temporary accommodation to house homeless people for long periods of time.

The Conservative governments of the 1980s and 1990s were unwilling to pressure reluctant local authorities to fulfil their responsibilities better; and, in 1996, enacted amending legislation to limit local authority responsibility in respect of homelessness to the provision of time-limited temporary accommodation. The Homelessness Act 2002 largely repeals the 1996 legislation, requiring local authorities to 'adopt a strategic approach in combating homelessness'. While this legislation removed the limitations on help for the intentionally homeless, it did include a provision where authorities could refuse to help those whose behaviour had been 'unacceptable' (see the discussion in Lund, 2006, p. 124).

It is single homelessness which has grown visibly, particularly in London. It has already been suggested that the roots of this problem lie in a complex of factors, only some of which concern housing policy. Certainly, however, the hard-pressed under-resourced local authority housing departments have been unable to pay much attention to the needs of this group, particularly if the individuals need some combination of housing and social care. It has been left to other special centrally supported initiatives for 'rough sleepers' to try to respond to the problem. The Blair government quickly made this one of their special concerns, referring the issue to the newly created 'Social Exclusion Unit'. This Unit recommended the injection of new resources and the setting up of special programmes on a nationwide basis. The result was the setting up of a Rough Sleepers Unit to co-ordinate responses from local authorities and voluntary groups. A controversial aspect of this policy has been a willingness to countenance coercive measures against begging and those unwilling to avail themselves of new facilities.

During 2005–6 94,000 households were accepted as homeless and in priority need by local authorities in England. There had been a fall in the numbers over recent previous years, but there is evident that this favourable trend has not applied in Scotland and Wales (National Statistics, 2007, pp. 135–6). There has been an effort to shift provision for priority homeless from temporary to more permanent accommodation.

Social Exclusion and Residualization

One housing issue which the Labour government have tried to address has been the deterioration of some social housing estates, therefore designated as 'problem estates'. The problems of such estates are seen as involving, as well as poor housing conditions, 'crime, disorder, unemployment, community breakdown, poor health, educational underachievement and inadequate public transport and local services' (Social Exclusion Unit, 1998). The government is addressing the issues about the physical conditions of these estates by making additional major repairs allowances available to some local authorities. At the same time it encouraged local authorities to consider transferring their stock to housing associations, who would be less restricted by the limitations on public sector borrowing. They are also encouraging 'private finance initiatives' to raise capital for stock improvements (see discussion of this phenomenon in relation to the health service on p. 156).

A full discussion of the issues about these estates would take us far from the subject of housing. It is important to note that efforts to tackle the physical problems of such estates have often failed, in the face of the wider issues needing to be confronted. But the extent to which the emergence and deterioration of these so-called problem estates has been a consequence of housing policies must be noted. Allocation of social housing involves achieving a balance between what people want, what they are deemed to need, and what is available. Under conditions of housing scarcity, individuals are in a weak position to assert their wants, unless their co-operation is required with a redevelopment scheme. Housing authorities allocate on the basis of assessments of need, attempting to make the most efficient use of the housing stock. However, in the past, they often gave attention to capacity to pay rent, and many were also disposed to make judgements about potential tenants' suitability for 'good' houses (see Pawson and Kintrea, 2002 for a good discussion of the complex ways in which allocation processes still influence social segregation).

In some areas, poorer houses were often only easily allocated to, for example, the homeless. Nevertheless, a reshuffling of tenants proceeds all the while, and those allocated the 'bad' houses seek transfers to better ones. Often they secure such transfers only if they have been 'good' tenants and, in particular, if they have been regular rent-payers. The only people who shift in the opposite direction are those who are punished for rent arrears or strikingly non-conforming behaviour, by eviction from 'good' houses and allocation of 'bad' ones. Government policy has become more repressive in this respect. At the time this book was being completed a housing minister even suggested that social housing policy should be used amongst the 'weapons' to enforce efforts to seek employment.

Social housing authorities now have stocks of houses and flats of various kinds: in particular, pre-war semi-detached houses, post-war 'semis' built when standards were low, modern houses built to high standards, flats in blocks of various sizes, good old houses acquired from private owners, and temporarily repaired houses with short lives pending demolition. Of course, these dwellings vary in popularity, with perhaps high-rise flats and short-life houses as the least popular. If, through allocation and transfer policies, there are various forms of segregation within an authority's housing stock, then the 'hierarchy of popularity' will have been influenced by social as well as architectural considerations. Indeed, these social factors may well complicate the hierarchy as certain estates, not necessarily characterized by severe design problems, also acquire reputations as 'rough' or 'respectable', perhaps as a result of some rather complex accidents of history. This can obviously tend to

involve differentiation by income, particularly if accessibility to employment opportunities influences tenant choices. Thus the unpopular areas may contain substantial
proportions of households dependent on social security benefits. Woods (1999),
p. 108 also notes:

> In addition to having concentrations of low income people local authorities have also
> had to contend with greater movement in and out of local authority housing ... A high
> turnover of stock makes it more difficult to develop community spirit and identity and
> makes it harder to achieve sustainable and supportive communities.

She goes on to paraphrase a Centre for Housing Policy report (1997) noting that:

> those moving out of the sector were generally couples aged under 45 where one or both
> people were working. On the other hand, those moving in to the sector were in the
> 16–29 age group and unemployed.

One crucial influence on this issue has been the sale of council houses, which further
enhances the social divisions, since houses on popular estates and on estates in which
the more prosperous tenants live will be more likely to be sold. This was a key controversial issue for housing policy in the last two decades of the twentieth century.
Now it has to be regarded as 'yesterday's issue'. Most people likely to be able to buy
council houses have done so. Transfers of local authority stock to alternative 'social
landlords' have become a much more important issue. A brief discussion of the
history and implications of the 'right to buy' policy is included in Box 10.3.

While the sale of council houses may been seen to be 'yesterday's issue', and certainly it faces no effective political opposition today, the damage is done. The so
called 'problem estate' is to some extent one of its products. Social segregation has

Box 10.3   The right to buy policy

The Housing Act of 1980 provided a statutory right to most tenants to buy
their own houses, at market prices less a discount based on length of tenancy.

The debate about the justification for selling social housing was partly a
technical one about the actual effect of such sales on the housing effort as
a whole and partly an ideological one about tenants' rights. There is a
trade-off here between the rights of actual tenants and the interests of
potential future tenants whose needs may not be met so easily because
public authorities have lost control over some of their stock. The trade-off
was made more evident by the refusal of the Conservative government to
let all the proceeds of sales be recycled into new investment in housing.
This is no longer the case.

(cont'd)

Box 10.3   *(cont'd)*

The houses that tenants bought were principally in 'good' popular estates. That development reinforced the gap between the 'good' estates and the 'bad'. In this way, it reinforced a situation in which renting of social housing is seen as a much inferior option to ownership. This development was influenced by government policies which pushed up rent levels, leaving subsidy to the benefit system. This increased the incentive for those required to pay full rents to seek to buy.

The provision of discounts weakened the economic arguments for sales; older houses that are, perhaps quite reasonably, sold to long-term sitting tenants at low prices still have to be replaced, if there is outstanding housing need, by new, expensive houses. Similarly inasmuch as the houses in the best state of repair were sold local authorities were left with a stock of deteriorating houses, whose repair costs had to be met out of a falling rental income.

The right to buy issue draws our attention to a variation of the same anomaly as exists within the owner-occupied sector: there is a vast gap between the original, 'historic' costs of housing and modern 'replacement' costs. In the local authority sector, a similar house may today be in theory yielding the local authority a 'profit'. In practice modern government policies on rent levels prevent any effective realization of that for the benefit of others.

The right to buy policy remains on the statute book, in a slightly tightened up form to eliminate some abuses that emerged. About 2 million tenants have become home owners under its provisions, but the numbers of new purchases is falling sharply.

been sharply increased, the social housing sector contains people who were and are unable to get onto the owner occupation ladder, even with the discounts offered under the 'right to buy'. The accompanying policies of raising rents for those left behind, operating to further incentivize efforts to buy, has had an effect. But that is irrelevant for the over 60 per cent of social tenants on housing benefit (Department for Communities and Local Government, 2006).

Conclusions

The latter part of this chapter has particularly emphasized the issues that have arisen from the interaction between Britain's various housing sectors with the growth of owner-occupation and the decline of private renting. The interactions here are complex. Studies of housing have given attention to movement between the sectors, examining the filtering hypothesis which suggests that the benefits of new houses, even at the

> ## Box 10.4   Alternative housing 'careers'
>
> - Early movement into, and then subsequent moves within the owner-occupied sector.
> - Movement from renting (either from a private or a social landlord) into owner occupation, and then mobility within that sector.
> - Movement from renting into owner occupation, but in poor quality housing from which it is difficult to move on and which may not appreciate significantly in value
> - Movement, either on separation from a parental home or via the private rented sector, to social housing, but then no further movement.
> - Movement into the private rented sector but then difficulty in moving on to the other sectors.

top of the owner-occupier market, filter down to contribute to the reduction of housing need. Superficially, this seems plausible. However, the 'chains' that have been traced resulting from new houses at the 'top' end of the system are often short. Typically, they extend down only to a young new entrant to owner-occupation, perhaps from that part of the private rented sector where the needs of the young mobile middle class are met, perhaps merely forming a new separate household for the first time (Forrest et al., 1990). The same seems to be true of purchased social housing when it is later sold by the original buyer.

Various different kinds of housing 'career' can be detected, and key examples are set out in Box 10.4. The optimistic assumption embedded in contemporary housing policy expects most people to achieve the first or second of these. Critics suggest that these careers are closed to many, and the residualization thesis involves arguing that this closure is contributing to a great divide in society. In any case, gone are the days when the planners of the 1940s envisaged people of different incomes and social statuses living side by side in mixed communities.

These divisions within the housing system may have equally serious implications for the allocation of opportunities and for territorial justice in our society. Owner-occupation conveys benefits which are passed on through inheritance, while the other sectors do not. These social divisions may be reinforced across time. However, even owner-occupation is increasingly stratified in terms of the age and quality of the housing and in terms of when individuals achieved that status.

Most seriously, though, while it is accepted that the concentration of social problems in certain areas raise policy concerns far beyond those of housing policy, it is important to recognize how housing policy has, and is, exacerbating these problems. Most fundamentally, it is disturbing that council housing which was conceived as housing 'for the working classes', or even a universal housing provision in a brief utopian dream in the 1940s, is now increasingly seen, like the comparable sector in the USA, as welfare housing, where the 'dangerous poor' are segregated and need to be contained. It is not clear that the agnosticism of the Blair governments, as expressed in the quotation above from Hilary Armstrong, offers a solution to this problem. The concerted efforts on the constellations of problems, proposed by the Social Exclusion Unit, is to be welcome, but surely the limitations of this approach are well expressed by Lee and Murie (1998, p. 37) when they say:

> If the situation where only those with no choice move into the social rented sector is to be avoided, a more radical rebuilding of that sector is required. That involves a new look at the structure of housing markets and the range of choice offered in different parts of it.

Now that issue is being joined by another issue, difficulties facing those forming new households in securing decent accommodation at costs they can afford. The decline of the social housing sector, and particularly the low rates of housing replacements in that sector, combine with rising prices in the owner occupation sector to severely limit the opportunities open to new households.

In many respects housing policy under the Labour governments since 1997 has had a 'Cinderella status', relative to the other areas of policy discussed in this book, with continuity with past Conservative policy very evident. Nevertheless since 2003 the government has shown some awareness that the consequence of this has been a growth in housing problems. Efforts to reverse this have so far been embedded in the strong commitment to owner-occupation and a lack of interest in developing social housing.

Suggestions for Further Reading

Key up-to-date texts on housing policy are Mullins and Murie (2006) *Housing Policy in the UK*, and Lund (2006) *Understanding Housing Policy*.

The Joseph Rowntree Foundation's web site may also be worth consulting (www.jrf.org.uk.). The website for the Department of Communities and Local Government is www.communities.gov.uk.

Chapter 11
The UK in the Wider World

Introduction

The preceding chapters have focused primarily on the countries of the UK, and often more specifically within that context, on social policy in England. This chapter aims to show that in order to understand social policy in its constituent countries or in the UK as a whole more fully, it is necessary to look outside national borders to the world beyond. There are a number of reasons why this is the case.

Historically, when looking at the shaping of UK social policy, the influence of other countries' welfare arrangements is discernible in all aspects of provision, from pensions to social work. This situation continues although now the notion of cross-national 'influence' has become much more formalized in ideas of 'policy transfer' and 'policy learning'. Industrialization, and the post-industrial landscape in much of the West, do throw up similar social and economic issues for the countries involved. However, as we shall see, all welfare states are not the same, and their development (or not) and quality (or lack of it) depends on more than economic advancement. In addition to questions of 'horizontal' similarity and difference between advanced economies in terms of their social provision and welfare outcomes, understanding the external influences on current UK policy also requires us to examine what are often termed 'scalar' relationships, that is, the interactions between policy actors at all the different levels of government from local activists to supranational and world regional organizations such as the World Bank and European Union. The discussion to follow begins with a summary of the traditional concerns of comparative analysis as a practical and theoretical exercise and highlights examples of both the promises and pitfalls of cross-national comparisons. The final part of the discussion moves to consider the significance of welfare debate outside the political spheres of national government and the location of the UK in relation to its neighbours and competitors.

Policy Learning

Countries at similar levels of economic development have always compared themselves to one another. In the past, concerns were located around imperial and military strength, the need for national efficiency (see Chapter 2, pp. 25–6) and the maintenance of international power. In the twenty-first century national interests have changed very little, with countries keen to secure and improve their positions in the global economy. Recent headlines and government reports in the UK have often bemoaned its ranking in the advanced nations, on a whole range of variables related to industrial achievement – adult literacy, numbers of graduates, skills (for example, the Treasury's Leitch Review of Skills, 2006). As George and Wilding (2002, p. 75) observe, 'comparison has become a significant emerging pressure in a nervously competitive global economy'. It is not only along industrial measures that countries concern themselves however, there are other dimensions of social policy which are deemed important cross-national indicators and relate much more to cultural issues and social behaviour. Thus media and government attention is also directed towards indicators such as the rate of teenage pregnancy, alcohol consumption and drug use, where it is often suggested that the UK compares 'badly' against its neighbours and competitors (see Box 11.1). Again much of this concern is with the condition of tomorrow's workers, but discussion of these issues is also used as a means to reflect on current and past policy and to consider what might be done to improve the UK's position in the future.

In many of these discussions national governments not only compare outcomes, such as the number of eighteen year olds with higher level qualifications, but also study the policy arrangements which are thought to contribute to positive outcomes elsewhere, and compare these with what goes on in their own countries. This process, where national policy analysts are tasked with scouting around their country's peers to identify successful policy measures in a particular area, and the capacity of the measures for success in their own country, is partly government driven as a response to global competition. However, it also results from domestic political pressures generated by the expression of comparative need, for example, reports that there are negligible waiting times for standard surgical operations in France, Germany and the US (Siciliani and Hurst, 2003). Comparison is particularly politically acute where need is transformed into demand, for example, in the case of British dental patients travelling to Poland in order to receive treatment to avoid the higher costs of private treatment, as well as limitations on the scope of NHS treatment in the UK. The mobility effects of a shrinking world bring a new international dimension to the

Box 11.1   One in seven under-13s have tried cannabis

- Britain worst in EU on child drug abuse, report finds
- Adult cocaine use rises, but cannabis levels down

Alan Travis in Brussels
Guardian, Friday 23 November 2007

Evidence of a growing pre-teen drug problem in Britain emerged yesterday with research showing that one in seven children have tried cannabis before the age of 13.

The study, reported by the EU's drug agency, says there has been an explosion in the number of children under 15 going into drug treatment across Europe.

The annual report from the European Monitoring Centre for Drugs and Drug Addiction shows that the UK's drug problem among young teenagers is far worse than in any other EU country. The research shows that 13% of British schoolchildren say they first tried cannabis before they were 13. This is much higher than any other European country – it compares with 8% in the Netherlands and Ireland – and is more than three times the EU average.

problem of 'middle-class flight' from state provided services, but also generate electoral concerns for governments who wish to gain or retain the support of those left at home.

Writing on the topic of comparative study, Richard Titmuss, the first Professor of Social Policy in the UK, states that 'When we study welfare systems in other countries, we see that they reflect the dominant cultural and political characteristics of their societies. But we have, nevertheless, to recognize that they are all concerned fundamentally with certain common human needs and problems' (Titmuss, 1974, p. 22). This insight into the starting point of comparative study has enjoyed a revival since the early 1990s both in the theorizing of cross-national comparisons which is discussed later, and (although largely unremarked) the development of a literature on 'policy-transfer' to which we now turn.

In an article published in 1991, Richard Rose describes an example of 'the traffic in lesson-drawing' thus:

A team of American public officials concerned with employment policies can go to Germany, Britain and France, and issue a report entitled *Lessons from Europe* (Carlson et al., 1986). A similarly motivated team of French policymakers concerned with creating jobs can journey in the opposite direction, producing a report entitled *Lessons from the United States*. (Dommergues et. al., 1989)

In this way, countries can learn from each other, both of the successes and the failures in the operation of policies. It is interesting in this example, that French policy analysts were looking towards the US for inspiration given that, to use George W. Bush's (in his use, pejorative) term, France represents the 'Old Europe' of social solidarity. It is more often the UK (Bush's 'new Europe' of social reform) which exhibits a trans-Atlantic preference when searching for ideas. For example, the shift in recent years towards a 'workfare' model of social security for unemployed people in the 'New Deal' is directly traceable to the debates around, and final content of, the 1996 Personal Responsibility and Work Opportunity Reconciliation Act in the US. More recently the Secretary of State for Work and Pensions has been keen to emphasize that social security policy ideas drawn from the US will not be adopted 'wholesale' (DWP, 2007), but as Rose notes, proximity in the sense of familiarity is the first port of call for the policy maker looking for an idea. It is thus unsurprising that Anglophone countries look to each other for policy influence rather than to closer neighbours.

Different kinds of international organizations also assist in creating the conditions for the voluntary sharing of policy ideas (see Chapter 3). The Organization for Economic Cooperation and Development (OECD) for example, an international 'think-tank', has a large and growing membership of high and middle income countries (from Germany to Mexico) and as Rose (1991) describes it, operates as a 'clearing house' for the statistical information required by governments in order to compare themselves with one another. Similarly, membership of regional organizations such as the European Union (EU) allows countries to explore policy developments with neighbours and, sometimes, for 'best practice' to emerge and become adopted across the group of countries. Occasionally this is based on measures of social need, but more often policy sharing is agreed in order to manage economic competition, the regulation of labour being a case in point.

While Rose (1991) argues that dissatisfaction is the driver for lesson-drawing, as with the dentistry case above, Dolowitz and Marsh (1996) suggest that although this may apply to voluntary engagement in policy transfer, there are numerous ways in which countries are coerced into adopting the policies of other countries. These more hostile contexts of policy transfer depend very much on the power relations exercised by political actors, including sub and supranational organizations in both the political and commercial arena. Some of the social policy issues arising from this are discussed below but here we can surmise that in the same way that these actors can coerce governments into action, they can also, should they prefer it, instigate or maintain inaction. Political infeasibility is one limitation on policy transfer, but in their early review of the literature, Dolowitz and Marsh (1996) summarize a number of additional constraints. These factors preventing the transfer of policy include the complexity of the problem to be resolved and the policy to be transferred, the predictability of outcomes and potential side-effects, the depth of understanding of the operation of the policy and the fact that policies are always layered onto existing policy contexts. It is this *context* that is argued to be more important in the more recent work of Lendvai and Stubbs (2007) that explores the travel of policies using the idea of 'policy translation' which is contrasted with the more linear and static notion of 'transfer'. They argue that translation better explains the process by which policies are identified, adopted and transformed amongst different countries, as the concept captures better both the continuous evolution of policy (see Chapters 3 and 4) and the fact (discussed further below) that policymaking happens more and more transnationally – outside the boundaries of national government, and amongst an expanded network of policy actors, public and private, local and global, socially concerned and economically driven (note: this is one aspect of the modern use of the concept of 'governance', see Box 4.5).

In terms of the content of policy transfer, there may be wholesale adoption of a policy package, or, as Dolowitz and Marsh (1996) identify, a number of different elements of policy which may be transferred alone or in bundles, ranging from goals to administrative techniques, institutions to ideology. Even if the whole package is embraced, it would be impossible for a policy to be transferred intact. As Lendvai and Stubbs suggest, policies which travel can never be reproduced exactly, it is not just their form but also their meaning which is subject to transformation in transit. The translation of policy is partly due to the specific policy context (the actors and their power relations and wider structural relations) but also a factor of language and the culture with which it has evolved. In the French and German languages for example, there is no single word for 'policy' as the words 'politiques' and 'politik' mean both policy and politics (Heidenheimer, 1986). These linguistic differences have implications for both the potential for shared understanding in policy communities – in the EU, policy documents now have to be available in 23 official languages, and the conduct of comparative research which has always struggled with the methodological issue of comparing 'like with like'.

For Rose (1991, p. 4) the most important aspect of analysis in relation to policy learning, is the circumstances under which, and the extent to which, policy measures in place in one country can be made to work in another. This leads us neatly into thinking about how we might answer this question and in order to do this we need to refer to the now well-established analytical framework of comparative social policy – welfare regime theory.

Explaining the Shape of Developed Welfare States

In the essay mentioned above, and in response to an earlier study of welfare development in the US (Wilensky and Lebeaux, 1965), Titmuss (1974) describes three models of welfare state: the industrial achievement model exemplified by Germany, the residual model exemplified by the US and the institutional model exemplified by Sweden. In classifying welfare states this way, Titmuss demonstrated that there is more to the character of welfare provision than can be determined by the study of public expenditure alone. This approach to comparative analysis contrasts with some of the work undertaken, particularly by US scholars around that time, which sought to develop grand theories of industrial development and emphasized similarity rather than difference in the progress of welfare states. These studies had tended to focus on levels of public spending with the assumption that the more economically advanced a country was, the more it spent on welfare and the better off its citizens were. This type of analysis was challenged again most forcefully by the publication in 1990 of Gøsta Esping-Andersen's *Three Worlds of Welfare Capitalism*, and this work has influenced the theoretical endeavours of comparativists ever since, in some ways to the detriment of what is essentially a broad and outward-looking field of study (see below). In Esping-Andersen's now well-worn phrase, a simple comparison of aggregate figures, whether spending or social contributions, 'camouflages more than it reveals'. This is because not only are high levels of spending not necessarily a good thing – a high spending country might have high levels of unemployment for example, which is a certain cause of diswelfare, but also because a figure on spending tells us nothing about the people on whom that money is spent – about the principles of distribution. Esping-Andersen was interested in the ways in which people's obligations to each other are translated into policy and not just how much it costs. Part of his original aim was also to show that rather than simply emerging as a result of industrial advancements, welfare regimes are active in the sense that their institutions and principles shape social and economic development as much as they are shaped by it.

Esping-Andersen's theory, based on a study of social security and employment in eighteen OECD countries, also identifies three regime types exemplified by the US, Sweden and Germany. He uses the concept of 'decommodification' to distinguish how far national social policies provide entitlements to benefits in ways which are relatively uninfluenced by the extent to which people are (or have been) labour market participants. The significance attributed to decommodification as a measure of welfare state quality, is rooted in the idea that social policy should contribute to social solidarity, that people should have equal status, and that they are worth more than the price at which they can sell their labour. The decommodified systems of Scandinavia are contrasted with corporatist and liberal systems which more clearly reflect labour market divisions and market ideologies. Goodin et al. (1999, p. 39) describe the three regimes as follows:

- The *liberal welfare regime* 'rooted in capitalist economic premises' confining the 'state to a merely residual social welfare role'.
- The *social democratic welfare regime* 'rooted in socialist economic premises' and assigning the state 'a powerful redistributive role'.
- The *corporatist welfare regime* 'rooted in communitarian social market economics' which 'sees the welfare regime as primarily a facilitator of group-based mutual aid and risk pooling'.

Clearly, on a range of indicators advanced economies can be broadly described by a small number of ideal types. These types do not correspond to every detail of a country's welfare system (or systems) but are intended to capture the essence of national social policy. Thus for example, believing that Canada is a liberal type welfare state we would expect social security policy to exhibit at least some of the characteristics associated with this type – principally means-testing of social provision to reduce the costs of welfare and deter claimants, low levels of benefits which are intended to preserve work incentives and support for private forms of welfare such as health insurance and private pensions, perhaps through tax subsidies.

Esping-Andersen's original 'regime' theory has therefore generated a wide range of challenges and alternative categorizations (see Arts and Gelissen, 2002, for a review of these). Some of them introduce other considerations than Esping-Andersen's central emphasis on the role of politics (for example the role of religion and the extent of male dominance) or stress policy areas neglected in his analysis (health and social care policy, for example). It is also important to bear in mind that the original analysis was confined to a limited number of countries for which good comparative data was available at that time. At the very least, there is a need to raise questions about countries in the world that have, or had at that time, even more weakly developed social policy systems.

In this last respect it is at least necessary to acknowledge the place of a fourth world of welfare, not found in Esping-Andersen's analysis, reflecting the view that the Mediterranean countries' welfare systems are not simply rudimentary or developing, but are of a qualitatively different type to the Conservative group, for example (where Esping-Andersen had placed Italy). The welfare systems in these countries are fragmented in the sense that they are funded and delivered by a range of mechanisms both state and non-state organized, and eligibility for transfers and services is complex and uneven. There continues to be a strong religious component to the governance of welfare and overall, the extended family remains significant in terms of its legal and practical responsibilities for the welfare of its members. Compared to the deindustrializing countries of northern Europe, the post-war economic trajectory of these countries has continued to rely heavily on agrarian production.

In addition to the fourth world of the southern European welfare states, some authors have argued that there are fifth, sixth or even seventh worlds of welfare which are constituted by the antipodean countries of Australia and New Zealand combined with the UK, a 'radical' group according to Castles and Mitchell (1993) due to their combination of the liberal preoccupation with work and the market and the demands of a strong Labour movement; the East Asian countries which have been termed 'Confucian' welfare systems (Jones, 1993) because of the alternative philosophy which has underpinned their development and their contrast to the capitalist democratic tradition in the West (Walker and Wong, 2004), and the post-communist central and Eastern European countries which have a typology all of their own (Deacon, 1993).

Whether the 'analytical parsimony' produced by restriction to three or four worlds is more fruitful than the foregrounding of difference that occurs where the number of worlds is expanded, is a matter for debate and in all probability depends on the use to which the typology is to be put. Deacon (2007), critical of what he sees as the domestically blinkered approach of comparative study, implies that in the face of global change comparative study is heading in the wrong direction, elaborating and reclassifying national welfare regimes when the struggle of and for policy ideas now takes place beyond national boundaries. He argues (2007, p. 175) that social policy-making has become 'multi-sited, multi-layered and multi-actored', thus rendering the regime framework redundant in terms of its capacity to assist in the analysis of social policy development outside the rich countries in the global North. James Midgely, long time critic of preoccupation with social policy in rich countries (MacPherson and Midgely, 1987), also remains concerned that comparative analysis continues to be constrained by the ideological models associated with the rich countries (social democracy versus neoliberalism) which, he argues, squeezes out the possibilities for more creative thinking about social policy development and its outcomes in the absence of welfare state institutions (such as the UK's NHS for example) and based on alternative perspectives on what the aims of social welfare should be (Midgely, 2004).

In an attempt to address some of these criticisms, Ian Gough and colleagues (Gough and Wood, 2004) have endeavoured to map a form of regime analysis onto the welfare contours of poorer countries in East and South Asia, Africa and Latin America. They agree that the typologies which frame much of the explanatory work done in comparative social policy are inapplicable to the rest of the world and suggest that globally, countries can be divided up into three 'welfare regimes': The 'welfare state regimes' of the rich global North, 'informal security regimes' where capitalist production co-exists with other forms of production, livelihoods are gained through a range of economic survival strategies, not just paid employment, and the state is both weak and one of many welfare actors; and thirdly, 'insecurity regimes' which are characterized by conflict and human suffering, smash-and-grab economics and absence in terms of both identifiable social policy (unless in the form of humanitarian aid) and of welfare institutions, often because there is no 'state' to speak of. Bangladesh and South Asian countries are broadly characterized by the 'informal security regime' while much of sub-Saharan Africa exhibits the characteristics of the 'insecurity regime'.

In all these accounts of social policy development, 'politics matters', that is to say that the direction and form of welfare systems is argued to depend on the outcomes of political (usually working-class) struggle, and the cross-class coalitions which happen in particular countries, at particular points in history related to particular issues and debates. Thus the Mediterranean and East Asian countries are argued to embody other worlds partly due to their different structures of political engagement and representation, and the informal security regimes of Gough and Wood, with their clientelist politics, are even further removed from the parliamentary democracies of the original 'three worlds'. However, in all of the discussion so far, the elephant in the room has been the role of 'the family' in cross-national welfare variation, and more specifically, the issues of gender difference and gender relations.

Gender, Diversity and Culture in Comparative Theory

One factor of variation across the welfare systems in the advanced economies which is used in many of the studies assessed by Arts and Gelissen (2002), can be broadly described as 'reliance on the family as a welfare provider'. However, although many of the mainstream typologies recognized the extent to which the family is counterpoised to the state and the market in the provision of welfare support and services, most also failed to account for the role of women as the providers of care (see Ungerson, 1997, 2000; and Daly and Lewis, 1998). This rather glaring oversight is all the more significant when we recognize that even in the social democratic welfare states (Sweden for example) where care work is most socialized and valued by the state, the vast majority of welfare is still provided by women within households. This includes the special care of children, older people and those who are sick or disabled as well as the execution of day to day household life. Without women's unpaid caring work, there would be no welfare. The exclusion of gender dimensions in the analysis of Esping-Andersen and some later typologies is largely explained by the focus on class politics as an explanatory variable and 'workers' within the analysis of data. Generally, women do not have access to the same social rights as men because they do not follow a full-time, lifelong employment trajectory and in most countries the social insurance principal disadvantages those with an intermittent work record and more limited earnings. Not only this, but many of the early comparative analyses involved in the design of typologies were solely concerned with social security at the expense of the other aspects of welfare.

With particular reference to Esping-Andersen's initial formulation of regime theory, feminist writers (see in particular Lewis, 1992; O'Connor, 1996; Sainsbury 1996; Daly and Rake, 2003) point out that while the idea of decommodification was that some welfare systems effectively reduce dependence upon the labour market, the issue for women in many societies is not dependence on the labour market but dependence upon men. In this sense the crucial distinction for women is between systems that link entitlements to 'the male breadwinner model', with women largely seen as 'dependants', and those that work with an 'individual' model which give women more equal status (Sainsbury, 1996). Paradoxically, systems that increase the commodification of women, by expecting them to be labour market participants, may contribute to reducing their dependence upon men. However, although the individual character of, for example, the Swedish model of social policy rests upon an expectation that there will be high labour market participation, this is in some respects coerced participation, given the expectations about work imposed by the social security system. While in the past this somewhat restricted both women and men's choices to undertake care rather than paid work, more recent policy around parental leave and other family-friendly policies are attempting to address the privileging of paid over unpaid work. This compulsion to take paid work is even more evident in nations where the rise of female labour market participation has been recent, such as the UK. It is also often participation in the least advantaged parts of the labour market where work is insecure and poorly paid. The high Scandinavian female labour market participation has partly been generated by a willingness of the state to pay women to carry out caring tasks which elsewhere have to be carried out by (generally female) parents and relatives themselves.

In the comparative analysis of social policy then, alongside issues about the working of the income maintenance system, there is a need to consider issues about provision for care: who provides it and whether and by whom it is paid, but also issues about the gendered expectations of the roles played by women and men in this regard. The examination of the ways in which the existence and operation of social policies supports or encourages particular patterns of gender relations – the male breadwinner model, contrasts with some of the more individualistic and voluntaristic accounts of gender difference which downplay the importance of welfare or 'gender regimes' and explain difference by way of simple choices made by women and men because they are biologically different (see Hakim, 2000). Of course women are not a homogenous group and they do make choices, but welfare institutions and social policies frame those choices and the frames differ cross-nationally.

The contributions of both Ginsburg (1992, 2004) and Williams (1995, 2001) are important in this regard as they both seek to develop an analytical framework which foregrounds the interaction between divisions of gender, race and class within and across welfare states. Ginsburg makes a case for the pursuit of a 'structured diversity' approach in comparatively accounting for the operation of these divisions, while Williams presents the dynamics of 'nation', 'family' and 'work' and their socially con-structed meanings over time as a way of better understanding the evolution and current arrangements of welfare states. Both of these analyses highlight the previously overlooked significance of ethnicity in comparative social policy and draw on the work of Castles and Miller (1993) in identifying types of migration regime and the consequences of different types for welfare relations between differing ethnic groups.

Elaborating further the view from a cultural perspective, comparative study has also been enriched by the questioning of our understanding of 'welfare states', or more particularly the idea of a 'nation' as an entity, found in the work of Clarke (2004), who argues that recognizing that 'nation' has a 'shifting and contested quality … might help us to think about how a complex of positions, relationships and identities is nested together in constructions of the people/nation and its ways of life' (2004, p. 152). From a similar perspective, Pfau-Effinger (2004) presents a gender analysis which attempts to bridge the divide between cultural explanations of relations between women and men, and those focused upon the impact of institutions. A focus on the particular in cross-national research is also found in Prue Chamberlayne et al.'s (2002) recent work which employs ethnographic methods in order to explore and compare the biographies of welfare subjects, that is, the life stories of social policy as experienced by ordinary people across Europe. What this wealth of approaches demonstrates is that comparative social policy is much more than a clas-sificatory exercise, it is about understanding, explaining and improving with a view to the world outside one's own country. While this section has summarized some of the more theoretical and abstract elements of comparative analysis, the following section provides a brief excursion into some of the more applied avenues of study. This approach emphasizes the particularity of different aspects of welfare provision rather than the more general shape of welfare states, and has become a core area of study due to the development of closer relationships between countries.

Comparing Social Policies

Comparative social policy research is as much about evaluation and the proposal of policy recommendations as it is about the theorizing of welfare state development and futures. Box 11.2 below contains the abstract of a clear example of how

Box 11.2   Abstract of R. Crompton, and N. Le Feuvre (2006), 'Gender, family and employment in comparative perspective: the realities and representations of equal opportunities in Britain and France', *Journal of European Social Policy,* **10 (4), 334–48**

In this paper, we will explore how contrasting national discourses relating to women and gender equality have been incorporated into and reflected in national policies. In the first section, we will outline the recent history of EU equal opportunities policy, in which positive action has been replaced by a policy of 'mainstreaming'. Second, we will describe the evolution of policies towards women and equal opportunities in Britain and France. It will be argued that whereas some degree of positive action for women has been accepted in Britain, this policy is somewhat alien to French thinking about equality – although pro-natalist French policies have resulted in favourable conditions for employed mothers in France. In the third section, we will present some attitudinal evidence, drawn from national surveys, which would appear to reflect the national policy differences we have identified in respect of the 'equality agenda'. In the fourth section, we will draw upon biographical interviews carried out with men and women in British and French banks in order to illustrate the impact of these cross-national differences within organizations and on individual lives. We demonstrate that positive action gender equality policies have made an important impact in British banks, while overt gender exclusionary practices still persist in the French banks studied. In the conclusion, we reflect on the European policy implications of our findings.

comparative research draws on the theoretical frameworks discussed above, compares specific policy arrangements cross-nationally and analyses the dimensions of similarity and difference in order to devise a range of policy recommendations which are intended to improve welfare outcomes, in this case, equal opportunities for women and men. What this abstract also highlights is the range of methods used in comparative research in addition to the quantitative measures found in the regime theorists' work.

The problem of comparing 'like with like' was mentioned above, and increasingly countries with membership of various supranational organizations such as the EU and OECD are obliged to collect and assemble data which conform to agreed definitions. It is now possible for example, to compare data on internet and mobile phone access in countries from Bahrain to Burkina Faso (UNDP, 2007). However, while these kinds of numeric data are relatively straightforward (you are either a mobile phone subscriber or you are not), comparative data on subjects such as 'poverty' rates and 'the family' are far from conceptually exact. Not only do concepts such as the 'family' differ and change geographically and linguistically, but data with which to compare such institutions and analytical units reflect these differences. Official definitions of the 'household' or 'part-time employment' for example, do not coincide cross-nationally, their classification resting on the norms which prevail in the society to which they belong. In Crompton and Lefeuvre's research (Box 11.2), the different cultural understandings of the concept of 'equality' in Britain and France clearly has implications for the policy recommendations which, if they are to be useful to both countries, have to accommodate cross-cultural variation.

In order to overcome the limitations identified above, numerous cross-national research networks have evolved, often funded by the EU, which, being made up of researchers from the countries involved are expected to overcome some of the linguistic and conceptual obstacles presented, through the pre-agreement of research terms and parameters (methodology and so on). Examples of work produced through these kinds of networks have already been mentioned (Gough and Wood, 2004; Chamberlayne et al. 2002) and are found in many mainstream social policy edited collections (see for example Taylor-Gooby, 2004). Much of this work is undertaken within the theoretical frameworks discussed in the previous section but this is not always the case. Box 11.3 below summarizes the process of ensuring comparability in a large EU-funded study of housing estates in ten European countries including three post-communist (or as they are now known 'transition' countries). This study

---

Box 11.3   Searching for successful policy: investigating national responses to the degeneration of large housing estates in Europe

Designing the research project
- Formulation and agreement of research questions (seven questions covering structural explanations of difference; policy philosophies; policy organization; who gains and who loses; perceptions of success and failure; generalizability and policy recommendations).
- Identification of research areas (cities and countries).
- Undertaking case studies in each country.
- Selecting research methods to be used in all countries: a two-phase approach:
  - a literature review, analysis of secondary sources and interviews with equivalent key stakeholders in each country that produced both quantitative and qualitative data;
  - policy analysis using secondary and interview data.

(Adapted from van Kempen et al., 2005, pp. 363–8 or see www.restate. geo.uu.nl)

is an example of comparative research undertaken outside of the welfare regime framework, but still seeking to identify similarity and difference, success and failure and a set of policy recommendations.

Social Policy from Above and Below

It was pointed out earlier on that one critique of comparative study questioned the centrality given to the nation state in analysis of social policy development and reform. Although it had long been recognized in development studies, another important statement from the policy transfer literature (see Dolowitz and Marsh, 1996) and originally restated in the context of social policy by Deacon et al. (1997), was that national governments might be coerced into adopting policy measures by powerful international governmental organizations (IGOs) of which they may or may not be a member. This has certainly been the case for poor countries in the global South, which have borrowed money from the international money-lending institutions set up along with the United Nations at the end of the Second World War. These institutions, the World Bank and International Monetary Fund have made these loans on strict conditions relating to the reduction of social spending and the restructuring of national economic goals. This conditionality, until recently expressed in the 'Structural Adjustment Programmes' designed for debtor countries has been widely condemned by many activist groups concerned with poverty and human rights issues as well as economic and social analysts who have pointed to the poor outcomes in terms of both the areas just mentioned and also in terms of the actual objectives of the programmes themselves.

The rich OECD member countries are largely immune to the strictures of the international money-lenders, but it is not just their influence in matters of social policy globally which is significant for the welfare of the majority of the world's population. From pension reform in Chile to the rules agreed through the World Trade Organization that affect global trade in services (notably, health services), the activities of global institutions impact on lives in local communities all over the world. Coercion is not the only means by which international governmental organizations can influence national policy and many governments in the rich countries are more eager to listen to the social policy recommendations of theoretical economists in the global institutions than they are to the findings of academic studies such as those outlined in the previous section. Many of these economists have been trained within the US in neo-liberal schools of thought but as Deacon (1997 and 2007) has shown, a whole range of perspectives on the solutions to ageing populations, the prevention and treatment of disease and the value of social policy more generally, are found both across and within the global institutions. In view of this, the idea that worldwide social policy is converging around a particular model (namely the residualist individualized US model) is mistaken. This is not only because there is policy disagreement at supranational level, but also because welfare regimes are very resilient and have tended to keep their shape remarkably well despite the pressure to be globally competitive (that is, to cut social expenditure and taxes, lower wages and reduce employment rights). Liberal regimes are obviously more receptive to liberal economic reforms but they too absorb pressures to be cheaper and more efficient in ways that maintain political stability (see Pierson, 2001). This notion that countries are 'path dependent', that they cannot stray too far from their institutional roots, is proposed as an explanation of the continuing diversity of welfare states and although the term itself suggests an arguable level of state passivity or political determinism, what is clear is that (national) politics still matter.

So, the story of global social policy should certainly not be read as one of fatalist acquiescence to the designs of superpowers, international lenders or big business. Nevertheless, the path dependency thesis does imply a less than revolutionary process of further evolution for developed welfare states within which policy is bounded by the preservation of interests of the strongest interest groups. Social policy and policy-making however, are not just the domain of the state and formal politics and this is true as much in the comparative and international context as it is in the domestic. There are non-governmental social policy actors working towards the improvement in human welfare 'from below' in many capacities (humanitarian and campaigning) and using a variety of strategies from simply sharing local practice with links in other countries, to becoming active in policy-making processes as brokers and consultants, to taking part in protest and direct action. In addition to the well-established aid charities such as Oxfam, an example of global social policy from below, familiar to UK readers, is the *Big Issue*, the magazine set up in the UK and bought and sold by homeless vendors. As an organization, the *Big Issue* currently operates in Australia, South Africa and Namibia and has links with similar street papers in many other countries. It might be assumed that skills and knowledge transfer in these operations travel one way, from North to South, but in this example, given the UK's limited success, there is surely potential for the sharing of policy ideas from South to North. Elsewhere, this process is already underway to some extent through professional organizations in the areas of social work and community development.

Conclusion: the UK in Comparative Context

Having explored some of the potential and limitations of comparative study, it is appropriate in a book that is concerned with social policy in the UK, that we conclude with some discussion of the UK in comparative and international context. Having examined some of the theoretical frameworks and reasons why a comparison of spending levels is insufficient on its own, it is also fitting that we begin this section with just such a comparison.

We can see from Table 11.1 that the UK comes below the OECD average and well below the average for the pre-accession countries included in the EU15, in both levels of taxation and social spending and shares this pattern with its Anglophone peers. Table 11.2 compares the UK poverty 'risk' (after taxes and benefits) with that for the pre-accession members of the EU ('risk' is the term used by the EU using the definition of poverty of 60 per cent of median income described in Chapter 5). It supports the view that there are no grounds for complacency about UK social policy.

Table 11.1 Social spending and taxation in OECD countries

	Public expenditure as a % of GDP		Taxes on the average worker as a % of labour costs*	
	1990	2003	1991	2003
Australia	14.1	17.9	...	28.0
Austria	23.7	26.1	39.1	47.5
Belgium	25.0	26.5	53.7	55.4
Canada	18.4	17.3	29.0	32.0
Czech Republic	16.0	21.1	....	43.2
Denmark	25.5	27.6	46.7	42.6
Finland	24.5	22.5	44.5	45.0
France	25.3	28.7	51.6 (1994)	49.8
Germany	22.5	27.6	20.1	51.5
Greece	18.6	21.3	33.0	37.7
Hungary	...	22.7	...	50.8
Iceland	14.0	18.7	20.1	29.2
Ireland	15.5	15.9	39.8	24.2
Italy	19.9	24.2	48.8	45.0
Japan	11.2	17.7	21.5	27.4
Korea	3.0	5.7	...	16.3
Luxembourg	21.9	22.2	33.9	34.1
Mexico	3.6	6.8	24.4	18.1
Netherlands	24.4	20.7	46.5	37.1
New Zealand	21.8	18.0	23.8	19.7
Norway	22.6	25.1	41.2	38.1
Poland	15.1	22.9	...	43.1
Portugal	13.7	23.5	33.2	36.8
Slovak Republic	....	17.3	...	42.9
Spain	20.0	20.3	36.5	38.5
Sweden	30.5	31.3	46.0	48.2
Switzerland	13.5	20.5	27.3	29.7
Turkey	7.6	....	41.2	42.2
UK	17.2	20.1	33.2	33.3
US	13.4	16.2	31.3	29.2
EU15 Average	21.9	23.9	41.5	41.8
OECD Average	17.9	20.7	36.0	37.2

Source: OECD Factbook 2007: Economic, Environmental and Social Statistics (online)
http://titania.sourceoecd.org/vl=781829/cl=28/nw=1/rpsv/factbook/
*The difference between the salary costs to the employer (including social insurance
contributions) of a single full-time employee earning the average wage and the amount
the employee takes home after tax.

Reflecting on some of contents of this chapter we can reconsider these figures in
the light of discussion around the welfare regimes and the nature of policy learning.
Although Esping-Andersen's original (1990) placing of the UK amongst the liberal
regimes was challenged, inasmuch as his approach did not take into account health

Table 11.2 The UK poverty levels compared with other European Union countries 2004

Country	Percentages at risk of poverty
Austria	13
Belgium	15
Denmark	11
Finland	11
France	14
Germany	24
Greece	20
Italy	19
Ireland	21
Luxembourg	11
Netherlands	12
Portugal	27
Spain	19
Sweden	11
United Kingdom	18

Source: Figures from European Commission (2007b), p. 95.

policy, later analyses, which accounted for the direction of policy in the 1980s and early 1990s reasserted its position clearly within the liberal model (Esping-Andersen, 1996, 1999). Whilst the role of social policy in the UK can be seen to be markedly more salient than is the case in the United States, the system compares unfavourably with those of the wealthier European Union nations. In Chapter 6 it was suggested that there is controversy about the future social trajectory of the European Union between advocates of the liberal model and those who favour a less market oriented approach. In that debate the UK is often to be seen as distinctly on the economic liberal side.

One view is that since Labour came to power in 1997, with a modernization agenda rather than an ideological hostility to the welfare state, the drift towards a US model has to some extent abated (Ginsburg, 2001). Some even suggest that globally 'the high tide of neoliberalism seems to have passed' (George and Wilding, 2002, p. 57) with the implication that the field is open as far as welfare state adaptation to twenty-first century life is concerned. In the UK where Labour are attempting to be all things to all people, seeking to 'reconcile centre-left objectives with market-friendly means' (Taylor-Gooby and Larsen, 2004) this is perhaps to the government's advantage.

In one area of social policy though, the UK is doing much of its policy learning from the US: the management of unemployment. As Jane Lewis and Susanna Guillari (2005) point out, many advanced economies, including the UK, are moving away from the male breadwinner model towards the Adult Worker Model (AWM) family as an underlying assumption in policy (even though, because many women work part-time, it does not necessarily exist in practice). This model assumes two adults both in paid work and reflects states' concern with dependency ratios and the affordability of the welfare state. The model retains the element of employment-related compulsion experienced by women in the social democratic regimes (whose citizenship depends on being counted as workers) and in the liberal regimes (whose financial survival often depends on it). In the UK, the AWM chimes with Labour's 'maximum participation' employment strategy and recent developments in social security and employment policy towards lone parents and the partners of unemployed people. Labour place a high value on paid work and so provision of childcare and financial support for working parents has improved (see Chapter 6) but this is at the expense of policy to support care as a human activity, and the sharing of this activity between women and men. With an ageing population and changes in the form and mobility of families, this is a serious policy oversight. It is especially serious for the UK because as a liberal regime it lacks both the cushion of family obligation found in the Mediterranean countries and the state commitment to care found in Scandinavia.

In this chapter we have seen that the raw statistics on social spending hide many interesting patterns of welfare provision. Comparative analysis of these patterns enables us to expand our understanding of the means by which a range of human needs are addressed within different social, historical, political, economic and cultural contexts and the specific interplay between the differing nature of social divisions and the various forms of welfare state. We have also seen that in addition to its theoretical contribution to social policy study, comparative analysis has a practical purpose in relation to the processes of policy learning and policy development. The need to cast the policy net more widely is ever more apparent, not just because the world is shrinking and global rather than domestic welfare has become a more salient issue, but also because as was observed in Chapter 2, the post-war welfare arrangements established across the rich countries have not provided a social panacea, and they are struggling to meet the needs of twenty-first century populations. It is with these issues that the following and final chapter in this book is concerned.

Suggestions for Further Reading

For an analysis of regime theory, its application to a range of policy areas and discussion of international divisions of welfare, readers are directed to Michael Hill's (2006) *Social Policy in the Modern World*. For those wishing to acquaint themselves with important debates, theoretical and methodological contributions to the field of study, Patricia Kennett's (2004) edited collection *A Handbook of Comparative Social Policy* is an excellent compilation which provides a mapping of the traditional concerns of comparative social policy within the shifting landscape of international welfare provision. A global approach to comparative study is provided in Midgley (1997) *Social Welfare in a Global Context*, which despite its age, usefully addresses both theoretical and applied issues of welfare provision in countries/regions around the world. With more of an interest in the global social policy process, Bob Deacon's recent (2007) book on *Global Social Policy and Governance* sets out the key ways in which social policy is articulated outside of national politics and introduces the range of policy actors involved.

There is a variety of good web resources:

- The International and Comparative Social Policy Group (ICSP) web site (www. globalwelfare.net) is maintained by the ICSP group of the UK Social Policy Association. It contains both research resources and resources specifically aimed at learning and teaching activities such as case studies and exercises. The site also includes extensive links pages covering governmental, non-governmental and activist organizations, research centres, and a direct link to the e-Library for Global Welfare (www.elibraryforglobalwelfare.org) a database that allows access to a wide range of international statistical indicators, policy documents and organizations.
- www.nationmaster.com provides access to a wide range of comparative data that can be specified and produced in graph format. Users are reminded to always check the source of the data (some comes from the CIA Fact Book for example) which is listed for all the material accessed through the site.
- The Global Social Policy Digest section of the journal *Global Social Policy* found at www.gaspp.org gives detailed quarterly updates on developments on a range of topics including redistribution, international actors and trade and social policy.

Chapter 12
Social Policy and Social Change

- Introduction
- Changes in the Family
- Changes in Working Life
- Changes in the UK Population
- Conclusions
- Suggestions for Further Reading

Introduction

In Chapter 1 we examined some of the theoretical and material concerns of social policy illustrated by examples of some everyday issues, problems and experiences which policy is expected to address and, ideally, solve. However, the subsequent chapters dealing with the policy process, policy learning and the various policy areas which are associated with the 'classic' welfare state, have shown that what is desired in policy terms and what is achieved, are not always the same thing, and even what is desired is open to question. Not only is policy-making often a contested and muddled activity, but the outcomes, the policies themselves, and their consequences, the impact on social life and relationships, are also often unintended, ineffectual or questionable. One of the themes running through the previous chapters has been the changing political context. We have at various points discussed the extent and implications of a UK, European and global shift to the neo-liberal economic agenda characterized in US policy, and how this is reflected in the politics of 'New Labour' in the UK. There is evidence to suggest both that a return to the Poor-Law mentality with its associated support for individualized, voluntaristic solutions to social problems, and a strong resistance to this, are both present in the current political climate in Europe, and that country's histories of welfare development are significant for their futures. Alongside an analysis of political factors impacting upon the evolution of social policy it is important also to recognize the influence of social change, since questions of, for example, gender relations and the meaning and place of kinship and family are central to the achievement of welfare. Questions of relations between social classes, generations and between ethnic groups are similarly significant in determining the distribution of welfare. With regard to social policy in the modern world, changes in the relationship between work (paid and unpaid) and welfare are also fundamental to the development of policy (see Williams 2001 for a discussion of the three themes of 'family', 'work' and 'nation' in the analysis of social policy).

What should also have become apparent from the discussions in the preceding chapters is that despite the welfare reforms introduced in the 1940s, the subsequent institutional reorganizations, and more radical shifts in the principles underlying social provision, diswelfare in the form of poverty, unemployment, homelessness and so on continues to exist. Added to the existence of the material manifestations of these problems (lack of social necessities, a job, a home) are the relational dimensions. These aspects of diswelfare relate to social inequalities based on class, gender, 'race' (which is placed in inverted commas because racial categories are a social construction not biologically fixed) and ethnicity, as well as along the dimensions of age, disability, sexuality and religion. The following sections will explore some of these social divisions in the context of social change over the last half century.

Changes in the Family

As discussed in Chapter 11, the share of public welfare is just the tip of the iceberg in terms of total welfare provision. Families provide a far greater proportion of care and emotional and financial support. We don't for example present ourselves at accident and emergency departments every time we catch a cold but we might expect our nearest and dearest to supply tissues and sympathy. In more material terms, studies of poverty have shown that it is to family that people turn when, for example, weekly income and food has run out and a meal or small loan is required (Dowler et al. 2001). For this reason, changes in the family, the reality of its supposed 'breakdown' and reassemblage, and the implications for social support, gender and generational relations are crucial to current and future policy debate.

Much has been made of the 'breakdown' of the family, and its implications for child welfare, crime rates and educational achievement to name but a few of the areas that have been identified as problematic. Much of the debate has, as the term 'breakdown' suggests, presented the changing shape of families in a negative light, viewing lone mothers in particular with opprobrium. However, the focus on lone mothers as benefit claimants which has dominated media representation, and the moralistic critique of lone parenthood which has come from the political right, obscures a realistic assessment of the family change that has actually occurred. As Therborn (2004, p. 182) shows, 'in Western Europe about as many people are married today as a hundred years ago, i.e. in the specific sense of women ever married by the end of their fertile life-period'. In the UK the percentage of never-married women by the age of 45–49 is just 8 per cent, less, in fact, than the 17 per cent of never-married women in Great Britain in 1900. Therborn argues that there is a 'northwestern European' socio-sexual order: a pattern of coupling and family formation which is typically characterized by young people leaving the parental home early, cohabitation followed by late marriage but often preceded by the birth of children (over half of children are born outside marriage in Sweden for example) and higher levels of marriage instability. This model contrasts with patterns for Southern Europe, Eastern Europe and the US, while central Europe, he argues, is moving towards the northern European model. Linda Hantrais (2004) comparing EU countries (including accession countries) also suggests that there is a clear difference between patterns of marriage and childbearing in northern, eastern, central and southern European countries. Others have suggested, however, that convergence towards the 'northern' pattern will continue, pointing to the falling birth-rate in southern Europe as an indicator of strains caused by conflicts between higher female labour force participation and traditional family models, in a context of low levels of state support (Castles, 2003).

The divorce rate and relatedly, lone parenthood have increased in almost all EU countries since the 1980s, but at the same time, lone parenthood is not a static status, lone parents generally enter new relationships, often resulting in remarriage. In this way reassembled or 'blended' families are created which contain step parents and step children and links to further extended family members such as grandparents, aunts and uncles and so on, who may not necessarily be biologically related. Children can often become part of new families created by both their parents and their subsequent partners including having siblings with whom they might not reside as well as step sisters and brothers. The idea of a 'family' then cannot be simply defined and policies which are intended to impact on the family such as child benefit payments, or even those which are indirectly influential such as housing policies are increasingly required to attend to the complexity of household formations and social relations. It is only in Labour's third term in office that a minister for the family has formally existed (the current title in 2008 is Minister for Children, Young People and Families). Prior to this in Britain, no explicit concern with family policy was discernible, in contrast to many continental European countries where a specific government department and ministers responsible for the 'family' have always been part of the welfare architecture. In other countries such as Sweden such a post does not exist, partly in recognition of the belief that 'family policy' can easily conflict with measures to achieve gender equality, which has had greater priority within the development of Sweden's social democratic welfare state. Interestingly, as can be seen by the title of the Department for Children, Schools and Families, Labour's concerns for the family are coupled with a focus on children rather than older generations. This is not just a semantic issue however. For social policy, one of the most significant aspects of family change is the impact it is having on caring relationships – the obligations and capacities of people who share some kind of kinship tie, to look after each other in times of physical or emotional need or other hardship.

In all three of the case studies set out in Chapter 1 we can identify dimensions of familial responsibility. In the cases of Daniel (Box 1.1, p. 2) and Sarah (Box 1.2, p. 6) there are obvious elements of parental obligation from both the perspective of a child in need of support to change the course of his life and also a parent who might be required to change the course of hers. Within both these cases however are possibilities for the involvement of wider family members, particularly grandparents, in the care of Sarah's children while she undertakes paid work for example, or in the case of Daniel, assisting in his upbringing in some way if his mother is ill and his father away working. Grandparents are an increasingly important source of child-care support for working parents (Wheelock and Jones, 2002). However, it is also important to recognize that while grandparents may well be happy to be involved in the lives of their grandchildren, if they are in their 60s or older, unpaid childcare on a daily basis might not have been part of their plans for retirement, and, given the increase in levels of labour mobility over the last two decades, the availability of older generations for the care of children certainly cannot be assumed. Given the government's desire to extend working life to the age of 68 by 2046, this care deficit is likely to increase as many grandparents will still be in the labour market when their grandchildren are young. On the other hand, later childbirth may also mean that grandparental childcare demands arise at a time when this older generation them-selves have care needs and cannot therefore take on childcare responsibilities. Thus there are questions here about the potentially contested terrain of obligations which older generations may have towards younger generations as well as the more obvi-ous questions raised by the case of Edith (Box 1.3, p. 8) within the more widely discussed 'problem' of elder care.

Family reassemblage also impacts on the nature of kinship obligations since the scope for family ties is increased and hence the capacity of individuals to undertake caring roles is stretched. Edith's children may wish for her to join their households but her son-in-law and daughters-in-law may well have obligations to their own parents, and if any of them are divorced and re-partnered then there may well be other people's interests to consider alongside those of their immediate family. In sum then (and leaving aside for now the economic issues) although the moral pressure to care for one's family members, especially younger and older members, still exists in UK society, the extent to which we can rely on this care as a basis for policy, is very limited. Even if our family members have the physical space and resources and want to care for us, there are many reasons why this may not be possible. It is for this reason that current policy in relation to health and social care as well as childcare requires creative reconstruction to meet the demands of modern life.

There is no doubt then that both the nature of 'households' and intimate relation-ships are changing and that this has implications for the expectations of state and citizenry regarding the provision and costs of care. This change is beginning to be explored through research such as that of Roseneil (2004) concerning the impor-tance of friends for example. While policy-making has yet to adjust to the realities of what families can and can't provide in terms of care and support in the twenty-first century, recognition of the diversity of families and family life is beginning to move onto the policy agenda. One change that has occurred in most European countries is the formal recognition of the legal and equality rights of same-sex couples through the introduction of civil partnerships, such as that introduced in the UK. The Nordic countries introduced these measures some years before most other European coun-tries although same-sex marriage, rather than a civil union, is legally recognized in Belgium, the Netherlands and Spain. A current debate in Sweden is moving towards this position as the Swedish church has announced that lesbian and gay couples should be given access to religious ceremonies as long as they are not called 'marriages'. In addition to their symbolic qualities, these developments also allow a more formal equality of legal status in terms of the transfer of assets and the right to be considered as 'next of kin' which is significant with regard to decision-making in the case of mental incapacity and terminal illness for example.

A final point to make in relation to transformations in family life is that there is an important gender dimension which we can only summarize here. The changes in the 'family' are in some part (explanation is the subject of continued debate) a result of women's struggles for independence through control of their own fertility and access to the public domain of politics and the labour market. Further discussion of changes in the labour market can be found in the following section, but it is impossible to decouple 'care' from 'work' in the social policy context. Women's increasing presence in the labour market reduces the time available for them to undertake the caring roles to which they have been assigned in the traditional male breadwinner family. Historically this has been a rather mythical household model given its restriction to mainly middle-class families and the fact that it was a post-war phenomenon which rapidly declined from the 1970s. While the male breadwinner family has been a model rather than a reality, the caring roles performed by men have not developed at the same rate as women's involvement in paid work. While in later life many men do find themselves caring for their female partners, the domestic division of labour has changed very little in terms of housework and childcare. The dawn of the twenty-first century has seen a surge of policy interest in 'fathers' however, with, on the one hand, a concern to responsibilize those who are regarded as not fulfilling their parental obligations as breadwinners and role models, and on the other, a concern to facilitate their engagement through paternity and parental leave schemes for example (see Hobson, 2002). The Labour government has tended to be more concerned with the former than the latter and even where the latter has been debated it remains within the context of family-friendly working. As Williams (2004) and Lewis (2006) have observed, if wider economic policy concerned with global competitiveness is to be pursued, then complementary social policies are going to have to recognize that for every adult worker there is not an adult partner undertaking care and other duties in the home.

Changes in Working Life

When Beveridge wrote his report in the 1940s, the basis on which he devised a system of national insurance and family support was not only a gendered division of paid and unpaid work but also an assumption that when adults (and thus excluding married women who were expected to have 'other duties' in the home) were in paid work, this would be undertaken on a full-time, life-long basis. Lisa Harker (1996) refers to this as the '48,48,48' model of employment – 48 hours a week for 48 weeks of the year for 48 years of working life. We can add to this the assumption that a permanent contract of employment would exist since casual labour was assumed to be confined to a small number of declining seasonal occupations (in agriculture or tourism for example) and perhaps the construction industry. The Beveridge plan did not therefore anticipate the tumultuous decline of heavy industry in the UK and the rise of a service sector which now for example includes such things as personal fitness trainers, dog psychologists, wedding planners and nail technicians – occupations which did not exist in the 1940s, carrying out activities that, where they were demanded, would have been the preserve of the very rich. Neither did the contributory system of national insurance allow for a shift from the full-time 'male' model of employment to models of non-standard employment which are both pre-industrial in terms of contractual variability (forms of self-employment and sub-contracting, zero hours and fixed term contracts for example) and 'female' in terms of the trend towards part-time and reduced hours working. The discussion in Chapter 2 identified some of the similarities in policy response to recurring public issues including unemployment (see also Chapter 6). Here we will consider the extent to which these public issues have a contemporary distinctiveness with implications for reconsidered policy responses.

The concern with a skills deficit in the UK (HM Treasury, 2006) has emerged in the context of a diminishing proportion of manual jobs and their replacement with jobs which require the use of information technology (IT) and have terms such as 'team leader' and 'co-ordinator' in the title. As Esping-Andersen (1999, p. 258) rightly observed at the end of the twentieth century: 'the most acute globalization problem that Europe and North America face may, indeed be that the market for unskilled labour has become international'. As manufacturing industries, attracted by lower wages in East and South Asia, have moved out of the UK and other advanced economies, the resulting unemployment is particularly concentrated amongst those with low skills.

Less skilled groups can be defined as those with no formal qualifications or those in the bottom 30 per cent of the education cohort each year (Gregg and Wadsworth, 2003, p. 87). According to the Leitch report, in the UK in 2005, 13 per cent of those aged between 19 and retirement age possessed no formal qualifications (HM Treasury, 2006). Gregg and Wadsworth (2003, pp. 287–9) report that even in the economic 'recovery' period in Labour's first term of office the less skilled continued to suffer chronic unemployment and 'inactivity' where individuals were not in paid employment and were not seeking paid employment (this category includes those who might have taken early retirement, those claiming incapacity benefits through sickness and disability as well as people undertaking caring roles and students). In 2002, 33 per cent of men with no qualifications were inactive while the employment rates for low skilled men were below 60 per cent and for women below 50 per cent. Lack of employment amongst people with low skills is also disproportionately a problem for younger (16–24) and older (50+) age groups. This is one reason why the Educational Maintenance Allowance was introduced in 2004 and it is also one reason why the more recent development of 'modern apprenticeships' occurred. These can be regarded as 'preventive' measures designed to reduce the numbers of unskilled school leavers joining the labour market each year. In terms of 'reactive' measures there has been much discussion in EU countries about 'active labour market policy', which concerns supply-side policies to make unemployed people employable. The New Deal is one such policy, and policies aimed at reducing 'social exclusion' are also concerned with those whom the so-called knowledge economy has left behind.

Labour's stress on labour market participation involves a faith in the long-run capacity of the market to deliver acceptable jobs, and to solve the problems of poverty and social exclusion. Linked with a view of the key role to be played by education and training, there seems to be an alarming dependence on a growth of opportunities for skilled workers. Yet the evidence on the way the labour market is developing gives little scope for optimism. As discussed in Chapter 6, there is a continuing polarization of work, characterized by Goos and Manning (2003) as a divide between 'Macjobs' and 'Mcjobs', and there is competition even for the latter. For those with a critical perspective on social policy, a key question is whether the more progressive policy elements in the Labour agenda can be sustained, despite a political context in which so much of the social and economic *status quo* is accepted.

As discussed in Chapters 1 and 2, part of the essence of the post-war welfare settlement was an attempt to lessen the salience of class divisions in the UK. While this never represented a quest for total equality, redistribution was regarded as a necessary component of a just and economically flourishing society. Thus the inequalities resulting from changes in employment are of central concern not just in terms of disparities in income but also in relation to the effects of social class on access to and experience of all the elements of welfare provision. The challenge for social policy of course is to mitigate these effects in pursuit of a more equal society. In considering the nature of class inequalities in post-war Britain, Richard Titmuss (1958) argued that there is a 'social division of welfare' where less visible private or tax subsidies mirror the more visible state provisions. Most importantly, the better-off gain more through the former thus reinforcing rather than mitigating class inequalities (see also Sinfield, 1978). The suggestion that middle-class people gain more from publicly provided and subsidised services is also supported in other studies (eg. Le Grand, 1982). Middle-class use of, and thus support for welfare services is of central concern in both historical analysis and prediction of future developments. The kind of analysis undertaken by Esping-Andersen to explain the diversity of welfare states is partly based on where middle-class loyalties have lain. With an eye to the future, Deacon (2007) raises the possibility that a lack of middle-class commitment to tax funded collective welfare provision will preclude the development of welfare states in many poor and middle-income countries.

In the UK context, Chapter 11 noted early signs of 'middle-class flight' in relation to international healthcare shopping. The chapters on social care and housing also pointed to the central thrust in privatization policy which has been to encourage private provision, concentrating support for poorer people through means tests. Health and education are the services from which the better-off gain most and so it is vital that support for these is not lost. What is also important however, is the more general principle of universalism in public welfare. Child benefit for example, which is paid in respect of every child, is a case in point. It may be 'wasted' in financial terms on the many well-off families who would not notice if it were abolished tomorrow (although some may 'redistribute' it privately through charitable giving), but its symbolic value as a public expression of the equal value of all children is inestimable.

Box 12.1   Korpi and Palme's 'paradox of redistribution'

We find that by providing high-income earners with earnings-related benefits, encompassing social insurance institutions can reduce inequality and poverty more efficiently than can flat-rate or targeted benefits ... The traditional arguments favouring low-income targeting and flat-rate benefits have focused on the distribution of money actually transferred and overlooked three basic circumstances. (1) The size of redistributive budgets is not necessarily fixed but tends to depend on the type of welfare state institutions that exist in a country. (2) There tends to be a trade-off between the extent of low-income targeting and the size of redistributive budgets. (3) And because large categories of citizens cannot or are not willing to acquire private earnings-related insurance and because of the socioeconomic selection processes operating, the outcomes of market-dominated distribution tend to be more unequal than the distribution found in earnings-related social insurance programs. Recognition of these factors helps us understand what we call the paradox of redistribution: The more we target benefits at the poor only and the more concerned we are with creating equality via equal public transfers to all, the less likely we are to reduce poverty and inequality (Korpi and Palme, 1998, pp. 174–5).

The alternative, often suggested by those on the right, of targeting child benefit payments only towards those with low incomes would not only be costly in terms of the administration of yet more means-testing but would also erode further the sense of *collective* provision which has underpinned the UK's welfare state. It may seem surprising that targeting is challenged in this way, surely – you may argue – targeting ensures that scarce resources are concentrated on those most in need. But we encounter here a point about the politics of welfare that Korpi and Palme have called 'the paradox of redistribution', that this approach may – in the longer run – undermine the quality of the support offered to those in need (see Box 12.1).

Given the related inequalities (in housing, education, income and so on) between those with higher skills and access to careers and those with low skills and access to the revolving door of McJobs, unemployment and government employment schemes, a drift away from universalism can only deepen class divisions. The case for universalism is expressed very powerfully in Richard Titmuss' work, where he argues that a shared service contributes to social cohesion and solidarity, a point he made poignantly when he was dying of cancer - referring to his participation in an out-patients clinic where the only discrimination involved treating patients in the time order of their arrival (Titmuss, 1974). If the low-skilled have become separated from the old working class, and state services such as local authority housing have become residual and 'last resort', there is a danger that the 'sloppy' sociology (Mann, 1994, p. 94) which allowed victim-blaming and behavioural explanations for disadvantage will flourish at the expense of those which question social and economic structures. With the adoption by the Labour government of the term 'social exclusion' as a policy concern, there is already a sense in which this has occurred through the term's 'moral underclass' dimension (see Levitas, 2005).

Changes in the UK Population

As Therborn's (2004) work shows, there has been a global decline in fertility, which began in the latter decades of the twentieth century. The two or three child family is the norm in most of the global North, and although the fertility rates in many poorer countries in sub-Saharan Africa remain high, rates have still decreased in most middle income and low-income countries in Latin America, South and South East Asia. In the advanced economies fertility rates have fallen dramatically in some countries with a consequent concern amongst policy-makers that they are below 'replacement' level. This means that populations are both ageing, and in some cases declining. In the pre-accession 15 EU countries for example, the total fertility rate fell from 2.23 in 1970–74 to 1.48 in 2000, well below the standard replacement rate of 2.1 children per woman (Hantrais, 2004, p. 20). With reference to UN Population figures, Therborn reports that 'by 2000 there were already more people of the age of 65 and older than there were children under 15 in Japan, and also in Germany, Greece, Italy and Spain. In 2015 this appears likely to be the case over the whole of Europe' (2004, p. 309). In the UK, 15.9 per cent of the population were over 65 in 2000 and this is projected to rise to 19.6 per cent in 2025 (Hantrais, 2004, p. 28). This means that by the time a good many of those currently completing a higher education course near their 40th birthdays, a fifth of the UK population will be over the age at which state retirement pensions are available.

Changes in the age structure of populations are of course nothing new, as human history is characterized by bulges and squeezes in age cohorts due to natural disasters, disease epidemics and wars. There was a post-war 'baby-boom' in Britain for example as couples were reunited, and in many African countries the prevalence of AIDS related deaths in mid-adulthood has left older generations to care for thousands of orphaned children. The welfare impact of ageing societies has however, become a topic of debate awash with predictions of unsustainable pension commitments and the collapse of intergenerational solidarity. Much of this debate is influenced by the negative association of ageing with a lack of productivity or usefulness, a decline in social status and physical degeneration, themes which are explored in much of the social gerontological literature.

In most ways these negative connotations can be shown to be highly inaccurate as people past retirement age make important contributions to society in a variety of ways. One example being the provision of childcare discussed earlier, another is the care of each other in later life when illness or disability is more likely to occur. Older people often continue to work past retirement age on a part-time basis or through voluntary activities and thus contribute to the economy in many invisible ways. Retirement age itself is an arbitrary 'marker' for the end of working life that has more to do with politics than biology (Hill, 2007, chapters 5 and 6). The value of older workers has more recently been recognized and is part of active recruitment strategies for some companies. Related to this and to combat the unfair treatment of older people which has characterized the periods of economic crisis over the last three decades, legislation now exists in the UK against age discrimination. The Equal Opportunities Commission, set up alongside sex equality laws in the 1970s, has merged with the Disability Rights Commission and Commission for Racial Equality to become the Equality and Human Rights Commission which is concerned with aspects of inequality along all social dimensions.

As with the evolution of family forms and the industrial structure, the challenges to social policy posed by an ageing population rest on the two core activities: care and work. The main care issues arising within an ageing population are the questions of who is going to provide it and who is going to pay for it. To some extent we have addressed these questions elsewhere (in Chapters 1 and 8 and earlier sections here). However it is worth reiterating that the care deficit is not restricted to the needs of children but also in respect of those (like Edith) who in later life might require varying levels of health and social care support services. The other side of this coin, of course, is that fact that due to improvements in health care and medicine, environmental health and working conditions, many more people are healthier in later life and may require little or no support at all.

In terms of paying for care, there is great political interest in the so-called 'dependency ratio', that is, the proportion of people of working age compared to the proportion of people below or beyond this age. Most of this interest is located in the prospective cost of pensions and the extent to which the UK's 'pay as you go' system of state pensions, where the national insurance contributions of current workers finance the pensions of retired workers, can survive in a situation where the latter become more numerous. UN (2003) figures suggest a ratio of 24 over 65s to those aged 20–64 in 2000 with a prediction that this will rise to a ratio of 39 to 1 by 2050. The futurology involved in contemporary policy-making around pensions means that scenarios tend to be based more on speculation than prediction. Changes in patterns of fertility have often surprised demographers in the past and there are even suggestions now that obesity, the disease of affluence, will lead to reductions in life expectancy. These alarmist forecasts of population change are merely conjecture and tell us more about the nature of scientific evidence than they do about social reality. Nevertheless, government policies aiming to maximize labour market participation are a consequence of worries that social security will become unaffordable since it now accounts for around half of public spending and around half of social security spending goes towards benefits for older people (including pensions, social assistance and disability benefits). Some of these policies such as the New Deal 50+, are targeted at improving the 'employability' of older workers themselves, particularly those with low or obsolete skills. Others such as the changes to incapacity benefit indirectly affect older workers more. Raising the retirement age will keep people economically active for longer, but at the same time the anticipated raising of the school leaving age will delay the labour market entry of younger cohorts. Clearly the grand aims of economic competition involve a great deal of policy plate spinning, and a lot of breakages (see Hill, 2007 for more detailed discussion of the 'problem' of pensions).

Box 12.2   Replacement migration as a solution to declining and ageing populations

In the global context, some countries are not as concerned as others regarding the decline of population. The UN *World Population Policies* (UN, 2008, p. 7) reports that 'Among the 50 least developed countries, the percentage of countries that viewed population growth as too high rose from 50 per cent in 1986 to 78 per cent in 2007.' Most of these countries were in Africa. Amongst the developed countries however, concern with the decline in the *working age* population is reported as a high priority. In its compilation of data, the UN (2001) sets out a range of 'scenarios' regarding the relationship between population decline and ageing and migration, including one which predicts levels of migration required to maintain working age populations 'at the highest level they would reach in the absence of migration after 1995'.

The findings of the 2001 study (p. 2–4) make interesting reading in the context of increasingly restrictive immigration policies across Europe. While for both the UK and the EU as a whole 'the numbers of migrants needed to offset population decline are less than or comparable to recent past experience', the magnitude of migration needed to address a declining working age population (scenario IV) is much greater and would be 'extraordinarily large' and therefore 'impossible' if the 'potential support ratio' or 'PSR' (similar to the dependency ratio) were to be maintained at current levels. In scenario IV, the UK, would require the entry of over 6 million migrants between 2000–2050 and in the EU the figure is predicted to be more than 79 million. As an alternative policy option for maintaining the PSR the report suggests that the upper age limit for the working population, in other words the retirement age, could be raised to 75.

One counterbalance to the trend towards an ageing population in the richest European countries is the impact of international migration (see Box 12.2). From the perspective of the countries of destination such as the UK, migrants may be desirable because they help to reduce skill shortages (nurses for example or those recruited through the Highly Skilled Migrant Programme) or because they are prepared to do the so-called 3-D jobs: dirty, difficult and dangerous (IOM, 2005) which local residents prefer not to do. The UK shares this view with other developed countries which either limit migration to those with specific skills, setup bilateral agreements to allow temporary entry for quotas of low-skilled 'seasonal' workers or both (UN, 2008). In this way migrants are pushed into extremely exploitative relationships. The recruitment of domestic workers in many societies falls into this category – linking gender roles and ethnic disadvantages in a particularly exploitative way (see Brah, 2001). One outcome of restrictive policies is the even more disturbing situation which arises with irregular migrants, vulnerable to trafficking and modern forms of bonded labour. However, in the current political climate there is more concern with the prevention of welfare tourism, moral panic about 'bogus' asylum seekers and a desire to limit even legitimate workers freely moving between EU countries.

Schierup, Hansen and Castles, in a challenging review of the responses of European welfare states to migration, stress the extent to which the relatively unregulated UK labour market may contribute both to driving significant numbers of migrants into poorly protected segments of the labour force, and increasing the 'latent tensions between exposed sections of the white British working-class and ethnic minority groups' (2006, p. 250). The extent of this exposure is debateable however, as the IOM (2005) have argued that evidence that migrants compete directly for jobs with local populations, or that they depress wage levels, is 'weak or ambiguous'. Nevertheless, with the political gains made by the far right in areas of London and the North of England and the rise in race-related crime (although as with all crime statistics there is some debate about the reporting of such crime), the Labour government is keen to stress the benefits of its 'managed migration' policies.

Back in the 1950s UK governments viewed the encouragement of immigration as a useful policy to combat labour shortages, but failed to consider the welfare of those invited to make a new life abroad or the racism they would encounter. The presence of both racism and xenophobia remains clearly discernible in both media portrayal and the day to day experiences of migrants to the UK. Existing ethnic divisions that reflect historically embedded forms of institutionalized discrimination and subordination, have denied the UK's minority ethnic groups access to the rights of citizenship. Racism is expressed in many different ways, sometimes direct and sometimes not. In the realm of social policy it concerns issues from a lack of cultural sensitivity in service provision to the practice of 'passport checking' by welfare service gatekeepers based on physical appearance. Physical appearance of course is not the only marker by which inequality due to ethnic difference is entrenched: culture, language and religion all operate as dimensions of social division, as has been the case in Northern Ireland, and with regard to Jewish and white Polish and other European migrants who have settled in the UK over the last century.

Whatever the policy stance on immigration today, the consequence of events in the past is that the UK is a multi-racial society, in which most members of ethnic minority groups (particularly children) were born in the UK (as noted in Chapter 9, p. 216) or have long-established citizenship rights. There was some discussion in Chapter 9, with specific reference to education, about the way in which cultural differences are dealt with in the delivery of services. It was pointed out that these issues apply to other services, such as health and social care too. There is an often proffered 'liberal' approach, which is flawed (even in its own terms). This is the view that such services should be ethnicity 'blind' – people regardless of 'race', creed or language are to be treated like everyone else. That, it is argued, is what an equal rights policy seems to require. The problems of this approach are as follows:

- First, it is a line of argument offered to resist scrutiny by officials who are actually discriminating. One cannot be confident about an egalitarian policy without the collecting of evidence to ensure that it is in operation (Henderson and Karn, 1987). The Parekh report (2000) refers to a continued inadequacy in the monitoring of discriminatory behaviour.
- Second, to operate without regard to people's actual needs and preferences may be discriminatory. Supplying houses or income maintenance benefits which do not enable people to meet their actual social obligations may severely disadvantage them. Supplying services which violate very deeply held beliefs and feeling – disregard of religious practices and holidays, medical services that have no regard to family cultural practices, education that imposes instruction in an alien religion – may alienate and lead to under-use of badly needed services.
- Third, and more complicatedly, induction into full citizenship requires acceptance that the history, the traditions, the culture and the language of the individual has a value along with that of the dominant society. To do anything less is to send the message that many of the things that create the individual's own sense of identity are not important – an implicit way of 'othering' and treating individuals as second-class citizens.

But in this context it is important to recognize the dynamic nature of culture. Individuals are not choosing between a culture from which they come and one which offers assimilation. Both are changing:

> The dynamic nature of culture lies in its capacity to link a group's history and traditions with the actual situation in the migratory process. Migrant or minority cultures are constantly recreated on the basis of the needs and experiences of the group and its interaction with the actual social environment. (Castles and Miller, 1993, pp. 33–4)

This theme is well explored by Brah (2001) who writes:

> For example, young African-Caribbean and Asian women in Britain seem to be constructing diasporic identities that simultaneously assert a sense of belonging to the locality in which they have grown up, as well as proclaiming a 'difference' that marks the specificity of the historical experience of being 'black, or 'Asian' or 'Muslim'. (p. 228)

There is a difficult line to be drawn in any effort to accommodate the conflicting demands of the new culture and the old one, between the extreme implied by the 'blind' approach and an opposite extreme of providing a separate socialization process for a separate people. This would be one which reinforces separation and tends to pass on disadvantages. People will then tend to remain separate whether they like it or not.

This is an issue about which there are strong feelings. There is a view taken by radical elements within some discriminated against groups that the prospects for the liberal model are so poor that separate institutions are preferable. Castles and Miller argue that culture is increasingly becoming politicized – exclusionary practices are based upon culture rather than overt arguments about racial superiority whilst 'the politics of minority resistance crystallize more and more around cultural symbols' (ibid., p. 35). Some fears about this as one of the directions in which UK policy is turning were highlighted in the discussion of the official encouragement of new schools run by religious groups in Chapter 9 (p. 217). To respond in this way may not do justice to the complex cultural identities highlighted by Brah. We all live in a changing and heterogeneous society, and conceding to demands for separate treatment for some groups will do little to help us come to terms with this. On the contrary there is a need to consider whether it is still appropriate to privilege certain indigenous cultural claims, particularly those of the Church of England whose popular support is now much diminished.

Language differences also pose particular problems inasmuch as failure to gain proficiency in a dominant language often leads on to severe economic disadvantages. Yet pressure to adopt the majority language may, if not handled properly, send discriminatory signals. In this respect it should be noted that the government has recently indicated that local authorities may be spending unnecessarily large amounts on interpretation and translation. Bilingualism offers a solution though dominant groups are rarely as ready to learn the less important language as subordinate groups are to learn theirs (a point that should not be lost on all those who, like the authors of this book, have the special advantage of having one of the world's dominant languages as their native tongue). There are also some very difficult issues where cultural differences involve beliefs and practices about which there are deeply held values on either side. A central example here is family practices, involving views about appropriate relationships between men, women and children.

For many of the less successful within the UK's minority ethnic groups there may be particularly strong forces which tend to ensure that they are found within the most disadvantaged sectors. Where discrimination has limited people to less well paid and less secure work, this will be reflected in minimal access to employment related benefits. Residential segregation, whether the result of explicit discrimination or produced by a combination of low 'market power' and the selection of areas where security and the availability of appropriate institutions (places of worship, voluntary organizations, etc.) may have an impact upon choices of houses, schools and health services.

At the time of the so-called 'race-riots' in the 1950s, more people were leaving the UK than coming in and this trend continued until the early 1990s. Migration figures are more 'guesstimate' than estimate since nationals of the European Economic Area are allowed to enter and leave the UK to work without official record, while general migration figures are captured in the International Passenger Survey which has its own methodological problems. The number of 'grants of settlement' is recorded, and this includes those seeking asylum as well as others wishing to remain in the UK for other reasons. In 2005, 38 per cent of grants were made in respect of asylum seekers, 35 per cent for employment and 21 per cent for those wishing to join already settled family members. This amounted to 179,100 people settling in the UK (Social Trends, 2007, p. 10). People seeking asylum are generally made up of younger age cohorts

(83 per cent of applications came from people aged under 35 in 2005) and the vast majority (71 per cent in 2005) are men. There are logical reasons for this demographic picture amongst which are the fact that women are traditionally less mobile given their caring responsibilities and are also less likely to be involved in political life and thus are not so often targets for political persecution. Despite popular belief, the UK does not attract asylum seekers due to its pole position in the 'Which' guide to advanced welfare states (within the EU25 the UK ranked 14th in 2005 for the rate of asylum seekers per 1,000 of population – 0.5, the EU average). Research suggests that is a mixture of colonial ties which continue to bind, and the ubiquitousness of the English language that draw people to the UK's ports of entry rather than any previous knowledge of the benefit system. In any case, all provision for asylum seekers is dealt with via the National Asylum Support Service and in this way they are excluded from the mainstream welfare systems and also barred from employment for the first six months of UK residence. In many ways asylum seekers are a test case for the humanitarian claims of welfare states. In the UK the result is very poor. Asylum seekers are treated as a social and moral residuum, and as the title of the book by Bommes and Geddes (2000) suggests, the more general relationship between immigration and welfare continues the challenge to the borders of the welfare state.

It was noted earlier that changes in intimate relations within individual societies have important implications for national policy. What also must be considered is what Hochschild (2000) has referred to as the 'internationalization of intimacy' which is apparent in the emergence of global care chains. The links in the chain are represented by female migrant care workers, who travel to rich countries to provide care services in a range of settings (within private and public organizations as well as in domestic households) while the better-off and better-educated women in the rich countries who previously bore the responsibility to undertake this work as unpaid carers, take paid employment. At the other end of the chain, many of the migrant women leave children and older generations for whom they have caring responsibilities in the charge of even poorer and less well-educated women from their own countries, financing this care with remittances from their meagre earnings. The welfare of *their* own families depend upon payments for the contributions they make to *ours*. Clearly as a response to the care deficit this evolution of the international division of labour does nothing to reduce the inequalities of gender, ethnicity or class.

Conclusions

This examination of social change and social policy has necessarily been rather limited and partial given the breadth of this topic and the myriad ways in which transformations in society render policy ill-fitting and archaic. However, what it has shown is that demands on social policy are high in that, whatever one's political persuasion it is expected to achieve grand aims (redistribution or economic competitiveness for example) while at the same time delivering quality and efficient services which at the same time improve collective and individual welfare. There has been much debate about whether state welfare provision can live up to these expectations while at the same time responding to the 'new risks' associated with changes in work and family life (see Taylor-Gooby, 2004). While those on the political right have argued for some time that it cannot, there is no reason or evidence which points to a failure of the 'welfare state' *per se* and much evidence to the contrary. As the previous chapters in this book have shown, depending on the objective one is measuring against, there are failures of particular policies and, leaving aside a critique of modern capitalism, failures of particular institutions (education for example) but this does not equate to a failure of collective welfare. It is hoped that readers will leave this book with the impression that both the failures *and the gains* of the past as well as the challenges of the present are ever present in their own lives. The future of social policy requires that we learn from the failures and nurture the gains in order to secure our vision of the good society.

Suggestions for Further Reading

A fascinating historical collection that addresses a wide range of social transformations over the last century and provides a good source of reference for social policy study is A. H. Halsey's (2000) *Twentieth Century British Social Trends*. For more up to date information on changes in British society the *Social Trends* series produced by the Office for National Statistics can be accessed and downloaded at www.statistics.gov.uk. This gives brief summaries of developments and statistical tables. In terms of changes within the family, Fiona Williams's (2004) report of key findings of the CAVA (Care, Values and the Future of Welfare) study *Rethinking Families* gives a clear insight into both changes that are occurring in British society and their policy implications. The policy implications of changes in working life and their relationship to family life are set out in Rosemary Crompton's (2006) book, *Employment and the Family*. A more generalist and economistic account of changes in employment in the UK can be found in Dickens et al.'s (2003) edited collection *The Labour Market under New Labour*, and for perspectives from social policy on a range of European employment issues see Jørgen Goul Andersen and Per Jensen's (2002) collection, *Changing Labour Markets*. Questions of pensions policy in an ageing society are examined by Michael Hill (2007) *Pensions*. With regard to migration and refugee policy, Rosemary Sales's (2007) *Understanding Immigration and Refugee Policy* provides excellent coverage of migration and welfare concerns in the British context, while Khalid Khoser's (2007) *International Migration* gives a scholarly and accessible introduction to migration from a global perspective. Finally, for a general introduction to the various dimensions of social division, Geoff Payne's (2006) collection *Social Divisions* is recommended.

References

Abel-Smith, B. and Townsend, P. 1965: *The Poor and the Poorest*. London: Bell.

Acheson, D. 1998: *Inequalities and Health*. London: HMSO.

Ainley, P. 2001 From a national system locally administered to a national system nationally administered: the New Leviathan in education and training in England. *Journal of Social Policy*, 30 (3), 457–76.

Alcock, P. 2006: *Understanding Poverty*, 3nd edn. Basingstoke: Macmillan.

Alcock, P. and Pearson, S. 1999: Raising the poverty plateau: the impact of means-tested rebates from local authority charges on low income households. *Journal of Social Policy*, 27(3), 497–516.

Alcock, P., Erskine, A. and May, M. 2002: *The Blackwell Dictionary of Social Policy*. Oxford: Blackwell.

Alcock, P., Erskine, A. and May, M. (eds) 2008: *The Student's Companion to Social Policy*, 3rd edn. Oxford: Blackwell.

Armstrong, H. 1998: Principles for a new housing policy. *Housing Today*, 83.

Arts, W. and Gelissen, J. 2002: Three worlds of welfare capitalism or more? A state-of-the-art report'. *Journal of European Social Policy*, 12 (2), 137–58.

Atkinson, A. B. 1975: Income distribution and social change revisited. *Journal of Social Policy*, (41), 57–68.

Atkinson, A. B. 1994: *State Pensions for Today and Tomorrow*. London: Welfare State Programme Discussion Paper 104.

Bache, I. 2003: Governing through governance: education policy control under New Labour'. *Political Studies*, 51(2), 300–14.

Baggott, R. 2007: *Understanding Health Policy*. Bristol: Policy Press.

Ball, S. J. 2008: *The Education Debate*. Bristol: Policy Press.

Bardach, E. 1977: *The Implementation Game*. Cambridge, MA: MIT Press.

Barker, K. 2004: *Review of Housing Supply, Delivering Stability: Securing our Future Housing Needs Final Report*. London: HMSO.

Barker, P. 1985: *The Founders of the Welfare State*. Aldershot: Ashgate.

Barr, N. A. 1981: Empirical definitions of the poverty line. *Policy and Politics* (1), 1–21.

Barr, N. 2001: *The Welfare State as Piggy Bank*. Oxford: Oxford University Press.

Barr, N. 2002: The Pension Puzzle. *Economic Issues* no. 29, New York: International Monetary Fund.

Becker, S. and Silburn, R. 1990: *The New Poor Clients*. Nottingham: Benefits Research Unit.

Beer, S. H. 1965: *Modern British Politics*. London: Faber & Faber.

Beveridge, W. 1942: *Social Insurance and Allied Services*. Cmnd 6404. London: HMSO.

Bommes, M. and Geddes, A. (eds) 2000: *Immigration and Welfare: Challenging the Borders of the Welfare State*. London: Routledge.

Booth, C. 1889–1903: *Life and Labour of the People in London*. 17 vols. London: Macmillan.

Brah, A. 2001: Re-framing Europe: gendered racisms, ethnicities and nationalisms in contemporary western Europe. In J. Fink, G. Lewis and J. Clarke (eds), *Rethinking European Welfare*. London: Sage.

Braybrooke, D. and Lindblom, C. E. 1963: *A Strategy of Decision*. New York: Free Press.

Bright, J. 2001: Wasteland. *Inside Housing* 9.2.01 14–15.

Burgess, S., Briggs, A., McConnell, B. and Slater, H. 2006: *School Choice in England: Background Facts*, CMPO Working Paper Series 06/159, Bristol: University of Bristol.

Butcher, T. 2002: *Delivering Welfare: the Governance of the Social Services in the 1990s*. Buckingham: Open University Press.

Butler, D., Adonis, A. and Travers, T. 1994: *Failure in British Government: the Politics of the Poll Tax*. Oxford: Oxford University Press.

Cahill, M. 2002: *The Environment and Social Policy*. London: Routledge.

Campbell, C. and Wilson, G. K. 1995: *The End of Whitehall: Death of a Paradigm*. Oxford: Blackwell.

Carlson, B., Koenig, J. and Reid, G. 1986: *Lessons from Europe: the Role of the Employment Security System*. Washington, DC: National Governors' Association.

Castles, F. 2003: The world turned upside down: below replacement fertility, changing preferences and family-friendly public policy in 21 OECD countries. *Journal of European Social Policy*, 13, 209–27.

Castles, F. and Mitchell, D. 1992: Identifying welfare state regimes: the links between politics, instruments and outcomes. *Governance*, 5(1), 1–26.

Castles, F. and Mitchell, D. 1993: Worlds of welfare and families of nations. In F. Castles (ed.), *Families of Nations: Patterns of Public Policy in Western Democracies*. Aldershot: Dartmouth.

Castles, S. and Miller, M. J. 1993: *The Age of Migration*. Basingstoke: Macmillan.

Central Advisory Council for Education 1967: *Children and their Primary Schools* (Plowden Report). London: HMSO.

Central Statistical Office 1995: *Population Trends*. Winter issue. London: HMSO.

Centre for Housing Policy 1997: *Contemporary Patterns of Residential Mobility in Relation to Social Housing in England*. York: Centre for Housing Policy.

Chamberlayne P., Rustin, M. and Wengraf, T. 2002: *Biography and Social Exclusion in Europe: Experiences and Life Journeys*. Bristol: Policy Press.

Child Poverty Action Group (CPAG) 2005: *Media Briefing on the Pre-Budget Report*. London: CPAG.

Churchill, H. 2007: Children's services in 2006. In K. Clarke, T. Maltby and P. Kennett (eds), *Social Policy Review 19*. Bristol: Policy Press, 85–106.

Clarke, J. 2004: *Changing Welfare, Changing States*. London: Sage.

Clarke, K., Maltby, T. and Kennett 2007: *Social Policy Review 19*. Bristol: Policy Press.

Cole, G. D. H. and Postgate, R. 1971: *The Common People 1746–1946*, Reprint. London: Routledge.

Colebatch, H. K. and Larmour, P. 1993: *Market, Bureaucracy and Community: a Student's Guide to Organisation*. London: Pluto Press.

Cousins, C. 1999: *Society, Work and Welfare in Europe*. Basingstoke: Macmillan.

Crompton, R. 2006: *Employment and the Family: the Reconfiguration of Work and Family Life in Contemporary Societies*. Cambridge: Cambridge University Press.

Crompton, R. and Le Feuvre, N. 2006: Gender, family and employment in comparative perspective: the realities and representations of equal opportunities in Britain and France. *Journal of European Social Policy*, 10 (4), 334–48.

Dahl, R. A. 1961: *Who Governs?* New Haven: Yale University Press.

Dahrendorf, R. 1985: *Law and Order*. London: Stevens.

Daly, M. and Lewis, J. 1998: Conteptualising social care in the context of welfare state restructuring. In J. Lewis (ed.), *Gender, Social Care and Welfare State Restructuring in Europe*. Aldershot: Ashgate.

Daly, M. and Rake, K. 2003: *Gender and the Welfare State*. Cambridge: Polity.

Deacon, A. 1976: *In Search of the Scrounger*. London: Bell.

Deacon, B. 1993: Developments in East European social policy. In C. Jones (ed.), *New Perspectives on the Welfare State in Europe*. London: Routledge.

Deacon, B. 2007: *Global Social Policy and Governance*. London: Sage.

Deacon, B. with Hulse, M. and Stubbs, P. 1997: *Global Social Policy*. London: Sage.

Deakin, N. and Parry, R. 1998: The Treasury and New Labour's social policy. In E. Brunsdon, H. Dean and R. Woods (eds), *Social Policy Review 10*. London: Social Policy Association, 34–56.

Dean, H. 2006: *Social Policy*, Cambridge: Polity.

Department for Communities and Local Government 2006: English Housing Survey 2005–6, www.communities.gov.uk/documents/housing/pdf/152636.

Department of Education and Science 1985: *Education for All* (a brief guide by Lord Swann to the Report of the Committee of Inquiry into the Education of Children from Ethnic Minority Groups), London: HMSO.

Department for Education and Skills 2003: *Every Child Matters*. London: DFES.

Department for Education and Skills 2007: *Referrals, assessments and children and young people who are the subject of a child protection plan or are on child protection registers, England – year ending 31 March 2007*. London: DFES.

Department for Education and Skills/ National Statistics 2007: *Children Looked after in England in the year ending 31 March 2007*, table 1. London: DFES.

Department of Employment 1971: *People and Jobs*. London: HMSO.

Department of Health 1995: *Child Protection: Messages from Research*. London: HMSO.

Department of Health 1997: *The New NHS*. London: HMSO.

Department of Health 1998a: *A First Class Service: Quality in the NHS*. Consultation Document. London: HMSO.

Department of Health 1998b: *Partnership in Action*. London: Department of Health.

Department of Health 2000: *The NHS Plan*. London: The Stationery Office.

Department of Health. 2002: *Shifting the Balance of Power: the Next Steps*. London: Department of Health.

Department of Health 2004: *Choosing Health, Making Healthier Choices Easier*. London: The Stationery Office.

Department of Health 2006: *Our Health, Our Care, Our Say: a New Direction for Community Services*. London: Department of Health.

Department of Health 2007: *Health and Personal Social Services Statistics*. London: Department of Health.

Department of Social Security 1998: *A New Contract for Welfare*, Cm 3805. London: HMSO.

Department for Work and Pensions (DWP) 2006: *Security in Retirement: Towards a New Pensions System*, White Paper Cm. 6841. London: DWP.

Department for Work and Pensions (DWP) 2007: *Ready for Work: Full Employment in our Generation*, Cm 2790. London: DWP.

Department for Work and Pensions (DWP) 2008: *Transforming Britain's Labour Market: Ten Years of the New Deal*. London: DWP.

DETR (Department of the Environment Transport and the Regions)1998: *Modern Local Government in Touch with the People*, Cm4014. London: HMSO.

Dex, S. 2003: *Families and Work in the Twenty-First Century*. Bristol: Policy Press.

Dex, S. and McCulloch, A. 1995: *Flexible Employment in Britain: a Statistical Analysis*. London: Equal Opportunities Commission.

Dickens, R., Gregg, P. and Wadsworth, J. (eds) 2003: *The Labour Market under New Labour: the State of Working Britain*. Basingstoke: Palgrave.

Dolowitz, D. and Marsh, D. 1996: Who learns what from whom: a review of the policy transfer literature. *Political Studies*, 44 (2), 343–57.

Dommergues, P., Sibille, H. and Wurzburg, E. 1989: *Mechanisms for Job Creation: Lessons from the United States*. Paris: OECD.

Dorey, P. 2005: *Policy Making in Britain*. London: Sage.

Dorey, P. (ed.) 1999: *The Major Premiership*. Basingstoke: Macmillan.

Douglas, J. W. B. 1964: *The Home and the School*. London: Macgibbon and Kee.

Dowler, E., Turner, S. and Dobson, B. 2001: *Poverty Bites: Food, Health and Poor Families*. London: CPAG.

Duncan, S. and Edwards, R. 1997: Lone mothers and paid work: rational economic man or gendered moral rationalities? *Feminist Economics*, 3 (2), 29–61.

Dunleavy, P. 1981: *The Politics of Mass Housing in Britain*. London: Oxford University Press.

Eardley, T., Bradshaw, J., Ditch, J., Gough, I. and Whiteford, P. 1996: *Social Assistance in OECD Countries: Synthesis Report*. London: HMSO.

Eckstein, H. 1960: *Pressure Group Politics*. London: Allen and Unwin.

Edgell, S. and Duke, V. 1991: *A Measure of Thatcherism*. Glasgow: Harper Collins.

Ennals, P. 2004: *Child Poverty and Education*. London: National Children's Bureau.

Esping-Andersen, G. 1990: *The Three Worlds of Welfare Capitalism*. Cambridge: Polity.

Esping-Andersen G. 1999: *Social Foundations of Post-Industrial Economies*. Oxford: Oxford University Press.

Esping-Andersen, G. (ed.) 1996: *Welfare States in Transition*. London: Sage.

Etzioni, A. 1969: *The Semi Professions and their Organization*. New York: Free Press.

European Commission 2007a: *Social Agenda: European Social Fund 50 Years of Investing in People*. Brussels: European Commission.

European Commission 2007b: *The Social Situation in the European Union*. Brussels.

Fimister, G. 1986: *Welfare Rights in Social Services*. London: Macmillan.

Finer, S. E. 1958: *Anonymous Empire*. London: Pall Mall.

Fink, J., Lewis, G. and Clarke, J. 2001: *Rethinking European Welfare*. London: Sage.

Fitzpatrick, T. 1999: *Freedom and Security: An Introduction to the Basic Income Debate*. Basingstoke: Macmillon.

Flaherty, J., Veit-Wilson, J. and Dornan, P. 2004: *Poverty: The Facts*. London: Child Poverty Action Group.

Floud, J., Halsey, A. H. and Martin, F. M. 1956: *Social Class and Education Opportunity*. London: Heinemann.

Ford, J. 1969: *Social Class and the Comprehensive School*. London: Routledge and Kegan Paul.

Forrest, R., Murie, A. and Williams, P. 1990: *Home Ownership: Fragmentation and Differentiation*. London: Unwin Hyman.

Franklin, B. (ed.) 1999: *Social Policy, the Media and Misrepresentation*. London: Routledge.

Fraser, D. 2002: *The Evolution of the British Welfare State*. London: Macmillan.

Fraser, N. and Gordon, L. 1994: Dependency demystified: inscriptions of power in a keyword of the welfare state. *Social Politics*, 1(1), 4–31.

Friedson, E. 1970: *Professional Dominance*. New York: Atherton.

Friend, J. K., Power, J. M. and Yewlett, C. J. L. 1974: *Public Planning: the Inter-corporate Dimension*. London: Tavistock.

George, V. and Wilding, P. 1994: *Welfare and Ideology*, 2nd edn. Hemel Hempstead: Harvester Wheatsheaf.

George, V. and Wilding, P. 2002: *Globalisation and Human Welfare*. Basingstoke: Palgrave.

Gillborn, D. 1992: *Race, Ethnicity and Education*. London: Unwin Hyman.

Gillborn, D. 1998: Race, selection, poverty and parents: New Labour, old problems. *Journal of Education Policy*, 13, 717–35.

Gillborn, D. 2005: Education policy as an act of white supremacy; whiteness, critical race theory and education reform. *Journal of Education Policy*, 20, 485–505.

Ginsburg, N. 1992: *Divisions of Welfare*. London: Sage.

Ginsburg, N. 2001: Globalization and the Liberal welfare states. In R. Sykes, B. Palier and P. Prior (eds), *Globalization and European Welfare States: Challenges and Change*. Basingstoke: Palgrave.

Ginsburg, N. 2004: Structured diversity: a framework for critically comparing welfare states? In P. Kennett, *A Handbook of Comparative Social Policy*. Cheltenham: Edward Elgar.

Glennerster, H. 1995: *British Social Policy Since 1945*. Oxford: Blackwell.

Glennerster, H. 2001: Social Policy. In A. Seldon (ed.), *The Blair Effect*. London: Little, Brown.

Glennerster, H. 2003. *Understanding the Finance of Welfare*. Bristol: Policy Press.

Glennerster, H. and Hills, J. (eds) 1998: *The State of Welfare*. Oxford: Oxford University Press.

Glennerster, H., Power, A. and Travers, T. 1991: A new era for social policy: a new enlightenment or a new Leviathan? *Journal of Social Policy*, 20(3), 389–414.

Golding, P. and Middleton, S. 1982: *Images of Welfare*. Oxford: Martin Robertson.

Goodin, R. E., Headey, B., Muffels, R. and Dirven, H-J. 1999: *The Real Worlds of Welfare Capitalism*. Cambridge: Cambridge University Press.

Goos, M. and Manning, A. 2003: Mcjobs and Macjobs: the Growing Polarisation of jobs in the UK. In R. Dickens, P. Gregg, and J. Wadsworth (eds), *The Labour Market Under New Labour: the State of Working Britain*. Basingstoke: Palgrave Macmillan.

Gordon, D. and Pantazis, C. 1997: *Breadline Britain in the 1990s*. Aldershot: Avebury.

Gough, I. 1979: *The Political Economy of the Welfare State*. London: Macmillan.

Gough, I. and Wood, G. (eds) 2004: *Insecurity and Welfare Regimes in Asia, Africa and Latin America: Social Policy in Development Contexts*. Cambridge: Cambridge University Press.

Goul Andersen, J. and Jensen, P. 2002: *Changing Labour Markets, Welfare Policies and Citizenship*. Bristol: Policy Press.

Gregg, P. and Wadsworth, J. 1995: A short history of labour turnover, labour tenure and job security 1975–93. *Oxford Review of Economic Policy*, 11(1), 73–90.

Gregg, P. and Wadsworth, J. 2003: Labour market prospects of the less skilled over the recovery. In R. Dickens, P. Gregg, and J. Wadsworth (eds), *The Labour Market Under New Labour: the State of Working Britain*. Basingstoke: Palgrave Macmillan.

Hakim, C. 2000: *Work– lifestyle choices in the 21st Century*. Oxford: Oxford University Press.

Hall, P. A. and Soskice, D. 2001: *Varieties of Capitalism: the Institutional Foundations of Comparative Advantage*. Oxford: Oxford University Press.

Halsey, A. H. (ed.) 1972: *Educational Priority*, vol. 1. London: HMSO.

Halsey, A.H. with Webb, J. (eds) 2000: *Twentieth Century British Social Trends*, 3rd edn. Basingstoke: Palgrave.

Halsey, A. H., Lauder, H., Brown, P. and Wells, A. S. 1997: *Education, Culture, Economy and Society*. Oxford: Oxford University Press.

Ham, C. 2005: *Health Policy in Britain*. Basingstoke: Palgrave Macmillan.

Hamnett, C. 1991: A nation of inheritors? Housing inheritance, wealth and inequality in Britain. *Journal of Social Policy*, 20(4), 509–36.

Hantrais, L. 2004: *Family Policy Matters*. Bristol: Policy Press.

Hantrais, L. 2007: *Social Policy in the European Union*. Basingstoke: Palgrave Macmillan.

Harker, L. 1996: *A Secure Future? Social Security and the Family in a Changing World*. London: CPAG.

Harris, B. 2004: *The Origins of the British Welfare State: Social Welfare in England and Wales, 1800–1945*. Basingstoke: Palgrave Macmillan.

Harrison, S. and Pollitt, C. 1994: *Controlling Health Professionals*. Buckingham: Open University Press.

Hay, C. 2002: *Political Analysis: a Critical Introduction*. Basingstoke: Palgrave.

Heclo, H. H. and Wildavsky, A. 1981: *The Private Government of Public Money*. London: Macmillan.

Heidenheimer, A. J. 1986: Politics, policy and police as concepts in English and Continental languages: an attempt to explain divergences. *The Review of Politics*, 48, 3–30.

Henderson, J. W. and Karn, V. A. 1987: *Race, Class and State Housing*. Aldershot: Gower.

Henwood, M. and Hudson, B. 2008: Checking the facts, article in the *Guardian*, 14.2.08, based on a report to the Commission for Social Care Inspection, *Lost in the System: the Impact of Fair Access to Care*.

Hill, M. 1972: *The Sociology of Public Administration*. London: Weidenfeld & Nicolson.

Hill, M. 2005: *The Public Policy Process*. Harlow: Pearson Education.

Hill, M. 2006: *Social Policy in the Modern World*. Oxford: Blackwell.

Hill, M. 2007: *Pensions*. Bristol: Policy Press.

Hill, M. (ed.) 1997: *The Policy Process: a Reader*, 2nd edn. Hemel Hempstead: Prentice Hall/ Harvester Wheatsheaf.

Hill, M. and Hupe, P. 2009 (forthcoming): *Implementing Public Policy*, revd. edn. London: Sage.

Hills, J., Le Grand, J. and Piachaud, D. (eds) 2007: *Making Social Policy Work*. Bristol: Policy Press.

Hills, J., Smithies R. and McKnight, A. 2006: *Tracking Income: How Working Families Vary through the Year*, CASE report 32. London: London School of Economics.

Hirsch, F. 1976: *Social Limits to Growth*. Cambridge, MA: Harvard University Press.

Hirschman, A. 1970: *Exit, Voice and Loyalty*. Cambridge, MA: Harvard University Press.

HM Treasury 2006: *Prosperity for all in the Global Economy: World Class Skills* (The Leitch Review of Skills), Final Report. London: The Stationery Office.

HM Treasury 2007: *Pre-Budget Report*. London: HM Treasury.

HMSO 1989: *Caring for People: Community Care in the Next Decade and Beyond*, Cmnd 849. London: HMSO.

HMSO 1998: *The Government's Annual Report, 97/98*. London: HMSO.

Hobson, B. 2002: *Making Men into Fathers. Men, Masculinities and the Social Politics of Fatherhood*. Cambridge: Cambridge University Press.

Hochschild, A. R. 2000: Global care chains and emotional surplus values. In N. Hutton and A. Giddens (eds) *On the Edge. Living with Global Capitalism*, 130–46. London: Jonathan Cape.

Hodgson, S. M. and Irving, Z. (eds) 2007: *Policy Reconsidered: Meanings, Politics and Practices*. Bristol: Policy Press.

Hood, C. 1991: A public management for all seasons. *Public Administration*, 69(1), 3–19.

House of Commons 1977: *Seventh Report from the Expenditure Committee: the Job Creation Programme*. London: HMSO.

Huby, M. 1998: *Social Policy and the Environment*. Buckingham: Open University Press.

Hudson, B. and Henwood, M. 2002: The NHS and social care: the final countdown? *Policy and Politics*, 30 (2) 153–166.

Humphries, S. and Gordon, P. 1994: *Forbidden Britain: Personal Stories of our Hidden Past*. London: BBC Books.

Hupe, P. and Hill, M. 2007: Street-level bureaucracy and public accountability. *Public Administration*, 85 (2), 279–300.

Hutton, N. and Giddens, A. (eds) 2000: *On the Edge. Living with Global Capitalism*. London: Jonathan Cape.

International Organisation for Migration (IOM) 2005: *World Migration 2005: Costs and Benefits of International Migration*. Geneva, IOM.

Jackson, B. and Marsden, D. 1962: *Education and the Working Class*. London: Routledge and Kegan Paul.

Jenkins, W. I. 1978: *Policy Analysis*. London: Martin Robertson.

Johnson, T. J. 1972: *Professions and Power*. London: Macmillan.

Jones, C. (ed.) 1993: *New Perspectives on the Welfare State in Europe*. London: Routledge.

Jones, K. 2000: *The Making of Social Policy in Britain from the Poor Law to New Labour*, 3rd edn. London: Athlone.

Jones, M and Lowe, R. 2002: *From Beveridge to Blair. the First Fifty Years of Britain's Welfare State 1948–1998*. Manchester: Manchester University Press.

Jordan, A. G. and Richardson, J. J. 1987: *British Politics and the Policy Process*. London: Unwin Hyman.

Joseph Rowntree Foundation. 2002: *Britain's Housing in 2002*. York: Joseph Rowntree Foundation.

Jowell, J. and Oliver, D. (eds) 2007 *The Changing Constitution*, 6th edn. Oxford: Oxford University Press.

Judge. K 1987: *Rationing Social Services*. London: Heinemann.

Kavanagh, D., Richards, D., Geddes, J. A. and Smith, M. 2006: *British Politics*. Oxford: Oxford University Press.

Kelly, A. (ed.) 1981: *The Missing Half*. Manchester: Manchester University Press.

Kennett, P. 2001: *Comparative Social Policy: Theory and Research*. Buckingham: Open University Press.

Kennett, P. 2004: *A Handbook of Comparative Social Policy*. Chelteaham: Edward Elgar.

Keynes, J. M. 1936: *The General Theory of Employment Interest and Money*. London: Macmillan.

Khoser, K. 2007: *International Migration: a Very Short Introduction*. Oxford: Oxford University Press.

Killeen, J., Turton, R., Diamond, W., Dosnon, O. and Wach, M. 1999: Education and the labour market: subjective aspects of human capital investment. *Journal of Education Policy* 14 (2) 99–116.

King, A. 2007: *The British Constitution*. Oxford: Oxford University Press.

Kings Fund 2006: *Securing Good Care for Older People* (Wanless Social Care Review). London: Kings Fund.

Klein, R. 1995: *The Politics of the NHS*. London: Longman.

Kleinman, M. 2002: *A European Welfare State?* Basingstoke: Palgrave.

Korpi, W. and Palme, J. 1998: The paradox of redistribution: welfare state institutions and poverty in the western countries. *American Sociological Review*, 63 (5), 661–87.

Labour Party. 1997: *Labour Party Election Manifesto*. London: Labour Party.

Laming, Lord 2003: The Victoria Climbié Inquiry Report, Cm 5730. London: The Stationery Office.

Land. H. 2004: Privatisation, privatisation, privatisation: the British welfare state since 1979. In N. Ellison (ed.) *Social Policy Review* 16. Bristol: Policy Press, 251–69.

Land, H. and Rose, H. 1985: Compulsory altruism for some or an altruistic society for all. In P. Bean, J. Ferris and D. Whynes (eds), *In Defence of Welfare*. London: Tavistock, 74–96.

Le Grand, J. 1982: *The Strategy of Equality*. London: Allen and Unwin.

Le Grand, J. 2001 We can save the NHS – if we are ready to pay for it. *Observer*, 21/10/01.

Le Grand, J., Mays, N. and Mulligan J-A. 1998: *Learning from the NHS Internal Market*. London: Kings Fund.

Leach, R., Coxall, B. and Robins, L. 2006: *British Politics*. Basingstoke: Palgrave Macmillan.

Lee, P. and Murie, A. 1998: Social exclusion and housing. In S. Wilcox (ed.), *Housing Finance Review*. York: Joseph Rowntree Foundation, 30–7.

Lendvai, N. and Stubbs, P. 2007: Translation, intermediaries and welfare reforms in South Eastern Europe, Paper presented for the 4th ESPANET conference, Bremen.

Levitas, R. 2005: *The Inclusive Society? Social Exclusion and New Labour*, 2nd edn. Basingstoke: Palgrave Macmillan.

Lewis, J. 1992: Gender and the development of welfare regimes. *Journal of European Social Policy*, 2 (3), 159–73.

Lewis, G., Gewirtz, S. and Clarke, J. 2000: *Rethinking Social Policy*. London: Sage/The Open University.

Lewis, J. 2006: The adult worker model family, care and the problem of gender equality. *Benefits*, 14 (1), 33–8.

Lewis, J. and Guillari, S. 2005: The adult worker model family, gender equality and care: the search for new policy principles, and the possibilities and problems of the capabilities approach. *Economy and Society*, 34 (1), 76–104.

Lindblom, C. E. 1977: *Politics and Markets: the World's Political-Economic Systems*. New York: Basic Books.

Lindsey, A. 1962: *Socialised Medicine in England and Wales*. Chapel Hill: University of North Carolina Press.

Lipsky, M. 1980: *Street-Level Bureaucracy*. New York: Russell Sage.

Lister, R. 2003: *Citizenship: Feminist Perspectives*. Basingstoke: Palgrave Macmillan.

Lister, R. 2004: *Poverty*. Cambridge: Polity.

Liu, S. 2001: *The Autonomous State of Childcare*. Aldershot: Ashgate.

Lukes, S. 2005: *Power: a Radical View*, 2nd edn. Basingstoke: Palgrave Macmillan.

Lund, B. 2006: *Understanding Housing Policy*. Bristol: Policy Press.

MacPherson, S. and Midgley, J. 1987: *Comparative Social Policy and the Third World*. Brighton: Wheatsheaf.

Macpherson, W. 1999: *The Stephen Lawrence Inquiry*, Cm4262-I. London: The Stationery Office.

Mann, K. 1994: Watching the defectives: observers of the underclass in the USA, Britain and Australia. *Critical Social Policy*, 41 (2), 79–99.

Marsden, D. 1973: *Mothers Alone*. Harmondsworth: Penguin Books.

Marsh, D. and Rhodes, R. A. W. 1992a: *Implementing Thatcherite Policies*. Buckingham: Open University Press.

Marsh, D. and Rhodes, R. A. W. 1992b: *Policy Networks in British Government*. Oxford: Oxford University Press.

Marshall, T. H. 1963: Citizenship and Social Class. In *Sociology at the Crossroads*. London: Heinemann.

Martin, D. 2002: Northern Toll. *Inside Housing*. 1.2.01 14–15.

May, M., Page, R. and Brunsdon, E. (eds) 2001: *Understanding Social Problems*. Oxford: Blackwell.

McKeown, T. 1980: *The Role of Medicine*. Oxford: Blackwell.

Means, R., Richards, S. and Smith, R. 2008: *Community Care, Policy and Practice*. Basingstoke: Palgrave Macmillan.

Midgley, J. 1997: *Social Welfare in a Global Context*. Thousand Oaks, CA: Sage.

Midgley, J. 2004: Social development and social welfare: implications for social policy. In P. Kennett (ed.), *A Handbook of Comparative Social Policy*. Cheltenham: Edward Elgar.

Millar, J. (ed.) 2003: *Understanding Social Security*. Bristol: Policy Press.

Minford, P. 1984: State expenditure: a study in waste. *Economic Affairs* (April–June), supplement.

Mishra, R. 1977: *Social Policy and Society: Theoretical Perspectives on Welfare*. Basingstoke, Macmillan.

Moon, J. and Richardson, J. J. 1985: *Unemployment in the U.K.* Aldershot: Gower.

Moran, M. and Wood, B. 1993: *States, Regulation and the Medical Profession*. Buckingham: Open University Press.

Mullins, D. and Murie, A. 2006: *Housing Policy in the UK*. Basingstoke: Palgrave Macmillan.

Murie, A. 2007: Housing policy, housing tenure and the housing market. In K. Clarke, T. Maltby and P. Kennett (eds), *Social Policy Review 19*. Bristd: Policy Press, 49–66.

Murray, C. 1990: *The Emerging British Underclass*. London: IEA.

National Statistics 2002: *Social Trends* 2002. London: Stationery Office.

National Statistics, 2007: *Social Trends 2007*. London: National Statistics.

Negrine, R. 1994: *Politics and the Mass Media in Britain*, 2nd edn. London: Routledge.

Newman, J. 2001: *Modernising Governance*. London: Sage.

O'Connor, J. S. 1996: From women in the welfare state to gendering welfare state regimes. *Current Sociology*, 44 (2), 1–130.

OECD 2006: *Starting Strong*. Paris: OECD.

OECD 2007: *Society at a Glance*. Paris: OECD.

Office for National Statistics 2007: *Social Trends, No. 37, 2007 edn.*, ed. Abigail Self and Linda Zealey. Basingstoke: Palgrave Macmillan.

Ofsted 1999: *Raising the Attainment of Minority Ethnic Pupils*. London: Ofsted.

Page, R. 2001: The exploration of social problems in the field of social policy. In M. May, R. Page and E. Brunsdon (eds), *Understanding Social Problems*. Oxford: Blackwell.

Page, R. 2007: *Revisiting the Welfare State*, Maidenhead: Open University Press.

Parekh, B. 2000: *The Future of Multi-Ethnic Britain*. Report of a committee chaired by B. Parekh. London: Runnymede Trust.

Parker, H. 1989: *Instead of the Dole*. London: Routledge.

Pascall, G. 1986: *Social Policy: a Feminist Analysis*. London: Tavistock.

Pater, J. E. 1981: *The Making of the National Health Service*. London: King's Fund.

Pawson, H. and Kintrea, K. 2002: Part of the problem or part of the solution: social housing allocation policies and social exclusion. *Journal of Social Policy*, 31 (4), 643–68.

Payne, G. (ed.) 2006: *Social Divisions*, 2nd edn. Basingstoke: Palgrave Macmillan.

Pensions Commission 2004: *Pensions: Challenges and Choices. The First Report of the Pensions Commission.* London: The Stationery Office.

Pensions Commission 2005: *A New Pensions Settlement for the Twenty-first Century. The Second Report of the Pensions Commission.* London: The Stationery Office.

Peters, T. and Waterman, R. 1982: *In Search of Excellence.* New York: HarperCollins.

Pfau-Effinger, B. 2004: *Development of Culture, Welfare States and Women's Employment in Europe.* Aldershot: Ashgate.

Pierson, P. 2001: *The New Politics of the Welfare State.* Oxford: Oxford University Press.

Piore, M. and Sabel, C. 1984: *The Second Industrial Divide.* Oxford: Blackwell.

Pitt, G. 2007: *Employment Law.* London: Sweet and Maxwell.

Pollitt, C. 1990: *Managerialism and the Public Services.* Oxford: Blackwell.

Pollitt, C. 2003: *The Essential Public Manager.* Maidenhead: Open University Press.

Pollock, A. 2004: *NHS plc.* London: Verso.

Powell, M. (ed.) 1999: *New Labour: New Welfare State?* Bristol: Policy Press.

Powell, M. (ed.) 2002: *Evaluating New Labour's Welfare Reforms.* Bristol: Policy Press.

Powell, M. (ed.) 2008: *Modernising the Welfare State.* Bristol: Policy Press.

Price, D. 2000: *Office of Hope: a History of the Employment Service*: London: Policy Studies Institute.

Rawnsley, A. 2001: *Servants of the People: the Inside Story of New Labour*, revd. edn. London: Penguin Books.

Richards, D. and Smith, M. J. 2002: *Governance and Public Policy in the UK.* Oxford: Oxford University Press.

Richardson, R. 2001: *Death, Dissection and the Destitute*, 2nd edn. London: Phoenix Press.

Rose, M. 1972: *The Relief of Poverty 1834–1914.* Basingstoke: Macmillan

Rose, R. 1991: What is lesson-drawing? *Journal of Public Policy*, 11 (1), 3–30.

Roseneil, S. 2004: Why we should care about friends: an argument for queering the care imaginary in social policy. *Social Policy and Society*, 3 (4), 409–19.

Rowntree, B. S. 1901: *Poverty: a Study of Town Life.* London: Macmillan.

Royal Commission on Long Term Care 1999: *With Respect to Old Age.* London: HMSO.

Sainsbury, D. 1996: *Gender Equality and Welfare States.* Cambridge: Cambridge University Press.

Sales, R. 2007: *Understanding Immigration and Refugee Policy.* Bristol: Policy Press.

Savage, S. P., Atkinson, R. and Robins, L. (eds) 1994: *Public Policy in Britain.* London: Macmillan.

Savage, S. P. and Atkinson, R. (eds) 2001: *Public Policy under Blair.* Basingstoke: Palgrave.

Schierup, C-U., Hansen, P. and Castles, S. 2006: *Migration, Citizenship and the European Welfare State.* Oxford: Oxford University Press.

School Food Trust 2007: *Second Annual Survey of Take-up of School Meals in England.* Sheffield: School Food Trust.

Schumpeter, J. 1950: *Capitalism, Socialism and Democracy.* New York: Harper and Row.

Seebohm Rowntree, B. 1901: *Poverty: a Study of Town Life* (2000, reprint). Bristol: Policy Press.

Seldon, A. (ed.) 2001: *The Blair Effect.* London: Little, Brown.

Seldon, A. (ed.) 2007: *Blair's Britain 1997–2007.* Cambridge: Cambridge University Press.

Semmel, B. 1961: *Imperialism and Social Reform.* London: Oxford University Press.

Siciliani, L. and Hurst, J. 2003: Explaining waiting times variations for elective surgery across OECD countries, OECD Health Working Papers. Paris: OECD.

Sinfield, R. A. 1978: Analyses in the social division of welfare. Journal of Social Policy, 7 (2), 129–56.

Sinfield, R. A. 1981: *What Unemployment Means*. Oxford: Martin Robertson.

Smith, B. C. 1976: *Policy Making in British Government*. London: Martin Robertson.

Smith, M. J. 1993: *Pressure, Power and Policy*. Hemel Hempstead: Harvester Wheatsheaf.

Social Exclusion Unit 1998: *Consultation on Deprived Urban Neighbourhoods*. http://www. cabinet-office.gov.uk/seu/1998/depneigh.htm

Spencer, S. 2007: Immigration. In A. Seldon (ed.) *Blair's Britain 1997–2007*. Cambridge: Cambridge University Press.

Spicker, P. 1995: *Social Policy: Themes and Approaches*. Hemel Hempstead: Prentice Hall.

Stacey, M. 1988: *The Sociology of Health and Healing*. London: Unwin Hyman.

Stanworth, P. and Giddens, A. 1974: *Elites and Power in British Society*. Cambridge: Cambridge University Press.

Stoker, G. and Wilson, D. (eds) 2004: *British Local Government into the 21st Century*. Basingstoke: Palgrave Macmillan.

Talbot-Smith, A. and Pollock, A. 2006: *The New NHS: A Guide*. Abingdon: Routledge.

Taylor-Gooby, P. 1985: *Public Opinion, Ideology and State Welfare*. London: Routledge and Kegan Paul.

Taylor-Gooby, P. and Larsen, T. 2004: The UK: a test case for the Liberal welfare state. In P. Taylor-Gooby (ed.), *New Risks, New Welfare*. Oxford: Oxford University Press.

Therborn, G. 2004: *Between Sex and Power: Family in the World, 1900–2000*. London: Routledge.

Thomas, R. and Dorling, D. 2007: *Identity in Britain*. Bristol: Policy Press.

Timmins, N. 1996: *The Five Giants: a Biography of the Welfare State*. London: Fontana.

Titmuss, R. M. 1958: *Essays on the Welfare State*. London: Allen and Unwin.

Titmuss, R. M. 1974: *Social Policy: an Introduction*. London: Allen and Unwin.

Tomlinson, S. 2001/2005 *Education in a Post-welfare Society*. Buckingham: Open University Press.

Townsend, P. 1979: *Poverty in the United Kingdom*. Harmondsworth: Penguin.

Townsend, P. 1993: *The International Analysis of Poverty*. Hemel Hempstead: Harvester Wheatsheaf.

Townsend, P., Davidson, N. and Whitehead, M. (eds) 1988: *Inequalities in Health*. Harmondsworth: Penguin.

Toynbee, P. 2003: *Hard Work*. London: Bloomsbury.

UN 2001: *Replacement Migration: is it a Solution to Declining and Ageing Populations?* ST/ESA/SER.A/206. New York: United Nations.

UN 2003: *World Population Prospects*. New York: United Nations.

UN 2008: *World Population Policies 2007*, ST/ESA/SER.A/272. New York: United Nations.

UN Population Division 2008: *World Population Policies 2007*. New York: Department of Economic and Social Affairs, United Nations.

UNDP 2007: *Human Development Report 2007/2008, Fighting Climate Change: Human Solidarity in a Divided World*. New York: UNDP.

Ungerson, C. 1997: Social politics and the decommodification of care. *Social Politics*, 4 (3), 362–82.

Ungerson, C. 2000: Thinking about the production and consumption of long-term care in Britain: does gender still matter? *Journal of Social Policy*, 29 (4) 623–44.

Urry, J. and Wakeford, J. (eds) 1973: *Power in Britain*. London: Heinemann.

Van Kempen, R., Dekker, K., Hall, S. and Tosics, I. (eds): 2005 *Restructuring Large Housing Estates in Europe*. Bristol: Policy Press.

Vick, N., Tobin, R., Swift, P., Spandler, H., Hill, M., Coldham, T., Towers, C. and Waldock, H. 2006: *An Evaluation of the Impact of the Social Care Modernisation Programme on the Implementation of Direct Payments*, unpublished report of the Health and Social Care Advisory Service to the Department of Health.

Walker, A. and Wong, C. K. 2004: The ethnocentric construction of the welfare state. In P. Kennett, *A Handbook of Comparative Social Policy*. Cheltenham: Edward Elgar.

Walker, R. 2005: *Social Security and Welfare*. Maidenhead: Open University Press.

Walter, J. A. 1988: *Basic Income: Escape from the Poverty Trap*. London: Marion Boyars.

Warmington, P. and Murphy, R. 2004: Could do better? Media descriptions of UK educational assessment results. *Journal of Education Policy*, 19, 293–9.

Webb, A. 1985: Alternative futures for social policy and state welfare. In R. Berthoud (ed.), *Challenges to Social Policy*. Aldershot: Gower, 46–71.

Wheelock, J. 1999: Fear or opportunity: insecurity in employment. In J. Vail, J. Wheelock and M. Hill (eds), *Insecure Times*. London: Routledge, 75–88.

Wheelock, J. and Jones, K. 2002: Grandparents are the next best thing: informal childcare for working parents in urban Britain. *Journal of Social Policy*, 31 (3), 441–64.

Wheelock, J. and Vail, J. (eds) 1998: *Work and Idleness: the Political Economy of Full Employment*. Boston, MA: Kluwer.

White, M. 1991: *Against Unemployment*. London: Policy Studies Institute.

Wilding, P, 1992: The British welfare state: Thatcher's enduring legacy. *Policy and Politics*, 20 (3), 201–12.

Wilensky, H. L. and Lebaux, C. N. 1965: *Industrial Society and Social Welfare*. Glencoe, IL: Free Press.

Williams, F. 1989: *Social Policy: a Critical Introduction*. Cambridge: Polity Press.

Williams, F. 1995: Race/ethnicity, gender and class in welfare states: a framework for comparative analysis. *Social Politics*, 2(2), 127–59.

Williams, F. 2001: Race/ethnicity, gender and class in welfare states: a framework for comparative analysis. In J. Fink, Lewis, G. and Clarke, J. (eds), *Rethinking European Welfare*. London: Sage.

Williams, F. 2004: *Rethinking Families*. London: Calouste Gulbenkian Foundation.

Williamson, O. E. 1975: *Markets and Hierarchies: Analysis and Antitrust Implications: a Study in the Economics of Internal Organization*. New York: Free Press.

Willis, P. 1977: *Learning to Labour*. Westmead: Saxon House.

Woods, R. 1999: No place like home?: Insecurity in housing. In J. J. Vail, J. Wheelock and M. Hill (eds), *Insecure Times*. London: Routledge, 105–18.

Wootton, G. 1970: *Interest Groups*. Englewood Cliffs, NJ: Prentice-Hall.

Young, P. and Irving, Z. 2004: *Changing Practices in Teaching Undergraduate Social Policy*. Bristol: SWAP itsn: www.swap.ac.uk/docs/learning/spUG practices.pdf

Index